READINGS ABOUT
CHILDREN'S LITERATURE

READINGS
ABOUT CHILDREN'S
LITERATURE

Edited by

EVELYN ROSE ROBINSON

DIVISION OF LIBRARY SCIENCE
SOUTHERN CONNECTICUT STATE COLLEGE
NEW HAVEN, CONNECTICUT

DAVID McKAY COMPANY, INC.

New York

1966

READINGS ABOUT CHILDREN'S LITERATURE

COPYRIGHT © 1966 BY DAVID McKAY COMPANY, INC.

LIBRARY OF CONGRESS CATALOG CARD NUMBER: 66-10430

MANUFACTURED IN THE UNITED STATES OF AMERICA

VAN REES PRESS • NEW YORK

PREFACE

As a teacher of children's literature, I encourage students to read not only trade titles but also books and articles about children's books. Now that classes are becoming larger, not enough copies exist of the recommended readings in the best stocked libraries.

In addition to students' needs, parents are asking for help in evaluating and selecting books for children. *Readings About Children's Literature* is, therefore, for students of children's literature and for parents as well as for teachers and librarians.

These *Readings* are grouped into nine categories including: developmental needs; reading interests; appropriate books and magazines to meet the needs of the average and exceptional young people (preschool through grades nine). The bibliographies listed in the articles are valuable for additional readings and assignments.

The selections, logically arranged, represent the available materials which best highlight the subjects and provide 1) an understanding of the child as a reader; 2) knowledge of criteria for and principles of book selection; 3) broad offerings of appropriate literature and its sociological background. These articles include excerpts from books, magazines, journals, and newspapers. Some articles had to be omitted owing to lack of space, which this Editor regrets exceedingly.

The data in some of the articles are out-of-date because newer editions of titles cited are now available. The articles, however, are still appropriate, and students can be encouraged to look up newer editions.

The Editor is grateful to the authors (many of whom she knows or has known personally) who so graciously and enthusiastically helped her. These authors are noted in the list of contributors. In addition to authors, my appreciation goes to the publishers who gave permission to reprint articles and helped to locate authors.

The task of reproducing materials was greatly lightened by the help of the Southern Connecticut State College Library Staff, and

v

by Marion C. Liebler, who typed the manuscript. To Dr. Evelyn I. Banning, Chairman of Education, Wheaton College, Norton, Massachusetts, the Editor also expresses gratitude for help in reading the manuscript. The responsibility for deciding on selections and their sequence is entirely mine.

NEW HAVEN, CONNECTICUT   EVELYN R. ROBINSON
JUNE 1, 1965

CONTRIBUTORS *

Richard S. Alm, Professor of Education, University of Hawaii, Honolulu, Hawaii; Editor of the *English Journal*

Siri Andrews, Retired Librarian, Concord, New Hampshire

May Hill Arbuthnot, Associate Professor Emeritus of Education, Western Reserve University, Cleveland, Ohio

Matilda Bailey, Visiting Professor, Slippery Rock State College, Slippery Rock, Pennsylvania

Augusta Baker, Coordinator of Children's Services, The New York Public Library, New York City, New York

Nora E. Beust, Formerly Supervisor of School and Children's Libraries, U.S. Office of Education, Washington, D.C.

Virginia Bright, *The Boston Globe,* Boston 7, Massachusetts

Learned T. Bulman, Coordinator of Youth Services, Free Public Library, East Orange, New Jersey

Dwight L. Burton, Head, Department of English Education, Florida State College, Tallahassee, Florida

Constance Carr, Formerly at the University of Minnesota, Minneapolis, Minnesota

Mary Ellen Chase, Author, Northampton, Massachusetts

Children's Book Council, Inc., New York, New York

F. E. Compton & Company, Chicago, Illinois

Marcus Crouch, Deputy County Librarian, Kent County Library, Springfield, Maidstone, Kent, England

Mildred A. Dawson, Professor of Education, Sacramento State College, Sacramento, California

Mary Gould Davis, Formerly Supervisor of Storytelling, New York Public Library, New York

Annis Duff, Editor, Junior Books, The Viking Press, Inc., New York, New York

Mary K. Eakin, Librarian, Youth Collection, State College of Iowa, Cedar Falls, Iowa

Mary E. Edes, Formerly an Assistant Editor of *Publishers' Weekly,* and Editor of their "Juvenile Forecast"

Sheila A. Egoff, Assistant Professor, School of Librarianship, University of British Columbia, Vancouver, British Columbia, Canada

* Only the senior author is listed here for articles with two or more authors.

vii

Yolanda D. Federici, Asst. to the Editor, Children's Book Department, Follett Publishing Company; and Lecturer on Children's Literature, Roosevelt University, Formerly Supervisor of Work With Children, Chicago Public Library

Phyllis Fenner, Author, Manhasset, New York

Carolyn W. Field, Coordinator of Work With Children, The Free Library of Philadelphia, Pennsylvania

Josette Frank, Director for Children's Books and Mass Media, Child Study Association of America and author of *Your Child's Reading Today*

Ruth Gagliardo, Director, Library Services, Kansas State Teachers Association

Doris Gates, Author, Carmel, California

Irene Smith Green, Formerly Supervisor of Work With Children, Brooklyn Public Library, Brooklyn, New York

Elizabeth Guilfoile, Consultant in Reading and Children's Literature and writer of children's books, Fort Thomas, Kentucky

Agnes G. Gunderson, Formerly Professor of Elementary Education, University of Wyoming, Laramie, Wyoming

Virginia Haviland, Head, Children's Book Section, Library of Congress, Washington, D.C.

May Bradshaw Hays, Book Reviewer, writer, and broadcaster over the Yankee Network (Station WIEC)

Paul Hazard, Author of *Books, Children and Men*

Robert A. Heinlein, Author, Colorado Springs, Colorado

Ruth C. Horrell, Librarian, Pontiac Township High School, Pontiac, Illinois

Leland B. Jacobs, Professor of Education, Teachers College, Columbia University, New York, New York

Clara J. Kircher, Children's Book Specialist, University of Maryland Library

Clifford J. Kolson, Professor of Education, Director of the Reading Center, State University College at Potsdam, New York

Nancy Larrick, Author and Editor, Quakertown, Pennsylvania

Lois Lenski, Author-Illustrator of *Strawberry Girl*, the *Mr. Small* Books and others, Tarpon Springs, Florida

Donald MacRae, Professor of Astronomy, University of Toronto, Ontario, Canada

Elizabeth MacRae, Assistant to Head, Boys and Girls Services, Toronto Public Libraries, Toronto, Canada

Cornelia Meigs, Professor Emeritus, Bryn Mawr College, Pennsylvania

Esther Millett, Librarian, The Mary R. Hillard Memorial Library, Westover School, Middlebury, Connecticut

Anne Carroll Moore, Author of *My Roads to Childhood,* Formerly Superintendent of Work With Children, New York Public Library

Amelia Munson, Retired. Formerly with the New York Public Library and Associate Professor in Adolescent Reading Interests and Appreciation, Columbia University, New York

Elizabeth Nesbitt, Retired. Formerly Associate Dean, Carnegie Library School, Pittsburgh, Pennsylvania

Ethel Newell, Librarian at West Junior High School, Mesa, Arizona

Charlemae Rollins, Retired. Formerly Children's Librarian, Chicago Public Library, Chicago, Illinois

Eulalie Steinmetz Ross, Children's Consultant, State Library of Ohio

Mabel Rudisill, Associate Professor of Education, Duke University, Durham, North Carolina

Julia L. Sauer, Retired. Formerly Head, Department of Work With Children, Rochester, New York Public Library

Ruth Sawyer, Author, Storyteller, Boston, Massachusetts

Ida Shroeder, Traveler and Linguist, New York, New York

Millicent E. Selsam, Author, New York, New York

Maurice Sendak, Author and Illustrator

Sister Mary Joan Patricia, Author

Dora V. Smith, Professor Emeritus in Education, University of Minnesota, Minneapolis, Minnesota

Frances Lander Spain, Director of Library Services, Central Florida Junior College, Ocala, Florida; formerly Coordinator, Children's Services, The New York Public Library

Ruth Hill Viguers, Editor of *The Horn Book Magazine,* Boston, Massachusetts

Hanor A. Webb, Professor of Science Education, Emeritus, George Peabody College for Teachers, Nashville, Tennessee

Sara Wheeler, Associate Professor, School of Librarianship University of Washington, Seattle, Washington

Paul A. Witty, Professor of Education, Northwestern University, Evanston, Illinois

World Book Encyclopedia, Field Enterprise Educational Corporation, Chicago, Illinois

Herbert S. Zim, Educational Director, Artists & Writers Press, Inc.

TABLE OF CONTENTS

PART ONE   The Child and His Reading

Give Children Literature • Leland Jacobs   3
An Enviable Possession • Elizabeth Nesbitt   8
Making Books Come Alive for Children • Nancy
    Larrick   14
Meeting Development Needs Through Reading
    • Paul Witty   20
Therapeutic Reading • Matilda Bailey   31
At the North End of Pooh: A Study of Bibliotherapy
    • Ethel Newell   40
Comic Books: A Teacher's Analysis • Dwight L.
    Burton   46
Substitutes for the Comic Books I • Constance Carr   51
Children's Preferences in Publishers • Clifford J.
    Kolson, Richard E. Robinson, William G.
    Zimmerman   63

PART TWO   Evaluation and Selection of Children's Books

What Are Good Books? • Paul Hazard   71
What Makes a Book a Good Book • Augusta Baker   74
Not Recommended • Ruth Hill Viguers   78
Children and Great Books • Doris Gates   81

PART THREE   Selection of Children's Books

Search for the Real Thing . . . • Virginia Haviland   89
Book Selection • Amelia Munson   96
The Selection and Acquisition of Books for Children
    • Frances Lander Spain   100
General Criteria for Selection and Use of Materials
    • Yolanda Federici   108
Buy Better Rather Than More • Mary K. Eakin   115
Periodicals That Will Benefit Elementary Children
    • Carolyn W. Field   118

PART FOUR   Children's Books—History and Trends

Literature For Children • World Book Encyclopedia   125
Books of Yesterday • Sheila A. Egoff   135

xi

Children's Books—Yesterday and Today • Dora
V. Smith   142
Editing the First Critical History of Literature for
Children • Cornelia Meigs   152
"My Father Says to Get a Classic" • Phyllis Fenner 158
Children's Books of 1930–1960 That Have Become
Modern Classics • Mary Elisabeth Edes   166
Frederic Melcher and Children's Books •
Ruth Gagliardo   172
The Newbery-Caldecott Medals: Legacy to Children's
Literature • Irene Smith Green   178
Salute to Children's Literature and Its Creators •
Marcus Crouch   183
A Brief History of National Children's Book Week
• Children's Book Council, Inc.   188

PART FIVE   Illustrations and Children's Books

Illustrating Books for Children • Anne Carroll
Moore   195
The Shape of Music • Maurice Sendak   201
Children's Preferences for Color Versus Other
Qualities in Illustrations • Mabel Rudisill   205

PART SIX   The Young Child and His Books

Recipe for a Magic Childhood • Mary Ellen Chase 217
What They Are Like: How to Identify Them
• Elizabeth Guilfoile   225
What Seven-Year-Olds Like in Books • Agnes G.
Gunderson   232
Mother Goose to Homer • Sister Mary Joan
Patricia, S.S.J.   239
How to Tell a Story • Ruth Sawyer •
Compton's Pictured Encyclopedia   248
The Story Hour: A Significant Program of Children's
Departments in Public Libraries • Nora E. Beust 255

PART SEVEN   Traditional and Modern Imaginative
Tales for Children

Fairy Tales and Their Effects Upon Children
Part I and Part II • Ruth C. Horrell   263
Folk-Tale Collections • Eulalie Steinmetz Ross   277

Traditional Scandinavian Literature for Children •
Siri Andrews   279
Memories of My Father, Joseph Jacobs • May
Bradshaw Hays   286
American Folk Tales • Mary Gould Davis   292
Children of the World Collect Pennies to Erect
Pinocchio Statue in Italy • Virginia Bright   299
Homage to Pinocchio • Ida Schroeder   302
Alice Liddell of Wonderland • Mary Elisabeth Edes 304

PART EIGHT   Fiction for Children and Young People

Literature of Human Understanding • Josette Frank 313
Making the World Safe for the Janey Larkins • Julia
L. Sauer   318
Regional Children's Literature • Lois Lenski   328
Books About Negroes for Children • Charlemae
Rollins   335
Foreign Books for Children • Clara J. Kircher   339
Some Funny Books • Annis Duff   345
The Glitter and the Gold • Richard S. Alm   351
"We Don't Even Call Those Books!" • Esther Millett 362
Science Fiction Writers: Prophets of the Future •
Hanor A. Webb   365
Ray Guns and Rocket Ships • Robert A. Heinlein   368

PART NINE   Nonfiction for Children and Young People

Informational Books—Tonic and Tool for the
Elementary Classroom • Herbert S. Zim   375
Nature Writing: Scientific and Nonscientific •
Millicent E. Selsam   383
Astronomy Books for Children • Donald and
Elizabeth MacRae   388
Which Anthropology Books to Choose for Children?
• Sara Wheeler   397
Poetry for Children • Mildred A. Dawson   404
Helping Children Enjoy Poetry • May Hill
Arbuthnot   410
Biographies for Teen-Agers • Learned T. Bulman 412

Index   425

Part One

THE CHILD AND HIS READING

GIVE CHILDREN LITERATURE *

Leland B. Jacobs

From the beginnings of the movement for free public education in this country, literature has held a place as a curriculum experience for children. It is true that, in the beginning, it was a rather sad and sorry kind of literature. One of the first bits of verse which colonial children were expected to learn reminded them dolefully that "In Adam's fall, we sinned all."

It is probably characteristic of so much of the literature given to those poor little Puritans that, as Dorothy Baruch said, "One would think from the kinds of reading experiences which were given to the young in those days that the adults of the community were in momentary fear of an infant revolt, and so they dangled them over hell-fire and brimstone to keep them in line."

OLD WORLD SOURCES OF CHILDREN'S LITERATURE

As our country first looked to the Old World for its traditions and culture, similarly, we looked to the Old World for our first children's literature. Later, we developed a literature for adults that represented our declaration of intellectual freedom from other parts of the world. In the absence of a true childen's literature, we gave to children some of the masterpieces of this adult literature.

ADULT'S LITERATURE NOT APPROPRIATE FOR CHILDREN

It is tragic that to this day, in some schools in the United States, the children's literary heritage is confined pretty much to the old classical adult material. In some third grades one still finds children reading:

> "Between the dark and the daylight,
> When the night is beginning to lower
> Comes a pause in the day's occupations
> That is known as the Children's Hour."

As one looks at this poem inside out, he discovers that it is the reminiscences of an old man looking back upon the joys of

* Leland B. Jacobs, "Give Children Literature," *Education Today*, Bulletin No. 22 (Ohio: Charles E. Merrill Books, Inc.)., n. d. Reprinted by permission of Charles E. Merrill Books, Inc., Columbus, Ohio, and the author.

having children in his household. If, in your school systems, you have any such individuals in the third grade, you should look at your promotional practices rather critically!

Frequently, in the fourth grade, one still finds nine-year-olds trying to get into the experiences expressed by "The little toy dog is covered with dust, but sturdy and staunch he stands," from "Little Boy Blue." If you analyze these lines sympathetically, you discover that this is the emotion of an adult who has lost a child. It is about a child—but not for children.

THE GOLDEN AGE OF CHILDREN'S LITERATURE

As we moved on toward the twentieth century there began to develop a movement for a literature that was distinctively for children. It was promoted by those who believed that the children of America deserve as significant a literature for them as do the adult readers in our culture. Our present age has seen the full flowering of this movement. The literature is here. This is truly the Golden Age of children's literature.

It is our job to provide literature in the elementary school so that children grow in reading taste. We have spent so much time on other aspects of reading, that we are in part to blame for the low level of adult reading habits in American life today.

There are six good reasons why children need literature in their lives.

1. Literature Is Entertainment

One reason why children need literature is that literature is entertainment. There should be no fear of entertainment as a noble end to education. The shortening of the working hours— for everybody but members of our profession, it seems—gives more time for leisure. Certainly, along with radio, picture magazines, movies, and television, some time ought to be reserved for reading. Unless children at school learn to love to read and enjoy reading for its own sake as entertainment, we are missing one of our wonderful citizenship opportunities. The teacher never needs to apologize to anyone when she is discovered in the classroom enjoying literature with the children. Literature as entertainment is a perfectly valid reason for including it as a curriculum experience.

2. *Literature Refreshes the Spirit*

The experience of reading fine prose and fine poetry helps to take us away from the urgencies of life that have become too urgent. For the moment, one learns to escape from the immediate cares and comes back to them recreated and refreshed. Unless children have many opportunities for this experience at school, they may never learn this wonderful value of literature in the refreshment of spirit. There are some books so impressive that when we rediscover them—long after we have forgotten their titles, incidents, and names of the characters—they make us recall what may be termed a "residue of meaning," an overtone of spiritual values. Because these books have such vital meanings for us, the spiritual quality of their entertainment comes to the fore.

3. *Literature Helps Explore Life and Living*

Children need literature in order to explore life and living. There is no other medium—television, radio, or any of the rest— that quite compares with that wonderful experience of getting into the life situations of another person in the ways that one can do it with literature. A fine author is so cautious, in the sense of being careful with life (the realities of life) that somehow or other he reaches out to the young reader, and together, they go exploring into the life and the living, the customs, the mores, the habits of thinking of another character. There are certain kinds of experiences that can come only vicariously through this kind of experience with literature. So, children need literature as an exploration of life.

4. *Literature Is a Guidance Resource*

It can serve as a guidance resource for letting a person get insights into himself so that he can possibly change behavior. Not all literature can do it, nor can it always be done prescriptively. But every one of us has in his life probably at least one book that helped to give him insight about himself at a time when he needed it.

5. *Literature Stimulates Creative Activities*

Children need literature as a springboard to creative activities in other areas. Creative reading of literature, coupled with a rich program in the arts, helps one art to feed another art. Reading stimulates drawing and rhythmic interpretation in dramatics. The richer the children's experiences in reading and dramatics, the richer they all become in the creative aspects of living.

6. Literature Is Beautiful Language

Children need literature in order to enrich their own language. Literature is beautiful language, and who among us do not want children to get the beauty of their mother tongue at its best?

BUT WHAT LITERATURE

But what kind of literature will provide the kind of values children need? There are three great parallels, which, if followed consistently, will provide the kind of literature program the children of today need.

Parallel 1. The New and the Old

Today's literature program needs a balance of new literature and old literature, for one's literary heritage has its source in the combination of the two. A child needs a great deal of the modern literature—the things that have been written for children in his own generation—because it is written in idiom and in style, mood, and tempo that he understands because he's living it. The great modern writers for children know what the inside of a child's mind is like, and they write with a tempo, style, and spirit that is Twentieth-Century modern.

The child needs a wealth of this type of material, but if his heritage is to be rich, he needs to know that before his time there came to us great stories, too—stories like "The Elephant's Child," who went down by the "great gray-green, greasy Limpopo River, all set about with fever-trees, to find out what the Crocodile has for dinner." Kipling is gone, but "The Elephant's Child" is with us yet. The child needs the old tales of Grimm, Asbjörnsen, Joseph Jacobs and all the rest of the wonderful group of folklorists who collected the old stories of the world. Children love this old literature. They particularly love it if they can share it with an adult who had it, too, as a child. This is the kind of literature that May Lamberton Becker said is like "the measles going through an orphanage." Generation after generation, the continuity of the literary experience going from the old to the young is a great experience.

Parallel 2. *Realistic and Fanciful Literature*

A second parallel is the balance between realistic and fanciful literature. A child loves the kinds of stories that acquaint him with his own world, whether he is close to it in time and space, or far from it. He loves animal stories. He wants and needs stories that take him out to the various parts of the United States, where people live like him as an American and yet differ from him because they belong to an area that is different.

But he also wants to go out in time and space beyond our own country to the Orient, to Europe, up into the hills of Switzerland with Heidi, over into Japan with the little farmer boy who was saved from the tidal wave. He wants to go back into time—to the time of Abraham Lincoln, when a little girl wrote and recommended that Lincoln would look much better on a platform if he had whiskers.

But along with these kinds of experiences in time and space with realistic literature, he also wants the kind of literature which takes him out of this world into the world of the impossible, the improbable, and the fanciful, such as: *Mary Poppins,* the "Three Wishes," and the fairy tales that transcend time and space. These are terribly urgent. Look what the child can do with such literature. He can get out of the plausible and the possible and look back on the real to get a greater perspective on both.

Parallel 3. *Prose and Poetry*

Unfortunately, in many schools today there is so little time for poetry. Some of the reasons for this are carried over from the past, such as: "mass memorization,"—forty times around the room, "I wandered lonely as a cloud"—until you hope you never see a daffodil again; "verse vivisection," during which you tear it to pieces to see how it ticks; "poetic preachment," where you impose poetry on children to improve their spirits, souls, and characters. This isn't the present-day idea of poetry for children. Today, we give them their wonderful heritage of poetry where they can read it and see it beautifully on a page, or hear it joyously.

THE PLACE OF LITERATURE IN THE CURRICULUM

Children need literature, then, for entertainment, for refreshment of spirit, for the exploration of life and living, for guidance, for creative activities, and for the enrichment of language.

There are some people who like to say that the social studies program is the backbone of the curriculum. Then there are some who think that mathematics gives muscle to the curriculum; while others feel that literature is mighty close to the heart of the curriculum. As Edna St. Vincent Millay has said so well:

> The world stands out on either side,
> No wider than the heart is wide.

Give children literature!

AN ENVIABLE POSSESSION *

Elizabeth Nesbitt

When attention has been drawn to it, it is striking to realize that the quality in children most frequently commented upon by adults is a sense of wonder. There is the much quoted passage from Kenneth Grahame, in which he speaks of children's simple acceptance of the mood of wonderment, of their readiness to welcome a perfect miracle at any hour of the day or night. J. Donald Adams, commenting on these remarks of Grahame's, writes "It (wonder) is the first possession that all of us have, and the first most of us lose. How rare are those few writers who, because their perception of the world is genuine and constantly renewed, are a help to us in retaining and renewing our own. They are the writers of the immortal stories of childhood; they are the truly great poets—and there are no greater benefactors of mankind."

* Elizabeth Nesbitt, "An Enviable Possession," *ALA Bulletin* 49 (November, 1955), 553–55, 578. This article is based on a talk given at the Children's Library Association program meeting at the ALA Philadelphia Conference, July 4, 1955. Reprinted by permission of the American Library Association and the author.

Walter De La Mare, although he does not use the word wonder, was thinking of that quality when he wrote in his introduction to *Bells and Grass,* "I know well that only the rarest kind of best in anything can be good enough for the young. I know too that in later life it is just... possible now and again to recover fleetingly the intense delight, the untellable joy and happiness and fear and grief and pain of our early years, of an all but forgotten childhood. I have, in a flash, in a momentary glimpse, seen again a horse, an oak, a daisy, just as I saw them in those early years, as if with that heart, with those senses." It is because Andersen saw things with that heart, with those senses, that his stories have genius; for as Rumer Godden truly says, Andersen never lost the "god-like power" of giving personality to things that have none, "not only toys, but sticks and stones, bannister knobs and footstools, cabbages." The most ordinary flower, the most insignificant insect were to him things of wonder, and each had its story. It was the crushing of this faculty of wonder and delight in children that Charles Lamb considered the greatest sin of the didactic age.

Although there is an apparent nostalgic mood in all these comments, there is also something more constructively meaningful than mere retrospective wistfulness. There is recognition that a child's ever readiness to wonder lends to life an expectancy, an exuberance, a significance, a variety of sensation, and that without it, there is too often only existence, a dreary futility, or a feverish attempt to compensate by labored and artificial means.

It is a usual and natural fallacy to associate the instinct of wonder with purely imaginative literature, with folk-literature and with fantasy. But the dictionary definition of the word wonder, as noun and as verb, leaves room for much broader associations. As a noun, it is defined as a cause of surprise or astonishment; a marvel, a miracle; and as the emotion excited by novelty, or by something strange or not well understood. As a verb, the definition is to marvel, and secondly to feel doubt and curiosity, to query in the mind. A sense of wonder may be aroused by realities and by fantasies. One may marvel at the indomitable nature of man in his progress as revealed in history, at the innate decency, goodness, and achievements of man as revealed in biography, at the curiosity, mental power, ingenuity, and resourcefulness of man as revealed in the records of discovery and invention, and science. One may feel astonishment and delight and pleasure at the phenomena and amazing complexities of the nat-

ural world, even though one knows that immutable laws govern
such phenomena and complexities.

If, as children's librarians, we agree that the capacity for
wonder that results in the ability to live with constant expectancy,
to revel in every new experience, to be quickened with excitement over every bit of new knowledge, is the quality that distinguishes childhood from adulthood, and is the most enviable
possession of childhood, then we must agree that it is a quality
to be fostered. To enforce this conclusion, may I bring one more
quotation to bear upon the point? And if this talk seems overfull
of borrowings from other minds, it is because there is importance
in the repetition and unanimity of emphasis. Clifton Fadiman
once wrote, "Unless our writers for the young can repossess that
sense of wonder which the nineteenth century for all its short-
comings was habitually familiar with, the books they fashion may
become more and more competent, skillful, morally sanitary,
and ideologically blameless, but within their pages the miracle
itself will not be wrought. And if it ceases to be wrought, the sense
of wonder will begin to die away in our children, and if that
happens, there's not much sense in their being children at all.
They might as well be born adults and have done with it." In
the same article, Mr. Fadiman makes a statement full of meaning
to all concerned with making available to children books of true
distinction and of vital appeal. He says, "It is easier to exploit
a subject than to delight the child by suddenly raising the curtain
on the human heart. But a book is not as good as its subject. It
is only as good as its writer." The last two sentences have implications which grow more and more comprehensive, until it becomes
almost impossible to confine them within the pattern of a single
talk. A story may fall into a favorite category of children's reading, a subject may be of provenly established interest to children.
But that is not enough. The test is whether the book recreates
in some way the spirit of childhood itself, so that the child loses
himself in the reading of it, and finds himself in the world the
book creates. The matter for analysis is not the story, not the
subject, but how the author tells the story, how he imparts his
wisdom, upon what knowledge, or recollection, or retention of
childhood he draws to create a book which the child will recognize as his own, whether it is intended for him or not. Indeed
it is a temptation to say with Mr. Fadiman that it would be a far
better and wiser thing if fewer authors wrote with the phrase
"child audience" in mind, since the very idea of such an audience

seems to have, at times, a paralyzing and inhibiting effect. Rather should they write out of a compulsive memory of a time of life when the world was a thing of wonder and delight, when joy and happiness and grief and pain too, were so intense as to be almost physical sensations. It is because *The Yearling* was so written that children have adopted it. It is because Beatrix Potter's books were so written that their vital appeal never grows less. Reduced to mere skeleton of story, her books might seem to be no different than those written in attempted imitation, footless, inane, shallow attempts to capture the excellence of her spirit. Again there is nothing particularly unique in the plot of *Treasure Island,* but there is great uniqueness in the writing. On the surface, *Robinson Crusoe* seems to have a dull, pedestrian realism, but it is an informed, a life-like realism. More importantly, the book has that epic quality of gathering together in one culminating moment the meaning and significance of the story. *Big Tiger and Christian* is an amazing panorama of human existence, with again one moment of illumination when the secret of the book and of human greatness seems close to revelation. The originality of Arthur Ransome's books lies in his capture of the seriousness, earnestness, and imaginative quality of the play spirit of childhood. The nonsense of *Mary Poppins* is nonsense inspired by the author's recognition of a child's readiness to accept the extraordinary, that which is wonder-ful, full of wonder. *Tom Sawyer,* and *Huckleberry Finn, Honk the Moose,* and *Homer Price* are books instinct with the spirit of boyhood. All these books which have become literature for children, in the true sense, have been books which have created some kind of world which some child recognizes as his own. Not every world is for every child. That some books have achieved what may be called universal popularity should not blind us to the fact that if we seek originality in children's books, then we must accept the fact that this same originality will bring into emphasis the individual differences among children, which are no less great than those among adults. Neither complete nor immediate popularity is the criterion. The former is rarely possible because each person's private world is uniquely his own. The second cannot be demanded because the greater the book the less immediately comprehensible it is. If easy and quick popularity were the gauge, there would be little need for trained children's librarians. The obligation of a children's librarian is to recognize the truth of the statement so often made that only the best is good enough for the young, that

the zest and eagerness, the sense of wonder, of youth is deadened
when it is fed the mediocre.

It is essential that we should look at the other side of each
book, at the world behind the surface qualities of plot and incident and character, which are but the outward manifestations
of the inner spirit of the book. If we find on the other side empti-
ness, or mere pedanticism, or artificiality deriving from substitu-
tions of adult interests and preoccupations then we may be sure
that this book is not a part of children's literature, though it may
be one that they will read and forget.

If we did this more often, if we learned to recognize when a
book has the power to give some child that almost "fearful"
sense of enlargement, as Mr. Fadiman calls it, we would incur
less frequently certain fallacies of book selection, both for the
collection and for the individual child. One of the constant problems is the trial and error aspect, the infrequency with which the
true response is correctly defined. To some degree, this is inevitable, since we are adults selecting and suggesting books for a
group of people very different from ourselves. This difficulty leads
to further incidental errors, to an inclination to distrust children's
appreciation of what seems to the adult too subtle or too difficult.
In turn, this inclination leads to a tendency to select in greater
numbers books of more obvious appeal, and those which do not
need thought and analysis on the part of the selector. Greater
attention to the inner spirit of a story might enlighten us to ways
in which we might introduce those books which need introduction. Neither for purposes of professional reviews, or of book talks
to children, least of all, of personal conversation with children,
is it enough to be able to give a mere résumé of a book. Perception of the other side of a story would help in avoiding superficial labelling of books by type of story. To type *The Doll's
House, Impunity Jane, Hitty, Miss Hickory,* and *Floating Island*
as doll stories is accurate as far as it goes, but it does not go nearly
far enough. The real stories have wide differences and it is these
differences which make the world of each book a different world.
So it is with adventure stories, with fantasy, with historic fiction, with any book or group of books that has quality and distinction because the authors have something to say and say it
well, so as to illuminate the theme or idea that has given rise
to the story. *Johnny Tremain* stands out among all fiction dealing with the Revolutionary period. And it does so, not so much
because it is well written, and based on sound knowledge, but

because of that one moment when James Otis, coming un-
bidden to a meeting of the leaders of the revolutionary movement, says, "it is for a simple thing that we ... fight ... that a
man may stand up." In that one moment, the whole impact,
not only of the book, not only of the American Revolution, but
of the entirety of man's long struggle for freedom, is expressed
with a simplicity impressive in its intensity.

The whole problem resolves itself into this—what is the most
distinguishing and the most precious characteristic of childhood?
Is it the sense of wonder with all the limitless suggestions involved in that word? And if it is, is that faculty a thing to be
envied, as the people quoted earlier believe? If it is, and if books
help to sustain and cultivate it, what kind of books? On this
point, it is not likely that there will be complete agreement. The
disagreement is part of a larger conflict, between admiration and
respect for all that is scientifically and objectively measurable,
and the fact that man's inner life consists of subjective states of
mind and emotion; conflict between the emphasis upon material
security and the fact that man's chief aim remains the pursuit of
happiness, a condition not guaranteed by physical or financial
security; conflict between conformity and individuality; conflict
between the literature of knowledge and the literature of power,
or, if preferred, between the literature of enlightened existence
and the literature of mere literalness. Certainly there can be no
denial of the value, the need, and the place of the literature of
knowledge. But that admission does not involve approval of the
subordinating of humane literature to didacticism and pedanticism. There is no intention here of imposing a point of view
upon a whole group. There is the intention of suggesting that the
writing, the selection, and the use of books with children show
evidence of a confusion which is part of a larger confusion, and
are therefore matters for thought and discussion. There is nothing more admirable than the concern of adults for children, and
yet that same concern often manifests itself in distortion. The
development of children's literature shows that in every period
of strain and stress books for children have become the vehicles
for the fears and preoccupations of adults. Equally the history of
children's literature shows that literature of power, convictions,
and permanence is created only when writers are freed from
the shackles of ulterior motives, of conforming to current and
popular theories. The censorship which prescribes limits within
which an author must write, subjects to which he must confine

himself, which tacitly approves the distortion of fact to serve a purpose of the present, is no better than any other form of censorship.

It is vitally important that children have knowledge. It is important, as they grow older, that they be able to face without evasion or cynicism or defeatism, the world in which they are going to live. But it is possible that the ability to do this will come not so much from knowledge as from the memory of a childhood filled with that peculiar happiness which is the unique possession of childhood and which the merely informed person can never know. It is not the elucidation of the mystery of life children need, but rather the kindness, the wisdom, the humor, and the imagination that arouses a sense of wonder over that mystery without attempting to explain it.

In the last analysis, all literature to children is first of all a story, and that story should be part of the literature of existence; a story that never ends, but goes on and on, though the people in the story come and go when their parts are ended.

MAKING BOOKS COME ALIVE FOR CHILDREN *

Nancy Larrick

"It's up to you!" says Nancy Larrick, author of *A Parent's Guide to Children's Reading* and *A Teacher's Guide to Children's Books.* She means you, you, and YOU who are in contact with children.

When a three-year-old brings you a book to read, don't be surprised if it is about a submarine rescue or a man-made satellite.

* Reprinted by permission of the Association for Childhood Education International, 3615 Wisconsin Ave., N.W., Washington 16, D.C. "Making Books Come Alive for Children," by Nancy Larrick. From *Childhood Education* March 1962, Vol. 38, No. 7, 311–15.

These are hot subjects today, even with the very young; and adults had better take heed.

If you would make books come alive for a child, I know of no better way to begin than with the child. He *is* alive. His interests and concerns will make the book come to life for him. Oddly enough many an adult tries to make books come alive for a child by beginning with his own childhood interests. Frequently they lead to a dismal letdown.

KNOW TODAY'S CHILDREN

Today's children are different from the children we remember we were. They have different interests; they are using different words. Indeed, they are living in a different world. A second grader made this dramatically clear to me when I used the term, "prehistoric times." "Do you mean prehistoric times before television?" he asked.

That stopped me in mid-sentence until I began to think of the shattering changes in our society since television began a new era.

Mass media bombard the modern home with world news. Technical terms are brought from their old hideout in the laboratory to become the language of the general public, including children. Nowadays children's interests are often as adult as their vocabulary. If you have any doubts, check the toy counter of the nearest five-and-ten. You will see space ships and submarines but few teddy bears and baby dolls. The little red wagon has almost faded away.

Librarians report growing demand for children's books about outer space and underwater exploration. Some first-graders are rejecting cowboy stories as too babyish. Instead, they are asking for books about electricity and radiation. Fifth- and sixth-graders often turn to adult books as more appealing than those written for young readers. *The Diary of Anne Frank* and *Thirty Seconds over Tokyo* are favorites with this age level.

Television producers receive quantities of juvenile fan mail about programs created for adults. Apparently children and their parents have the same reading interests and are viewing the same television programs. Many of these deal with the conflicts and confusions of what we have been calling the adult world. It is small wonder, then, that today's child turns to books with different expectations from the child of 1930 or even of 1950. Through television, in particular, a child is likely to establish certain habits which affect his approach to books. For one thing, he is

used to making a choice. His television set permits him to select
the program he will view. If one channel does not please him he
switches to another, much as he swaps one comic book for another. He is used to being part of the adult world, watching the
same television programs with his parents and exchanging views
on an equal basis.

BY WAY OF CONTRAST

Imagine a child coming from this kind of world into the traditional classroom. He reads, "Oh! Oh! See. See. Come. Come,"
in a book selected for him. He meets with a group, also selected
for him, to hear others read the same colorless words at a pace
that is not his own. And, as one youngster put it, "We read and
read, but nothing ever happens in the story."

But something may be happening in the mind and heart of the
child himself. He may be deciding that reading is deadly dull and
therefore not for him. He may be finding out that this kind
of book talks down to him ("Come, children," says Mother.
"Come.") while television makes a man out of him, giving him
the same straight talk that it gives his parents.

Further, he may rebel against the slow pace of the three-group
lock step that means *read, listen, and wait.* He may not register his
protest verbally. But, television-trained as he is, he may tune out
that which is not appealing. Daydreaming is one way to do it.
Wriggling and squirming and interrupting are other ways.

LET HIM CHOOSE THE BOOKS

When a child is given the opportunity to choose the book he
will read, he begins to see things in a different light. This is what
he has done all his life with television. It is the procedure approved by the big, exciting grown-up world outside of school.

If each child is to have a choice, there must be many books
from which to select: easy books for the slow reader; more advanced books for the better reader; baseball books; fairy tales;
biographies; books about jet planes and outer space, about the
moon and deep-sea diving. There must be fiction and nonfiction,
poetry and prose.

Unless a child has been used to selecting books for himself, he
will need some guidance. He may resent guidance of the "see-
see-read-read" variety. But he will welcome guidance that is as
straightforward as a newscaster's report.

The third-grader who follows the world series is a natural for

How Baseball Began in Brooklyn,[1] by LeGrand. His sister, a horse fan, will thank you for a steer to *Misty of Chincoteague*,[2] by Marguerite Henry or *Little Vic*,[3] by Doris Gates. Space enthusiasts of all ages will be eager to know about *You Will Go to the Moon*,[4] by Mae and Ira Freeman; *A Book of Satellites for You*,[5] by Franklyn Branley; and that delightful bit of spoofing, *Miss Pickerell Goes to Mars*,[6] by Ellen MacGregor.

A book comes alive when it is in the hands of an interested reader. When an interest is already astir in the child, all you have to do is help him find the book which will kindle that interest further. That is the easiest kind of guidance.

To make it even simpler, there are numerous book lists which group favorite children's books by subject and age level. By using the index in the book list and reading the annotations, you have some guidelines by which to aid children in selecting books. Soon fourth- and fifth-graders will be consulting the same book lists when they choose books. Today's children like self-service, even in books.

MAKE THE INTRODUCTION ALIVE AND PERSONAL

Beyond this, it is important to introduce children to new interests and to open new vistas which will lead to books. This is where the fun begins—the challenge, if you will—for a child's adventures into new kinds of books and new kinds of subjects depend in large part on the introduction he gets from adults.

A printed list of recommended books won't do it. Certainly, required reading selected by adults won't do it—not today, when children are accustomed to the spoken word of radio and television, to hearing enthusiastic, firsthand reports of world affairs and commercial products.

Take a tip from television and make your introduction of a new book just as vital, just as personal. First read the book your-

[1] LeGrand. *How Baseball Began in Brooklyn* (Nashville, Tenn.: Abingdon Press, 1959).

[2] Marguerite Henry. *Misty of Chincoteague* (Chicago: Rand McNally & Co., 1947).

[3] Doris Gates. *Little Vic* (New York: Viking Press, Inc., 1951).

[4] Mae and Ira Freeman. *You Will Go to the Moon* (New York: Random House, Inc., 1959).

[5] Franklyn Branley. *A Book of Satellites for You* (New York: Thomas Y. Crowell Co., 1959).

[6] Ellen MacGregor. *Miss Pickerell Goes to Mars* (New York: Whittlesey House, 1951).

self; reread it if there's been a time lapse, letting yourself bask in its humor or pathos or whimsy.

Then while you are still aglow with it, read a chapter or two to children. Your delight in the book will show in the way you read it, and children will sense your enthusiasm. Soon they will want to be a part of it and ask for more.

Some of the real gems of children's literature need this kind of read-aloud introduction. Tell a 10-year-old that *Charlotte's Web,*[7] by E. B. White, is about a talking spider, and he may shy away. But read aloud part of that remarkable book, and Charlotte will have another devotee. The interest and sympathy in your voice and the magic of Charlotte's personality will do the trick.

The Borrowers,[8] by Mary Norton, and *Half Magic,*[9] by Edward Eager, profit from the same kind of introduction. Indeed, any book does. Read aloud a few chapters of a book you have already read and are sold on, and a listener's indifference is likely to vanish.

This is true for poetry, too. But you will have to read and reread before you meet your audience. The misreading of poetry can be as discordant as a soloist off key, and a dull listless voice will deaden interest from the start.

If your children have not been reading poetry, begin with something light, even humorous. Fourth- and fifth-graders love "The Tale of Custard the Dragon," by Ogden Nash. *The Golden Treasury of Poetry,*[10] selected by Louis Untermeyer, and *Time for Poetry,*[11] edited by May Hill Arbuthnot, are excellent collections of poetry for all ages. *Poems To Read to the Very Young,*[12] selected by Josette Frank, is just right for preschoolers.

Remember, too, that children today are used to seeing as well as hearing, so share the pictures as you read. In *Charlotte's Web,* Garth Williams' pictures of Wilbur the pig are irresistible. Even

---

[7] E. B. White. *Charlotte's Web* (New York: Harper & Bros., 1952).

[8] Mary Norton. *The Borrowers* (New York: Harcourt, Brace & Co., Inc., 1953).

[9] Edward Eager. *Half Magic* (New York: Harcourt, Brace & Co., Inc., 1954).

[10] Louis Untermeyer. *The Golden Treasury of Poetry* (New York: Golden Press, 1959).

[11] May Hill Arbuthnot. *Time for Poetry* (Chicago: Scott, Foresman & Co., 1952).

[12] Josette Frank. *Poems To Read to the Very Young* (New York: Random House, Inc., 1961).

the most hard-bitten fifth-grade missile expert will soften before Wilbur's contented smile as he stands under Charlotte's web.

When you read *I had a little . . .*[13], by Norma Levarie, hold the pages so children can see as you read. The drawings are as gay as the text with suspense at the turn of every page. First- and second-graders, by the way, will soon be guessing what the next rhyming surprise will be.

YOUNG AND OLD ALIKE

Read *I had a little . . .* the next time you have guests to dinner, and I think you will find they are as charmed as the children. Or read a chapter from *Charlotte's Web* to some of your contemporaries, and watch the reaction. These books have a quality that appeals to young and old alike. They have a subtlety, a sophistication if you wish, that lifts them above any grade-level label.

Watch for this as you search for books to introduce to today's children. Before you bring a book to a class, give it the read-aloud test. If it flows rhythmically to your adult ears, the chances are it will appeal to readers atune to adult oral-language media. If it speaks in the straight-forward manner accorded grown-ups, children will be pleased.

If you are intrigued by the information in a book of nonfiction or glowing with satisfaction over a book of fiction, you can be sure that most children will do likewise.

It's up to you!

13 Norma Levarie. *I had a little . . .* (New York: Random House, Inc., 1961).

MEETING DEVELOPMENT NEEDS THROUGH READING*

Paul A. Witty

> In this article ... Dr. Witty examines reading as a means
> of satisfying developmental needs—that is to say, read-
> ing as "bibliotherapy." His article surveys recent thought
> on the important subject of bibliotherapy and serves as
> a stimulating introduction to the articles that follow.

Many students believe that education should be regarded as a
process in which the maximum development of every boy and
girl is sought according to his unique nature and needs. Parallel-
ing this concept, "developmental reading" has gradually replaced
older concepts of the reading process. At one time, it was held
that the child first "learned to read and later read to learn." Today most educators insist that the reading experience of every
boy and girl should be meaningful from the beginning, and that
reading should be associated with interests and needs as children
mature.[1]
Throughout the history of American education, the value of
reading in changing attitudes and behavior of boys and girls
has been assumed. The content of the New England primer reflected the conviction that religious attitudes could be affected
or strengthened through reading. Later a nationalistic ideal was
suggested by the content of reading textbooks. To some degree at

* Paul A. Witty, "Meeting Development Needs Through Reading," 84, 451–
58. From the April, 1964 issue of *Education*. Copyright 1964 by the Bobbs-
Merrill Co., Inc., Indianapolis, Indiana, with permission of the author.

1 Paul A. Witty, "Relation of Reading to Personality Development." Supplementary Educational Monograph, No. 72. *Keeping Reading Programs
Abreast of the Times*. Chicago: The University of Chicago Press (October,
1950), pp. 172–77. See also the writer's article "Promoting Growth and Development Through Reading." Report of Proceedings, 1963 Spring Conference, Chicago Area Reading Association, May 11, 1963, for an extended
treatment of methods and of suitable materials.

least, the ideals of each era have been mirrored by the materials chosen for textbooks.

Moreover, it has been assumed that individuals are influenced not only by textbooks, but also by other printed materials. Again and again, the importance and worth of turning to textbooks for information, inspiration and deep satisfaction have been stressed, since as Thomas Carlyle long ago indicated, "All that mankind has done, thought, gained, or been: it is lying as in magic preservation in the pages of books."

BIBLIOTHERAPY AND READING PROGRAM

It is, however, only in recent years that reading has been advocated as a means of satisfying personal and social needs, and the term "bibliotherapy" employed as a method of need fulfillment. As defined by David H. Russell and Caroline Shrodes, bibliotherapy is a process of strong interaction between the reader and literature which may be utilized effectively in helping children to solve problems and to develop effectively. They state:

> ... This definition suggests that bibliotherapy is not a strange, esoteric activity but one that lies within the province of every teacher of literature in working with every child in a group. It does not assume that the teacher must be a skilled therapist, nor the child a seriously maladjusted individual needing clinical treatment. Rather, it conveys the idea that all teachers must be aware of the effects of reading upon children and must realize that, through literature, most children can be helped to solve the developmental problems of adjustment which they must face [1].

DEVELOPMENTAL TASKS AND READING

At Northwestern University, the writer and his associates have long believed that all children referred as problems to the Psycho-Educational Clinic may be best understood and helped by studying their behavior in relationship to basic human needs (2). This approach has proved effective in dealing with the various types of cases sent to the Clinic regardless of whether the referral is because of reading difficulty, personality maladjustment, or some other problem.

After a child has been carefully studied, reading experiences are frequently recommended in accord with "derived needs" or "developmental needs" as differentiated from basic human needs.

The "derived needs" resemble the "developmental tasks" set forth by Robert J. Havighurst and others. According to Havighurst, a "developmental task arises at or about a certain period in the life of an individual, successful achievement of which leads to happiness and to success with later tasks, while failure leads to unhappiness in the individual, disapproval by society, and difficulty with later tasks..." (3, 4).

Following is the list of "developmental needs" which has been employed for guiding reading at the Northwestern University Psycho-Educational Clinic:

1. Developing competency in physical skills or recreational pursuits.
2. Understanding oneself and developing an adequate, satisfying ideal of self.
3. Understanding one's social environment and adjusting oneself to one's peers.
4. Understanding one's place in a family group and achieving independence of adults.
5. Achieving academic competency.
6. Developing skills in oral and written expression and in reading.
7. Understanding and making desirable adjustments determined by the role of sex.
8. Achieving an understanding of vocations and of occupational demands.
9. Understanding the basic promises of our society and recognizing one's responsibility for successful participation in democratic life.
10. Developing an appreciation of scientific discovery and of life in the modern technological world.

Does Reading Affect Attitudes?

Many teachers and specialists in reading have expressed their belief in the influence of reading on attitudes and behavior. But studies have shown quite clearly that the nature and amount of change vary greatly.

For example, Nila B. Smith (5), reported a study in which elementary school pupils were asked to indicate books, stories, or poems which had changed their thinking or their attitudes. Although almost two-thirds reported that changes in attitudes had resulted from their reading, only about ten per cent stated that changes in behavior had also transpired. Significant was the fact that "with one exception, no two children in any room mentioned the same book as one which had changed their thinking or attitudes." It appears that reading does affect pupils, but that the results of reading are highly individual. Somewhat similar results were obtained by Samuel Weingarten in a study of junior college students (6).

Studies of the effects of reading have shown too that adults may be affected little, if at all, by their reading. During an election campaign, one writer examined the reaction of hundreds of adults to reading materials dealing with political topics, and concluded that "People of the same kind seem to hold the same political opinions whether they read books a great deal or not at all [7]." Nevertheless, individuals do continue to report changes in their attitudes and behavior resulting from reading.

Of course, pupils do not always show the attitudes anticipated from their reading. Their reaction to materials may be affected by their previous experiences, predispositions, or prejudices (8). Despite this fact, changes have been revealed in some studies in accord with anticipation. Thus, Deborah Elkins used a sociometric approach to study "rejected" children as well as leaders. She also asked the pupils to write about their wishes and their worries (9). It was found that the items of concern fell under two large headings, peer and family relations. Books and short stories on these topics were assembled. The reading and discussion of these materials seemed to have a beneficial effect on the pupils.

Despite such investigations and reports from case studies, we still have little reliable data concerning the effects of reading upon pupils. David Russell has pointed out that although we have established many facts about eye movements, interests, and tastes in reading, "we don't know much about what reading does to people [10]."

PREVENTIVE BIBLIOTHERAPY

Writers at present are becoming more and more cautious in using the term "bibliotherapy" to describe the association of reading with pupil needs. Thus, Richard L. Darling points out that "bibliotherapy" seems to be a misnomer when applied to such practices generally.

... since there is little difference between bibliotherapy as we have described it in this sense and teaching in the classroom and reader guidance in the library. Certainly it is mental hygiene but it lacks the basic requirement of therapy which seems to require that an illness be present to treat [11].

It seems desirable to consider the use of books to meet the needs of groups as preventive bibliotherapy, a practice designed to foster mental health.

Bibliotherapy as a "preventive" measure or guidance in reading according to individual needs is gaining acceptance as may be noted in widespread applications with exceptional pupils (12, 13). The writer of this article has indicated varied ways in which the classroom teacher may use books to satisfy the needs of slow-learning and of gifted pupils (14, 15).

For example, a balanced program provides the gifted pupil with opportunities to satisfy some of his personal and social needs through reading. An identification with a character in a story is sometimes beneficial. Thus, a gifted boy recovering from rheumatic fever experienced great personal satisfaction by reading Marguerite De Angeli's *Door in the Wall,* a narrative laid in seventeenth century England, which portrays the ways in which Robin, the son of a nobleman, stricken on the eve of departure for the contests, overcame his affliction and won the king's recognition.

Similarly, Eleanor Estes' *The Hundred Dresses* proved of value to an insecure girl through her discovery of the successful course followed by another girl in obtaining group sanction. Elizabeth Yates' *Amos Fortune: Free Man,* a story of a boy's rise above his environment, tells of the problems faced and overcome by an African prince sold in slavery. His devotion to the needy and his many sacrifices provide a heartening picture of what man can be at his best. This book afforded the stimulation needed by a gifted Negro pupil in developing appropriate goals and aspirations.

In the excellent biographical literature now available, gifted pupils may find additional inspiration as well as a sound basis for the formation of an ideal of self that is in keeping with their outstanding abilities and promise. Regional books such as Lois Lenski's *Strawberry Girl* and *Cotton in My Sack* and family stories such as Eleanor Estes' *Ginger Pye* may also help some gifted children understand people better. Many other books contain materials suitable for helping to fulfill other needs of exceptional pupils.

READING PROMOTES UNDERSTANDING

We have seen that reading to promote personal and social development has long been advocated, not only for exceptional children, but also in the regular classroom for all pupils. As early as 1940, when the significance of mental health in effective education became somewhat widely accepted, the importance of books in satisfying personal and social needs was also stressed (2, Ch. 3). This emphasis continued throughout the following years as writers indicated the important role played by reading in the lives of boys and girls (16).

Muriel Crosby has recently set forth her convictions with reference to books on the following words:

> Within books are the sources for helping a child
> to become aware of the beauty and power of words
> to recognize that he is not alone in a hostile world
> to identify himself with a great cause or a great idea
> to develop values to live by
> to find a life's work or avocation
> to discover the world of imagination
> to sustain an ideal which will guide him throughout his life
> to become inspired to be a Schweitzer, a Salk, a Hemingway
>   of the future [17].

Crosby also describes enthusiastically and sympathetically the role of books in helping children attain the above goals. She states:

> All children like all adults, have problems. Books will not by themselves solve children's problems or adults' problems. But books may help ... A skillful teacher ... is seeking constantly for ways to help children face problems, see them in perspective, and deal with them adequately. One of these ways is centered in books and reading [17].

It is not only children who may be helped through books to satisfy their basic needs, but also adolescents who may be similarly aided, as Frieda Heller suggests in the two paragraphs below:

> If the adolescent wishes help in understanding himself there will be titles similar to Bro's *Let's Talk About You,* Strain's

Teen Days, Fedder's *A Girl Grows Up,* Fosdick's *On Being a Real Person,* or Schacter's *How Personalities Grow.*

For those students who plan to take on marriage and family responsibility immediately on leaving school, Strain's *Love at the Threshold,* Landis' *Building a Successful Marriage,* Grove's *Your Marriage and Family Relationships,* or Landis' *Your Dating Days* will be helpful [18].

Geneva R. Hanna and Mariana K. McAllister have devoted much of their recently published book to describing the role of reading in helping to satisfy the developmental needs of adolescents. Their analysis of a large number of appropriate books is penetrating and timely (19).

In order to engage successfully in a developmental reading program, the high school teacher, similar to the elementary school teacher, needs to be acquainted with many books, as well as with other reliable sources for information. Some of these materials will be known to the teacher. Others may be chosen from lists of books included in the references cited in this issue of the magazine.

Teachers at all levels will find helpful suggestions set forth by Muriel Crosby and her associates in the fourth edition of *Reading Ladders for Human Relations* (20). They indicate the complexity of using reading to foster human relations and stress the significance of related experience.

Similarly the writer of this article believes that books are most effectively used for meeting needs when reading is associated with firsthand experience, when identification with characters in books are discussed, and when additional related reading is introduced. To obtain the maximum results it is desirable to study home conditions and community influences and to obtain the cooperation of the home. The entire process aims to promote normal, wholesome growth and development and to serve as a preventive measure. Accordingly, the writer believes that the term "bibliotherapy" should be used with discretion and limited to the specialized endeavor described by Ruth M. Tews:

Bibliotherapy is a process of selected activity involving reading materials, planned, conducted, and controlled as a treatment under the guidance of a physician for emotional and other problems. It must be administered by a skilled, professionally trained librarian within the prescribed purpose and goals [21].

Once again, we should bear in mind the relatively unpredictable and highly individual nature of children's reactions to books which they read.

Case Study

We should, however, recognize the value of the teacher's efforts to use reading as part of a program designed to promote sturdy individual growth (22). We should recognize the fact that reading alone is rarely, if ever, sufficient to satisfy pupil needs (23). In association with discussion and related experience, it may help greatly. Let us examine a pupil and his improvement, traceable in part to the use of books to satisfy his interests and "developmental needs."

John, age 10, was brought to the Psycho-Educational Clinic by his mother who asserted that John never read anything but the comics. Moreover, he was said to be just like his father who "never reads." His weaknesses and limitations were stressed in his presence with reiteration of the statement that John never read anything but the comics. At the conclusion of this recital, the examiner asked Mrs. X to name a few books that she had read recently. After considerable hesitancy and embarrassment, she recalled one title only—a book she had read at the time she had seen the movie of the same title.

John's health and general physical condition were excellent. Moreover, his IQ was 128; his academic achievement was slightly above his grade placement. However, he had received low, average, or poor marks in every school subject. When he was questioned concerning his wishes, he replied: "I want to be just like my father and do the things he does." To questions about his vocational ambitions and his favored recreation, his responses reflected his admiration for his father. John's father, it seemed, was a man thoroughly acquainted with airplanes, horses, and the customs of people in South America. John indicated also an attachment to his cousin—a former lieutenant in the army. If he were unsuccessful as a representative to South America, John said, he might enlist in the army.

Here was a clear case of thwarted developmental needs—status in group, understanding of oneself, and recognition for successful attainment.

John's program of reading was planned in accord with his interests and was designed to meet his needs. Accordingly he was provided with short stories about airplanes and South America. The stories presented a reading difficulty on the level of his demonstrated ability. He progressed rapidly in reading several *New World Neighbor* books about South America. He stated that two travel books illustrated by Disney contained the best stories he had ever read. Suitable books about horses were then procured. John enjoyed several of the stories in Fenner's *Horses, Horses, Horses.* He read Farley's *The Black Stallion,* James' *Smoky, The Cow Horse,* and Henry's *King of the Wind.*

By this time, John was enjoying reading. To assure further mastery of habits and skill in reading, he received systematic training in several books devised for use in the army. These experiences proved particularly pleasant. He reported his satisfaction in discussing the contents of these books with his cousin.

In John's case, many factors contributed to his progress. His reading gains were attributable in part to the close association of his experience with developmental tasks and interests. Some of his improvement was undoubtedly traceable to improved conditions and modified attitudes at home, as well as to the associated reading of books describing various patterns of effective home life. After several weeks, John's mother telephoned stating that "everyone is now reading at home." John's gains were fostered, too, by his discussions of books with his father and with his cousin, as well as by opportunities to contribute to class projects information he had acquired through reading.

CONCLUDING STATEMENT

Many teachers believe that reading instruction will become more beneficial when increased efforts are made to associate reading with interest and needs. The problem of identifying needs is difficult. Lists of needs and suggestions for studying them may prove helpful to the teacher. In addition, the teacher may find assistance through the use of interest inventories, observations, interviews, and discussion.

The selection of books to meet specific or general needs is not a simple task. Fortunately, however, there are excellent book lists which may guide this activity. And pupils should be encouraged to employ self-selection in fulfilling their interests and needs. It should be recognized, too, that the teacher should work closely with the librarian in a mutual effort to provide books to meet highly individual needs. Finally, in this endeavor the cooperation of the parent is necessary to obtain the maximum benefits and greatest satisfactions from reading.

References

1. Russell, David H., and Shrodes, Caroline. "Contributions of Research in Bibliotherapy to the Language-Arts Program," I, *The School Review,* Vol. LVIII (September, 1950), p. 335.
2. Witty, Paul A. "Children's Needs—The Basis for Language Programs," *Pupils Are People,* Nellie Appy, Chairman. National Council of Teachers of English (New York: D. Appleton-Century Company, 1941), Chapter 3, pp. 37–58.
3. Havighurst, Robert J. *Developmental Tasks and Education.* (Chicago: University of Chicago Press, 1948), p. 6.
4. Corey, Stephen M., and Herrick, Virgil E. "The Developmental Tasks of Children and Young People," *Youth, Communication and Libraries,* edited by Frances Henne, Alice Brooks, and Ruth Ersted (Chicago: American Library Association, 1949), pp. 3–13.
5. Smith, Nila B. "The Personal and Social Values of Reading," *Elementary English,* Vol. XXV (December, 1948), pp. 490–500.
6. Weingarten, Samuel. "Developmental Values of Voluntary Reading," *The School Review,* Vol. LXII (April, 1954).
7. Berelson, Bernard. "The Public Library, Book Reading, and Political Behavior," *The Library Quarterly,* Vol. LXV (December, 1945), pp. 298–99.
8. Waples, Douglas, Berelson, Bernard, and Bradshaw, Franklin. *What Reading Does to People.* (Chicago: University of Chicago Press, 1940).
9. Elkins, Deborah. "Students Face Their Problems," *The English Journal,* Vol. XXXVIII (November, 1949), pp. 498–503.
10. Russell, David H. "Some Research on the Impact of Reading," *The English Journal,* Vol. XLVII (October, 1958), p. 396.

11. Darling, Richard L. "Mental Hygiene and Books," *Wilson Library Bulletin,* Vol. XXXII (December, 1957), pp. 295–96.
12. Cahoe, E. "Bibliotherapy for Handicapped Children," *National Education Association Journal,* Vol. XLIX (May, 1960), pp. 34–36.
13. Sister Mary Jerome. "Retarded Children Can Enjoy Reading," *Catholic School Journal,* Vol. XIX (February, 1959).
14. Witty, Paul A. "Needs of Slow-Learning Pupils," *Education,* Vol. LXXXI (February, 1961).
15. Witty, Paul A. "A Balanced Reading Program for the Gifted," *The Reading Teacher,* Vol. XVII (May, 1963).
16. Burrows, Alvina Treut. "Caste System or Democracy in Teaching Reading," *Elementary English,* Vol. XXVII (March, 1950).
17. Crosby, Muriel. "Reading for Human Relations," *The Packet,* Vol. XVI (Winter, 1961–1962).
18. Heller, Frieda. "The Library in the School's Reading Program," *The High School Journal,* Vol. XXXIX (December, 1955), pp. 161–65.
19. Hanna, Geneva R., and McAllister, Mariana K. *Books, Young People, and Reading Guidance* (New York: Harper and Brothers, 1960), preface, xi–xii.
20. Crosby, Muriel (ed). *Reading Ladders for Human Relations,* Fourth edition (Washington, D.C.: The American Council on Education, 1963).
21. Tews, Ruth M. (issue ed.) "Bibliotherapy," *Library Trends,* Vol. XI (October, 1962), introduction, p. 99.
22. Witty, Paul A. "Promoting Growth and Development Through Reading," *Elementary English,* Vol. XXVII (December, 1950).
23. Larrick, Nancy. *A Parent's Guide to Children's Books* (Garden City, N.Y.: Doubleday and Company, 1958).

THERAPEUTIC READING*

Matilda Bailey

Reading for information is undoubtedly the kind used most widely in the public schools. However, English teachers talk of another type. It goes by a number of different names—"leisure reading," "free reading," and even the spirit-killing "extra-credit reading." Obviously, there is much overlapping in the two kinds of reading: reading for information often yields tremendous enjoyment, and reading for enjoyment frequently results in added information. As a consequence, it is difficult to pigeonhole kinds of reading according to any ironclad classification.

Therapeutic reading is not a third kind of reading, and it is certainly not a new type. Therapeutic reading is merely a new name for an old idea. The term *therapeutic* indicates that it is "of or related to the healing art." Surely boys and girls, as well as adults, are beset with all kinds of problems which bore into their hearts and minds. Often we can only vaguely guess at the things which are giving hurt. With such hazy appreciation of their problems, we naturally have difficulty in finding the right remedies. Fortunately, there is another way. Through the medium of books, children can find duplications of their problems and can see the ways by which other children have met their difficulties. Thus, therapy in reading occurs.

VALUE OF THERAPEUTIC READING TO BE SEEN IN MANY INSTANCES

Illustrations of the value of therapeutic reading are endless. One adolescent girl suffered agonies because of her bright red hair and her bountiful and unbeautiful crop of freckles. All her friends were of the peaches and cream variety. Then one day she discovered L. M. Montgomery's *Anne of Green Gables;* and by identifying herself with Anne, who also had red hair and freckles, her problems were solved. A well-known fiction editor tells of

having lost her father when she was very young. For a time the
world seemed entirely black, and then one day she found a story
about a little girl her own age who had lost both her father and
mother. Through a storybook character, who exemplified courage, she found solace.

Physical handicaps are frequently crushing blows to youngsters.
An example of what a make-believe story can do is seen in the experience of a boy named Jim. Jim was born with one leg shorter
than the other; and he was always forced to wear a built-up
shoe, which he hated because it clumped-clumped when he
walked. That built-up shoe seemed to be a nemesis; and because
of it, an otherwise normal boy was becoming moody and anti-
social. Then one day his father found a story about a boy, like
Jim, who had a built-up shoe. That boy played football, and he
was a star because with his heavy shoe he could kick harder than
any of the other players on the team. Because of that story, the
real boy, Jim, took hope. Last spring he was graduated from high
school. For his prowess in football as the best kicker in the district, Jim was awarded a special distinction. A book and a father's guidance had done the trick.

In an Anglo-Saxon community, the influx of "foreigners" often
presents a problem in the schools. One teacher wisely anticipated
difficulty by reading aloud to her class Eleanor Estes's *The Hundred Dresses.* The pupils quickly recognized that the little girl
in the story, with her strange and almost unpronounceable name,
was a very nice little girl made extremely unhappy by the Browns
and Smiths and Joneses in her class.

One girl said after the reading of the story, "I wish she were in
our class. We'd be nice to her."

Thus far the matter rested entirely in theory. However, one
morning a few weeks later, three new little faces appeared in the
classroom; their names were not easy to spell or to pronounce.
There was a moment of silence—this was the acid test. Then suddenly smiles of welcome appeared on the pupils' faces, and the
three new and rather frightened children smiled back. *The Hundred Dresses* had saved the day.

Many schools have the problem of the children of migrant
workers. The children are here today and gone tomorrow. Certainly something can be done to make the today that they are
here a happy one. If they are treated like outcasts, as they are
very frequently, all their todays will be a dreary and lonely pro-

cession. Many teachers have found that Doris Gates's *Blue Willow* can do much to ease the way.

Parents are often more conscious of the value of books in character building than teachers seem to be. After all, we may argue, we are so busy taking care of facts and "figgers" that we haven't the time to "Build thee more stately mansions, O my soul." Let the parents take care of that problem! Recently in a public library two mothers were heard to ask the librarian, "My little boy tells lies. Do you have a book that would be good for him to read?" and "I want a book for my son. He can't play with the other boys on our street without fighting with them." Certainly we shall agree that parents and teachers both need to be concerned with fundamental qualities of character and personality.

METHODS OF USING BOOKS IN THERAPEUTIC READING

The first step, obviously, is to determine whether there are any serious personality problems in a class. If there are—and there usually are—the next step involves an analysis of them. Some may be aggravated cases, and others may be simply incipient. Some may be individual problems, and some may be classwide. Not one can be solved with the mind alone. A little bit of love and understanding can go farther than all the statistics in an educational notebook. Hence, in speaking of the method to be used in therapeutic reading, one must agree with Parks that the teacher is always the best method.

Many of the problems in an average class are highly personal. Marie's family has had to go on relief, John's father and mother are getting a divorce, Ellen is an adopted child, Kathie lives on the wrong side of the tracks, Bob's father has died and he must help with the support of the family. Ted is fat and awkward, Carol's clothes look "funny." Bob has a new baby sister and no one at home is paying any attention to him. Little things, like a pair of squeaky shoes, can grind into the soul. Even such a little thing as "lining up" leaves one or two hurts: the first in line is always the "smallest," and the last in line is always the "biggest." Extremes can be painful.

As a consequence, personal hurts and problems should be dealt with individually. Often a sympathetic word or two and an understanding pat can do wonders. However, sometimes pride enters in; and the method has to be indirect. In the latter situation, it is usually best for the child himself *incidentally* to "discover" the book. Then there is no danger of his feeling that the privacy of his individual hurt has been invaded.

When a problem is a class problem, the matter can be brought into the open and discussed with all the pros and cons. Prejudices and fears and hates can be aired as common property. A story is told of a prominent contemporary painter, who in his early paintings had a lion phobia. In each of the pictures, a part of a lion could be seen; it would be crouching back of a column or tree or bush. The whole lion was never seen. Then one day the artist painted a picture and put a whole lion in the very center of it. That was the end of the lion phobia; he had brought the lion out in front, and that was the end of the complex.

When we bring our "lions" of hate and prejudice out in front, we usually are able to conquer them. Children pick up stereotyped adjectives to describe persons of minority groups. These adjectives set character appraisals: all persons belonging to those minority groups are what the adjectives say they are; there are no exceptions. Stories which give realistic pictures of persons of other races and of other creeds can do much to dispel wrong stereotyped thinking. Stories of this sort plus healthful class discussions are means by which the lion is brought out in front.

Often such discussions can begin with a single story read aloud by the teacher or read by the pupils themselves. If interests are aroused and thinking is challenged, the search for other stories dealing with the problem is certain to begin. Every possible source should be tapped. As the reading continues, interesting discoveries will be made. Thus, ideas can be pooled and evaluations made. The opportunities are endless.

Possible Books to Be Used in Alleviating Personal Problems

The bibliography given here includes books dealing with some of the most serious of the personal problems. It is merely a scratching of the surface, but it suggests possible remedies for the varied personal problems in each classroom.

The grade placement of the books, covering grades 1 through 12, is only approximate. The numbers immediately after the name of the book give the approximate grade level. Each teacher will know best the problems, the interests, and the reading abilities of her pupils and will use the books accordingly.

Appearance

FAT: Engelbretson, Betty, *What Happened to George,* 1–2
Evers, Helen and Alf, *Plump Pig,* 1
Felsen, Henry G., *Bertie Comes Through,* 8–10

SIZE: Beim, Jerrold, *The Smallest Boy in the Class,* 1–2
Felt, Sue, *Rosa-Too-Little,* k–1
Field, Rachel, *Hepatica Hawks,* 7–9
Harris, Leonore, *Big Lonely Dog,* 2–3
Krasilovsky, Phyllis, *The Very Little Girl,* k–1
Lipkind, William, *Even Steven,* K–3
Seuss, Dr., *Horton Hears a Who,* k–3
Ward, Lynd, *The Biggest Bear,* k–3

PLAIN: Gates, Doris, *Sensible Kate,* 6–7
McGinley, Phyllis L., *The Plain Princess,* 3
Palmer, Nena, *That Stewart Girl,* 8–10
Reyher, Rebecca, *My Mother is the Most Beautiful Woman in the World,* 2–3

Physical Handicaps

VARIOUS: Herman, William, *Heart Courageous,* 8–10

BLIND: Aldis, Dorothy, *Dark Summer,* 10–12
Bretz, Alice, *I Begin Again,* 10–12
Dickson, Marguerite S., *Bramble Bush,* 9–11
Knight, Ruth Adams, *Brave Companions,* 8–11
Putnam, Peter, *"Keep Your Head Up, Mr. Putnam!"* 10–12
Sherriff, Robert C., *Chedworth,* 11–12
Spellman, Francis J., Cardinal, *The Foundling,* 10–12

DEAF: Ehrlich, Bettina, *A Horse for the Island,* 10–12
Field, Rachel, *And Now Tomorrow,* 11–12
Murphy, Grace E. Barstow, *Your Deafness Is Not You,* 10–12
Warfield, Frances, *Cotton in My Ears,* 11–12

CRIPPLED: Angelo, Valenti, *Hill of Little Miracles,* 6–8
Baker, Louise, *Out on a Limb,* 9–12
Burnett, Frances Hodgson, *The Secret Garden,* 6–8
Menotti, Gian Carlo, *Amahl and the Night Visitors,* 9–12

PARALYZED: Barton, Betsey, *And Now to Live Again,* 10–12
Beim, Lorraine, *Triumph Clear,* 7–8

Berry, Erick, *Green Door to the Sea,* 8–10
Walker, Turnley, *Rise Up and Walk,* 10–12
Walters, Anne B. and Marugg, James K., *Beyond Endurance,* 10–12

HARELIP: Webb, Mary, *Precious Bane,* 11–12

SCAR: Leao, Sylvia, *White Shore of Olinda,* 11–12
Macken, Walter, *Rain on the Wind,* 11–12

Traits of Character and Personality

TIMIDITY: Cavanna, Betty, *Lasso Your Heart,* 8–10
Dalgliesh, Alice, *The Bears on Hemlock Mountain,* 3–4
Treffinger, Carolyn, *Li Lun, Lad of Courage,* 6–7
Williams, Gweneira, *Timid Timothy,* 1–2

CONCEIT: Boyle, Kay, *The Youngest Camel,* 5–6
Pope, Edith, *The Biggety Chameleon,* 1–3
Silliman, Leland, *The Daredevil,* 8–10
Tunis, John R., *Highpockets,* 8–12
Walden, Amelia E., *Marsha-on-Stage,* 8–10

LONELINESS: Bishop, Claire, *All Alone,* 4–6
Garner, Elvira, *Little Cat Lost,* 2–3
Glenn, Elsie and Morris, *Dumblebum,* 2–3
Smith, Dorothy E., *O, the Brave Music,* 10–12
Woolley, Catherine, *Ginnie and the New Girl,* 3–5

GREEDINESS: Cutler, Lin, *Peg-a-leg,* 2–3
Lipkind, William, *Finders Keepers,* k–3

SELFISHNESS: Bradbury, Bianca, *One Kitten Too Many,* 3–4
Cadell, Elizabeth, *The Cuckoo in Spring,* 9–12
Cavanna, Betty, *6 on Easy Street,* 8–10
Harkins, Philip, *Southpaw from San Francisco,* 8–10
Henry, Marguerite, *Geraldine Belinda,* 2
Latham, Frank B., *The Law or the Gun,* 5–8
Sigsgaard, Jens, *Nils All Alone,* 2

ACCEPTING RESPONSIBILITY: Beskow, Elsa, *Pelle's New Suit,* 1–2
Buck, Pearl, *The Big Wave,* 3–6

Du Soe, Robert C., *Three Without Fear*, 5–7
Farley, Walter, *The Black Stallion's Sulky Colt*, 8–10
Fisher, Aileen, *Homestead of the Free*, 5–8
Gray, Elizabeth J., *Adam of the Road*, 7–9
Hader, Berta and Elmer, *Cock-a-Doodle-Doo*, 2–3
Hazeltine, Alice I., comp., *Selected Stories for Teen-Agers*, 8–10
McFarland, Wilma, comp., *Then It Happened—*, 8–12
Rankin, Louise, *Daughter of the Mountains*, 7–8
Sperry, Armstrong, *Call It Courage*, 4–6
Stuart, Jesse, *A Penny's Worth of Character*, 4–5
Thompson, Mary W., *Pattern for Penelope*, 8–11

Poverty

Crone, Anne, *This Pleasant Lea*, 10–12
Gates, Doris, *Blue Willow*, 5–7
Giles, Janice, *Miss Willie*, 10–12
Sawyer, Ruth, *Maggie Rose; Her Birthday Christmas*, 4–7
Seredy, Kate, *Tree for Peter*, 4–6

Family Relationships

EVERYDAY LIFE: Alcott, Louisa May, *Little Women*, 7–9
Beim, Jerrold, *Kid Brother*, 2–3
Brink, Carol, *Family Grandstand*, 4–6
Carroll, Gladys H., *Christmas without Johnny*, 10–12
Cleary, Beverly, *Henry and Ribsy*, 4–5
Enright, Elizabeth, *Spiderweb for Two*, 5–7
Estes, Eleanor, *The Moffats*, 4–7
———, *The Middle Moffat*, 4–7
———, *Ginger Pye*, 4–7
Gilbreth, Frank B., Jr. and Carey, Ernestine G., *Cheaper by the Dozen*, 9–12
Holberg, Ruth, *Tomboy Row*, 4–6
Lenski, Lois, *Papa Small*, k–2
Millar, Margaret, *It's All in the Family*, 10–12
Partridge, Basil, *The Penningtons*, 10–12
Rawlings, Marjorie K., *The Yearling*, 9–12
Reynolds, Barbara L., *Pepper*, 4–6
Smith, Madeline B., *The Lemon Jelly Cake*, 10–12
Turnbull, Agnes S., *Gown of Glory*, 10–12
West, Jessamyn, *Cress Delehanty*, 9–12
Wilson, Hazel, *More Fun with Herbert*, 4–6
Woolley, Catherine, *Holiday on Wheels*, 3–5

NEW BABY: Flack, Marjorie, *The New Pet*, 1
Hawkins, Quail, *The Best Birthday*, k–2

TWINS: Du Jardin, Rosamond, *Double Date*, 8–10
Haywood, Carolyn, *The Mixed-up Twins*, 2–4

BROKEN HOME: Beim, Jerrold, *With Dad Alone*, 2–4
Cronin, A. J., *Green Years*, 11–12
L'Engle, Madeleine, *Camilla Dickinson*, 10–12
Lewiton, Mina, *The Divided Heart*, 8–10
Moody, Ralph, *Man of the Family*, 9–12
Smith, Dorothy E., *He Went for a Walk*, 10–12
Stone, Amy, *P–Penny and His Little Red Cart*, 3–5

ADOPTED CHILD: Daringer, Helen F., *Adopted Jane*, 4–5
De Leeuw, Adele and Cateau, *The Expandable Browns*, 3–6
Doss, Helen, *The Family Nobody Wanted*, 9–12
Goudge, Elizabeth, *City of Bells*, 11–12
Montgomery, L. M., *Anne of Green Gables*, 8–10
Rose, Anna P., *Room for One More*, 9–12
Runbeck, Margaret Lee, *Our Miss Boo*, 8–12

ORPHAN: Eustis, Helen, *The Fool Killer*, 10–12
Gallico, Paul, *The Small Miracle*, 10–12
Horgan, Paul, *One Red Rose for Christmas*, 9–12
Stuart, Jesse, *The Beatinest Boy*, 4–6

Boy-Girl Relationships

Bro, Margueritte, *Stub, A College Romance*, 10–12
Cleary, Beverly, *Henry and Beezus*, 4–5
Craig, Margaret, *Julie*, 10–12
Daly, Maureen, *Seventeenth Summer*, 9–12
Du Jardin, Rosamond, *Boy Trouble*, 8–10
Gray, Elizabeth J., *Sandy*, 9–12
Horner, Joyce, *The Wind and the Rain*, 9–12
Stolz, Mary S., *To Tell Your Love*, 8–11
Summers, James L., *Girl Trouble*, 8–10

Relationships with Persons of Other Races and from Other Countries

Bannon, Laura, *Hat for a Hero* (Mexican), 1–3
Bard, Mary, *Best Friends* (French), 5–7
Beim, Lorraine, *Two Is a Team* (Negro), 1–2

Bemelmans, Ludwig, *Madeline's Rescue* (French), 1–3
Benary-Isbert, Margot, *The Ark* (German), 7–9
Blanton, Catherine, *Hold Fast to Your Dreams* (Negro), 9–10
Bontemps, Arna, *Lonesome Boy* (Negro), 1–3
Church, Richard, *Five Boys in a Cave* (English), 6–7
Clark, Ann N., *Secret of the Andes* (Inca Indian), 4–7
Davis, Norman, *Picken's Treasure Hunt* (African), 2–4
De Angeli, Marguerite, *Bright April* (Negro), 4–6
———, *Elin's Amerika* (Swedish), 4–6
———, *Up the Hill* (Polish), 4–6
Decker, Duane, *Hit and Run* (Negro), 8–9
Estes, Eleanor, *A Hundred Dresses* (Polish), 4–6
Flack, Marjorie, *Story about Ping* (Chinese), 1–3
Goetz, Delia, *Other Young Americans* (Latin Americans), 8–9
Guareschi, Giovanni, *Don Camillo's Dilemma* (Italian), 10–12
Lewis, Elizabeth F., *Young Fu of the Upper Yangtze* (Chinese), 7–9
Liang, Yen, *Dee Dee's Birthday* (Chinese), k–1
Lipkind, William, *Boy with a Harpoon* (Eskimo), 4–6
Long, Eula, *Faraway Holiday* (Mexican), 1–2
McSwigan, Marie, *All Aboard for Freedom* (Czech), 6–7
Mirsky, Reba P., *Thirty-one Brothers and Sisters* (African), 4–6
Papashvily, George and Helen, *Anything Can Happen* (Russian), 10–12
Politi, Leo, *Little Leo* (Italian), k–3
Prishvin, Mikhail M., *The Treasure Trove of the Sun* (Russian), 5–7
Ritter, Elizabeth, *Parasols Is for Ladies* (Negro), 4–6
Rugh, Belle D., *Crystal Mountain* (Lebanese), 4–7
Schartum-Hansen, Ingvild, *Ingvild's Diary* (Norwegian), 5–8
Seredy, Kate, *Good Master* (Hungarian), 5–7
Shannon, Monica, *Dobry* (Bulgarian), 5–8
Tunis, John R., *All-American* (Negro and Jewish), 8–11
Unnerstad, Edith, *The Saucepan Journey* (Swedish), 4–7
Walden, Amelia E., *Daystar* (Italian), 8–10
Woody, Regina J., *Starlight* (Negro), 6–8

Prevention or Cure: Both Are Possible in Well-Chosen Books

The kind of reading described in this *A B C Language Arts Bulletin* may result in something that may be even more valuable than therapy. If we can anticipate difficulties, there is no need

for remedy. For example, if we can help boys and girls to understand appreciatively the people of other races and from other
countries, prejudices may be forestalled. If we can recognize in a
child personality traits which may later grow into personality
problems and if through books we can give him insight, we have
been good teaching "doctors." If we can throw light upon all the
dark crannies of the mind and heart before fear and hate and
bias creep in, then we have gone a long way in educating healthy-
minded boys and girls.

Therapeutic reading may be a kind of "laying up treasures."
Today is good, but tomorrow may bring heartaches. When heartaches and failures and rejections come, what is the bulwark? It
may be knowing someone who has had the same experience. It
may also be a book, read years before, in which a character met
and solved a similar problem. Thus, "remembrance of things
past" may be the therapy for tomorrow.

AT THE NORTH END OF POOH:
A STUDY OF BIBLIOTHERAPY *

Ethel Newell

Pooh Bear began to sigh, and then found he couldn't
because he was so tightly stuck; and a tear rolled down
his eye, as he said:

"Then would you read a *Sustaining Book,* such as
would help and comfort a Wedged Bear in Great Tightness?"

So for a week Christopher Robin read *that sort of
book* at the north end of Pooh, and Rabbit hung his
washing on the south end.

* Ethel Newell, "At the North End of Pooh: A Study of Bibliotherapy,"
Elementary English 34 (January, 1957), 22–25. Reprinted with the permission
of the National Council of Teachers of English and Ethel Newell.

And at the end of a week, Christopher Robin said, "Now." And Pooh Bear came free. (*Winnie, The Pooh—* Milne).

Wedged Bear in Great Tightness

Pooh Bear was in a jam. A sustaining book was read to him during the time of trial, and at the end of the week Pooh came free. How splendid if all bibliotherapy held such promise! But many people, young and old, do not even know they are in a jam—others know them as maladjusted, some who know they are in trouble will not ask or look for the sustaining book; others, when they read, fail to transfer from the book world to their reality.

The child has been called a modern discovery, for from this era of psychology has grown a new and tender regard for childhood. Today children are people, with an age of their own, with feelings, desires, fears, and hurts, and, above all, needs—great needs to grow and to be allowed to grow, needs for understanding.

We are convinced today that the best way we can give our child what he needs most is to become informed parents, teachers, and librarians. In becoming informed, we learn among many things, that children are individuals and that they have problems. Children of all ages fear some form or other of "horrible heffalumps" —the unknown, the strange, problems, struggle.

In Rumer Godden's newest book, children are called sparrows, so vast and lively is their cheeping. We are inspired to greater responsibility in remembering that though they sold for only three farthings, not one should fall to the ground.

From the day our child walks away from his own door yard, the problems arising from interaction with others are forever after his to solve. And "ensemble living" is without rehearsal. Annis Duff reminds us—not the same thing at all as ensemble playing where a pattern tells us where to take the leading part and when to twitter away quietly in the background. Here inexperienced players feel their way through an unwritten score.

The Sustaining Book

Now we remember that Pooh was too fat and that bibliotherapy was prescribed as an aid in the crisis. We ask, *is* there *real* help to be found in books for the personal problems of children? . . . . What kinds of help and how much? . . . . How sure? . . . . In what books?

Real help? Bibliotherapy is grounded in the theory that there is a relationship between personality and vicarious experience. A child will identify with a character who is having trouble similar to his own, his tension will be relieved, and he may imitate the hero on the battlefield, bringing about the hoped-for transformation.

The testimony of Margaret Benary-Isbert in a recent issue of *The Horn Book Magazine* is but one of many on the values of bibliotherapy:

> I have proof enough in my own life that books can be a great help and inspiration. What a reassurance it was for us in the war, when the enemy planes dropped bombs on our cities, to read Thornton Wilder, Tolstoy, and Samuel Butler! Books helped to keep alive in us the knowledge that even wars cannot destroy the world of the spirit and the heart.

Ministers, counselors, and other therapists, including librarians and teachers, relate many case histories demonstrating the values of bibliotherapy. As we examine the books they recommend, we see differences in use and in standards for selection, but all agree that therapeutic stories have value.

As educators and librarians, we have already learned to believe, with Lillian Smith and others who have made scholarly studies, that childhood is much too fleeting to allow time for anything but the best. One and all, we agree that with the vast amount of superlative literary material with which we can nourish and arm our young today we should know what that material is and recognize the criteria which prove useful in evaluating forthcoming books.

At the outset then, considering the case for children's literature, shall we not honestly ask—can any book so didactic as to admit a cure as its aim stand sufficiently high on our own measure? Or are we wrong in measuring books and books-for-therapy by exactly the same yardstick?

The answer seems to be no and yes.

Perhaps the question is not really so much one of the value of therapeutic stories as it is one of the degree or nature of the value.

What kind of help? Help from books is of two general kinds and of many degrees: first, the slow, steady *growth into a deepened self* from the experiences of reading real literature; second, an immediate first aid for emotional illness, which may be found in the here-and-now books with a mission, not lasting literature, but as necessary as a shot of penicillin for a particular infection.

Information itself is one kind of armor against difficulty. The fears of a child going to the hospital may be eased by information about our doctor friends, the pleasant nurses, the child companion in the next bed, the comic books on the table. But *real* armor, it seems, is strength for the battle. Annis Duff *(Longer Flight)* says that the most and least we can aim at is the development of such inner strength that, *come what may*, the child need never be afraid. Inner strength will come from emotional experience, and only real stories (not informational books dressed in story clothing) can satisfy emotions.

The strongest appeal then, now in need, and always, is for the book to grow on. And formulas and missions do not seem to produce great literature. Nevertheless, simple, realistic stories of present-day children hold an important place in children's reading today and are often delightful, but their value is in their *timeliness*, rather than in excellence of writing.

How sure? The values recorded in book lists such as those of Kircher, LePlante and O'Donnell, and Taba are largely useful as general analyses of content. But just because *Timmy and the Tiger* is listed under "overcoming fears" does not mean that a certain Johnny we know will recognize or accept the similarity between himself and Timmy and profit by the experience. To him it may be just another story. Research is a little discouraging about the chances of transfer.

Clara J. Kircher in the bibliography *Character Formation Through Books* says there are two ways in which reading of books may be essential aid in treating the problem child: (1) the child reads of a similar problem and obtains emotional relief, and (2) the child gleans principles of conduct which enable him to better manage himself. But she adds,

> We must not delude ourselves with the idea that once a moral principle gains entrance to the mind of the child it determines conduct. I have been deeply interested in observing a child acquire a good moral principle, see its beauty and recognize its validity, but refuse to apply it to his own personal problem.

If the chosen material is good in itself, the theory that children will become like their heroes does no harm since children are "past masters at pulling their own particular plums out of any pie" (Betzner and Moore, *Every Child and Books*). However, all such plans tend to invite preachment and personal application which children resent, to narrow the range of choice, to encourage in adult leaders false hopes of an easy road to a supreme end.

In what books? In all books which have the power to soothe, awaken, probe, and inspire—fiction, poetry, drama, biography—and those factual books which are written with imagination and with grace of style.

Among much of the American realism we choose, we will note an emphasis upon a single child, with which the reader's ego is easily identified. Among writers who already have made notable contributions are Eleanor Estes, Newbery winner whose Moffat family books and the *Hundred Dresses* stand out as classics; Doris Gates, author of *Blue Willow* and other stories of migrant and socially insecure children; Marguerite De Angeli, author-artist, from whose pen have come the Newbery winner *Door in the Wall* and a group of charming little stories of minorities people— *Bright April, Yonie Wondernose, Up The Hill,* and others; Ruth Sawyer, author of *Old Con and Patrick, Roller Skates,* and the newer *Maggie Rose;* Florence Crannell Means, who writes excellent stories of the minorities and their regions; Lois Lenski, author of American regionalism; Mabel Leigh Hunt, who wrote the modern Negro story *Ladycake Farm;* John R. Tunis, author of the best on school sportsmanship; Ann Nolan Clark, Elizabeth Janet Gray, Elizabeth Enright, Kate Seredy, Claire Huchet Bishop, Florence Hayes, Mary Stolz, Meindert De Jong.

The books will be largely concerned with realism, the "can happen" books, but let us never forget that laughter is a great unifier and tension breaker, that poetry is one of the most powerful instruments to inspire; and Jessie Orton Jones would have us understand ourselves and others as a religious experience, beginning with the rhythm of "evening and morning" refrain in that great poem of creation, the first chapter of Genesis.

How may we know them? We will apply the same criteria and measure to the books for growth that we have applied to all imperishable literature. Character portrayal which comes from both skill and understanding of children will give these books intense reality.

As criteria for judging that first-aid book, valuable chiefly for its timeliness in the life of an individual child with an individual problem, we will ask that it be well written; that purpose does not obscure the story; that it be written subtly; and that the author avoid the sentimental mood which results in a book about children rather than for them.

As librarians and teachers, we may choose to conclude our study with a resolution that not a single sparrow in our flock, not one troubled young heart within our reach, will fail to find guidance, either for growth or for cure, in the words which Kipling knew— words which "come alive and walk up and down in the hearts of men."

Bibliography of Background Reading

Adams, Bess Porter. *About Books and Children*. Holt, 1953.

Arbuthnot, May Hill. *Children and Books*. Scott-Foresman, 1947. (*Note:* A new edition was published in 1964.)

Benary-Isbert, Margot. "The Need of Understanding in Our Shrinking World," *The Horn Book Magazine,* June, 1956.

Betzner, Jean and Moor, Annie E. *Every Child and Books*. Bobbs-Merrill, 1940.

Duff, Annis. *Bequest of Wings*. Viking, 1944.

———. *Longer Flight*. Viking, 1955.

Ferris, Helen. Editor. *Writing Books for Boys and Girls*. Doubleday, 1952.

Jones, Jessie Orton. "Books, Children, and Religion," *The Horn Book Magazine,* February, 1954.

Kircher, Clara J. *Character Formation Through Books, a Bibliography*. Catholic University of American Press, 1952.

Lewis, Claudia. *Writing For Young Children*. Simon and Schuster, 1954.

Meigs, Cornelia, and others. *A Critical History of Children's Literature*. Macmillan, 1953.

Russell, David H. "Guidance Resources in Literature" (Leaflet No. 5, *Adventuring in Literature with Children,* A.C.C. Int. 1953).

Shrodes, Caroline. "Bibliotherapy," *The Reading Teacher,* Vol. 9, No. 1, International Council for the Improvement of Reading Instruction, October, 1955.

Smith, Lillian H. *The Unreluctant Years*. A.L.A., 1953.

Yashima, Taro. "On Making a Book for a Child," *The Horn Book Magazine,* February, 1955.

COMIC BOOKS: A TEACHER'S ANALYSIS*

Dwight L. Burton

Comic books are back in the headlines. Much of the current
public furor is traceable to a book by Frederic Wertham,[1] a New
York psychiatrist, who contends that comic books promote, among
other undesirable outcomes, illiteracy, unwholesome states of
mind, and delinquent behavior. The *NEA Journal,* in its November, 1954, issue,[2] designates Dr. Wertham's book as "the most
important book of 1954" and admonishes local education associations and parent-teacher associations to "see that it is widely
read and that the community takes steps to protect children from
the menace it describes."

Children and adults now buy more than one billion comic
books each year, and, with deadly regularity, studies of children's
voluntary reading show comics heading the list, particularly
among children in grades four to eight. Public and professional
concern over this interest in the comics is not new. A check of
the *Readers' Guide to Periodical Literature* shows that since 1945
more than 250 essays and articles on comics have appeared in
American periodicals, including such journals as the *Saturday
Review, The Atlantic Monthly, The New Yorker,* and Phi Beta
Kappa's *American Scholar.*

Teachers long have shared in the general concern over the wide
reading of comic books and their impact upon children's minds.
Several years ago the National Council of Teachers of English

* Dwight L. Burton, "Comic Books: A Teacher's Analysis" *Elementary
School Journal,* 56 (October, 1955), reprinted by permission of The University of Chicago Press, Copyright October, 1955.

1 Frederic Wertham, *Seduction of the Innocent.* New York: Rinehart & Co.,
Inc., 1954.

2 Joy Elmer Morgan, "Seduction of the Innocent," *NEA Journal,* XLIII
(November, 1954), 473.

published an article entitled "Substitutes for the Comics."[3] As professional people, teachers should make sure that lay groups are familiar with the materials mentioned and with others, such as the December, 1941, issue of the *Journal of Experimental Education* and the December, 1949, issue of the *Journal of Educational Sociology,* which present research relative to comics. The findings of research, in the main, fail to support the conclusions of Dr. Wertham. Without acting as an apologist for objectionable comic books, the teacher has an obligation to make research findings available to groups discussing the matter.

BASIC APPEALS OF THE COMIC BOOKS

Elementary school teachers interested in developing reading interests and tastes of children have an additional stake in understanding children's zest for the comic books. Might not the comics be a foot in the door to success in guiding children to more profitable reading experiences? Carr has advised:

> If the teacher or parent is concerned about a child's growth in appreciation of "good" books, let him start with the present level of the child and initiate him into books that attract him with the same qualities of adventure, excitement, and humor that he is meeting in comic books.[4]

What, then, are the basic appeals of the comic books?

Probably the most obvious appeal of the comics lies in the ease with which they can be read and understood. The vocabulary of the comics is not particularly easy; one study estimates the difficulty level at fifth to seventh grade.[5] This is unimportant, however, for the actual text need not be read at all. Looking at the pictures and reading a word here and there are enough to get the story. Superior readers may read as many comics as inferior readers, but the poor reader especially may be attracted to the comics if the required or recommended reading in class is continually beyond him.

Certainly another of the basic attractions of the comic books is that they appeal immediately to more senses than does straight

[3] Constance Carr, "Substitutes for the Comics," *Elementary English,* XXVIII (April and May, 1951), 194–200, 276–85. These articles were reprinted in a pamphlet, which is now out of print while undergoing revision.

[4] *Ibid.,* p. 194.

[5] Robert L. Thorndike, "Words and the Comics," *Journal of Experimental Education,* X (December, 1941), 110–13.

reading. Little imaginative effort is necessary to read them. The reader need not conjure up his own images. The characters, complete with bulging biceps and golden tresses or patently evil visages, and the situations are there already in bright colors. The comics are therefore a haven for the lazy or sluggish imagination.

Then, too, the content of the comic magazines is highly compatible with the nature of children in preadolescence or early adolescence, the period when comics are at their peak of popularity. Although the content is highly varied, common to all the comic magazines are the magic ingredients of action, suspense, mystery, and adventure—adding up to "punch" in the mind of the young reader. The frequent stress on the fantastic or the bizarre is in line with the wild flights to which the imagination is inclined in late childhood and early adolescence. The main characters in the comics tend to be either supermen, who represent a kind of ideal fulfillment, or simpletons to whom one can feel superior. Says Al Capp, creator of Li'l Abner, "When Yokum speaks, he speaks for millions of morons."

The appeal of the comics is rooted, too, in the fact that their picture of life and the assumptions underlying it are naturally acceptable to the immature mind of the reader. This is true of all "trash" literature and of many motion pictures and radio and television programs. That life is an exciting physical adventure is one assumption of the immature mind. Another is that people are either all good or all bad, with no intermediate degrees, and that one can tell the difference usually by physical appearance alone. One just knows that clean-cut Roy Rogers is a "good guy" while his unshaven adversaries are crooks. The outlaws in "Dick Tracy" and "Batman" usually have revolting physical characteristics and mannerisms. Another assumption undergirding comic-book experience is that romantic love and money lie at the heart of the problems of life. Still another is that the end justifies the means: it matters not that Superman kills a few people here and there and destroys countless dollars' worth of property, for he is on the side of right. In the comics, people in authority—policemen, mayors, senators, teachers, parents, corporation heads—tend to be stupid, pompous, or sadistic, and inevitably they are humiliated. How appealing is this to the youngster who is so much under the thumb of adult authority! The rebellion against authority, whether of the Bugs Bunny or Li'l Abner variety, is a very real appeal.

Finally, of course, the success of the comic books is aided by their low cost and their availability.

Transition Books

Once the teacher has made an analysis of the basic appeals of the comic books, he is in a position to construct a ladder out of the aesthetic wasteland which they represent by steering pupils to selections which contain the same basic appeals yet represent a step upward toward a more mature and wholesome reading experience. What qualities should these "transition" materials have?

1. They must be easy to read, appropriate to the reader's level. Difficulty in recognizing more than one in one hundred words will quickly kill the pleasure element in reading. Though the reading level is low, the selection still may be aesthetically satisfying, as writers like Eleanor Estes, Doris Gates, and Stephen Meader have demonstrated.

2. It is also most important that transition materials reflect experience close to that of the reader. Identification with characters and situations is a keystone of appreciation in reading and, for most pupils at the early adolescent and late childhood level, this identification must be literal. Only mature readers develop the ability to make abstract identifications with characters and situations. It is psychologically impossible for the pupil to jump from the comics to a pleasurable reading of *Evangeline*. Preferably, characters in these transition selections should be of about the age of the reader, and their experiences should be of the familiar or the exciting kind with which the reader wants to identify.

3. Transition books must avoid the gross distortion of experience that is characteristic of the comics. Yet the experience represented should be simple, since life for most young readers is relatively uncomplicated. Action still will occur mostly on the physical plane, but the plots should avoid the wild coincidence and improbability of many of the comics. True, the young protagonists often will do surpassing things in a world curiously detached from adult control, but perhaps we can accept this at this stage. Traumatic experiences involving excessive violence and the sordid should be avoided.

4. These materials must have the magic ingredients of "punch"; action, suspense, peril are the watchwords. Pupils should not get

the idea that the books on the teacher's recommended list are
likely to be dull.

5. Finally, transition materials must be made as available as
possible. Classroom libraries, book exhibits and bazaars, bulletin-
board displays of book jackets will help. Parent-teacher associations and other lay groups interested in combating the comic-
book "menace" might concern themselves with making other
reading materials more plentiful and available for children.

What are some selections and types of selections which fit these
characteristics? The area of folklore offers rich possibilities as an
antidote for comics. Each region of the country has its folklore,
which can be appreciated at various levels of awareness but which
has much in common with the comics: the lusty, sometimes slap-
stick, humor; the action; the quality of the unusual and amazing;
the superheroes. Yet all of this is of a much richer, more wholesome, and more artful fabric than the comics display.

Many of the selections in such series as the Bobbs-Merrill
(Indianapolis) "Childhood of Famous Americans," with its simple biographies of Davy Crockett, Narcissa Whitman, and others,
fit this transition category for third and fourth graders. So might
the "Landmark" and "World Landmark" books of Random House
(New York), with the stories of General Custer, the FBI, and the
Battle of Britain, among many others, serve this purpose with
fifth and sixth graders. The "American Adventure" series of
Wheeler Publishing Company (Chicago) and the "Real People"
series of Row, Peterson and Company (Evanston, Illinois) are in
the same category. These books are useful as supplementary materials in the social studies field, and some of the selections provide
literary experiences in their own right. A few examples of writers
whose books fill the transition need in grades seven and eight are
Jim Kjelgaard, Montgomery Atwater, Doris Gates, Shannon Garst,
Stephen Meader, Kenneth Gilbert, and Howard Pease.

A healthful viewpoint toward comic books is summarized in a
statement of the faculty of the Whittier Elementary School in
Minneapolis:

> Those of us who hope to guide children's tastes and espe-
> cially their reading interests must certainly take note that the
> comics are a form of reading each child takes to without
> coaxing....

> With adult guidance the comics may serve as a bridge to
> the reading of more lasting books. We must help our children

discover good books that are exciting too and teach them to discriminate among comic books; then we may safely accept our children's comic reading for what it is—a stage in their growth—provided we also help them toward wider horizons of interest and appreciations.[6]

[6] *Guide to the Teaching of Reading in the Elementary School,* p. 130. Minneapolis, Minnesota: Division of Elementary Education, Public Schools, 1950.

SUBSTITUTES FOR THE COMIC BOOKS*

Constance Carr

Does Hop Along Cassidy or Superman ride or fly your household or schoolroom? Does Bugs Bunny call in a raucous voice, "What's up, Doc?" If so, you are probably not alarmed over the children's natural imitation of the heroes they know best. But perhaps you are alarmed over a child's addiction to the comic books to the exclusion of more profitable reading.

Comic books have been the subject of many violent arguments for the past ten years. We could name outstanding people supporting either side with acceptable reasons. But rather than to divide the issue into sides, what about joining forces to suggest books that will fill the needs of children now reading comic books?

If the teacher or parent is concerned about a child's growth in appreciation of "good" books let him start with the present level of the child and initiate him into books that attract him with the same qualities of adventure, excitement, and humor that he is meeting in comic books.

Let us take a look at the most popular comic magazines and

* Constance Carr, "Substitutes for the Comic Books I," *Elementary English,* 28 (April, 1951), 194–200, 214. Reprinted with the permission of the National Council of Teachers of English.

comic strips named in the Witty study [1] and find what types they portray. We find two main classifications—adventure and humor. The adventure comics may be broken down into types of "fantastic adventure," "general blood and thunder," "cowboys," "jungle stories," and "detective stories." The humor comics can be broken down into types such as "adults in ridiculous positions," "getting ahead at great odds" and "little heroes."

As we find books to substitute for all these types we are also going to include a section called "real boys and girls," which is a cross section of adventure and humor not met in the comics.

We want to emphasize strongly several obvious implications about the books to be substituted and their use:

1. They must be easily accessible.
2. There must be a quantity of them from which to choose.
3. There should be no forcing of reading or forcing of book reports, only fun in sharing a good story.
4. Many of the books should be quick reading—at one sitting.
5. They will be more enticing to the young reader if they have many illustrations which carry along the plot of the story. They have the added advantage of usually having larger and better pictures.
6. The adult must know the kind of comics each child prefers and then know what books make similar appeal. The adult must see that such books are accessible to the child.
7. If the adult is working with a group of children, he should attempt to build group acceptance of books. These group attitudes should make the books as acceptable as the possession of comic books in the peer relationship.

While the level of difficulty of the comic books, estimated in one study,[2] ran between fifth- and seventh-grade reader level, it is obvious that many slow readers have been attracted to them. Whether or not those people are actually reading the text of the comic books, we want to make provisions for them in books they can really read. So the books suggested will be classified into difficulty areas of "below fourth grade," "fourth through sixth grade," and "above sixth grade."

[1] Witty, Paul A., "Children's Interests in Reading the Comics," *Journal of Experimental Education*, 10 (December, 1941), 100–104.

[2] Thorndike, Robert L. "Words and the Comics," *Journal of Experimental Education*, 10 (December, 1941), 110–113.

"Sure Fire" Authors

There are certain authors whose books are outstanding in meeting the challenge of the comic books because they meet the same needs that are met in the comic books. Their books could be classified under many different headings; they combine various exciting situations with rare humor. We will start by listing their contributions first because they are "sure fire" and should be in any library. Most of these authors are still producing, so watch for their new books as they come off the press.

Below Fourth Grade

Dr. Seuss (Theodore Seuss Geisel) has books full of color, fantastic adventure, humor, and some excitement. They are books short in number of running words and full of large "laugh appealing" pictures. From the kindergarten to the grandparent, people will enjoy the nonsense; so the over-age, slow reader can feel respectable if caught with one of Dr. Seuss' books.
And To Think That I Saw It on Mulberry Street. Vanguard, 1937.
The Five Hundred Hats of Bartholomew Cubbins. Vanguard, 1938.
Bartholomew and the Oobleck. Random, 1940.
Horton Hatches the Egg. Random, 1940.
If I Ran the Zoo. Random, 1950.
The King's Stilts. Random, 1939.
McElligot's Pool. Random, 1947.
Thidwick, the Big Hearted Moose. Random, 1948.

Richard Bennett's books are well illustrated, short, well-told stories packed with fun in interesting settings.
Mick, Mack, and Mary Jane. Doubleday, 1948.
Mister Ole. Doubleday, 1940.
Shawneen and the Gander. Doubleday, 1937.
Skookum and Sandy. Doubleday, 1935.

Fourth through Sixth Grade

Robert Lawson has humor, real boys who get into fantastic situations, mystery, excitement, and animals that are believable though thoroughly and imaginatively delineated. Lawson's wonderful detailed drawings are worth poring over at any age. His books are well set up with large print and wide margins. Don't

let children miss these books! The last two are more difficult
reading and belong in the sixth-reader-level bracket.

Ben and Me. Little, 1939.

I Discover Columbus. Little, 1941.

Mr. Twigg's Mistake. Little, 1947.

Mr. Wilmer. Little, 1945.

Rabbit Hill. Viking, 1944 (Newbery Award).

Robbut—A Tale of Tails. Viking, 1948.

Fabulous Flight. Little, 1949.

Smeller Martin. Viking, 1950.

MUNRO LEAF'S books illustrated by Robert Lawson are good.
They are short stories full of humor and some excitement. All
are full of silly situations.

The Story of Ferdinand. Viking, 1936.

Simpson and Sampson. Viking, 1941.

Wee Gillis. Viking. 1938.

PHIL STONG should be included because his books are about
"all-boy" characters, usually living in the Middlewest, who get
into a variety of humorous situations. There is variety of humorous situations. There is plenty of excitement and often a mystery
to be solved. The illustrations by Kurt Wiese are most effective
in catching the fun of the stories.

Captain Kidd's Cow. Dodd, 1941.

Censored, the Goat. Dodd, 1945.

Cowhand Goes to Town. Dodd, 1939.

Farm Boy; A Hunt for Indian Treasure. Dodd, 1934.

Honk: The Moose. Dodd, 1935.

Missouri Canary. Dodd, 1936.

No-Sitch: The Hound. Dodd, 1936.

Way Down Cellar. Dodd, 1942.

Young Settlers. Dodd, 1938.

JAMES THURBER'S books will not appeal to all readers because
he is often subtle or satirical, which is bewildering to some children. But his stories are usually humorous and fantastic. They
are short, with well-spaced margins and suitable print. The excellent illustrations catch the mood of the story.

The Great Quillow. Harcourt, 1944. (Illustrated by Doris Lee)

Many Moons. Harcourt, 1944. (Illustrated by Louis Slobodkin)

The White Deer. Harcourt, 1945. (Illustrated by Thurber and
Freeman)

WANDA GÁG'S folk tale books will delight children with their
well-told stories and amusing, detailed pictures. The folk tales
are funny rather than of "blood and thunder" variety.

Gone is Gone. Coward, 1935.

Tales from Grimm. Coward, 1936.

Three Gay Tales from Grimm. 1943.

PHYLLIS FENNER is doing a marvelous job of making collections of stories from all sources. There is a well-chosen collection for almost each of the categories listed later. The stories are well illustrated. Share one or two stories with a group and then let them browse for themselves. Children need not read every story in a book.

Adventures, Rare and Magical. Illustrated by Henry Pitz. Knopf, 1945.

Cowboys, Cowboys, Cowboys. Illustrated by Manning de V. Lee, Knopf, 1950.

Giants and Witches and a Dragon or Two. Illustrated by Henry Pitz, Knopf, 1943.

Princesses and Peasant Boys. Illustrated by Henry Pitz. Knopf, 1944.

There Was a Horse—Folktales from Many Lands. Illustrated by Henry Pitz. Knopf, 1941.

Time to Laugh; Funny Tales from Here and There. Illustrated by Henry Pitz. Knopf, 1942.

Fools and Funny Fellows. Illustrated by Henry Pitz. Knopf, 1947.

Above Sixth Grade

WILLIAM DU BOIS' books will not appeal to all children because he, too, includes subtle satire. Neither will his illustrations please all readers. His style matches well the characters of his stories and best of all he includes diagrams of some of the fantastic inventions discussed in the story.

Twenty-One Balloons, a Newbery Award winner, makes a slow start and the suggestion is to get children over the first part to where the professor starts his balloon journey. The first three of the books listed below can be read by children with fourth-reader level of reading ability. The others are for those above sixth-reader level.

The Flying Locomotive. Macmillan, 1941.

The Great Geppy. Viking, 1940.

The Three Policemen or Young Bottsford of Farbe Island. Viking, 1938.

Peter Graves. Viking, 1950.

The Twenty One Balloons. Viking, 1947.

STORIES OF HUMOR AND FUN

It is easiest to substitute for the really "funny" comic books. The stories are usually shorter, they have the gayest of illustrations, and the appeal is general—for all ages. The slow reader will find much success in these materials.

There are many animal stories included. Mickey Mouse and his foibles and Donald Duck and his temper have characteristics of the human world rather than of the world of mice and ducks. We laugh at their "cheeky" tricks which we won't let children try, and somehow the irrepressible little fellows come back for more. Such a character is Pinocchio and a host of other "heroes" of these stories. The suggested books are durably bound, with print that is better for the eyes and with illustrations that have more aesthetic appeal.

The common element in all of these stories is the complete absurdity of the situation. But sometimes the appeal is strengthened for children because the adult is put in a foolish position. Sometimes it is the smaller (or supposedly duller) person outwitting the larger, older, or more authoritarian person as in the case of the Katzenjammer Kids.

Most of these stories can be read easily with fourth-grade reading ability. Only a few are long stories such as those by Brooks in his Freddy the Pig series, or Lofting's Dr. Dolittle stories, and Mary Poppins. The *Peterkin Papers* are stories complete in the chapter and the whole books need not be read at one time.

Authors having more than one book fitting the needs and qualifications of the "funny" stories:

WALTER R. BROOKS has written a number of stories humanizing the personalities of the animals of the barnyard. They have the foibles of humans and get into many difficulties but always manage to outwit their enemies in clever and humorous ways. Freddy, the pig, is the main character. The books are illustrated by Kurt Wiese.

Freddy Goes to Florida. Knopf, 1949. (Originally published as *To and Again.*)

More To and Again. Knopf, 1930.

Freddy, the Cowboy. Knopf, 1950.

Freddy, the Detective. Knopf, 1932.

Freddy, and the Perilous Adventure. Knopf, 1942.

MARIE HALL ETS has whimsy and clever illustrations in her books.

Oley, the Sea Monster is printed in comic book style of strips across the page. Viking, 1947.

Mr. Penny. Viking, 1935.

Little Old Automobile. Viking, 1948.

HUGH LOFTING'S DR. DOLITTLE stories are now popular with the second generation. The *Voyages of Dr. Dolittle* was the second Newbery Award winner. Since then six other stories have been written about the kind little doctor who befriended the animals who in turn shared many ridiculous adventures with him.

The Story of Dr. Dolittle. Lippincott, 1920.

The Story of Mrs. Tubbs. Lippincott, 1923. (Third-grade reading level)

HANS A. REY has four easy little books that are fun for boys and girls. The ridiculous antics of Curious George and Cecily G. are very satisfying to children and are enlivened with Rey's clever illustrating.

Cecily G. and the Nine Monkeys. Houghton, 1942.

Curious George. Houghton, 1941.

Curious George Takes a Job. Houghton, 1947.

Elizabite. Harper, 1942.

PAMELA TRAVERS' Mary Poppins, who comes and goes with the wind, is a heroine who is funny to some children. Some are too literal to care for these stories. The books are long. They are illustrated by Mary Shepard.

Mary Poppins. Reynal, 1934.

Mary Poppins Comes Back. Reynal, 1935.

Mary Poppins Opens the Door. Reynal, 1943.

ATWATER, FLORENCE and RICHARD: *Mr. Popper's Penguins;* illustrated by Robert Lawson, Little, 1938. This is a "sure fire" story of a house painter who acquires penguins and has various accommodations to make for them. But the penguins learn an act and finally go to the North Pole with Mr. Popper.

BALET, JAN: *Ned and Ed and the Lion;* Dodd, 1949. A merry-go-round lion carries the boys off to the jungle for adventures. A delightfully imaginative book with pictures to match.

BLOUGH, GLENN: *The Monkey with a Notion;* illustrated by John De Cuir, Holt, 1946. This is a possible story with a gay monkey who lets the other animals in the pet shop out at night. Miss Peasley, the owner, doesn't like children, but she overcomes her aversion when a little boy solves the mystery.

BRIGHT, ROBERT: *Georgie;* Doubleday, 1944. George is a sweet, lovable little ghost who accidentally gets eliminated from his home. He searches for another but finally gets back to the Whittakers and puts them back on schedule. There are delightful black and white pictures which fit the humor of the story.

CHALMERS, AUDREY: *Hundreds and Hundreds of Pancakes;* Viking, 1942. Mr. Fizzlewit's family is surrounded by animals released from the zoo but Mrs. Fizzlewit feeds them pancakes until they can be recaptured.

CHASE, RICHARD: *Jack and the Three Sillies;* illustrated by Joshua Tolford, Houghton, 1950. An American version of the folk tale of Jack who barters his cow for a stone. His wife searches until she finds three people sillier than Jack.

GARBUTT, KATHERINE and BERNARD: *Hodie;* Aladdin, 1949. Hodie has trouble persuading the farmer he can be a good farm dog, for he is a French poodle with a fancy haircut.

HALE, LUCRETIA: *The Peterkin Papers;* illustrated by Harold Brett, Houghton, 1924. A series of hilarious stories about the Peterkin family who get into trouble and can't get out logically until they get advice from the "lady from Philadelphia."

HENRY, MARGUERITE: *Little-or-Nothing from Nottingham;* illustrated by Wesley Dennis, Whittlesey, 1949. A small dog wanders into a traveling circus and becomes part of it. But he is constantly thwarted over burying his bones and not finding them the next morning.

HURD, CLEMENT: *The Race;* Random, 1940. A monkey and a crocodile have a race; they hop into cars, into boats with first one ahead and then the other. This is extremely easy reading and has proved very popular with children.

LE GALLIENNE, EVA: *Flossie and Bossie;* illustrated by Garth Williams, Harper, 1949. Bossie was the queen of the barnyard and Flossie the overlooked hen. Each has a brood of chickens and their characters are brought to a test. This is a delightful story.

McGINLEY, PHYLLIS LOUISE: *The Horse Who Lived Upstairs;* illustrated by Helen Stone, Lippincott, 1944. A city horse dreams of the country but finds he likes his old home best when he has a chance to try the country.

NEWBERRY, CLARE: *Herbert, The Lion;* Harper, 1956. Herbert was such a pet that no one could punish him, not even after he ate grandmother, grandfather and on through the family. Children really enjoy this story.

SLOBODKIN, ESPHYR: *Caps for Sale;* Wm. Scott, 1947. This is a story of a cap peddler who carried his wares stacked on his head. The caps are stolen by some monkeys and he can't get them back until the surprise ending.

ADULTS IN RIDICULOUS POSITIONS

A child makes so many mistakes growing up and adults seem to make so few to a child's eyes. Or, perhaps it is because adults are always telling children what to do that makes any story about adults in ridiculous positions particularly funny.

Below Fourth Grade

ANDERSEN, HANS CHRISTIAN: *The Emperor's New Clothes;* illustrated by Virginia Lee Burton, Houghton, 1949. This is the clever story of the Emperor and his court who are afraid they aren't fit for office but a child recognizes the true state of affairs. The Burton pictures make it even more delightful.

BISHOP, CLAIRE HUCHET: *The Man Who Lost His Head;* illustrated by Robert McCloskey, Viking, 1942. When a man loses his head what can he do but try a pumpkin and a parsnip and get into difficulties. It takes a boy to help him out.

JORDAN, MILDRED: *"I Won't" Said the King or The Purple Flannel Underwear;* illustrated by Roger Duvoisin, Knopf, 1945. The King acts childish and gets into trouble. A small boy helps to solve the most pressing problem of counting the printuplets.

GETTING AHEAD AGAINST GREAT ODDS

Children are always facing great odds—there are so many adults to say "Do this!" or "Do that!" They have to learn to get along with so many kinds of people—some the same age, younger children, and older children. These next stories are absurd and fantastic because the hero manages to achieve through being different.

ADAMS, VEOTTA McKINLEY: *Captain Joe and the Eskimo;* illustrated by Barney Tobey, Wm. Scott, 1943. Captain Joe is trying to rescue a marooned Eskimo boy. But the boy doesn't know what to do with the things thrown to him and manages to escape by making different use of them.

BROWN, MARCIA: *Stone Soup;* Scribner's, 1947. Three soldiers can beg no food from the villagers but they outwit them by making stone soup—they supply the stone and the villagers the vegetables that go into it.

BRYANT, SARA CONE: *Epaminondas and His Auntie;* illustrated by Inez Hogan, Houghton, 1938. This old story is forever popular with children. A little boy who always does the wrong thing by following the instruction he has been given last.

DAVIS, ROBERT: *Padre Porko, The Gentlemanly Pig;* illustrated by Fritz Eichenberg, Holiday, 1948. Padre is an interesting character who dresses beautifully and is very witty whenever he is consulted by the other animals who are in trouble. The book is a series of short stories.

MEADOWCROFT, ENID L.: *The Adventures of Peter Whiffin;* illustrated by Beatrice H. Bennett, Crowell, 1936. An easily read story with big print and pictures. The elephants and horses maintain their own characteristics yet the adventures are exaggerated.

WEBB, WHEATON P.: *Uncle Swithin's Inventions;* illustrated by Glenn Rounds, Holiday, 1947. Uncle Swithin is considered queer and worthless by the other adults of the community. But to his nephew, Dennis, his liar-proof fishhook which catches the electric eel makes him a hero.

THE LITTLE HERO

How wonderful to have the person who succeeds no bigger or older than yourself! Especially since some of the difficulties they get into are like your own—or some you wish you could try. The next group of stories have small heroes and heroines that succeed and carry on in spite of handicaps.

COLLODI, CARLO (LORENZINI): *The Adventures of Pinocchio;* illustrated by Attilio Mussino, Macmillan, 1927. This irresistible, mischievous little wooden boy's adventures have satisfied children of several generations.

DAUGHERTY, JAMES: *Andy and the Lion;* Viking, 1938. It is not surprising that Andy, who has read every book about lions he can get, should meet one and remove a thorn from his paw. Andy is rewarded for his deed when the circus comes to town and he is recognized by his friend lion and so becomes a hero.

DICKENS, CHARLES: *The Magic Fishbone;* illustrated by F. D. Bedford, Warne, 1868. Alicia is the oldest of the king's 19 children so must assume much responsibility although she is but 7 years old. She has a magic fishbone to use in case of emergency and because she uses it so wisely she is well rewarded by her Fairy Grandmarina.

GORDON, PATRICIA: *The Witch of Scrapfaggot Green;* illustrated by Wm. DuBois, Viking, 1948. Sam and Daisy are the only members of a village not upset when the witch returns after her grave has been disrupted.

GRAHAME, KENNETH: *Bertie's Escapade;* illustrated by Ernest Shepard, Lippincott, 1949. Bertie, the pig, and his two rabbit friends go out on Christmas Eve and eventually they ransack Mr. Grahame's kitchen and celebrate on his provender.

HUTTER, DON: *Abraham, the Itinerant Mouse;* illustrated by Kurt Wiese, Dodd, 1947. There are three stories about the adventures of Abraham, who is a gallant, brave, little fellow. He gets into serious predicaments but gets out by clever thinking and maneuvering.

WHITE, E. B.: *Stuart Little;* illustrated by Garth Williams, Harper, 1945. Adults may stumble over the first remark that Mrs. Little's second son was not much bigger than a mouse but children are thoroughly thrilled and amused over his adventures.

REAL BOYS AND GIRLS AS HEROES

In this area the books we are recommending tell their story better than the comic books. There are no comic books able to depict real boys and girls doing everyday activities in good stories involving humor and excitement that is probable. I am sure that such a comic book would rate close to the top in popularity. There are a few comics that have heroes in the "bobby sox" age with some action centered in the romances of the teens, and others dealing with problems of the parent, but they are few.

Many teachers and librarians have spoken of the popularity of these books which we will list next. Children like them because the situations, emotions, and problems are like their own. Most of these books can be read with reading ability of fourth- through sixth-reader level.

ELEANOR ESTES writes of the Moffat family in a human and humorous way. The stories appeal because each of the children is an individual very like some child you know. Each of the chapters can be read as a separate story. Louis Slobodkin is known as the "Moffat maker" because his few lines show character and action.

The Moffats. Harcourt, 1941.
The Middle Moffat. Harcourt, 1942.
Rufus M. Harcourt, 1943.

ROBERT MCCLOSKEY's illustrations have long pleased us and now he has two books that are particularly satisfying because of their "boyness." *Homer Price* can be read as individual stories and *Lentil* is a very short book.

Homer Price. Viking, 1943.

Lentil. Viking, 1940.

MONTGOMERY, LUCY MAUD: *Anne of Green Gables;* illustrated by E. R. Withington, Page, 1908. This is the first of a series of stories about Anne who was an ordinary girl but who managed to get into extraordinary scrapes. The books carry Anne from her 10th through her 17th year and so introduce an element of romance which is very satisfying for girl readers.

SAWYER, RUTH: *Roller Skates;* illustrated by Valenti Angelo, Viking, 1937. Lucinda is 10 and spends a year, while her folks are away, making friends all over New York. She has adventures galore and learns through her mistakes. The sequel, *The Year of Jubilo* (Illustrated by Edward Shenton, Viking, 1940) is not as exciting but very appealing to girls in their teens. Lucinda learns to cook and to fall in and out of love.

STREATFEILD, NOEL: *Movie Shoes;* illustrated by Susanne Suba, Random, 1949. This is one of the vocational series which is also a well-written story. Jane is the ugly duckling of the family but lands a movie contract because of it. She discovers the work is not all glamor and has some personality lessons to learn. Other books about children with careers are:

Ballet Shoes. Illustrated by Richard Floethe, Random, 1937.

Circus Shoes. Illustrated by Richard Floethe, Random, 1939.

Theater Shoes. Illustrated by Richard Floethe, Random, 1945.

BOTHWELL, JEAN: *Peter Holt, P.K.;* illustrated by Margaret Ayer, Harcourt, 1950. Peter is a "Preacher's Kid" but that doesn't keep him from developing two enemies. How he solves his difficulties is a very satisfying story.

BRINK, CAROL RYRIE: *Caddie Woodlawn;* illustrated by Kate Seredy, Macmillan, 1935. (Newbery Award) Caddie lives in the wilds of Wisconsin in the 1860's. She doesn't want to assume her woman's role and in most of her escapades she doesn't. But she comes to see her place in the world in the process of a good story.

CLEARY, BEVERLY: *Henry Huggins;* illustrated by Louis Darling, Morrow, 1950. Henry has trouble carrying his dog Ribsy home in a paper sack but that is only the beginning of this story of a real boy, his dog and the problem of living with that combination.

NORTH, STERLING: *Greased Lightning;* illustrated by Kurt Wiese, Winston, 1940. When a boy has to sell his pet pig he feels badly but when he catches him in the greased pig contest at the Fourth of July celebration it is a good story.

ROBINSON, TOM: *Trigger John's Son;* illustrated by Robert Mc-Closkey. Viking, 1949. Trigger John is a combination of Homer Price and Tom Sawyer. His decisions are not always conventional to adults but very satisfying to boys. Everyone will enjoy the way he handles the "Goosetown Gang."

WILSON, HAZEL: *Herbert;* illustrated by John Barron, Knopf, 1950. Herbert has a can collection for which his family built an addition to the house but then complications arise. An uncle helps to resolve them and many more in this funny story.

CHILDREN'S PREFERENCES IN PUBLISHERS *

Clifford J. Kolson,
Richard E. Robinson, and
William G. Zimmerman

In this article ... What books do children prefer? Do they have preferences in publishers, and do they examine new books critically? Tentative answers to these and other questions are given in this report of an investigation of children's examination of books.

The major purpose of this study was to determine whether children show a preference for publishers of children's books through self-selection activities.

In 1944 Marie Rankin (1) reported the surprising finding that the Newbery Books selected by adults were not held with equal enthusiasm by children. Ten years later, after a study of the

* Clifford J. Kolson, Richard E. Robinson, William G. Zimmerman, "Children's Preferences in Publishers," *Education* 83 (November, 1962), 155–57. Copyright 1962 by The Bobbs-Merrill Co., Inc., Indianapolis, Indiana. Reprinted by permission of the authors.

readability of the bestsellers in children's books, Craig (2) came to the conclusion that "... children's books, like electric trains, are bought for the gratification and edification of the parents."

These and similar studies have more or less pointed out the discrepancy between the judgment of adults and that of children concerning books written for children. If parents are to avoid the "Craigian Assumption" made earlier, some guide must be found for the selection of books for children.

In the past, attempts to find such a guide have been oriented toward content and illustrations. Averill (3) concentrated on the ideal character. Butterworth and Thompson (4) investigated subject matter. Malter (5) concerned himself with the illustrations. Although the contributions of these studies should not be minimized, the divergence between children's and adults' preferences is still with us.

Perhaps the answer might be found in "brand names." Housewives quite frequently do not bother to determine what should be in a can of peas to make it superior. They merely find a brand they like and then purchase by "brand name" thereafter.

The publisher's name on a book is the "brand name." If it could be determined that children prefer one publisher over another, perhaps one would be safe in buying by that brand name.

METHOD OF PROCEDURE

The present study was an observation-frequency normative survey. It involved the observation of 750 children, ages 6, 7, and 8.

One hundred and fifty children were observed in the following five cities: Fort Myers, Florida; Arlington, Virginia; Pittsburgh, Pennsylvania; Portland, Oregon; and Los Angeles, California.

These children had separated from their parents and were browsing in the children's book section of large department stores. The frequency tabulations were made by observing which books the children examined initially and which books they eventually selected for more prolonged examination. The list of publishers was limited to those who had books in the book sections of the stores in all five cities.

Thus it was felt that the study substantially satisfied these criteria:

1. *Freedom from influence.* The design should be so constructed as to prevent adult influence on the child's selection of books.

2. *Wide choice.* The children involved should have the opportunity to choose from a large selection of books.

3. *Naturalness of setting.* The observations should take place in an environment familiar to the child.

4. *Geographical inclusiveness.* The sampling should come from as wide a geographical area as possible.

5. *Level of application.* The study should be designed for a particular age group.

RESULTS

It appears that the discrepancy between children's choices of a book and adults' choices of a book is still very much with us. Clerks in the book sections reported that: (1) Most children's books were purchased by adults unaccompanied by children; (2) even when children were present adults tended to select the books. Our observations substantiated these facts.

It was found that publishers' books which rank high in adults' preference ranked low in children's preference. For example, table 1 shows that books of publisher F were the first choice among adults. Although a large number of children (231) chose to examine publisher F's books initially, only 71 examined them at length.

As can be noted in the table below, there is an inverse, though not proportional, relationship between child and adult preferences in publishers' books. Moreover, there seems to be no significant relationship between the books that a child initially examined and those he examined carefully.

FREQUENCY TABLE

Publisher	Number of Children Initially Examining Publisher's Books	Number of Children Selecting Publisher's Books for Prolonged Examination	Rank order of total volumes sold
A	93	179	6
B	78	154	4
C	78	137	5
D	103	115	2
E	167	94	3
F	231	71	1
Total	750 children	750 children	

As a result of this study, the suggestion is offered that perhaps it would be desirable for parents to allow their children to browse in book sections and purchase that book the children choose for prolonged examination.

We are quite familiar with the common phenomenon wherein children read and reread certain books, never seeming to tire of them. Sundry other books which have been purchased by parents or given as gifts by relatives seem to be thrust into the background. Obviously, children do have a distinctive hierarchy of values for books.

It has been argued by some of our colleagues that certain publishers' books have such a large volume of sales the child is undoubtedly familiar with the books, probably having several of them at home. The contention is that he would tend to read something with which he is not familiar.

However, we noted a high incidence of initial examination of the more "popular" books notably those of publisher F and publisher E. Prolonged examination was accorded to the less "popular" books of publishers A and B. Obviously, children do examine books critically and then exercise discernible value choices.

It seems apparent that the results of this study are in accord with the earlier studies made by Craig and Rankin.

The findings of this study indicate that children manifest a strong preference for books by certain publishers through self-selection activities.

References

1. Rankin, Marie, *Children's Interests in Library Books of Fiction,* Teachers College Contributions to Education, No. 906 (New York: Bureau of Publications, Teachers College, Columbia University, 1944).
2. Craig, James Calvin, "The Vocabulary Load of the Nation's Best Sellers from 1662–1945: A Study of Readability," Unpublished Doctoral Dissertation, University of Pittsburgh, 1954.
3. Averill, Lawrence A., "The Impact of a Changing Culture Upon Pubescent Ideals," *School and Society,* Vol. LXXII (July 22, 1950).

4. Butterworth, Robert F. and Thompson, George C., "Factors Related to Age-Grade Trends and Sex Differences in Children's Preferences for Comic Books," *Journal of Genetic Psychology*, Vol. LXXVIII, First Half (March, 1951).
5. Malter, Morton S., "Children's Preferences for Illustrative Materials," *Journal of Educational Research*, Vol. XLI (January, 1948).

Part Two

EVALUATION AND SELECTION
OF CHILDREN'S BOOKS

WHAT ARE GOOD BOOKS?*

Paul Hazard

Liberators will come, from Grimm to Andersen; and there will be others later on, but before them, beside them, around them, how many pedants and fools there were! How many exploiters trying to make a profit from worthless merchandise! What a cemetery! You may say: It is all very well to look disgusted. What does please you, anyway, and just what are you asking for? Stories, nothing but stories? Do you grow angry as soon as knowledge or morals is mentioned? And for a book to satisfy you, must it contain absolutely nothing? First of all, I reply, there are good books of every kind; and when one of them is good, even though it does not contain what I ask for, let it be welcomed gratefully. I will enumerate the kind of books which seem to me good.

I like books that remain faithful to the very essence of art; namely, those that offer to children an intuitive and direct way of knowledge, a simple beauty capable of being perceived immediately, arousing in their souls a vibration which will endure all their lives.

And those that provide them with pictures, the kind that they like; pictures chosen from the riches of the whole world; enchanting pictures that bring release and joy, happiness gained before reality closes in upon them, insurance against the time, all too soon, when there will be nothing but realities.

And books that awaken in them not maudlin sentimentality, but sensibility; that enable them to share in great human emotions; that give them respect for universal life—that of animals, of plants; that teach them not to despise everything that is mysterious in creation and in man.

And books which respect the valor and eminent dignity of play; which understand that the training of intelligence and of reason cannot, and must not, always have the immediately useful and practical as its goal.

I like books of knowledge; not those that want to encroach upon recreation, upon leisure, pretending to be able to teach anything without drudgery. There is no truth in that. There are

* Paul Hazard, "What Are Good Books?" in Chapter I *Books, Children and Men* (Boston: The Horn Book, Inc., 1960), pp. 42–45. Reprinted by permission of The Horn Book, Inc.

things which cannot be learned without great pains; we must be resigned to it. I like books of knowledge when they are not just grammar or geometry poorly disguised; when they have tact and moderation; when, instead of pouring out so much material on a child's soul that it is crushed, they plant in it a seed that will develop from the inside. I like them when they do not deceive themselves about the quality of knowledge, and do not claim that knowledge can take the place of everything else. I like them especially when they distill from all the different kinds of knowledge the most difficult and the most necessary—that of the human heart.

A Perrault, while he is relating marvels to us, teaches us with wit and charm not to be mistaken about men, women, and children; he is full of observation and he is never ponderous. He has so many delightful traits, so just and so true, that they penetrate the soul deeply; so full of strength that they will ripen gradually in the spirit to blossom some day into wisdom! In "Hop o' My Thumb": "She was indeed poor, but she was their mother." "This Peter was her eldest son whom she loved above all the rest, because he was somewhat carroty, as she herself was." "It is quite possible that the woodcutter was more vexed than his wife, but she kept teasing him and he felt as many other people do who admire women who say the right thing, but find extremely tiresome those who never say anything but the right thing." In "Puss in Boots": "The King lavished caresses upon him, and as the fine garments he had given him enhanced his good looks (for he was well made and very handsome) the King's daughter found him very much to her taste and the Marquis de Carabas had no sooner cast two or three glances towards her, very respectfully and tenderly, than she fell madly in love with him." In the story of "The Sleeping Beauty," who has been asleep for a hundred years, and whose first words, when she wakens and sees before her a charming prince, are: "Is it you, my prince? I have waited long for you to come." These tales, as Fénelon said of poetry, are more useful and more serious than common persons realize.

Finally, I like books that contain a profound morality. Not the kind of morality which consists in believing oneself a hero because one has given two cents to a poor man, or which names as characteristics the faults peculiar to one era, or one nation; here snivelling pity, there a pietism that knows nothing of charity; somewhere else a middle-class hypocrisy. Not the kind of morality that asks for no deeply felt consent, for no personal effort, and which is nothing but a rule imposed willy-nilly by the strongest.

I like books that set in action truths worthy of lasting forever, and of inspiring one's whole inner life; those demonstrating that an unselfish and faithful love always ends by finding its reward, be it only in oneself; how ugly and low are envy, jealousy, and greed; how people who utter only slander and lies end by coughing up vipers and toads whenever they speak. In short, I like books that have the integrity to perpetuate their own faith in truth and justice. Listen once more to what Perrault says to us:

> Is it not praiseworthy of fathers and mothers, when the children are not yet old enough to taste strong unpleasant truths, to make them like them, and if I may put it this way, to make them swallow them by enveloping them in tales that are pleasant and suited to their tender years? It is unbelievable how eagerly these innocent souls, whose natural goodness has not yet been corrupted, receive these subtle teachings. We see them sad and depressed as long as the hero or the heroine is unlucky, and shouting with joy when the time for their happiness arrives; in the same way, having endured impatiently the prosperity of the wicked man or woman, they are overjoyed when they see them finally punished as they deserve.

I know very well that these conditions are difficult to fulfill. They are even more imperative than when it is a question of a good book for men, which in itself is not so easy to produce. But to misshape young souls, to profit by a certain facility that one may possess to add to the number of indigestible and sham books, to give oneself too easily the airs of a moralist and scholar, to cheat in quality—that is what I call oppressing children.

WHAT MAKES A BOOK
A GOOD BOOK *

Augusta Baker

A small girl was a frequent visitor at the Central Children's Room of the New York Public Library. She would spend a long time browsing among the books, examining the pictures, and dipping into the stories. Then, each time, she would take the L. Leslie Brooke edition of *The Three Bears* (Warne) to the charging desk, have it properly stamped, and carry it home. This devotion to one book finally caused the librarian to ask, "Why do you always take this same book?" The little girl promptly replied, "Because I know it's good."

Here is a small adjective but an all-important one. What makes a book a *good* book? What are the qualities of good children's literature? Elizabeth Nesbitt gave an address in California in 1939 entitled "Hold to That Which Is Good." She said then, "Literature is immeasurably above and beyond the printed work, of a significance transcending the merely informative, varied as is human destiny, nonexistent without the twin qualities of beauty of idea and beauty of expression." It is here that one finds the books which are full of wonder and imagination.

The mass production of uninspired "real-life" stories and fact books of all kinds has swamped the truly creative, imaginative story. The child brought up on an exclusive diet of the ordinary, factual book may be quite intelligent, but he will be a poor, dull soul. How much better it would be if that same child could have his facts mixed with some originality of idea and individuality of presentation. Ravielli's *An Adventure in Geometry* (Viking) has these qualities. *Mr. Popper's Penguins* (Little) is about an ordinary American family, as is *The Peterkins Papers* (Houghton), but in both books the everyday happenings have been

* Augusta Baker, "What Makes a Book a Good Book," *The Instructor* 73 (November, 1963), 47–48. Copyright 1963 by F. A. Owen Publishing Company; reprinted from *The Instructor* by permission.

transformed by humor and imagination, and it is this transformation that delights the children and not the uninteresting recognition of facts found in so many curriculum-inspired books.

Children like the realistic and familiar if there is some spark
of imagination. Fact books must be lively and well presented.
Shaw said, in *Back to Methuselah,* "Imagination is the beginning
of creation. You imagine what you desire; you will what you
imagine; and at last you create that will."

Beauty of expression denotes quality, and quality cannot be
found in the vocabulary-controlled book which is so popular
today. Introduce the child to new words and let him stretch for
them. A rubber band is enlarged by stretching it. The average
child must be bored with the avalanche of "I Can Read" books
which are pouring from many of our publishing houses. Yes, he
can easily read these books, but as Clifton Fadiman has said,
"What the child-mind measurers call a feeling of mastery is often
only a feeling of boredom. Virtue lies in a little frustration."
Quiller-Couch reminds us, "Great authors never oppress any-
body with condescension." Language should be accurate because
language expresses thought; and, if we lack the skill to speak
precisely, our thought will remain confused and ill-defined.

Language should also be beautiful, colorful, and descriptive.
Compare the following two versions of "The Golden Goose":

> There was once a man who had three sons, the youngest of
> whom was called the Simpleton. He was laughed at and de-
> spised and neglected on all occasions. Now it happened one
> day that the eldest son wanted to go into the forest, to hew
> wood, and his Mother gave him a beautiful cake and a bottle
> of wine to take with him, so that he might not suffer from
> hunger or thirst. When he came to the wood he met a little
> old grey man, who, bidding him good-day, said: "Give me a
> small piece of the cake in your wallet, and let me drink a
> mouthful of your wine; I am so hungry and thirsty." But the
> clever son answered: "If I were to give you my cake and my
> wine, I should have none for myself, so be off with you," and
> he left the little man standing there and walked away. Hardly
> had he begun to cut down a tree, when his axe slipped and
> cut his arm, so that he had to go home at once and have the
> wound bound up. This was the work of the little grey man.
> (From *The Golden Goose Book,* by L. Leslie Brooke; Warne.)

Now read the same part of the story from *Favorite Fairy Tales to Read Aloud* (Grosset).

There was once a man who had three sons, the youngest of whom was called Dummling.

One day, the eldest son decided to go into the forest to cut some wood. Before he started his mother packed a lunch for him so that he might not suffer from hunger or thirst.

In the wood at midday, he stopped work and sat down to eat. Just then, a little old man appeared before him and said, "May I have a crust of bread and some milk? I am so hungry and thirsty."

But the young man said, "If I do, I shan't have enough for myself. Be off with you!"

He left the little man standing there and went on his way. But he had not been long at work, chopping down a tree, before he cut himself and had to go home to have it bandaged.

Now this was no accident. It was brought about by the little man, who had magic powers, and had decided that anyone as selfish as this fellow should be punished.

The second version has had a stamp of approval put upon it by a "distinguished panel" of experts which includes two educators and one librarian. But how much of color and beauty of style will be lost to the child who reads it rather than the other!

Closely related to the vocabulary-controlled book is the oversimplified one. Not every child in the fourth or fifth grades can read with ease and enjoyment *The Wind in the Willows* (Scribner), but is that a good reason for rewriting it? So many books are being specifically written for use by remedial-reading teachers that the rewriters should not desecrate the best in children's books.

Such authors as Robert Louis Stevenson, Louisa May Alcott, and A. A. Milne wrote out of themselves unaware of whether they were overstepping a child's "experience." E. B. White said, "What am I saying to my readers? Well, I never know. Writing to me is not an exercise in addressing readers, it is more as though I were talking to myself while shaving. ..." L. M. Boston, author of the "Green Knowe" books, said, "I deplore the tendency to come down to a supposedly childish level in subject and in language; to make it easy, to provide predigested food ... to eliminate, in fact, the widening of the horizon ..."

Rewriting and adapting the classics is unforgivable unless the result is a literary tour de force. Walter de la Mare used the poet's skill when he created *Tales Told Again* (Knopf) and *Stories from the Bible* (Ryerson).

A creative writer cannot be confined by restrictions. He must be free to soar to the heights and take with him his young readers. No limits, such as age or series will ever attract the writers who have imagination, wisdom, sincerity, charm, and distinction of style, all of which are essential qualifications of a good book. *Little Bear* (Harper) and *The Cat in the Hat* (Random) are rare exceptions. It was Anatole France who remarked, "When you are writing for children, do not assume a style for the occasion. Think your best and write your best. Let the whole thing live."

Perhaps something should be said about the artwork in children's books. Drawings should be made by the greatest artists, since exposure of a child to fine art and beauty cannot begin too early. A child can develop an appreciation for beauty through his handling of well-illustrated books. He should be able to meet, in his books, such artists as Kate Greenaway, Beatrix Potter, Randolph Caldecott, Howard Pyle, as well as such modern artists as Marcia Brown, Marie Ets, and Robert McCloskey.

Writing for children is an art, and one should never forget this. A good book is an experience to a child; and, as he reads, he adds to his growth as an individual. He is able to receive new impressions and ideas, and he gains a certain indefinable something which can never be taken from him. Good children's books have sound and direct values which are implicit in the writing. Here are truths to which they can hold. In *My Roads to Childhood* (Horn Book, Inc.), Anne Carroll Moore gives some advice to a promising young writer. "Writing for children, like daily living with them, requires the constant sharpening of all one's faculties, the fresh discovery of new heights and depths in one's own emotions, the saving conviction that children have as many varied tastes in reading as grown-ups. Kenneth Grahame says they have just as much 'sense,' that it is only 'experience' they lack. In the matter of their reading, I think they have more sense since they are entirely unconcerned with other people's opinions of books. When they are bored, they stop reading the book. 'I didn't like that book,' is reason enough, and it admits no arguments."

So, likewise, it was reason enough when the small girl clutched *The Three Bears* and put her stamp of approval on it with, "Because I know it's good."

NOT RECOMMENDED*

Ruth Hill Viguers

Ever since Alice M. Jordan's first Booklist in the September-October 1939 *Horn Book,* her precedent has been followed by later reviewers: the reviewing only of books worth recommending from the point of view of creative writing, original and accurate presentation of a subject, good illustrations, and bookmaking. This has seemed the logical course for a magazine with the space limitations of a bimonthly publication which aims to present not only book reviews but articles relating to children's books and reading, and in view of the variety of *The Horn Book* subscribers (parents, authors, artists, editors, and other individuals, as well as libraries), the wide geographical extent of the circulation (international, even including a few subscribers behind the Iron Curtain), and the tremendous number of children's books published each year.

Often, however, in their discussions together, the reviewers take a strong stand against books which are merely uninspired duplications of what is already available and publications which insult the taste and intelligence of children. Now seems to be a time when, at the sacrifice of space for recommending books, our stand should be expressed in the magazine.

While the mass publication of garish, shiny-covered "flats" has a number of years' start, there have been, coincident with the merging of trade publishing houses with textbook publishers, increases in the number of companies entering the children's book field for the first time, large increases in mass publications for children, and "refinements" in new promotion.

The announcement of the first list from a new publishing company is always awaited with interest. Will this company have something fresh and original? The Golden Gate Press books have, so far, been a great disappointment. Six books at once, none of

* Ruth Hill Viguers, "Not Recommended," *The Horn Book Magazine,* 39 (February, 1963), 76–78. Reprinted by permission of The Horn Book, Inc., Boston, Massachusetts, and the author.

which is very different from hundreds of others, make an unfortunate beginning. Harmless, ineffectual, all in slim picture-book format, though three are geared in text to children of the middle years, the stories have little that is new in plot, background, or viewpoint. *Woody's Burro* by Hester Hawkes would have made a good chapter in a longer book, but it is too slight to stand alone. The illustrations are inferior in every case.

Parents' Magazine has been around long enough to have learned a few things about the importance of giving children the best, whether in baby food or diapers; but they seem not to be aware of the best or even the better in books for children and they have evidently been quite taken in by the money-making potentialities of publishing for children. The result is a collection of "flats" under the imprint of the Parents' Magazine Press that are as unneeded as they are lacking in distinction in style, format, or illustration.

Just when parents are beginning to realize that restricting their children to vocabularized books in their out-of-school pleasure reading is a blatant form of retardation, notice comes of a new series from the Crowell-Collier Press: "Modern Masters' Books for Children," by Louis Untermeyer, John Ciardi, Robert Graves, Arthur Miller, Phyllis McGinley, and others. "The authors," says the promotion release, "have been limited to the use of words drawn from a controlled vocabulary list of less than 800 words.

If these writers want to write school readers, that is their prerogative, and their work should be so recognized and advertised; if they want to play with vocabularized writing as a new discipline or parlor game, they should confine their efforts to books for their contemporaries; but permitting their names to be used as a new promotion trick to snare naïve adult book buyers into thinking that they are giving their children the best to be had is playing into the hands of the kind of business that is aimed only at profit and has no consideration for the child. Finally, allowing themselves to be coerced into writing within restrictions that destroy their art is a perversion of their talents.

Those who believe sincerely that children are entitled to the best and who work toward that end may well have their faith in certain writers destroyed by this kind of activity. At this writing, three of the series have been published. None is worthy of its author. The writers in each case have been very conscious of writing beneath them. They would be ashamed to have their names associated with comparable books for adults.

In September, 1960, Phyllis McGinley wrote an article for *Glamour* magazine called "Talking Down." Many librarians read it with delight when it was reprinted in the *Wilson Library Bulletin* in April, 1962. Her premise was that in childhood tastes are forming and children should have the best; in the good children's books can be found what is not often available in books for adults—integrity, good style, well-drawn characters. She went on to say that, while among current books these qualities can be found with searching, most of the writing is "limp, listless, unoriginal, mediocre, and humdrum," and deplored "that leech among publishing structures—the Law of the Right Vocabulary."

"How wonderful," we parents, children's librarians, and reviewers thought. "She is saying so well just what we all believe and have been working for all our lives."

Six months after her article appeared in the *Wilson Library Bulletin* comes Phyllis McGinley's own contribution to the "Modern Masters' Books for Children." It is called *The B Book*. The writing, which is limited to the use of 364 words, is "limp, listless, unoriginal, mediocre, and humdrum." In addition, it is coy, contrived, and condescending. In her article Miss McGinley remembers the joys of books in her childhood and speaks of children today deserving the "brave books." Undoubtedly, experiences with her own children prompted her in her article to defend good words in children's books and to emphasize that children do not fear difficult words but love them. ". . . who cares about stumbling in the delightful race toward knowledge?"

Does she believe that her grandchildren will be of a lesser breed? Do not they also deserve the "brave books"?

Has the importance of money today completely eclipsed the importance of children, the development of taste, the education of mind and heart as well as intellect?

The literary heritage is one of the great human opportunities. We would expect that the "Masters" of American letters would be the last to hinder anyone's realization of this right.

CHILDREN AND GREAT BOOKS *

Doris Gates

This is an age which has been called many things. It has been called an Age of Anxiety, and certainly none of us would have any quarrel with that. If Lewis Carroll were alive today, he might call it an Age of Muchness. There is too much of almost everything. There are, for example, too many children's books. There are some 1,500 new titles published every year. Often they aren't worth a child's time or the money they cost.

Still, we must remember that every one of the great children's books we have today was once new. I can even now remember with joy the morning many, many years ago when I walked into my library and saw a flat package on my desk and, on opening it, discovered *The Story of Ferdinand*. I knew that here was a landmark in the field of children's literature, as it has proved to be.

TAKING A NEW LOOK AT OLD FAVORITES

The Little Mermaid was once new, as was *The Ugly Duckling*. Just because a book is new, therefore, doesn't necessarily mean that it can't be good. On the other side of the coin, it doesn't follow that because a book is old, it must be great. When I think of *Mrs. Wiggs of the Cabbage Patch* or *The Five Little Peppers and How They Grew* or *Little Lord Fauntleroy* and compare them with some recent books, I think we have made strides.

If the new books may be good, and the old books may be bad, how are you going to know what to offer children? A definition of literature may help. Here is one I came across many years ago. It is not a definition of children's literature alone, but a definition of all literature. *Literature is immeasurably above and beyond the printed word, of a significance far transcending the merely informative, varied as is human destiny, nonexistent with-*

* From Doris Gates, "Children and Great Books," in *Contributions to Reading*, no. 31 (Boston: Ginn and Company). Reprinted by permission of Ginn and Company, Boston, Massachusetts.

out the twin qualities of beauty of idea and beauty of expression.[1]
Let us analyze this.

WHAT MAKES A BOOK GREAT?

First, there is "immeasurably above and beyond the printed word." What does this mean? I consider that it means the power of a book to speak to the reader from between the lines. By means of symbol and imagery and story, literary artists say more in a book than they actually state. That is why a great book deserves more than one reading. It would be unfortunate if we never repeated the reading of great books later in our lives when we had more to bring to them; for we can only get from a book as much as we have to bring to it. To illustrate this, consider a portion of a great book, *The Velveteen Rabbit* by Margery Williams. The book was published by William Heinemann, Limited, London, in 1926 and is still popular, although not nearly widely enough known.

"The Rabbit, who very much wanted to become real, is talking to the Skin Horse, who is very old.

" 'What is real?' asked the Rabbit one day. 'Does it mean having things that buzz inside you and a stick-out handle?'

" 'Real isn't how you are made,' said the Skin Horse, 'it's a thing that happens to you. When a child loves you for a long, long time, not just to play with, but really loves you, then you become real.'

" 'Does it hurt?' asked the Rabbit.

" 'Sometimes,' said the Skin Horse, for he was always truthful. 'When you are real, you don't mind being hurt.'

" 'Does it happen all at once, like being wound up?' he asked. 'Or bit by bit?'

" 'It doesn't happen all at once,' said the Skin Horse. 'You become. It takes a long time. That's why it doesn't happen to people who break easily or have sharp edges or who have to be carefully kept. Generally, by the time you are real, most of your hair has been lugged off, and your eyes drop out, and you're getting loose in the joints and very shabby. But these things don't matter at all, because once you are real you can't be ugly, except to people who don't understand.' " [2]

---

[1] Proceedings of the Institute on Library Work. Univ. of California, "Hold to That Which Is Good," by Miss Elizabeth Nesbitt.

[2] From *The Velveteen Rabbit* by Margery Williams; by permission of the publishers William Heinemann, Limited, London.

READING BETWEEN THE LINES

This is real literature, and for little children. From it they gain some idea, they absorb some notion, of what it means to be real and to be loved. Other such stories are ... *And Now Miguel, Call It Courage, The Adventures of Odysseus,* and *The Arabian Nights;* all these stories speak from between the lines and are immeasurably above and beyond the printed word.

Now let us take the next idea, "far transcending the merely informative." We have a great many factual books dealing with facts in isolation. We also have a great many histories, offering history as a series of anecdotes. I should love to see children reading again, as they did once upon a time, a book by Hendrik van Loon, called *The Story of Mankind,* in which they get some sense of the continuity of life upon this planet, in which they get a sense of the philosophy of history. It is a spacious book with vision, wit, and humor, showing what man has endured to reach modern times; it gives children a view through the arches of the years and builds in them what Edith Hamilton has called "eternal perspectives."

INFORMATION PLUS ...

When I think of geography and the many stories of other lands which are coming today, I always think of that beautiful book by Selma Lagerlöf, called *The Wonderful Adventures of Nils.* This was a geography commissioned by the Swedish government and written by a Nobel Prize winner. I also think of books like *Lost Worlds,* by Anne Terry White, which deals with the great archaeological finds and which has stimulated the interest of many children in that period of world history. John and Jean George's nature study books, *Vulpes, The Red Fox* and *The Masked Prowler: The Story of a Raccoon,* are examples of books that far transcend the merely factual. These happen to be rather long books, but this should not deter a child from reading them unless he has been required to read a given number of books. In that case he is apt to choose very thin ones—in more ways than one. Let us stop measuring a child's reading experience by the number of books he has read. It is quality, not quantity, that matters in a reading experience. Lyman Bryson once said that a well-read person was not someone who knew a lot of books, it was someone who knew a few great books well enough to quote from them.

MYTHS AND LEGENDS

Going on to "varied as is human destiny," I think I have already
suggested the wide range, the infinite variety of children's literature. But there are two vitally important categories in this literature. I refer to mythology—mythology, folklore, and legends—and
to that other large field which we call "nonsense." I shall mention
only three things about mythology: first, it is important that children should know it because it shows them that the concerns of
man today are exactly the same as they were before recorded time.
Trial and triumph, fear and hope, and the cross-motives of mankind are the elements with which myths are concerned. Every
generation doesn't start brand-new; it comes along with all the
knowledge acquired in the past, and myths give a sense of this.
Second, myths allow children to identify with an adult world. In
myths and in folklore events occur in a grown-up world in which
the child participates. Third, myths give children an experience
with true nobility of language; sometimes children meet real
literature for the first time in the myths and folklore they encounter in their reading.

NONSENSE IS NEEDED

When we come to nonsense, we come to a subject that is very
hard to discuss for the simple reason that so often one person's
idea of nonsense is not another's. The crux of the whole business
with respect to nonsense is that you just have to have faith in it.
Some critics of American culture have said that the greatest product of the American imagination is our sense of humor; we are
a laughing people. In this age of anxiety especially children need
to be merry. Under the cloak of nonsense, moreover, a great many
wise things can be said. Children need Lear, Laura E. Richards,
Lewis Carroll, Carl Sandburg, the *Just So Stories* by Kipling, and
all the rest of the books that are such fun.

THE WONDER OF WORDS

Taking the last segment of the definition, "nonexistent without the twin qualities of beauty of idea and beauty of expression," we'll concede, I think, that beauty of idea is desirable in
all books for children. The value of literature, however, extends
beyond the beauty of idea to the language in which the idea is
expressed. Great children's books let us help children develop a
vocabulary. Our thoughts, for all practical purposes, can only be

as good as the vocabulary in which we express them. So it is important that children should learn the value of words, the excitement of words. There is no reason why children, if they have read great children's books, should not have acquired a knowledge of words or an ability to use them that will make them want to continue to add to their vocabularies by reading when they reach the secondary level.

ENTHUSIASM IS CATCHING

How are you going to guide your children toward these great books? Since nothing succeeds like enthusiasm, you must be enthusiastic about the books, and the only way you can be is to know them, to know them at firsthand. You can read a few books each year, each term, and thus be able to recommend them with genuine enthusiasm. There are many lists available from which to make selections of your great books. One of the best of them, I think, is a very personal list in that it includes only 230 titles. It's called *Children's Books too Good to Miss*, and it's published by the press of Western Reserve University. The list has been arranged according to age and includes picture books, factual books, and fanciful tales.

Above all, give books status in your classroom. I believe in classroom libraries as much as I believe in central school libraries. I think books should be immediately available when children want them.

Don't assume that this kind of reading won't work with your class. You would be surprised at the children who respond to great literature when given a chance to know it. There is a reason why the great stories for children have lived. They have been kept alive by the children's own love for them.

Part Three

SELECTION OF CHILDREN'S BOOKS

SEARCH FOR THE REAL THING

Among the "Millions and Billions and Trillions" of Books *

Virginia Haviland

The selector of books for a children's library today is offered the largest number of widest range of possibilities in history. Therein lie problems of choice so time-consuming and difficult as to lead him to question where we are going and whether we shall manage to distinguish what we may call the *real thing* from something we may designate as *fool's gold*.

If the large library with opportunity to read and discuss new books before purchase feels hard-pressed by sheer quantity of attractiveness and high intentions, what can there be but acute frustration for the conscientious one-man children's department and the jack-of-all-trades librarian who must select all his books without seeing or reading them first. Perhaps many are trapped like the one-man selector who admits, unhappily, "The less time I have, the more titles I buy. It is so easy to be taken in by a title that sounds as if it would fill a need."

The number of new titles selected in one year for a children's collection varies greatly from library to library, and is not in proportion to size of library. Figures for a sampling of libraries vary from 302 to 1,276 of the 1960 publications selected. A majority of libraries chose from 500 to 700, but a few, both larger and smaller, purchased some 900 different new titles, and another few about 300. Certainly there can be no fixed number as most desirable, since factors of budget, use of library, and publishers' output itself are all variables. However, *differences in number selected* for libraries of similar size and budget may be due to *differences in ability to separate the real thing from the fool's gold*—which we may recognize as differences in standards and policy for selection as well as in opportunities to see and know the new books.

While lamenting our inability to handle this huge output with ease and assurance, we must acknowledge that the greater total of new titles available offers greater *potential* for choosing the

* Virginia Haviland, "Search for the Real Thing; Among the 'Millions and Billions and Trillions' of Books," *Library Journal*, 86 (December 15, 1961), 4332–36. Published by R. R. Bowker Company.

real thing, greater variety of books on the same subject, and large coverage of subjects—on more reading levels—to meet new curricular developments and widening individual needs and interests. We must only hope that haste, chance, and heavy promotion will not lead us first to the less good, rather than to the better, choice.

We are fortunate indeed in the wealth of truly beautiful and appealing books being published for children. There is no lack of creative vigor in the writing of fiction, biography, and history. (Our discouragement is in plowing our way to it.) We have splendid access to new poetry and old, and to folklore in fresh collections and newly illustrated, newly translated editions. The United States is envied abroad for the best of our picture-book production—for the rich variety in art and design, as well as in storytelling. We are envied also for our wide range of informational books, so well produced and on so many levels of interest and reading skill.

At the same time, we in this country are fortunate in the widening, enriching stream of books coming to us from abroad. Distinctive color work appears in picture-story books printed in Germany, Switzerland, and Holland. There is continued excellence in fantasy and historical fiction from England; in accounts of exploration and archaeology from Germany; in fantasy, mystery, and tales of adventure from these two countries and from France and Scandinavia—all strengthening our list of books presenting foreign backgrounds.

These books will be discovered. But the wise books selector knows that haste and human limitations may slow the discovery and result in failure to recognize some of the subtly disguised pitfalls to good selection.

Are we taking adequate time to determine what we really have or are we being taken in by pretentious bookmaking? Are texts actually worthy of their lavish illustration, perhaps even without value apart from their pictures? Is the book with glossy exterior, lush art work (several media in one volume), and out-size page giving us more than is the modest volume with more limited illustration which allows the eye to follow the text without distraction? Are we training children to expect more and more color, and less and less text in proportion to illustration? Do we perhaps presume that a child wants an "eye-smiting array" of color? Let us recall that among the most widely beloved picture books are Wanda Gág's *Millions of Cats,* Robert McCloskey's *Make Way for Ducklings,* and Lynd Ward's *The Biggest Bear.*

On a day when I toyed with *Fool's Gold or the Real Thing in Children's Books?* as a possible title for a forthcoming library association talk, a mountain of new books lay nearby ready for the weekly book-review committee meeting. In it was a heavy proportion of informational material. More than half of the total number appeared to be books belonging to series, some with confident titles indicating *absolute* authority and *complete* coverage. A startlingly greater number than usual reported on their jackets the specific number of different words used in their texts, an ever smaller number of words for easier and easier reading. Everything was colorfully packaged, aimed to beguile the selector.

SERIES FALLACY THREATENS

The series fallacy is increasingly with us, presenting real problems in discrimination. We are offered "deals" for bargain buying of series of biography, social studies, and science. We are not expected to inspect the quality of individual titles, to be aware that a poorer item in a series benefits from acclaim for preceding, more outstanding companions (although we have seen that some authors do less than their best in a series and that others, even though writing superbly, suffer from being compressed into a series' standard dimensions). Too, the popularity with young readers of some well-known series, with magic in their names, continuously poses a threat to balance in library expenditure.

In the increasing flood of "vocabularized" books, are we finding the "easy-to-read" book with its word-list tag also *worth reading?* Added to the enormously successful new stories for beginners, we find informational material and classic tales reworked in a word-count formula and reduced to the monotony of a textbook primer. This new flood of *vocabularized* books brings back to me the heated discussion at a reading conference two years ago when reading supervisors loudly insisted that they did *not* want their pupils' individualized reading (outside of basal texts) to be done in word-list books. How, they asked, will children learn new words? There is David Fletcher's strong statement, too, on the blurb of his *Confetti for Cortorelli:* "If this age is to produce any worthwhile children's books, authors must not be made the slaves of 'age groups' and 'readability,' or confined to words of two syllables." We must all recognize that factors other than word count—the look of the page, the space between lines, the amount of illustration, and size of margins—contribute to making a book easy to read.

Again we may ask whether we are being attracted to fool's

gold by a false snob appeal of the term "classic," if we accept
abridgments and watering-down of texts because we believe that
the slow or lazy child must read *Alice in Wonderland* or *Treasure
Island* in one form or another. Is it not dishonest to allow children to think they are truly reading the classics when they read
them in abbreviated form?

Are we being pressured into accepting for purchase any and all
titles on certain subjects because teachers require a long list of
library references for assigned topics? If so, we need to educate
those creating such pressures. Too much emphasis on correlating
public library book collections with school work, and coercion
to spend disproportionate amounts of the budget for such nonfiction, may mean too little thought for leisure reading. One child
insists on more and more titles on jet propulsion, while another
makes a quieter request for Jules Verne or Mark Twain. Attractive editions of such stories must be available for these moments;
they may never come again for these individuals.

Awareness Creates Anxiety

Our anxieties in book selection will vary in proportion to our
awareness of limitations, not only of the lack of sufficient man-
hours for reading and thinking but of special knowledge needed.
Frequently we need a scientist's knowledge for judging books in
the growing specialized area of science. And, lest we become captivated by some adult appeal or dismiss some book too readily,
we need, just as often, the reactions of small children themselves
to books produced for them. Kindergarten classes have pointed
out more surely than book committee members the significance
of Edward Emberly's *The Wing on a Flea,* a new picture book
which stimulates small children to distinguish different shapes in
the world about them.

Anxiety in selection will vary also, of course, with conscientious-
ness in use of the book budget and depth of perception of fundamental aims and values. There must be awareness of *differences*
in books if we are to do our own job of selection well and also
help those interested in children to become aware that there is
something beyond mediocrity and that reading alone is not
enough. We must recognize with Lillian Smith that "to tolerate
the mediocre and commonplace is to misunderstand the purpose
of book selection and the significance of literature" (*The Unreluctant Years,* ALA).

With salesmen and book dealers actively circulating and with
brightly written promotion on every side attracting attention to

the newest books, it is natural, even inevitable, that selectors—pressed for time, unable to examine books at leisure or to review them or hear them reviewed—should give ear and eye hastily to the unknown. *Is there need for haste?* Is the selector being trapped into buying more than he wishes later he had bought? Is it too difficult to return approval copies? Is it really a bargain to accept quickly, as a "package deal," a dealer's or publisher's selection or all of a given series, because the discount is bigger?

Small libraries, without approval copies at hand, must usually rely on printed reviews and approved lists and on visits to bookstores and exhibits. The need for a variety of reviews with their different emphases and coverage is greater for the small library than it is for the larger one with an orderly system of reviewing. There is special help in the "For the Small Library" recommendation in *Booklist;* in the unfavorable as well as favorable verdicts expressed in both *School Library Journal* and the *Bulletin of the Center for Children's Books,* with a helpful key also in the latter to "marginal" and "special" values; in the inclusion of illustrations from books and a scientist's reviews in *The Horn Book.*

For the small library, even more important guidance than that of current reviews (and, says a one-man department, it is "less difficult and time-consuming") is that offered later in selective lists and in catalogs with annual supplements, in which entries are starred and double-starred. ALA's annual "Notable Children's Books" appears each spring; *The Horn Book* "Fanfare" summary is printed in its August issue; during Book Week and before Christmas many lists of the year's outstanding books are printed by large libraries and newspapers. No single summary or review medium is sufficient, but a number of them together become a substitute for reading and examination of the books themselves.

COOPERATIVE REVIEWING EFFORTS

Fortunately, in some areas, the limitations are lessened by regional, county, or state cooperative arrangements for sharing book reviewing and discussion. In the offering of facilities, books and leadership, large libraries and state, county, or regional centers provide indispensable aid for book selection.

Without formal ties a group of children's librarians in any area may evolve a joint working arrangement. Such a group has met for over a year in the Boston Public Library, having been organized because of the need expressed by a former staff member who in a new small-city position was frustrated by lack of a book-review system. This Greater Boston Children's Book Review

Committee includes a few elementary and junior high school librarians among the large number of suburban public-library staff members and has the help of the state library extension office in handling details of meeting and book approval service. Each member of the group is responsible for reviewing books, on an alphabetical author arrangement, approval copies being mailed by a dealer to member libraries ("A" authors to one member, "B" authors to another, etc.).

Some other large-city libraries have for years welcomed children's librarians of their metropolitan areas at regular children's librarians' meetings. In Miami, Florida, a different service exists; a Joint Book Selection Committee of the Miami Public Library and the Dade County School Libraries has been organized. Its members prepare an annotated list each semester and offer guidance at a book display, set up on the day the list is issued, to librarians from school and public libraries of the surrounding area who come to see the books.

Helpful annual or semi-annual meetings with book-fair-type exhibits and oral reviewing are sometimes held at city libraries or state meetings. In Philadelphia, for example, there is an annual spring review and display of the outstanding books published in the preceding year. Young adult books are reviewed in the morning and children's books in the afternoon. Lists of the books on display are distributed to the librarians, teachers, parents, and other interested adults attending.

In Oklahoma, the Children's and Young People's Division of the Oklahoma Library Association and the Extension Division of the State Library cooperate so that small-town librarians in the state may see new children's books and talk with other librarians about them. A panel of reviewers from city, county and school libraries share in presenting the books.

Experiences like these indicate that success is possible wherever there are leadership, available review copies (from dealer, state library, or large-city library), and a meeting place geographically convenient.

Discussion, with resulting development of policy, is needed for preservation of the best of the older books as well as for selection of the best of the new. *Regular* reevaluation of the book collection is required if it is to be kept fresh and up-to-date—free of the dead wood that is dated as fiction and no longer accurate and serviceable as informational material. The budget must be stretched to cover replacement of worn-out copies of excellent, still meaningful older books, for, as we know, an old title in fresh covers can still be a new book, especially when a librarian remembers her earlier enthusiasm. "We need more talk about the older books," says our friend, the struggling selector. "Remember what happened in the Washington Children's Services Division meeting with *Big Tiger and Christian?*" (See *Top of the News,* Oct. '59).

A growing number of library systems have developed well-organized schemes for replacing older books, based on periodic issuing of lists of books reevaluated and found worth their keep. A specified percentage of the book budget may be assigned for replacement orders—from two-thirds of the total budget in some large systems down to 40 per cent in some smaller cities and towns and 20–25 per cent in others. It appears easier to order new books, known to be in print and in stock, without weighing the new and the old, unless a library follows a definite plan for replacement ordering. A larger percentage of the budget must be spent on new titles in the small town or branch library, where basic titles and classics wear out less rapidly, in order to provide the variety required by avid readers. Larger units must do more replacing, but also need multiple copies of outstanding popular books, new or old.

Out of group discussion and reviewing will come not only specific information valuable to purchase of new books and replacement of old titles, but also a clearer recognition of criteria for different kinds of books and training in the application of critical judgment. Basic policy will develop.

From exchange of points of view about controversial books comes strength for rejecting or supporting them. A library will not select those books which present untrue or stereotype situations for a minority group, but will purchase religious and human-relations books when these reduce prejudice and ignorance *and* meet general literary standards. The library will not accept as gifts any books which do not meet generally accepted standards. It will categorically reject stories in endless, cheaply produced series. It will distinguish between the responsibilities of the school and the public library to supply textbook materials, purchasing nontextbook materials to *supplement* school study, and purchasing textbooks (titles not used in its schools) only when nothing else is available. It will recognize that it is now possible to substitute easy-to-read trade books for textbook readers.

BOOKS FOR THE FEW

If we have discovered books that we can recognize with confidence as being worthy of purchase, knowing why *this* is the real thing and *that* is fool's gold, we have yet a further question. Do we accept our responsibility to select for the few as well as for the many? One librarian who spends hours of thought on this *either/or* knows that "a book might mean everything to the individual, next to nothing to the group." It might be a book on raising rabbits; it might be *The Hobbit*. Another, having made her choice of an unusual book, lives up to her responsibility to know and do something about it; she starts a run on *Tistou of the Green Thumbs* by talking about it and reading it aloud. We are all living up to this responsibility each time we buy and place on the parents' shelf that book which might not get to the child unless it is read aloud, that book which is too difficult to be read by the age for which it has the greatest appeal. In whatever measure we are selecting and introducing such books, we are giving creative publishing its chance.

BOOK SELECTION *

Amelia H. Munson

BOOK SELECTION

Now, having had a good look at your young people and their interests, all of which you expect to reflect in your book collection, do you want to draw up a set of procedures for yourself or working criteria for book selection? Let's take the latter first. What are the things to remember about your young people when it comes to selecting books?

That there will be representatives of all reading levels, the slow, the normal (if there are any such), and the advanced; and

* Amelia H. Munson, "Book Selection," Chapter 8 in *An Ample Field* (Chicago: American Library Association, 1950), pp. 81–85. Reprinted by permission of the American Library Association, and the author.

of all interests, the prosaic and the poetic, the fanciful and the practical. There will be those concerned with schoolwork and those concerned with making a living. There will be some who will quickly outstrip you in the breadth and the technicality of their reading, and others who will require time and patience before they even begin to experience pleasure and satisfaction from the printed page. For all of these there must be something, but the very multiplicity of books and the normal limitations of book budgets require that there be selection. And the expressed aim of the American Library Association is as valid today as when it was first proposed: "the best books for the greatest number at the least cost."

THIS IS THE GENERAL IDEA

In your whole collection, try to have: Scope, coverage, variety, readability, and attractiveness.

Scope. Start, of course, with the known interests of young people so as to set up the inviting element of familiarity. Add to this books that will broaden their interests. The idea back of this special collection is not so much to relieve your adult clientele from the annoying proximity of the younger set as to facilitate for these young people their transition to a large, sometimes a frighteningly large, collection of adult books. There should, therefore, be samples of practically everything; certainly every sizable division of the Dewey Decimal System will be represented. The preceding chapters have outlined the most important ones.

Coverage. Several different meanings are combined in this term. (1) The same subject may be presented in different forms. This follows from the breaking down of fiction and nonfiction barriers, as suggested in the previous chapters, and recommends your gathering material on a subject from factual, fictional, biographical, poetic, dramatic, and all other possible fields that add just the angle needed. (2) A few books should be available both for reference and for circulation. It is desirable that they be taken home for leisurely perusal but imperative that they be on hand for consultation, in case someone else has reached the circulation desk first. These are not primarily reference books; they may not even be considered informational. They may pertain to local interests or seasonal, but, as you work directly with your young people, you will discover what they are and you should act upon your discoveries promptly. (3) There is frequently a temptation to cover a subject—say, Sherlock Holmes—by the purchase of an omnibus volume. This may seem economical but it makes for poor distribution and, as a rule, is not so inviting in appearance as the separate volumes.

Variety. The same subject may appeal to a wide age range. Therefore it should be presented in books widely differing in treatment and in vocabulary; although for the latter, it is well to remember that when a person's interest in a subject is really aroused, he tends to read far beyond his native capacity. It stands to reason that, if your collection has scope and coverage, as described above, it is bound to have variety.

Readability. Sometimes this is a matter of format, sometimes of vocabulary, sometimes of construction. In general, prefer the concrete to the abstract, the simple to the involved, and the broken page to long, solid paragraphs. Again, consider your clientele. Readable for whom? If there are young people with reading difficulties, there should be simple written books with adult content, a difficult group to assemble.[1] (*Note:* This is not, by any devious twist of reasoning, to be interpreted as a recommendation of rewritten or watered-down classics.)

Attractiveness. Mostly a matter of format. See that the suspicion of juvenilia does not attach to a book, but by no means exclude all illustrated editions. Look for: clear type, not too small; wide margins; a sufficiently heavy paper to be opaque; and eye-catching but not blinding jackets.

CONTENT

As for content, in *nonfiction* look for awareness of present-day discoveries and techniques, accuracy of research and of presentation, a style suitable to the content, and a certain persuasiveness of writing. In *fiction*, your care should be to select books that have vitality, either from character or incident or atmosphere, and that are true to the most fundamental concepts of life.

ARE YOU UP TO THE BEST BOOKS?

It will be wise, I suppose, to have mediocre books that will be read rather than superlative books that simply sit on the shelves. But you will be justified in spending the taxpayers' money on

---

[1] Valuable assistance may be found in *Gateways to Readable Books,* by Ruth Strang and others (H. W. Wilson, 1944), which not only lists a great many books of this kind for young people, with reading level indicated, but gives excellent advice in its introduction, "What makes a book easy to read?" New edition in 1958 (Editor's note).

those finer books, if you will train yourself to introduce them to your would-be readers at the right time, if you will learn to know your young people so well that you can recommend when occasion arises and they will accept your recommendation even though the book seems to lack the accustomed immediate appeal, and if you yourself are so versed in good writing and so imbued with its quality that it becomes the most natural thing in the world for you to talk about it. One of the hindrances to the growth of literary appreciation in the library profession is the compulsion we are under to read the latest books, whatever they are, and to keep in touch with all contemporary expression, no matter how inept, in order to answer our inquiring readers. We need to extract time somehow for ourselves, to cultivate our own reading tastes, to follow our own special delights in reading.

It is good for us to remember, too, that much disservice has been done literature (poetry especially) by the air of sanctity with which we have invested it, so that "the classics" occupy a world apart. Sometimes it is because we ourselves have found them formidable and, although recommending them for others to read, we cannot bring ourselves to talk of them with the ease and informality that lighten our discussion of other books. We need to increase our acquaintance, to be more casual in our approach, and to be able to talk about them with the naturalness we use toward the movies and the comic strip. We need to become so familiar with these books that we can—in the other sense of the phrase—be *familiar* with them. More people are lured into reading by someone's contagious enthusiasm for a book than by any number of remarks about the values of reading or the beauties of literature.

But Watch! Wait!

We need patience, too, as we watch the sometimes tortuous unfolding of adolescence. Forced growth may exact its own penalty, and every state of awareness can be so provocative, so challenging in itself, that we can afford to be patient in dealing with it. In guiding the reading of young people, one starts with the human being, wherever he is, and goes on as he goes on. The fact we must always keep in mind is that he *does go on,* that he isn't the same person day after day, that we can't even be sure his growth will be according to chart. We must rediscover him frequently and be alert to the opportunities he gives us.

There are writers who have so much of significance to say to your young people that the thought of its never reaching them should be a reproach to haunt your hours. After all, we have chosen to work with books because of our belief in their power. We must be constantly in touch with the sources of that power. The advice Maxwell Anderson gives in "Whatever Hope We Have" is applicable to us:

> ...if you practice an art, be proud of it, and make it proud of you.... turn to the art which has moved you most readily, take what part in it you can, as participant, spectator, secret practitioner, or hanger-on and waiter at the door. Make your living any way you can, but neglect no sacrifice at your chosen altar. It may break your heart, it may drive you half mad, it may betray you into unrealizable ambitions or blind you to mercantile opportunities with its wandering fires. But it will fill your heart before it breaks it; it will make you a person in your own right; it will open the temple doors to you and enable you to walk with those who have come nearest among men to what men may sometime be.[2]

[2] Maxwell Anderson, "Whatever Hope We Have," *Essence of Tragedy* by Maxwell Anderson, 1939. Used by permission of William Sloane Associates, Inc.

THE SELECTION AND ACQUISITION OF BOOKS FOR CHILDREN *

Frances Lander Spain

The scope of this paper will be limited to a discussion of the methods of acquisition of books for children by public libraries and by public school libraries. It will avoid on one hand the

* Frances Lander Spain, "The Selection and Acquisition of Books for Children," *Library Trends* 3 (April, 1955), 455–61. Reprinted by permission of the University of Illinois, and the author.

Scylla of principles of book selection and on the other the Charybdis of order work. Both have been covered ably in books and periodicals.

Material on the general practices and variations in the area of acquiring new titles and replacing old ones for schools and children's collections is scarce. Order procedures and routines are reviewed in the standard works on school library administration and in public library work with children. A few articles in periodicals handle the topic briefly. However, the overall programs followed by librarians generally to maintain a collection of books for children are not described in detail. Librarians throughout the country have furnished the data upon which this paper is based. They represent school and public libraries in large, medium size, and small governmental units in several parts of the United States.

Librarians working with children have established criteria, principles, and standards for books that are to be used with children. In order to build up working collections of suitable books, it is necessary to survey the output of books published for children, to apply standards to them, to select and reject new and old titles, and to establish procedures for accomplishing this.

Supervisors of library service to children in public libraries and in school systems regularly check, or have checked by an assistant in their offices, book announcements from publishers, book lists, and reviews in such standard publications as: *A.L.A. Booklist, The New York Times, New York Herald Tribune, Saturday Review, Bulletin of the Children's Book Center University of Chicago, The Horn Book, Junior Bookshelf, Junior Reviewers,* and the like. School librarians also check reviews appearing in general professional education and subject field periodicals. From these announcements and reviews, checklists of books to be considered for their collections are compiled and book-ordered for evaluation.

Review copies of books suitable for school and public library children's rooms are sent by publishers to some large, strategically located systems. Other books are ordered "on approval" from publishers and jobbers, and single copies of some titles are bought for examination before quantity orders for branch and school distribution are placed. Most large school library systems and children's library departments approve for inclusion in the collections only books that have been examined, that have been read and reviewed by staff members, and that are available for further examination by the individual librarian selecting books for his school library or public library children's room.

All librarians responsible for selecting books for children would prefer to see books before ordering. However, those who live and work in small towns and out-of-the-way locations have little access to many children's books and must depend upon reviews and selected lists. They see books only when they go to cities with good bookstores, when they attend professional meetings where book exhibits are held, or when they visit Book Fairs, Book Week celebrations, and other special exhibitions. State departments of education, especially if there is a school library consultant in the office, and state library commissions often have sample or display collections of books that are open for examination. Small collections of books are available to school and public libraries from some of these state agencies. School librarians in some systems are allowed school time to visit such exhibits. One of the great problems in the acquisition of books for children is the availability of books for examination before a decision to purchase them must be made.

Book selection and recommendation of books are done by all professional school and children's librarians in a system. They are appointed to book-reviewing committees for periods of from two to four months. All members of the staff have an opportunity, therefore, during a year to participate in this basic activity connected with book acquisition. Appointment may be to a general book-reviewing committee or it may be to a subject committee; in either case, the librarian's interests and particular knowledges are used. Specialists in subject fields are often invited to review books and in the schools, teachers, elementary supervisors, and often administrators sit on review committees.

New books, after they have been recorded in the offices of supervisors of school and children's library services, are sent out to committee members to be read and evaluated. Reviewers make definite recommendations about each book. The Office of Children's Services of the New York Public Library, for example, has two categories of recommendation: for reading rooms—a book that is distinguished and should be in the collection of fine books kept permanently in the children's rooms for reading and enjoyment there; and for circulation—a book that is good, but not outstanding enough to become part of the reading-room collection. Besides essential and approved titles, the Department of Work with Children of the Schenectady County (New York) Public Library designates some books "revolving." Two copies are bought to circulate among the branches as a tryout before extensive ordering is done.

In many libraries recommendation for purchase by a particular branch is a common practice. Because of neighborhood needs or local interests, a book not suitable for the collection in general may be approved for a special children's room. An example of this is the great demand in sections of New York City for Spanish language books for the Puerto Rican children.

If there is a question about a book, it may be read by a second or third reviewer. Problem books are always read carefully by the supervisor with final decision left to him. In the Los Angeles and Denver school systems there is an advisory or reviewing committee which is called in to settle serious problems.

Reviews are written on "p" slips or order forms for permanent filing in the supervisor's office where they may be consulted when needed. In many public libraries the reviews are also given orally at regular meetings of the whole staff of children's librarians. Here books may be discussed and questions about the reviews asked. The Work with Children Department of the Los Angeles Public Library invites to its monthly meetings children's librarians of the surrounding smaller cities so that they may participate in and benefit from the discussion and examination of books not otherwise available to them. School librarians do not generally have regular system-wide meetings for book discussion. In the Los Angeles area, though, the Southern Section of the School Library Association of California sponsors a monthly book breakfast on Saturday mornings during the school year when current books are reviewed and discussed.

Many supervisors of work with children in public libraries and some in school libraries issue lists of titles approved for purchase. These lists are based on the reviews and recommendations of staff book committees and in some systems become the order form. Large public libraries seem to use lists more than small public libraries or large and small school library systems. In some school systems, lists of approved titles are offered for discount bids and thereafter for the period of the bid carry the discount price. These lists then may be used as order forms without further bids. Instead of issuing separate lists of approved books many school systems recognize standard lists—the three *Basic Book Collections* for elementary, junior high, and senior high schools. *The Children's Catalog* and its supplements, *The Stand-*

ard Catalog for High School Libraries and its supplements, and
state lists—and accept for inclusion in their collections any titles
appearing on them. Special lists are compiled where needed. Because of the great range of books used in the high school libraries, their librarians are generally free to order books they require, clearing titles with their supervisors.

Lists of approved titles are sent to the children's and school
librarians prior to the book-order period and are used in con-
junction with ordering. They are not for public distribution,
but are kept as a record of books that have been approved for
purchase, as a second check of the titles ordered by each unit, and
in some systems as an order form from which composite order
slips are made. The Boys and Girls Department of the Carnegie
Library of Pittsburgh, Pennsylvania, has discontinued its monthly
annotated lists, but continues a list, revised every five years, of
titles that form the nucleus of every branch children's collection.
In Chicago, the supervisor of school libraries issues an annual
list of three to four hundred books which is a supplement to the
Approved List of Library Books for the Chicago Public Schools.

Whether books approved for inclusion in the collection appear
on a list or not, they are available for examination by all children's and school librarians in those public libraries and school
systems where review and on-approval copies are provided. Regular book-order periods are scheduled at which time the individual school or children's librarian handles the books; reads the
reviews, or listens to them as they are given orally in a meeting,
or both; and makes his decision regarding the need his unit has
for them. Books not approved are also available for examination
with reviews suggesting the reasons the book was not recommended. Usually a school or children's librarian may question
a review or request a reconsideration. He may also ask that a
book not being considered for the collection be reviewed.

Each school and children's librarian is free to select and order
the books he wishes and the number of duplicates his library
can use. When inexperienced or untrained persons are responsible for school library or branch children's room service, the
supervisor's office through the supervisor or an assistant, gives a
great deal of direction in book selection. Experienced librarians
of good judgment and extensive book knowledge require little
supervision. Though each librarian is given wide freedom in
selecting books for his library, some departments of children's
services have overall system-wide requirements for all units. In

Pittsburgh every children's room of the Carnegie Library must have a copy of the approximately 500 books on the basic list which is the nucleus of the children's collections.

The frequency with which children's books are ordered varies greatly. Orders for books to be used in children's rooms of public libraries seem to be placed more often than those books to be used in school libraries. The former are placed generally on a monthly basis, the latter on an annual or semester basis.

Books selected by individual school and children's librarians for units within a system are cleared generally through the office of the supervisor. He is responsible for checking orders, approving or disapproving them, and forwarding them to the order department or business office for purchase. In secondary schools books ordered, especially if from a previously approved list, may go through the office of the principal directly to the business office for purchase.

Orders for school library books are usually sent out for bids. Small orders may be placed without bids, and in some systems comprehensive discount bids cover all titles on approved lists for a specific period. Public libraries are not so frequently required to have bids on book orders. However, books are bought where best discounts are obtained. Books for children are usually purchased from jobbers and publishers, and only occasionally from local bookstores. Foreign children's books are ordered directly from importing houses and stores, and prebound books directly from prebinding companies.

Books in prebound, library, and school editions are purchased more extensively for use in the elementary school libraries than in children's rooms of public libraries. However, when publisher's bindings are weak or books will have hard and long use, the general practice seems to be to order them in reinforced bindings whether they are for elementary or secondary school libraries or for the children's rooms of public libraries. Picture books, large flats, paperbound books, fiction, and titles that promise to be popular are most often bought in prebound editions.

School libraries and children's rooms of public libraries usually have portions of the budgets of their central agency allocated to them to cover the cost of book orders during the year. For the school library the amount is based on the average daily attendance in the school and is, in many states, governed by state-adopted school library standards. For children's rooms the amount is based on circulation, special needs of the children who use the rooms, high percentage of replacements, additional language requirements, condition of the book stock, and other pertinent factors. The librarians in charge of these units may order books —new titles and replacements—as they wish under the general direction of the supervisor.

While school librarians and children's librarians of public libraries are selecting new titles they are also concerned with the maintenance of their collections, with the replacement of specific titles and with the evaluation of their holdings. Methods of accomplishing this vary from simple, incidental reordering of single books by individual librarians to highly organized checking of scheduled lists.

The collections in children's rooms of public libraries are reevaluated according to a carefully developed plan that in many systems is almost as important as the acquisition of new titles. In order to keep their collections live and active, children's librarians are constantly reviewing their contents. In Atlanta, Los Angeles, and New York the departments of work with children have monthly lists of replacements which cover fiction, picture books, easy books, and subjects by classification so that in any year the whole collection is revised.

The quality of service given in school libraries and in children's rooms of public libraries depends upon the overall collection. The selection of new books, reevaluation of older ones, decisions to withdraw or replace specific titles are professional responsibilities of the librarians developing these collections of books for children. There are many details, numerous steps, multiple forms, and procedures to the process of acquiring books. The larger the system and the greater the number of units, the more elaborate the process seems to be, but large or small, the reason for the procedure is to determine for any library the books that will be of most value in it and to set up routines for acquiring those books economically and quickly.

INDIVIDUALS AND INSTITUTIONS CONTRIBUTING INFORMATION

Ruth Adams, head, Work with Children Department, Schenectady (N.Y.) County Public Library; Wilma Bennett, librarian, Covina (Calif.) High School Library; Helen Canfield, supervisor of Children's Work Department, Hartford (Conn.) Public Library; Virginia Chase, head, Boys and Girls Department, Carnegie Library, Pittsburgh, Pa.; Mrs. Harriette H. Crummer, supervisor of children's library service, Evanston (Ill.) Library and Board of Education; Mrs. Mary P. Douglas, supervisor of city school libraries, Raleigh (N.C.) Board of Education; Lois Fannin, assistant supervisor of library service, Long Beach (Calif.) Public Schools; Mrs. Carolyn W. Field, director of work with children, Philadelphia (Pa.) Free Public Library; Kathleen G. Fletcher, coordinator of school libraries, High Point (N.C.) City Schools; Helen Fuller, supervisor of work with boys and girls, Long Beach (Calif.) Public Library; Jewel Gardiner, supervisor, Sacramento (Calif.) Elementary and Junior High School Libraries; Elizabeth Gross, coordinator of work with children, Enoch Pratt Free Library, Baltimore, Md.; Marjorie Halderman, supervisor, Astoria (Ore.) High School Libraries; Virginia Haviland, readers' advisor for children, Boston (Mass.) Public Library; Sue Hefley, supervisor of materials center, Webster Parish Schools, Minden, La.; Ruth E. Hewitt, superintendent of work with children, Seattle (Wash.) Public Library; Marjorie B. Hill, head of children's department, Warder Public Library, Springfield, Ohio; Anne Izard, chief of children's department, Mount Vernon (N.Y.) Public Library; Marion James, librarian, Mason Junior High School Library, Tacoma, Wash.; Rosemary Livsey, director of work with children, Los Angeles (Calif.) Public Library; Florence Longman, librarian, Beaumont (Tex.) Senior High School Library; Dilla MacBean, director of division of libraries-public schools, Chicago (Ill.) Board of Education Library; Virginia McJenkin, director, Fulton County School Libraries, Atlanta, Ga.: Margaret Martignoni, superintendent of work with children, Brooklyn (N.Y.) Public Library; Mrs. Elizabeth D. Miller, librarian, Roswell (N.M.) Senior High School Library; Evelyn G. Peters, librarian, Orleans Parish School Board Professional Library, New Orleans, La.; Evelyn C. Thornton, supervisor of libraries, Arlington (Va.) County Public Schools; Mary Ann Wentroth, boys and girls librarian, Oklahoma City Libraries; Elizabeth O. Williams, supervisor of library and textbook section, Los Angeles (Calif.) Board of Education; Mrs. Paul Carson, librarian, Rock Hill (S.C.) Public Library; Mary Lee Keath, director of library service department, Denver (Col.) Public Schools; and Maxine LaBounty, coordinator of children's services, Public Library of the District of Columbia, Washington, D.C.

General References

Boyd, Jessie: "The Selection of Material in the Oakland Public School Represents Wide Participation." *Bulletin of the School Library Association of California,* 25 (March, 1954), (31).

Fargo, Lucile F.: *Library in the School.* 4th ed. Chicago, American Library Association, 1947.

Gardiner, Jewel: *Administering Library Service in the Elementary School.* 2nd ed. Chicago, American Library Association, 1954.

Long, Harriet G.: *Rich the Treasure.* Chicago, American Library Association, 1953.

Power, Effie: *Work with Children in Public Libraries.* Chicago, American Library Association, 1943.

Willett, Mary A.: "It Works in Lakewood" (Ohio). *Library Journal,* 76 (May 15, 1951), 833–44.

GENERAL CRITERIA FOR SELECTION AND USE OF MATERIALS*

Yolanda Federici

A talk given at Joint Conference of Illinois Association of School Librarians and Children's Librarians' Section, ILA, Peoria, March 21.

The National Library Week issue of the *Saturday Review* for March 22. 1958, carried an article entitled, "Pollyanna Rides Again" (page 37). It cleverly impales the well-known stereotype in the field of library service, "the sisterhood of juvenile librarians," who worship "sacred bovines."

Some of these statements have some element of truth which

* Yolanda Federici, "General Criteria for Selection and Use of Materials," *Illinois Libraries,* 40 (June, 1958), 504–509. Reprinted by permission of the *Illinois Libraries,* and the author.

could be said to apply to a few individual "juvenile librarians," but never to the group or to their standards. A lack of knowledge of the professional preparation of children's and school librarians and of their aims, as well as a total lack of knowledge of childhood and early adolescence, and a blind approach to the definition of a children's or a young people's book, can create this kind of misunderstanding.

During the eighteenth and nineteenth centuries, books for children and young people appeared regularly and in some quantity. Regularly, the children ignored them and read those adult books of general appeal which offered to them some enjoyment. A few of these are now "classics."

Toward the end of the nineteenth century, some astute publishers and some brave authors actually produced children's books, like *Little Women,* instead of books for children and young people.

These emancipators realized that children were interested in anything and everything but that their understanding, and, therefore, their enjoyment, had limitations according to their chronological age. They realized that children understood death—at least, as well as most adults—but not suicide; unhappiness but not despair; disappointment but not hopelessness; frustration but not bitterness; cruelty but not viciousness; love but not passion; justification but not rationalization.

In short, they granted to children the outstanding qualities of childhood: logic and literal-mindedness. Those adults who retain or regain these simple characteristics are said to have childlike qualities rather than childish or juvenile qualities. It has also been conceded that these characteristics develop into wisdom.

Children's and school librarians, being adults, sometimes also forget the straight line, the perfect circle, and fall into the complexities of jagged tangents. In examining general criteria for the selection and evaluation of library materials, a few definitions, perhaps, to clear the communication channels will help.

In the semantics of library service, evaluation cannot be confused with selection. Evaluation is the appraisal, selection is the purchase, of a book. Although inextricably related, evaluation comes first; selection follows. Evaluation defines the quality of a book; selection defines the quality of a book collection.

For the appraisal of a book, there is no substitute for personal reading; but, even then, printed reviews are important in order to be aware of as many opinions as possible. Judgment is more accurate when a single one is tested and tempered by many.

A book review gives information about a book. This is the main function of newspaper and magazine reviews. Sometimes, the book's positive negative qualities are indicated, but the positive usually predominate.

Publishers' catalogs have annotations and descriptive notes.

Professional library journals have critical book reviews which are both an appraisal and a recommendation for or against purchase. The number of times which a book is recommended for purchase becomes a guide to the librarian. Keeping a possible purchase file is wise, since, happily, so many books on a subject are published annually that refined selectivity can be achieved.

The possible purchase file is not only useful for the selection of new or current titles, but also in developing an initial book collection and for maintaining an existing collection when replacing titles or adding copies.

Therefore, selection has three parallel phases—current books, initial collection, and maintaining the existing collection.

In all book purchases, in addition to evaluation for quality, other and extraneous factors influence selection—the type of community, of library, and of readers, for example.

When an agency is an isolated one-agency library, purchase problems increase, but may be lessened if the community also maintains other unrelated units which provide books for research, circulation, or buying.

When a library agency is not only in a community where books are available elsewhere but is also a branch or a school library in a large organization—city, county, state—some titles need not be selected at all by every agency since these may be borrowed when needed from within the larger organization. This situation permits more emphasis on selection for the general and average reader at the specific branch or school library.

The reader group, if it is normal, will have 10 per cent who are gifted and special readers and 80 per cent who are average, approaching at the top the gifted group, but at the bottom touching the slow, uninterested 10 per cent of nonreaders.

But the reader-group may have 40 per cent gifted; 50 per cent average; 10 per cent slow. These variations will influence selection. Here, selection then diverges from evaluation which remains constant.

Selection by librarians has been criticized, but never as severely as the evaluation of books. When we are accused of worshiping sacred cows, these bovines are all branded with an "E" for evaluation. The fact that we attempt to set standards annoys some people exceedingly. Either they think so little of children's books that they do not feel the need for standards, or they themselves, being now out of the chronological age of childhood, find themselves perfectly adequate as evaluators of all childhood things—including books. Unfortunately, this attitude exists among the general staff of librarians who challenge the specialist on his own ground—something that would frighten them if they happened to be in a position to challenge specialists in other professions. But standards developed by knowledge and refined by experience are guides without which no one and nothing can operate. They set the line between "no" and "yes." If we haven't learned when to say "no," our "yes" is not a standard.

It is true that standards can be carried to petty lengths. For instance, I have heard children's and school librarians with adequate knowledge and long experience state emphatically that they will not buy a book for children which has a gun in an illustration. An historical book on firearms is also taboo. This is laughable because a bread knife can be just as deadly.

No doubt you have also heard authors tell the story of their experiences with librarians and children's book editors who have told them that a junior novel for the early teen years must not have more than one or two discreet kisses exchanged by Romeo and Juliet in order to pass the morality test for children's books. Yet, a book can have no kisses and plenty of innuendo and be offensive.

The plain fact is that realism is essential in children's and young people's books, but it must remain moral and within the comprehension of the age-range by which it will be read.

To a five-year-old child, potatoes, washing machines, and guns are fine playthings. They do not know and cannot conceive the idea that there could be any danger in playing with them. Therefore, when a picture book shows a child playing with guns—toy guns or real ones—the book has false concepts which the literal-minded child accepts. This is not laughable; this is dangerous.

In the teen-age novels, *Rowan Farm* (Benary-Isbert) and *Sarah* (Bro), humorous phases of affection and love, including the physical, are well depicted and felt by the reader. I doubt that either Mrs. Benary-Isbert or Mrs. Bro counted the number of kisses in their books; neither did the librarians or the children's book editors.

When we speak of concepts in children's books, we refer to ideas developed naturally and carefully, with multiple degrees of action within the conception and understanding of children. It is not the subject or the action, but the treatment, which distinguishes a children's book and a young people's book from an adult book. Complexity of language has nothing to do with this; complexity of concepts does.

The normal 12-year-old reader can read the words in the books by William Faulkner, but what will he get out of them? On the other hand, oversimplification of ideas is undesirable.

The portrayal of family loyalty versus personal ambition and pride demands a wide range of choices for actions which involve moral values and personal integrity. An eight-hundred page adult novel could be written on the subject; yet Ruth Sawyer presents these mature concepts adequately for 10-year-old children in her small book, *Maggie Rose*.

As I have said before, complexity of language has no relation to complexity of concept; neither does it denote literary quality. A book with complex grammatical structure and many-syllabled words can have literary quality in spite of these handicaps.

Put under a microscope, the style of writing and its quality refers entirely to the author's choice of words, short or long, which transform a written expression into a vivid mental picture —with "vivid" as the key word. The authors who have a distinguished literary style use descriptive sounds, tastes, smells, the feeling of touch, the immediacy of sight, as well as action to vivify the characters and the plot.

Originality in metaphors and similes gives the book a fresh and creative literary style. Here are some examples from *The Silver Branch* by Rosemary Sprague. The first is a short dialogue (p. 96).

> "She touched the bundle in the napkin. 'Take it with you and eat on the road.'
> " 'We will,' Flavius said, 'We will indeed; for we're both of us as empty as wine-skins after Saturnalia.' "

A pedestrian style would have read: "We certainly will. We're starved."

Here is another quotation (p. 97).

> "That evening they got into conversation with several owners of small, hopeful-looking vessels...."

And another (p. 98):

> "The babel of voices and the beat of the wind in the striped awning, the warmth of the braziers and the smell of broiling meat and crowding humanity, made the whole place seem so bulging full, that Justin thought, the walls must be straining apart at the seams, like a garment too tight for the person inside it."

This imagery carries over into characterization and gives life to the names in the story, as in this description (p. 99):

> "The smile puckered his plump, clean-shaven face rather pleasantly, and Justin saw with sudden liking that he had the eyes of a small contented child."

Literary quality actually simplifies reading because each description, each idea, is clarified.

Standards for concepts and literary style also involve motivation, in a dual interpretation—the action which moves the plot to its conclusion and the reason or motive which spurs a character into action. This is the "why" of an action.

The *Trojan War* by Olivia Coolidge is more than a story from Homer. It is an example of the exploration of motives. Not even the edition by Church, which has long been a standard title in library collections, presents so thoroughly why these Greek and Trojan men fought; why Ulysses finally agreed to fight; why Hector went to his certain death. While a child is reading this book, he is stirred and thinks about honor, loyalty, love, affection, coexistence, rather than carnage and brutality which were plentiful in the Trojan War.

After an appraisal of quality has been made, selection begins. For an initial collection, distinguished examples in each subject area are the first consideration; but some current titles, although evaluated as not of lasting value, need inclusion, otherwise the collection is top-heavy. Each year, from the thousand new titles published for children, perhaps one hundred have lasting value. Next year, some that had been selected as quality books will be down-graded slightly when compared to the new crop of quality books.

In maintaining an existing collection, this constant reevaluation before selection is essential so that the degree of basic value of a book to a collection will be clarified. Beyond the classics and the Newbery and Caldecott Award books, each subject area has some titles which are giants that should appear and be maintained whether they do or do not have high popularity value for circulation figures and factual usefulness for quick reference.

The books by Katherine Shippen, for example, are neither wildly popular nor can they be used for quick reference to answer a school assignment. But these books are giants in each subject field. From them the reader gathers factual information, but also the philosophy of a subject, the why, and a fine literary style.

Let's take a specific classification, 200–299 for an exercise in selection. These titles: *The Tree of Life, The Lord Is My Shepherd, Many Mansions, Small Child's Bible, Small Rain, This Is the Way;* the books by Fitch, *One God, Their Search for God, Allah, The God of Islam; Greek Myths* by Olivia Coolidge; Hawthorne's *Wonderbook* and *Tanglewood Tales;* Colum's *Children of Odin,* are basic no matter how small the collection is.

A second degree of basic value would then include at least, *A First Bible,* illustrated by Helen Sewell, and *The Bible Story* by Elsie Egermeyer. Optional titles which have current value would then include Mary Alice Jones' books, *Tell Me about God, Tell Me about the Bible,* etc., *Rainbow Book of Bible Stories,* and so on. Special items for specific needs would bring in *The Oldest Story* by Blanche Thompson; *In the Beginning* by Alfred Evers, and others. Historically valuable books, as part of children's literature, that is, would include the *Children's Bible,* by Sherman and Kent, for the extensive collections.

No mention has been made of illustration and of general format, both of which influence evaluation and selection, because content and the more intangible values seemed of primary importance.

General criteria for the selection and use of library materials for children and young people would demand an examination of the following: (1) Concepts—clarity and suitability; (2) Literary style—simplicity and originality; (3) Integrity of motivation—in characterization and in plot; (4) Continual comparison of titles even in the quality field before initial purchase and maintenance; (5) Maintenance of a core collection of essential materials without regard for popularity or for quick reference value.

It is my belief that the evaluation and selection of children's and young people's books is not a duty, but a trust given to each children's and school librarian.

BUY BETTER RATHER THAN MORE*

Mary K. Eakin

Ever since Sputnik went into orbit and precipitated the whole question of the quality of American education, there has been a steadily increasing awareness on the part of adults of the value of more and better books for children and an ever increasing pressure on schools to make such books available. Impetus in the areas of science, mathematics, and the social studies has been provided by funds supplied through the National Defense Education Act.

Encouragement and guidelines for establishing well-balanced collections have been made available through the recently published *Standards for School Library Programs* and the work of the various School Library Development Projects sponsored by the American Association of School Librarians. Publishers have responded promptly, sometimes overwhelmingly, to the requests for more materials in all subject areas and at all reading levels. As a result there are few subjects known to mankind that have not been at least attempted in books for children at all levels from elementary school on.

With increased funds for purchasing books and with ever increasing numbers of books available for use by and with children, many schools are finding themselves in a position that paraphrases the television commercial—they are buying more books, but are giving the children less to read. Quantitative measures alone are not enough to insure good library service. All too frequently schools find themselves to be liberally supplied with books, numerically speaking, but inadequately supplied in terms of materials that meet the standards of good book selection and good teaching.

* Mary K. Eakin, "Buying Better Rather Than More," *The Instructor*, 73 (November, 1963), 67–69. Copyrighted 1963 by F. A. Owen Publishing Company. Reprinted from *The Instructor* by permission.

More and more it becomes evident that today's teachers and librarians, to do an adequate job of book selection for a school, must be supplied with a wide variety of selection tools and with adequate time for examining those tools carefully and thoughtfully. Book selection today is a far more time-consuming job than it ever was in the past. It takes time to read the many reviews and to sift from them the books that are actually of value. It takes time to examine new books and see if they really do meet the needs of a particular school, and since a librarian cannot be an expert in all fields of knowledge, it takes time to enlist specialists' help in various fields.

Not all administrators have recognized these aspects of the book selection problem. In their zeal to provide the books that are needed to meet rapidly changing teaching methods and the ever widening areas of children's interests, they have sometimes resorted to the questionable practice of buying by the series or by the job lot, without first examining the books or finding reviews of them. Or they have provided funds for increased purchases of books, but have not allowed librarians or teachers sufficient time to do a good job of selection.

It is no longer possible to resort to a standard book selection tool, such as *Children's Catalog* (H. W. Wilson), and a single current reviewing tool, such as *The Horn Book* or *Booklist,* as the only sources of book information. Too many books are being published in a single year for any one tool to review them all, and too many books require a specialized kind of reviewing.

Some of the specialized book-selection problems faced by teachers and librarians may be worth examining. Children have long been interested in all aspects of modern scientific developments. Long before adults were willing to admit it, many seven-year-olds were able to understand the basic principles of jet propulsion. Because of the concern about improving education in science, the market is flooded with books of science for children from the primary grades on up. Some of these are quite good, others are little more than scissors-and-paste jobs, hastily contrived and dependent on subject matter and brightly colored pictures for their sales appeal.

Few librarians have the science background that would enable them to evaluate such books and so it becomes necessary to depend on other sources for help in weeding out the superficial and inaccurate from the useful. In this area, the standard reviewing tools are not much help unless the reviews are written by specialists in the field—specialists who not only know science, but who also have some understanding of children and respect for their needs and abilities. Such reviewing is done annually in the December issue of *Natural History Magazine,* an excellent source of help for librarians. Here the user not only reads sound evaluations of current science books, but also finds the kind of clear, objective statements that help the uninitiated to establish criteria for evaluating other kinds of science materials. By using these reviews, and those by scientists and science teachers in *The Horn Book* and *Library Journal,* librarians and teachers can be assured of providing books that will truly meet the science needs and interests of children. They will no longer find themselves in the embarrassing position of having children point out to them the inaccuracies in the books supplied by the library, or of having secondary teachers complain of the misinformation children acquired in the grades.

A second problem area is the social studies. It has become a problem as a result of an over-abundance of histories and books about other countries ranging from very good to hopelessly poor. Here, again, the publishers have responded to the numerous requests from teachers and librarians for more books to help elementary children understand their own history and the present-day lives of people in other lands.

Unfortunately this subject area lends itself beautifully to series books and it is a rare publisher who has not succumbed to the temptation to publish a series on American history, biographies of famous people, or stories of other countries and cultures. Some of these series have been almost uniformly good. Others have shown all the weaknesses to which the series are prone— patterned writing; padding to make a slight subject fill the required number of pages; superficial treatment of more serious subjects; too hasty writing and editing.

The obvious answer to such books is, of course, to ignore the fact of series and to evaluate and select each book on its own merits, with no regard for the series of which it may be a part. Unfortunately, it is much easier to buy by the series than to take time for individual book selection. But the schools that make a practice of buying by the series and of encouraging children to read by the series are truly "buying more and giving less."

A third problem area includes beginning reading books. The trend toward writing trade books for children who are just emerging as independent readers is a worthy one, but many of the

products that have resulted are no better than the basal readers
to which so many people have objected. The good ones—Seuss,
Minarik, Selsam—are very good indeed and children ought to
have access to them. However, the child's need for this kind of
material is of short duration; he goes very quickly into the
stories by Haywood, Mason, Cleary, and so on. It is not necessary
for a library to stock other than the very best of the beginning
reading books to satisfy the needs of the children. Multiple copies
may be needed, but the number of individual titles can be kept
to a minimum.

PERIODICALS THAT WILL
BENEFIT ELEMENTARY CHILDREN *

Carolyn W. Field

Although the American people do not lead in the reading of
books, they do read numerous magazines; and children mimic
adults by looking at magazine pictures or reading them for pleasure and information. This characteristic of children makes magazines particularly useful in school libraries. Not only do they
provide information on subjects too recent to be available in
books, but also the pictures and the brevity of the articles will
appeal to the reluctant or slow reader as well as the average or
gifted. A magazine article may encourage a child to delve deeper
into a subject in an encyclopedia or a book.

Although there is no single magazine for children with the
universal appeal or literary quality of the beloved *St. Nicholas,*
there are several general magazines and many in subject areas
written for adults that will appeal to and be suitable for children.
The number of titles suitable for an elementary school library depends on the needs of a particular school, other library and class-

* Carolyn W. Field, "Periodicals That Will Benefit Elementary Children,"
The Instructor, 73 (November, 1963), 56–58. Copyright 1963 by F. A. Owen
Publishing Company; reprinted from *The Instructor* by permission.

room resources, *and* the budget, rather than on an arbitrary figure.

A good source for criteria for judging children's magazines is a brief pamphlet called *Evaluating Library Resources for Elementary School Libraries* by Mary V. Gaver and Marian Scott (SSH Press). They point out that each magazine should be judged according to format and appearance, content and activities. The paper should be of good quality, the type easy to read and properly spaced. The illustrations should be simple and attractive with clear, sharp black and whites and good color reproduction. The cover design and size of the magazine should be suitable for the potential reader.

The content should include a variety of short stories and poetry as well as accurate informational articles by competent writers on subjects of interest and comprehensibility for the age level for which they are written. The activities section should contain clear, simple directions and call for materials easily accessible and noninjurious to the child who uses them.

Many magazines, especially those indexed in the *Readers' Guide to Periodical Literature* or the abridged edition, are useful for reference and should be kept on file for two or three years, depending on the curriculum of the school. In order to provide copies of a magazine such as *National Geographic* for both reference and circulation, it is often expedient to order duplicate subscriptions of fewer titles, choosing the most useful ones.

School libraries should subscribe to the *Readers' Guide* or the abridged edition. It is invaluable as a reference tool for both student and teacher for up-to-date information on older subjects as well as new areas of knowledge. Whether the school library subscribes to all the periodicals listed is immaterial. The entries will point up information available in magazines that can be found at home or in another nearby library.

Periodicals ready for discard are useful for the clipping file and even single gift copies of magazines contain pictures or articles suitable for this vertical file.

This leads me to the subject of a written policy for the selection of library materials. Every school library should have a written policy covering selection of magazines as well as books, and it should be followed when considering gifts—either books or magazines.

What are the magazines that every elementary school library

should have? For general interest to children, I would suggest *American Girl, Boys' Life, Highlights for Children, Jack and Jill, National Geographic, Popular Mechanics,* and *American Junior Red Cross News.*

For use by teachers and some students there should be *The Horn Book, Plays, School Library Journal, Elementary English,* and the *University of Chicago Children's Book Bulletin.*

Assuming that *My Weekly Reader* and the Scholastic Magazines publications are available in the classrooms, my second string would include *Nature and Science* (formerly *Junior Natural History*), *Life, Sports Illustrated,* and *Audubon Magazine.*

The school with a budget large enough to provide magazines for special interest might have *Scott's Monthly Journal, Arizona Highways,* and *Science News Letter* as well as a general magazine like *Children's Digest,* or some similar to those already in the collection, such as *Popular Science.*

More detailed information on children's magazines can be found in the chapter on "Perioricals" in Wofford's *Book Selection for School Libraries* and in *The Dobler International List of Periodicals for Boys and Girls.*

Good magazines for children whether for reference or browsing are an integral part of every library and should be carefully selected to serve the specific needs of a particular school.

Annotated Bibliography

(Those starred are indexed in *Readers' Guide*.)

The American Girl (monthly). Girl Scouts of the U.S.A., 830 Third Ave., New York 22, N.Y. Short stories, a serial, articles on beauty hints, personality problems, and fashions, book and movie reviews, contributors' section, and jokes.

American Junior Red Cross News (monthly—from October to May). American National Red Cross, 18th and D Streets, N.W., Washington 6, D.C. Articles on animals, holidays, science, and other lands.

* *Arizona Highways* (monthly). Arizona Highway Department, Phoenix, Arizona. Magnificent colors pictures and interesting articles on life in Arizona.

* *Audubon Magazine* (alternate months). National Audubon Society, 1130 Fifth Ave., New York 28, N.Y. Official organ of the society, with popular articles and book reviews.

Boys' Life (monthly). Boy Scouts of America, New Brunswick, New Jersey. Short stories, special articles, a serial, and reviews of books, movies, and records.

Children's Digest (monthly except June and August). Parents' Institute of Parents' Magazine, 52 Vanderbilt Avenue, New York 17, N.Y. Stories, fairy tales, games, puzzles, comics on "eye-ease" tinted paper of cheap quality.

The Dobler International List of Periodicals for Boys and Girls, Muriel Fuller, P.O. Box 193, Grand Central Station, New York 17, N.Y. Detailed information on 350 periodicals for children —general, religious, school, foreign, and foreign language.

Elementary English (monthly from October to May). National Council of Teachers of English, Champaign, Illinois. Excellent articles on current trends in the language arts, research reports, articles on authors, and book reviews.

Evaluating Library Resources for Elementary School Libraries, by Mary Virginia Gaver and Marian Scott, SSH Press, 54 North Drive, Lawrence Brook Manor, East Brunswick, New Jersey; 1962. Easy-to-use criteria for evaluating reference books, trade books, children's magazines, and supplementary textbooks.

Highlights for Children (monthly except June and August), 37 East Long Street, Columbus, Ohio. Stories, poems, activities, and a contributors' page.

* *The Horn Book* (alternate months), The Horn Book, Inc., 585 Boylston Street, Boston 16, Mass. The only magazine devoted entirely to children's books, authors, and illustrators with contributors' section.

Jack and Jill (monthly). Curtis Publishing Co., Independence Square, Philadelphia 5, Pa. The best general magazine for the younger elementary grades with short stories, a serial, information articles, puzzles, poems, and a contributors' section.

* *Life* (weekly). Time, Inc., Time and Life Building, Rockefeller Center, New York 20, N.Y. This magazine should be familiar to everyone.

* *National Geographic* (monthly). National Geographic Society, 1146 16th Street, N.W., Washington 6, D.C. A must for all libraries.

Nature and Science (monthly). American Museum of Natural History, 77th Street and Central Park West, New York 24, N.Y. Articles of interest to children.

* *Plays* (monthly October to May). Plays, Inc., 8 Arlington St., Boston 16, Mass. Short plays for all ages with emphasis on holidays. Production notes. Radio scripts.
* *Popular Mechanics* (monthly). Popular Mechanics Co., 250 West 55th St., New York 19, N.Y. Articles on mechanical sciences. Directions on home projects.
* *Popular Science Monthly* (monthly). Popular Science Publishing Co., 355 Lexington Ave., New York 17, N.Y. Similar to *Popular Mechanics* though emphasis is given to the sciences.

Readers' Guide to Periodical Literature, H. W. Wilson Co., 950 University Avenue, New York 52, N.Y. (Provided on a service basis).

* *School Library Journal* (monthly except July and August). R. R. Bowker Co., 1180 Avenue of the Americas, New York 36, N.Y. Articles on children's reading, authors, and curriculum aids. Book, record, and film reviews.
* *Science News Letter* (weekly). Science Service Inc., 1719 N. Street, N.W., Washington 6, D.C. Articles and news notes relating to the industrial, applied, and natural sciences. Book reviews.

Scott's Monthly Journal (monthly). Scott Publications, Inc., 1 West 47th Street, New York, N.Y. For stamp collectors.

Sports Illustrated (weekly). Time, Inc., Time and Life Building, Rockefeller Center, New York 20, N.Y. Excellent photographs and articles on sport events, athletes, and techniques.

University of Chicago, *Bulletin of the Center for Children's Books,* The University of Chicago Press Journals, 5750 Ellis Avenue, Chicago 37, Illinois. Reviews current books to use in the curriculum.

Wofford, Azile, *Book Selection for School Libraries,* H. W. Wilson Co., 950 University Ave., New York 52, N.Y.; 1962. Excellent for teacher, librarian, or volunteer interested in the school library or general introduction to the selection of materials, criteria, and specific suggestions of titles for all parts of the curriculum.

Part Four

CHILDREN'S BOOKS—
HISTORY AND TRENDS

LITERATURE FOR CHILDREN *

Books written especially for children are a relatively new kind of literature. In fact, such literature is little more than 100 years old. Before about 1850, writers tried to teach and improve children. The only books for children taught lessons on how to behave and what to believe. They also contained lessons on the ideas of history and science at that time.

Children found these books dull and tiresome, and turned instead to stories that their parents and older friends enjoyed. Many children still read and love books that were written primarily for adults, such as Daniel Defoe's *Robinson Crusoe,* Jonathan Swift's *Gulliver's Travels,* and Washington Irving's *Rip Van Winkle.*

Children today can choose from thousands of books written and illustrated especially for them. Good books make it possible to live more lives than one. By opening a book or going to a story hour at a library, children can share the experience of a boy clinging to the back of a goose flying high over Sweden, a tomboy growing up in Hungary, or a man cast away on a desert island. Through good literature, children can find new friends, laughter, knowledge, and an understanding of people of all ages in all parts of the world.

THE HISTORY OF CHILDREN'S LITERATURE

Even as far back as the A.D. 600's, in the Old English or Anglo-Saxon period, monks and other learned men wrote "lesson books" for children. These men wrote in a form of English which children today could not read. It requires long months of study to be able to read this Old English or Anglo-Saxon language.

The Early Beginnings

Aldhelm (640?–709), the abbot of Malmesbury and bishop of Sherborne, was probably the first man to write lesson books for children. His *De Septenario, de Metris, Enigmatibus, ac Pedum Regulis* contained a long essay on the meaning and use of the number seven in the Bible. The title of his book is translated

* From "Literature for Children," *World Book Encyclopedia,* Vol. 12, pp. 316–21, 1965. Reproduced from *The World Book Encyclopedia* with permission. Copyright © 1965 by Field Enterprises Educational Corporation. International Copyright © 1965. All rights reserved.

in this way: "Concerning the number seven, meter, enigmas (riddles, puzzles), and the rules of feet." Some of the ideas were probably Aldhelm's own, but he took the riddles from older manuscripts. Aldhelm discussed the meaning of the number seven as it was used in the Bible. The *meter,* or feet, referred to Latin verse forms. The riddles and puzzles which the pupils were asked to solve were written in Latin.

Aldhelm set the pattern of children's writing. Until about 1500, all books of instruction used the question and answer form or were written in verse.

The Venerable Bede (673–735) was another early writer. For 52 years he was a teacher at the monastery school of Jarrow, in Durham County in England. He was an outstanding author of lesson books. Bede showed more imagination than Aldhelm and was more creative. His *De Natura Rerum* was a book that contained all the knowledge then known of natural science, natural history, and the study of plants and flowers and the stars. Bede was widely read. He could write for his pupils in clear, plain, understandable Latin. This textbook was a small spark of intellectual light during the Dark Ages when men made little progress in learning.

The next great teacher was Egbert of York (?–766?). He collected the works of monks like Aldhelm and Bede. In his library were also the works of Orosius, who was an authority on history, and books by the outstanding Greek and Roman authors. Learning now began to widen a little. Egbert founded the famous school at York. There, Alcuin (735–804) studied. He wrote a wide variety of lesson books, still using the question and answer, or *dialogue,* form. Many of his books were on grammar. He went farther than authors who came before him. Alcuin was tutor to the king's sons and to several girls of the household at the court of Charlemagne (742–814), in Aachen. This is one of the earliest records of coeducation, or educating boys and girls together. It is even more remarkable because, at that time, girls were seldom taught to read.

Alfred the Great (849–899) was a great hero of England. He drove back the invasions of the Danes. Later, he proved himself equally great in the ways of peace. Alfred translated Latin literature into Anglo-Saxon, with the help of a number of scholars. Children in the schools in monasteries had to read and speak Latin in and out of school until about 1350. But Alfred had the best of the literature of his time translated from Latin into Old English, and made it understandable to the common man.

Aelfric (955?–1020?) was a teacher in the monastic school in Winchester. He was the leading educator of the A.D. 900's, and was called *Grammaticus*. He wrote his *Colloquy* also in the question and answer form, and used subjects from everyday life. The *Colloquy* is a dialogue between the pupil and the teacher, with the pupil "begging to be taught," and the teacher answering questions on occupations and trades. The book gives much information on manners and customs of the times. Details of what people ate and how they lived every day are sometimes amusing and always interesting. The "ponies," or language translations, which students of Latin sometimes use today, originated nearly 1,000 years ago. The *Colloquy* of Aelfric was written in Latin, but between the lines there was a translation into Anglo-Saxon. This is one of the last notable writings in Anglo-Saxon, which is sometimes called Old English.

Another highlight of this period was the first encyclopedia for children. It was written by Anselm (1033–1109), the archbishop of Canterbury, and called *Elucidarium*.

The Middle English Period

William the Conqueror and his Norman French knights won England in 1066, and French became the language of the nobility. Many French words were taken into English at this time. This period was called the Middle English Period. It lasted until the invention of the printing press and the coming of the Renaissance around 1450. The children of the nobility received instruction in manners and morals during this period. Some treatises were addressed to servants. One of the best known was *The Babees Boke, or, A lytle Reporte of how Young People should behave.* There is an introduction of fifty-six lines to this book. Then "the whole duty of children" is set forth in one hundred and sixty lines. Another rhymed one was *The Boke of Curtesye,* which was well known before the beginning of printing. The 848 lines of this book are divided into three parts. The first tells how children should act. It describes the correct behavior of a guest who is dining at the home of a nobleman. It gives rules of proper table manners. The second part gives moral instruction. The third explains in detail the duties of all the servants in a nobleman's household.

Much like this book is William Caxton's *Book of Curteseye,* which was printed by Caxton (1421–1491), the first English printer. It dates from about 1477, and contains rules of behavior much like those found in earlier books. It also suggests books which are suitable for young persons to read. Boys of noble families often received training in the households of other nobles, and such books helped them know how to act. There were also at least two books in manuscript form especially for girls. These were *How the Good Wife Taught Her Daughter* (about 1430) and *The Booke of the Enseynements and Teachynge that the Knight of the Toure made to his Daughter.* This second one was translated from the French and printed by William Caxton. Another translation which Caxton made from the French was the *Myrrore of the Worlde,* much like Anselm's *Elucidarium.* This was published in 1481.

Still another encyclopedia was *The Wyse Chyld of Thre Yere Old.* This was first printed in Cologne in 1470. It was translated into English from the original Latin and printed in 1495 by Wynkyn de Worde, who followed Caxton. Caxton also printed Sir Thomas Malory's *Noble Historyes of King Arthur,* Aesop's *Fables, The History of Reynard the Fox, Guy of Warwick,* and *The Seven Champions of Christendom.* He printed many other moral and *didactic,* or teaching, works to educate and instruct his readers.

The Renaissance

Printed books were much too expensive to be generally used by children in early days. Instead, the hornbook was made for them about 1550. The hornbook was not really a book. It was a printed page pasted on a square piece of wood that had a handle at one end. The page was protected by a transparent piece of horn, somewhat like clear plastic. It was often bound by a metal rim. A cord could be put through a hole in the handle and fastened to a child's belt or girdle. The text always started with the crisscross, or christcross. This was followed by the alphabet, first in small letters and then in capital letters. Groups of syllables were below this. They were followed by the words, "In the Name of the Father and of the Son and of the Holy Ghost, Amen." Then came the Lord's Prayer.

After the hornbook, rhymed alphabets and primers were published for children. Among these was the forerunner of the *New*

England Primer, which was first published by Harris in Boston about 1690. It was called the *Royal Primer.* Here each letter of the alphabet was the key letter of a still familiar verse, such as:

> A—In Adam's fall
> We sinned all

running down to:

> Z—Zaccheus he
> Did climb a tree
> His Lord to see.

The *Royal Primer* was popular. Probably more than 5,000,000 copies were sold during the hundred years that it was used as a textbook for younger children.

Puritan Times

In the 1600's, children's books in England and America were rather gloomy. They reflected the Puritan outlook. The Puritans were much more interested in the fear of God than they were in the love of life. James Janeway's *A Token for Children, Being an Exact Account of the Conversion, Holy and Exemplary Lives, and Joyful Deaths of Several Young Children,* is typical of this time. These lines show how Janeway felt:

> When by spectators I am told
> What beauty doth adorn me,
> Or in a glass when I behold
> How sweetly God did form me,
> Hath God such comeliness bestowed
> And on me made to dwell,
> What pity such a pretty maid
> As I should go to Hell!

English parents also recommended John Foxe's (1516–1587) *Book of Martyrs* and John Bunyan's (1628–1688) *Divine Emblems.*

In America, the books for children were either reprints of English publications, or local writings that were even drearier. Some of their titles sound very sad indeed: *Young People Warned, the Voice of God in the Late Terrible Throat Distemper;* and *A Dying Father's Legacy to an Only Child.* Cotton Mather (1663–1728) wrote a *Token for Children of New England, examples of chil-*

dren in whom the fear of God was remarkably budding before they died.

The one really outstanding book of this Puritan period of gloom was John Bunyan's *Pilgrim's Progress*. It has lived because it has universal truth in it. *The Pilgrim's Progress* is an allegory on the development of the human soul. The characters themselves represent various qualities, such as despair, gloom, perseverance, and hope. Children still read this book as a good adventure story. *The Pilgrim's Progress* is one of those books which never grow old and which mean different things to a person as he lives on through life.

Two other books which were written for older people in the late 1600's and early 1700's have become children's classics. They are Daniel Defoe's (1660–1731) *Robinson Crusoe* and Jonathan Swift's (1667–1745) *Gulliver's Travels*. Like *The Pilgrim's Progress,* the story of Robinson Crusoe was also an allegory in which there were deeper meanings, but it is now enjoyed as an adventure story. *Gulliver's Travels* was written as a political satire. But children love it as humor, especially the first book, telling of Gulliver's travels to the land of the *Lilliputians* (little people).

One of the first important illustrated textbooks for children was *Orbis Sensualium Pictus* (Visible World), written by John Amos Comenius (1592–1670) in 1651. It was the first textbook in which pictures were as important as the text. Comenius was a bishop of Moravia, and an educator who believed in teaching children by means of letting them see things with their own eyes. In his book, he used pictures to teach language. He wrote the book in Latin and German. It was translated into English by Charles Hoole in 1659. Comenius also believed in the conversational method of teaching languages, and in teaching the language of the people instead of Latin. He thought that men and women should receive the same education. He wanted to unite all nations through a common system of education.

The 1700's

At last someone appeared on the scene who recognized that children had special interests, and who tried to meet them. This man was John Newbery (1713–1767), a writer, publisher, and bookseller of Saint Paul's Churchyard, London. He published a series of books for children. The first of them was the *Little Pretty Pocketbook* in 1744. A copy of this book was printed in the United States in 1944, on the two hundredth anniversary of its first appearance. Newbery also printed *chapbooks*. These were cheap little paper editions which were sold on the streets by *chapmen* (peddlers). They contained ballads and folk tales. The ordinary person could afford to buy these books. Samuel Johnson and Oliver Goldsmith were friends of John Newbery. Probably they both wrote some of these chapbooks. The style of *The History of Little Goody Two-Shoes* (1765) shows humor like Goldsmith's, but the authorship has never been proved. This book is known as the first book of fiction written solely to entertain children, and was printed 100 years before Lewis Carroll's *Alice's Adventures in Wonderland*.

Like Caxton, Newbery published translations from the French. Among these was *Tales of Mother Goose* by Charles Perrault (1628–1703), a member of the French Academy. In Perrault's time, it was beneath the dignity of authors to write books for children. As a result, books by Perrault were published without any name attached to them. It is generally believed now that either Perrault or his son wrote *Blue Beard, The Three Witches, The Sleeping Beauty, Puss in Boots,* and *Red Riding Hood*. In the Tuileries gardens in Paris there is a statue of Perrault. It shows him seated, with figures of gay little children dancing around him. Newbery also published a collection of Mother Goose nursery rhymes. The first American edition of *Mother Goose's Melodies* appeared in 1785, eighteen years after Newbery died.

Two years after John Newbery died, one of his helpers, Benjamin Collins, originated the *battledore*. This was a folding three-leaved cardboard. On it were numerals, easy reading lessons, alphabets, and little woodcuts. Unlike the hornbook, it contained no religious instruction. The battledore was entertaining, instructive, and cheap. It was popular until about 1850.

In France, at about the same time, Jean Jacques Rousseau (1712–1778) was startling his country and the world with a new theory of education. He described it in his book, *Émile*. Rousseau wanted to see men grow up naturally. Misunderstanding of his theory set in motion the *didactic* (teaching) school of writing. Prissy, smug, good little boys were always successful in these stories. Bad little boys always came to a bad end.

An immediate follower of Rousseau's *Émile* was Thomas Day's (1748–1789) *Sanford and Merton* in 1783. It was a story about a good little boy named Harry Sanford and his tutor, Mr. Barlow. These two tried to reform bad little Tommy Merton, but had very little success. Three other writers of this time influenced children's literature. Mrs. Anna Letitia Barbauld (1743–1825) worked with her brother, Dr. Aikin, to write *Evenings at Home*. This book combined real science with unreal science. Mrs. Sarah Kirby Trimmer (1741–1810) wrote Sunday-school stories. Her *History of the Robins* (1786) was the first children's story to have a theme of "kindness to dumb creatures." Maria Edgeworth (1767–1849) was a really skillful writer. She had a true understanding of children, but her work was still rather didactic and moralizing. Even so, many of the tales in *Parent's Assistant* (1796) and *Moral Tales* (1801) are delightful. They are still read today, a fact which proves their lasting quality and truth.

William Blake (1757–1827) published his *Songs of Innocence* in 1789 and *Songs of Experience* in 1794. These are songs *about* children rather than *for* children. Blake struck a new note in his sensitive verses. They have a delicacy and imaginative quality that appeals to some children.

The 1800's

At the beginning of the century, in 1800, literature for children took a new turn. It became more honestly creative. There was and still is much writing for children that is cheap and common. But the time had come when real literary geniuses could write openly for children without harming their reputations.

Charles and Mary Lamb, brother and sister, worked together to write the first children's version of Shakespeare's plays. Their *Tales from Shakespeare* was published in 1807. They did a superb job. Charles Lamb followed this in 1808 with a second adaptation, *Adventures of Ulysses*. In 1809 Charles and Mary Lamb worked together again to produce *Mrs. Leicester's School* and *Poetry for Children*.

The Lambs frankly wrote to give pleasure to children. Other writers began to follow their example. The didactic writers began to put more lifelike characters and fewer prigs into their books. Mrs. Mary Martha Sherwood (1755–1851) wrote the *History of the Fairchild Family* in 1818. There were long religious discussions in this book, but the children were much more natural.

Jane Taylor (1783–1824) and her sister Ann (1782–1866) were didactics with a smile. Together they published *Little Ann and Other Poems* in 1804. A new edition of *Little Ann* was published in 1883. It had charming illustrations by Kate Greenaway (1846–1901). In 1904 an anniversary edition called *Original Poems and Others* was edited by E. V. Lucas and delightfully illustrated by

Francis D. Bedford. Children today still enjoy these stories in spite of their moralizing tone. Each new generation still enjoys Jane Taylor's famous little poem, "Twinkle, Twinkle, Little Star."

Period of Change

During the next 50 years, great authors wrote many books that are still enjoyed. These books had a powerful influence on the writing for children that followed. Many of these authors are common household names today. The Grimm brothers, Jacob Ludwig and Wilhelm Carl, traveled around Germany, talking to the people and collecting their folk stories. *Popular Stories* was translated into English in 1824. Because of their work, most later collectors of fairy tales followed the stories as the people told them, instead of changing them. In 1841, Hans Christian Andersen's great fairy tales were translated into English. These works are called *modern* fairy tales, because Andersen actually wrote them. He copied old ways of telling stories.

About this same time, other authors began to write children's stories that contained good characterizations and accurate description. Harriet Martineau's (1802–1876) *Feats of the Fjord* was published in 1841. Her *Crofton Boys* (1841) was one of the earliest school stories. This was followed in 1857 by *Tom Brown's School Days* by Thomas Hughes (1822–1896). Charlotte Mary Yonge (1823–1901) wrote a number of interesting historical stories, such as *Dove in the Eagle's Nest* in 1866 and *Little Duke* in 1854. In this same general period James Fenimore Cooper was writing the *Leatherstocking Tales*.

Another American who wrote at this time was Washington Irving (1783–1859). His *Legend of Sleepy Hollow* (1819) and *Rip Van Winkle* (1819) are imaginary tales about the Hudson River Valley. They are still so popular that attractive new editions are published from time to time. His *Knickerbocker's History of New York* (1828) was edited in 1928 by Anne Carroll Moore and illustrated by James Daugherty. The result was a book which was much more attractive and less wordy than the original edition. The *Tales from the Alhambra* (1832) has also been edited and published in recent editions.

The *Peter Parley* books by Samuel Goodrich (1793–1860) were a long series of informational works. They were much copied by other writers. Then came the Abbotts, Jacob (1803–1879) and his brother John Stevens (1805–1877). Jacob Abbott wrote the

Rollo Books and *Franconia Stories,* as well as a long series of biographies and travel books. Some of these he wrote with his brother. In 1923 *Franconia Stories* was published in attractive format. It is a pleasant children's book that tells of the daily life in New England in the middle 1800's.

Charles Kingsley and Nathaniel Hawthorne both retold the Greek myths in simple prose. Kingsley's *Heroes* in 1856 and Hawthorne's *Wonder Book* and *Tanglewood Tales* in 1851 are still read by children.

Fun for its own sake began to appear in children's literature about this time. *The Butterfly's Ball* by William Roscoe (1753–1831) was published in large type and illustrated with gay, colored pictures. In 1846 Edward Lear published his *Book of Nonsense.* The type of poem called the limerick was here to stay. Two years later, in 1848, Heinrich Hoffmann-Donner's *Struwwelpeter* was translated into English. It was followed some years later, in 1901, by *Clean Peter, or the Children of Grubbylea* by Ottilia Adelborg (1855–1936).

Many well-known writers of books for older people continued to write fine books for children. Sir Walter Scott (1771–1832) wrote *Tales of a Grandfather* between 1828 and 1830. *The Rose and the Ring,* by William Makepeace Thackeray (1811–1863), appeared in 1854. Charles Dickens (1812–1870) wrote *Child's History of England* in 1854 and 1855, *A Christmas Carol* in 1843, and *The Magic Fishbone* in 1868. John Ruskin (1819–1900) wrote *Dame Wiggins of Lee and Her Seven Wonderful Cats* in 1885, as well as *King of the Golden River* in 1851. In 1865, Lewis Carroll (1832–1898) wrote *Alice's Adventures in Wonderland,* a landmark in children's literature.

1850–1900

In this half century, children's books came into their own. This period was made notable by the contributions of such persons as Mary Mapes Dodge (1831–1905), Howard Pyle (1853–1911), Frank R. Stockton (1834–1902), Mark Twain (1835–1910), James Otis Kaler (1848–1912), John Bennett (1865–1956), Louisa May Alcott (1832–1888), Thomas Bailey Aldrich (1836–1907), Joel Chandler Harris (1848–1908), Kate Douglas Wiggin (1856–1923), Laura E. Richards (1850–1943), Gelett Burgess (1866–1951), Frances Hodgson Burnett (1849–1924), and Palmer Cox (1840–1924).

English authors of the same period include George Macdonald (1824–1905), Christina Rossetti (1830–1894), Robert Louis Stevenson (1850–1894), Rudyard Kipling (1865–1936), Sir James M. Barrie (1860–1937), Walter De La Mare (1873–1956), William H. Hudson (1841-1922), and Kenneth Grahame (1859–1932).

Special Collections

Several noteworthy collections of children's literature for the student include the following:

Boys and Girls House, Toronto—The Osborne collection of early children's books.

Connecticut Historical Society—Children's books published in the United States before 1836.

Harvard University—Chapbooks.

Huntington Library and Art Gallery, San Marino, Calif.—Illustrated children's books.

Library of Congress—Books published in the United States before 1900.

New York Public Library—Early children's books.

Philadelphia Public Library—The Rosenbach collection of children's books, chiefly English and American.

Pittsburgh, Carnegie Library of—Historical collection, especially of the years 1750–1800.

BOOKS OF YESTERDAY *

Sheila A. Egoff

> There are ABC's, battledores, chapbooks, and other delightful English children's books in the Osborne collection at Toronto.

At Boys and Girls House, the headquarters of children's library work in Toronto, Canada, there are two rooms, slightly Vic-

* Sheila A. Egoff, "Books of Yesterday." Reprinted from *Library Journal,* 77 (February 15, 1952) 273–77, published by R. R. Bowker Company, by permission of author and publisher.

torian in decoration, which house a collection of quaint, curious, as well as well-known books for children, the products of 250 years of writing and illustrating for boys and girls on the part of English authors and artists.

Wandering about these rooms you might pick up a little book and open it to read:

> A Tailor who sail'd from Quebec
> In a storm ventur'd once upon deck;
> But the waves of the sea
> Were as strong as could be,
> And he tumbled in up to his neck.

"Edward Lear," you say triumphantly. Not at all. The crude little hand-colored pamphlet in your hand is dated 1820—a quarter of a century before Lear published his verse form that made him known as "the father of the limerick." It is called *Anecdotes and Adventures of Fifteen Gentlemen.* The author has descended into anonymity, but can probably be credited with providing inspiration for *The Book of Nonsense.* In the display case at one end of the room is a four part chapbook edition of *Gulliver's Travels* published by Tabart, an intriguing figure in the history of publishing for children. These frail midgets of book production, whose survival seems almost miraculous, not only provide an insight into some of the publishing methods of the years 1800 to 1810, but show how completely by that time Swift's bitter satire was accepted as a child's adventure story. Pulling a little gray book out of its case, dated 1811, you are amused by *Frank Feignwell's Attempts to Amuse His Friends* exhibited in a series of characters which show Frank as a king, a harlequin, a barber, with appropriate removable costumes—an early toy book which proves there is nothing really new under the sun. After browsing through the shelves of dreary Moral Tales and books of manners mostly addressed to "young ladies" and filled with advice, injunctions, and exhortations such as to avoid "the custom of laying rouge upon your cheeks" because it is similar to telling a lie, of the reading of novels because they are "pernicious," it is a relief to fall upon a bit of comical nonsense such as *Authentic Memoirs of the Little Man and the Little Maid With Some Interesting Particulars of Their Lives.* After a most sincere proposal of marriage upon the part of the little man,

> The little maid replied,
> Should I be your little bride,
> Pray what shall we have for to eat, eat, eat?
> Will the flame you're only rich in
> Light a fire in the kitchen,
> Or the little god of love
> Turn the spit, spit, spit?

Women were as practical then as now.

These are but samplings of the 1800 early children's books given to Boys and Girls House, Toronto Public Library, by Edgar Osborne, County Librarian of Derbyshire, England.

How It Began

About 25 years ago Edgar Osborne began collecting the more important early, and often rare, children's books. His reasons were real and important. Being firmly convinced that the basis of good adult-reading habits is laid in childhood, and springs from the books read in the nursery library, he hoped to discover, by examination, what the qualities are in children's books which have kept some of them alive for many generations whilst others are neglected and even completely forgotten. Also, in his perambulations as a book collector, he was disturbed to find that not only were many of these old children's books rapidly disappearing from the bookseller's market, but also that many of the popular, well-produced, and attractively bound books of the Victorian period were becoming very difficult to obtain.

As the years passed Edgar Osborne found himself in the alarming position of the sorcerer's apprentice, with the collection growing by leaps and bounds and rapidly overflowing his library. He had also the collector's urge to have his efforts and experience put to a practical use. Finally he decided to let the books go where the need for them was great.

Here we may let him speak for himself. In his offer of this wonderful gift he said: "You may wonder why I wish this collection to pass out of England. I make the offer because I realized when I was in Canada some years ago that the opportunity for people in the Dominions to acquire books of this character is lacking. Also, I have always felt that the link between British librarians and those from the Dominions is not so close as it might be, and I hope therefore that this gesture on my part will help towards a closer understanding between librarianship in this country and overseas."

WHY TORONTO?

His reasons for giving it to Toronto are equally specific. "I feel that Boys and Girls House, Toronto, is a splendid, imaginative, and conscious effort to encourage children to read sound literature ... I am sure that you and the staff you have at Boys and Girls House would know as soon as the collection came into your hands that Canada, and Toronto in particular, would possess an asset that might make your library unique in the Dominions, as far as bygone children's books are concerned ..."

To see and handle these books which we in this country could only have known through written histories of children's literature is an experience as great as seeing an original painting after having looked for years at a small printed reproduction. Sometimes one must "make do." But in the field of early children's literature we in Canada have an outstanding collection of priceless "originals." So, here they are, books that were actually used, many of them more than 200 years ago, and most of them in their original bindings. In a few cases, the only known copy now rests with us.

BATTLEDORES

All types of children's books are represented, from ABC's, battledores, and chapbooks to the elaborately bound and finely illustrated books of the later years of the nineteenth century. The quality of the story told or the style in which it is written is not the only criterion for inclusion. The interest is as much historical as literary. There are many examples of the efforts made by publishers, printers, binders to provide attractive books for children. The illustrators are especially well represented both in line and color, with an emphasis upon those of the nineteenth century. These range from the much-beloved Caldecott to the little-known Grisset. The Kate Greenaway collection is practically complete in first issues; so is that of Walter Crane. There are examples of the works of Richard Doyle, George Cruikshank, Christina Rosetti, to mention only a few.

Through this collection we can trace the development of children's literature from the chapbooks to the famous Puritan book *A Token for Children*, 1671, down to Beatrix Potter. To demonstrate the special branch of book illustrations a sequence could be arranged from an *Aesop's Fables* dated 1566, with woodcuts, down to modern artists such as Arthur Rackham. The same could be done for printing, binding, and related subjects. These books are, moreover, pieces of social history. One can see mirrored in them the whole of the ages they cover. The reflection is scaled, it is true, to Lilliputian proportions; but it is the way of mirrors to be faithful and exact no matter what their size. These children's books are of their particular period in their style and content. Moreover, there are tones in these children's books, overtones and undertones for those who will put them together and listen.

All the landmarks of children's literature are here in first or very early editions. Thomas Day's *History of Sandford and Merton* with a Stothard frontispiece in the third volume; Catherine Sinclair's *Holiday House; Coral Island* with the author's own illustrations. Two of the rarest items are the two parts of Marie Edgeworth's *Harry and Lucy*, 1801, which epitomize the influence of Rousseau in English children's literature. These also are in their original state. There are first editions of *The Water Babies, Alice's Adventures in Wonderland, The Rose and the Ring* (very scarce), and the classic blood-and-thunder, *Treasure Island*.

There are many "association books." Most of the Ewing collection came from the Gatty family and some of the books bear the signature of Mrs. Ewing's sister. Some of the most important books belonged to the Nightingale family and many bear Florence's signature in a juvenile hand. In later years Florence Nightingale knew what to choose to delight other young people as is proved by a deluxe edition of *The Adventures of Baron Munchausen* inscribed "To my dear Louis with Aunt Florence's New Year's love." It is dated 1879.

There are splendid sections of fables, animal stories, and Robinsonnades. One could follow the whole rise, development, and fall of the children's periodical through the examples brought together and chronologically arranged. There is not a book in the collection that has not its own special place or significance.

THE LIBRARY'S GUARANTEE

The Toronto Public Library Board in accepting this gift has undertaken to preserve the collection as a complete unit, to maintain and repair it, to add to it, and to publish a catalog which, it is hoped, will be a guide and a key to the history of children's literature. The Board has undertaken to make the collection fully available to students of librarianship and to all others interested in children's literature. These "others" may be publishers, illustrators, teachers interested in early educational books (for there is a large section of books of instruction), those interested in the bibliographical aspect of books, or simply those who love children, or books, or both.

It is fitting that these books at Boys and Girls House should be located next to a modern working collection of books for boys and girls. They not only cast a light upon children's books of today but make us realize that "though" time may have shifted the emphasis it has not changed the fundamental art of writing for children.

In the great and glorious scheme of book-writing and book-making, the children were for a long time neglected. Through the centuries when manuscripts were giving place to the printed books, when the House of Elzevir was laying the foundations of modern publishing business and making the printed word easily available for the first time to the common man, even when the great flood of printing came in the Victorian age, it did not occur to adults to provide children with suitable books. They, the children, were forced to prey upon books not even written for them such as *Pilgrim's Progress, Robinson Crusoe,* and *Gulliver's Travels.* The development of a special literature for children came very slowly. In 1865 when Lewis Carroll wrote *Alice's Adventures in Wonderland,* and so opened the door to children's literature, he stood alone on the threshold for a long time. Today, children's books pour from the presses in the thousands, few of them up to the standards that most thinking adults demand in their own books. To many adults any children's book is still a good book.

THE CHILDREN DECIDE

The emphasis has shifted from famine to surfeit. Fortunately the children themselves have had, and will continue to have, a word or two to say about the books provided for them, and have themselves set the standards for "a good book."

Here in this collection we can see the fruits of their judgments. The children in Mrs. Sherwood's *The Fairchild Family* who obeyed through fear have been replaced by the enterprising children created by Arthur Ransome; Harry and Tommy, of Thomas Day's *Sandford and Merton,* who were nourished on moral tales told by the estimable Barlow, have yielded to happy-go-lucky boys like Tom Sawyer and Homer Price. The books of Mrs. Barbauld and Mrs. Cameron and Peter Parley, which banished the fairies and provided only instruction, are now museum pieces, while the hero stories, Grimm, Andersen, *Goody Two Shoes, At the Back of the North Wind, The Little Duke* have been saved to offer joy to each generation.

The writers of the "awful warning" school of poetry of the early nineteenth century warned the children of the swift, inevitable consequences of even minor wrongdoings. In *Original Poems* by Ann and Jane Taylor we find young Harry who was so cruel that he caught fish. One day when he was putting his fish on a dish in the pantry a large meat-hook caught him on the chin:

> Poor Harry kicked, and called aloud
> And screamed, and cried, and roared,
> While from his wound the crimson blood,
> In dreadful torrents poured.

The children themselves warn just as definitely of the danger of oblivion to those writers who do not give them pleasure. Among the oppressors of children was one A. Berquin, a follower of Rousseau, who had tremendous success with English parents and governesses. In 1800 there was an English translation of his *The Looking-glass for the Mind; or, Intellectual Mirror: Being an Elegant Collection of the Most Delightful Little Stories; and Interesting Tales . . .* with 74 cuts. On the opposite page, written in a child's hand, is a comment on this book. It reads: "The looking-glass for the mind; or, *un*intellectual mirror; being an *in*elegant collection of the most disagreeable, silly stories and uninteresting tales with 74 ugly cuts." It is signed Mary Graves, 13, 1848.

CHILDREN'S BOOKS—
YESTERDAY AND TODAY *

Dora V. Smith

Book Week, 1956, put on such a show as America has seldom seen. Books were everywhere and of every kind, from poetry to scientific fact, from folk tales of the nations to *The Wonderful World of Mathematics,* from the cave dwellers to adventures in space, from the world's great heroes to the child at play—and all of them in format and illustration representing the best that artist, editor, writer, and producer could do together. There were books for the beginner and books for the mature; books for the skilled reader and easy books for those over-age children who need adult concepts presented to them in simple form.

The encouraging number of books was equalled by the variety of places in which they appeared. City art galleries, libraries, and department stores played host to communitywide Book Fairs. From nursery school to college classroom and library, teachers and pupils displayed both new and old in books for children. Scouts and Camp Fire Girls joined in the celebration. Women's clubs and Parent-Teachers' associations showed a zeal that kept schools and libraries hard-pressed for speakers to send to them. Writers who once confessed with reluctance that they wrote for children were guests of honor everywhere. Behind the movement were more than sixty children's book editors, devoting full time to the production of good books for young people. (In 1919 there was one.) Not only that, but publishers everywhere boasted of the sales in children's books which help float their entire publishing business in ways unknown in the past. And it is rumored that the children of today don't read!

Newspapers devoted whole pages to books for children, some of them like the *New York Herald Tribune, The New York*

* Dora V. Smith, "Children's Books—Yesterday and Today," *ALA Bulletin,* 51 (April, 1957), 254–59. Reprinted by permission of The American Library Association and the author.

Times, The Washington Post, and the *Chicago Daily Tribune,* publishing a whole section of ten to twenty pages on children's books alone. Monthly domestic, educational, and literary magazines plan every November a substantial article on books for children. This could not happen in any other nation on earth. It is due primarily to the persistent efforts of a small number of people determined to give our children the best.

There is no cure for discouragement with *what is,* like taking a backward glance at *what has been.*

In colonial days the *Bible, The New England Primer,* and *The New England Psalter* made up the chief reading of boys and girls in a period when even the advent of a book "to make learning to read a diversion rather than a task" failed to dispel the gloom of children who "were afraid they should go to Hell and were stirred up dreadfully to see God."

Next followed a period of reading for patriotism's sake, for industry, and for good citizenship, which culminated in the famous *McGuffey Readers,* devoted to character-building and oratory.

A welcome release from the tiresome admonitions of a somber tutor in *Sanford and Merton* then came, in the realistic stories of Maria Edgeworth who, although she discouraged Mother Goose and the fairy tales, knew a real child when she saw him.

THE ADVENT OF THE SUNDAY SCHOOL LIBRARY

By 1824 the famous Sunday School libraries began to spread throughout the land. Their motley array of titles lives in the memory of many a reader grown gray in the service of better books for children: *Thou God Seekest Me,* the story of a little girl whose ring on her finger, as the sun gleamed on it, reminded her to keep her temper because God was looking at all times; the *Life of Ulysses S. Grant; The Wide, Wide World,* or the sorrows and sentiment of Ellen Montgomery; and Sophie May's *Dotty Dimple,* whose entertaining moods alternated between childish glee and remorseful penitence as her young readers revelled in her unpredictable pranks. Together with Prudy, she helped move girls' stories away from exemplary childhoods to more normal activities, along with Elizabeth Ward's *Gypsy Breynton,* and Susan Coolidge's *What Katy Did,* at home, at school, and in the country.

By 1870 there came a flood of adventure stories, from *Green Mountain Boys* and *Masterman Ready,* to Beadles' notorious paperbound dime novels. Cheap series rose to 116 volumes, like Oliver Optic's *Outward Bound* stories with their riotous mutineers and their stilted conversations, and Horatio Alger's endlessly repetitive plots and glorification of material success.

THE COMING OF LIBRARIES FOR YOUTH

Into this melee came the voice of Caroline Hewins, at that time librarian of the Young Men's Institute Library at Hartford, Connecticut, pleading for library work with children, for encouraging a love of good reading among boys and girls. She had seen a wealth of new books of a very different sort come across the water—the tales of the Grimms and of Hans Christian Andersen, Ruskin's *King of the Golden River,* and Kingsley's *Heroes* and *Water Babies.* She had experienced the new delight in the ridiculous which came into children's literature with *Alice in Wonderland.* She recognized the artistic power of Walter Crane's illustrations for children, the freshness and humor of Randolph Caldecott's new picture books, and the grace and charm of Kate Greenaway. Howard Pyle too, with his *Robin Hood,* had brought a new distinction into children's books on this side of the Atlantic. Numbers of these writers had been introduced to American readers by three notable magazines for children: *Our Young Folks,* Horace Scudder's *Riverside Magazine for Young People,* and Mary Mapes Dodge's *St. Nicholas.*

Miss Hewins knew, however, that these books were "little bread in comparison with the works of the 'immortal four,' who were then writing series at the rate of two or more volumes a year. Oliver Optic, Horatio Alger, Harry Castleman, and Martha Finley, author of Elsie Dinsmore, and twenty-five years later, refused to be forgotten." She made a plea for special shelves or rooms for young people, she wrote editorials to warn parents of what their children were reading, she prepared annotated book lists for young readers, and she compiled annually a report of what libraries were doing to stimulate better reading among boys and girls.

LITERARY READINGS IN THE SCHOOLS

About this time, the schools "went literary." America had had her own golden age of literature. The renown of New England's men of letters had spread throughout the country—first Emerson, Hawthorne, and Thoreau; then Longfellow, Holmes, and Lowell; and, finally, Melville, Whitman, and Parkman. They must have a place in American schools. At the same time, *Little Women* had arrived to give *Elsie Dinsmore* stiff competition. *The Story of a Bad Boy* and *Tom Sawyer* had brought a new sense of reality into stories for boys, and *Treasure Island* had come from overseas.

In 1880, the Indiana State Department of Education published a report urging the schools to awaken a permanent interest in literary materials "which would be a cultural asset to the individual in adult life." It inveighed against giving a child "the ability to read, while failing to cultivate in him a taste for the pure, the elevating, and the instructive. In view of the attractive garb in which vicious literature is clothed, he will be more likely to read to his injury than to his profit."

Both the "adult life" and "the pure and elevating" stayed with the schools for a long time. The College Entrance Examination Board, receiving candidates from the far reaches of the country, where academies were few and where individual preparation was spotty, began to "set classics" for study. Harvard and Michigan published such lists, including *The Courtship of Miles Standish, The Lady of the Lake, Julius Caesar, The House of Seven Gables,* and *Silas Marner.* By 1890 a tradition was established which still held the literature program in its grip in 1932, when the National Survey of Secondary Schools took place. Four classics a year was the average reading diet, with "reports" on books of similar literary types every sixth Friday.

No doubt there were some lovers of literature who created in young people a hunger for more but, in general, detailed dissection of classics, paraphrasing of poetry, and emphasis upon literary history, precluded any real joy in the reading. Selections were chosen for their literary merit alone, without regard to their difficulty or suitability for the readers concerned. The whole procedure led John Dewey to remark that literature had become a peg on which to hang the dictionary and the encyclopedia. Knowledge and, sometimes, appreciation of the classics, was engendered in the few, but preference for literature escaped the many.

In the elementary schools the old readers took on a more literary character, as their names indicate. *Story Hour Readers* and *Stepping Stones to Literature* gave to children a program of imaginative literature and reading intended for pure enjoyment, which had never been achieved before. The Grimms, Hans Christian Andersen, the Greek and Roman myths, the stories

of Charles and Mary Lamb, Kingsley's *Heroes* and the *Water
Babies* and Ruskin's *King of the Golden River,* were all there
as an outgrowth of the desire to inspire a love of literature and
a sustained interest in reading.

New Influences

Meanwhile, free libraries for children spread throughout the
country, under the auspices of the American Library Association
and stimulated later by the generous gifts of Andrew Carnegie.
By 1895 they ranged from Boston and Hartford, through Minneapolis and Denver, to Seattle and San Francisco.

The next year Anne Carroll Moore began her distinguished
career as head of the children's department of the Pratt Institute Free Library in Brooklyn, a decade later to assume for 35
years, leadership in the field of children's books as Superintendent of Library Work with Children in the New York Public
Library. Story hours for boys and girls introduced them to the
world's great fairy tales and hero stories. The changing seasons,
the great holidays, came and went, and were utilized as occasions
for bringing in poets and their verses and storywriters and their
tales relating the best in books to the lives of the children.

In 1911 the National Council of Teachers of English began
its career of stimulating good reading among young people; in
1924 C. C. Certain established *The Elementary English Review;*
and, during these years also, what is now the Association for
Childhood Education International was developing its bibliographies for children's reading and its *Told Under* series of collections of literature.

A Significant Era

The years from 1915 to 1930 were at once the most exciting
and the most stormy in the field of children's reading. They
represented a period of significant beginnings and great issues.
At the outset of the period May Massey was editor of *The Booklist* and, by 1923, had gone to Doubleday's in charge of the children's book department. Louise Seaman Becktel had held a
similar position at Macmillan's since 1919. Anne Carroll Moore
was writing occasional articles on children's books for *The Bookman,* and in 1924 began the famous *Three Owls* weekly page
for the *New York Herald Tribune,* uniting in the minds of everyone the three-fold yet single task of writer, illustrator, and critic.
Never did anyone do children's books a greater service than she

did in upholding standards for authors, illustrators, and publishers through the work of the critic. In 1924 Bertha Mahony Miller established *The Horn Book,* through whose influence for more than thirty years, teachers, librarians, writers, and parents have been guided in the direction of books which have dignity, integrity, and literary value for young readers.

Like the White Stag in Kate Seredy's story, these four women stood at the crossroads and led the way into the promised land of children's books, encouraging struggling artists and authors, studying new techniques of printing and of illustrating, ferreting out the needs of boys and girls for this book and that as the years passed. No greater monument to their devotion, their talent, and their persistent courage is needed than the array of children's books which, through their efforts and the efforts of others who have followed them, is now placed before American boys and girls. This remarkable entente between author, artist, publisher, critic, and those who work directly with children in school and library must never be allowed to lapse.

Meanwhile, the library within the school, with its ready access to every child in the land, began to make itself felt, and in 1918 both schools and libraries joined in the preparation of standards of organization and equipment for their work through the efforts of the American Library Association, the Department of Secondary Education of the N.E.A., and the North Central Association of Secondary Schools and Colleges. Other sectional groups have since done the same for every part of the country. In 1925 parallel committees set similar standards for elementary school libraries. Today, with broad unit instruction accepted throughout the country, the first step in the planning of any teacher is to consult with the librarian about books available for pupils of all levels of ability.

In 1919 Frederic C. Melcher promoted the first Children's Book Week which, with the backing of the Children's Book Council, has exerted a powerful influence throughout the country. In 1922 he suggested and made possible the first American Library Association Newbery Award for the most distinguished book of the year for American children. By 1937 picture books had achieved a distinction all their own, and he suggested the Caldecott Award for them, and donated the medal given annually by the children's librarians of the ALA.

John Dewey's analysis of learning through the solving of real problems, instead of through the storing up of knowledge, was beginning in the third decade of the twentieth century to influence the schools. Children were to begin by understanding the wonders and the working of the life about them. The psychology of child development turned attention to those stages in the growth of children which were to become guides to the making of the curriculum. Books and more books were needed to bring sound information and a wealth of vicarious experience to bear upon children and the life around them. The library was to be the heart of the school program, and leaders like Nora Beust, Mildred Batchelder, Frances Henne, Mary Peacock Douglas, and Ruth Ersted later worked to make it so.

When schools first began to talk about work-type reading, they sought help in finding good books which would open up to a child his own small world of domestic animals, the larger world of new and exciting modes of transportation, of the changing seasons, of the motion picture and the radio. But the children's literature world had little to offer. *The Bookman* for 1920 contained an article and book list to guide parents in directing the reading of their children under ten. The emotional and imaginative world of little children was well cared for by Stevenson's *Child's Garden of Verses, The Tale of Peter Rabbit,* and Hudson's *Little Boy Lost;* but there were more sorties into the land of fairies, of giants, and of nonsense than into the world of reality. The books were excellent, of high literary quality, but limited in the aspects of life with which they dealt.

Meanwhile, World War I had made possible the testing of intelligence and of ability in reading. More and more children were pouring into the schools—all of the children of all of the people. Objective evidence was available of what they could read and of what they knew or did not know about their world.

One year after *The Bookman* list of January and February, 1920, Lucy Sprague Mitchell's *Here and Now Story Book* appeared with simple, unpretentious little stories in it of the milkman, the postman, the child's own pets, and things that move. Her plea was that little children must become familiar with their immediate environment through stories written on their own intellectual level. The argument was on. "Only the blind eye of the adult finds the familiar uninteresting," it maintained. The retort was, "Loss of vision is never compensated for by gain of sight." A remark of Florence Barry about Maria Edgeworth is reminiscent of the debate that followed:

"If she never understood the 'fairy way of writing,' it was because she had built a school upon the fairy circle of her village green. Her children were so happy in and about the village that they never discovered the enchanted wood; they planted trees instead of climbing them; they knew all about the roads to Market, but nobody showed them the way to fairyland."

Happily for children, the upshot of the struggle was that there is room for both the fairy circle and the school; that happiness belongs to the village green as well as to the enchanted wood; that trees may sometimes be planted for the sake of climbing and sometimes for more practical purposes; and that, seen through the eye of the imagination, the road to the market may be as enchanting as the road to fairyland. Who today would deprive children of either?

In 1925 came the first of three yearbooks on reading of the National Society for the Study of Education which, for thirty years, have guided the educational world in the direction of a balanced program based on a careful analysis of the many functions of reading in everyday life. Emphasis shifted to silent reading as obviously the major kind required by modern youngsters and their elders. Furthermore, the years 1920–1930 saw more than one hundred studies of children's interests in reading, in an effort to adjust the offerings of school and library to the normal interests of boys and girls and to use these interests as a point of departure for better choices in reading. The studies had both good and bad effects. Some people mistook what *was* for what *might be* and went about giving children only what they were "interested in" or what they could read without effort at the moment. Others fixed their eyes only on norms and forgot the individual child. Still others, knowing little about the values in books, categorized them superficially as "child-life" or "community-life" stories, or "Westerns" or "tales of pioneer life," forgetting that these same books have intimate personal values for individual readers which may be lost in a catchall classification.

But these same reading studies were valuable in other ways. For one thing, as a result of them, we left behind forever the tendency then prevailing to base choices of books for all children upon personal recollections of childhood reading by deeply sensitive and imaginative adults. We were face to face with the real choices of many children and gained a new consciousness of how individuals differ one from another in both interests in reading and in power to read.

THE FLOWERING OF BOOKS FOR CHILDREN

Fortunately, the will to broaden the reading of children, to relate books to all the experiences of life coincided with the upsurge in production of more and more beautiful books for boys and girls. The efforts of the leading editors began to bear fruit. New processes in color, print, and design made possible the work of such distinguished artists as C. B. Falls, the Petershams, Wanda Gág, Boris Artzybasheff, and Lynd Ward. By good luck, some of these artists have been productive over a long period of time. The Petershams, beginning with *Poppy Seed Cakes* in 1924, did *The Christ Child* in 1931, won the Caldecott Award for *The Rooster Crows* in 1946, and then produced their distinguished *Silver Mace* in 1956. Lynd Ward illustrated Elizabeth Coatsworth's 1931 Newbery Award book, *The Cat Who Went to Heaven* and himself won the Caldecott Award in 1953 for *The Biggest Bear*.

Perhaps the best way to conclude this quick overview of three hundred years of publishing for children is to take an appreciative look at the services which books have rendered to boys and girls in the United States during these last twenty years, and which they are continuing to render today. The needs of children have been carefully examined and writers found who can meet them on a high level of performance.

THE CHILD'S OWN WORLD IN BOOKS

Today children can find themselves and their activities in books of rare distinction. They can have fun with animals and nature. They can find their questions about science answered in terms which they can understand. They may even learn from the beautiful and highly imaginative picture books that loss of vision need not accompany gain of sight. They may delve deeply into the past to find the roots of the present, especially into the past of their own country, which has been made vivid to them in fiction, biography, and history. They may make excursions into the America of today with its diverse cultures and its fascinating variety of customs and of scenes. They may make friends with children around the world. They may lose themselves in poetry, in a rich wealth of legendary lore, and in modern imaginative stories, or they may find the charm of novelty in the things of every day. This is the rich fare which children's books in mid-century America offer to our boys and girls.

No other nation on earth offers so much to its children in the field of literature and reading. No other nation has so much money to spend on making good books available to boys and girls. Expert librarians and teachers are at work together to entice our children to read.

Studies of the training of elementary school teachers throughout America in 1928 revealed only a few courses in Children's Literature for teachers, and most of them represented chiefly "the sixteen-must-haves before the eighth grade." In 1937 two of the ten teachers' colleges visited in the Regents Inquiry in New York State had courses in books for children. Today few colleges would dare to send out teachers without some background in this field.

The wide range in reading ability represented in our schools makes the problem especially critical. Time was when those who could not read left school for work—to remain untouched by books the rest of their lives. These young people today are in school, and appropriate reading materials must be found for them. They must find the information, the fun, and the challenge they need in wholesome books suited to their level of ability. There is no other way to reach them, however much we should like to offer them only the literary and the best. Large numbers of adults in America today will never read above the seventh-grade level. Progress for them, enrichment of their lives through reading, must come by reaching out in all directions rather than upward, by finding more and more books suited to their capacities which will broaden and deepen their experience.

The forward march of books for children has led us into a promised land, flowing with both milk and honey. The scouts have gone ahead. They have laid open the treasure. How long will it be before all of the children of all of the people are privileged to enter into their inheritance? The answer is in our hands.

EDITING THE FIRST CRITICAL HISTORY OF LITERATURE FOR CHILDREN *

Cornelia Meigs

Cornelia Meigs served as editor-in-chief of "A Critical History of Children's Literature," which Macmillan published on June 22, opening day of the 1953 ALA Convention, and as author of the first quarter of this distinguished book. She is the author of more than 25 books for children and a winner of the Newbery Medal.

If, as we are assured, there are three generations to a century, it is the middle lifetime of the 1900's which entered on the world amid a full burgeoning of children's books. They have grown from a small and much sought-after element in the life of a thinking child into an ever-present and all-pervading commodity. As human beings do, we have taken such a development rather as a matter of course, nor have we tried very much to explain to ourselves what has happened, any more than did Jack of Beanstalk fame, as he sat back on his heels and watched his vegetable phenomenon spring up before him and mount to the sky. Such astonishing growth of children's reading matter must have some preceding causes, and surely it will have striking results, for good or ill, upon young mankind.

There is a challenge in the very difficulty of seeing some pattern in this bewildering abundance of young people's books, in the new varieties of subject and manner of writing, in the intensified color of presentation, in the wider exploitation of the charms of both largeness and smallness. Certainly it is true that now, in this moment of time, is the occasion for beginning to

* From Cornelia Meigs, "Editing the First Critical History of Literature for Children," *Publisher's Weekly*, 164 (July 4, 1953), 21–24. Reprinted by permission of the R. R. Bowker Company and the author.

think, not in terms of "children's books," of "reading for Johnny or Elizabeth" but in terms at last of children's literature as a whole. With longer delay we can easily lose our bearings in the flood of excellent or mediocre output, or in the subtle influence of those publications which do rather worse than waste our children's time.

With the growing quantity, with the distinct improvement in the general average of children's books, it is happily true that there has advanced also the criticism which goes by right with any developing literature. It came on the scene rather earlier in the century than this wide extension of children's reading; it had indeed much to do with focusing the attention and furthering the production in the field of children's books. Anne Carroll Moore's able essays on juvenile literature were speedily followed and supported by the founding of *The Horn Book* as a magazine devoted entirely to the consideration of books for the young. The body of such criticism has been slowly gathering, but not until now has it come in any way close to a survey of the whole field, a discussion of kind and quality, of the sweep of development through the years, of which a critical history must be composed. Many people have realized that the next step of criticism must be just that one, but it looked not like a step but the stride of seven-league boots. It is not difficult to know, from a literary point of view, what were good to be done, but it calls for personal and individual stimulus to carry someone to the point of actually doing it.

In "From Rollo to Tom Sawyer," a series of papers by Alice Jordan, supervisor of work for children in the Boston Public Library, she refers to "that complete history of American children's books, greatly needed and as yet unwritten." It is a prickling phrase, an arresting thought—needed, yes, but why unwritten? Added to this there dropped soon after into one person's consciousness another stimulating suggestion. Paul Hazard, in his enchanting essay "Books, Children and Men," speaks of children's literature as "that sparkling river of life." Could there be a more apt and imaginative figure, or one that could more sharply arouse intellectual curiosity? A river, indeed, but whence comes its flow and to what sea is it making its way? Under the stress of these and similar questions, slowly accumulating, one begins to be impelled, like Rikki-Tikki-Tavi to "run and find out."

The idea of a critical survey of children's books was an alluring one, but also forbidding. It makes the page look very broad, as the typewriter carriage inches across it, when the subject has no opening dates, no fixed boundaries, no thoroughly settled conclusions with which to concur or disagree. A free field is not often the lot of the literary researcher and critic, but how widely scattered and elusive, consequently, would be the source material. Interest in even an enticing project may falter and hang back unless it is upheld by other interest. The whole idea might have perished still-born if it had not been for Bertha Mahony Miller.

Did she have a feeling in her extremely intuitive bones when she accepted an invitation to a weekend in Vermont, and listened, sitting by the fire on a cold, rainy afternoon, to the unfolding of a plan which had so many possibilities both beckoning and forbidding? Bertha Miller, it is to be remembered, was founder of the Bookshop for Boys and Girls in Boston, as well as of *The Horn Book*. Under her editorship the high quality of that magazine's criticism was so well established that it has not lost any degree of it since her retirement. She herself is a critic of rare ability, and she has retained what so many critics lose, a spirit of warm enthusiasm. "I have a sense of *triumph* that any children's book should be so good," she once wrote personally to an author whose work she approved, words which, needless to say, brought to the author an unforgettable glow of pleasure. All the warmth of her spirit responded to this idea of a literary history; she gave advice, she gave reassurance. The task would not be too difficult, she declared, there should be little trouble in finding a publisher, in gathering colleagues—for it was plain at once that the book could not be written by one person alone—in reaching ultimate readers. It sounded almost easy as long as she was there. She drove away next morning with the clouds lifting above the mountain pass which she must cross, but the force of her encouragement stoutly remained.

She was right about finding a publisher, for Doris Patee of Macmillan saw at once beyond the difficulties and knew that here was an opportunity for real contribution if the work were properly done. She had also all of a skilled editor's perceptive knowledge of how much can practically be enclosed between covers, brought into a not undue number of pages and a nonprohibitive price. Her mind's eye immediately envisioned a consultive committee which should contain Anne Carroll Moore and Frederic Melcher, she arranged a luncheon for everyone who would be helpful to talk the matter over with everyone else. Hers was the real, the practical impetus that put the work actually in hand. By her means the writers of the four parts were chosen and the first consultations arranged. There was much to do in bringing the plan into working shape, in settling the division of the whole sequence into periods, in deciding who was to work on which portion of the whole. Mr. Melcher has a maxim, often quoted by those who have heard him expound it, that "what belongs to you sticks to you." Nowhere could it have been more fully proved than here where the different authors gravitated to their most fitting parts. The original promoter of the enterprise, retired professor of English at Bryn Mawr College, came into possession of the earliest and first portion, because of a special bent for history. It would be necessary to go far back in literary records, if there was to be understanding of why the English-speaking peoples should have produced, out of a rich heritage, a greater and more significant body of writing for children than had any other nation.

To Anne Thaxter Eaton, school librarian, teacher, and author of children's reading, there fell the second, the Victorian period. Her cordial, her friendly understanding and rarely appreciative approach does justice to that age over whose very name people used to smile because of its chignons and bustles, but which is now beginning to be more and more valued with the realization of how it carried the world forward. Its chief work was not merely to produce Queen Victoria, a stout lady in a black bonnet, or to secure a society which sat safely reading in stuffed armchairs and ignoring comfortably most of the less palatable facts of living. Among its immense new ideas of social justice and scientific evolution was a sure and growing knowledge of how to write for children. Such beloved favorites as Charlotte Yonge, Mrs. Molesworth, and Mrs. Ewing emerge under Miss Eaton's touch as more real, more closely connected with our own age, more to be appreciated than ever.

Elizabeth Nesbitt is associate dean and professor of children's literature of the Carnegie Library School in Pittsburgh, and is an established critic of children's books and author of "Books and Children" and of many magazine articles. Her share in this collaboration has been to treat of a momentous period when a significant number of truly great geniuses concerned themselves directly with books for the young: Kipling, Stevenson, Beatrix Potter, Walter De La Mare, and Howard Pyle. Her clear-cut, precise, and discerning critical analysis goes well below the surface of simple acceptance of the great good fortune of children's literature to have such noble names upon its record. She makes it clear why these writers wrote so greatly and so signally enriched children's reading during that space of 30 years between 1890 and 1920. One knows, through her, what has been the fullness of their gifts to young readers past and present.

Only a person of remarkable ability in literary organization and constructive analysis could have made plain, as Ruth Viguers has done, the foundation, the pattern, and the future promise of the vastly extended literature for children today. She had worked with Anne Carroll Moore in the children's section of the New York Public Library; she has done library work abroad in many interesting connections; she lectures on children's literature at the Simmons Library School in Boston and she is the mother of three rising readers of her own. She has faced "a mountain of books" with the boldness of an Alpine climber and also with the patience of a tapping geologist who finds ultimately the basic formation under the tall cliffs and supporting ledges. No one knows, who has not witnessed it, the amount of work which went into the examination, the classification, and the illuminating comment concerning that mass of books belonging to what we think of as our own age, the middle lifetime of the century.

It was fortunate for the completeness of the enterprise that a distinguished historian, Henry Steele Commager of Columbia, who has written so widely in the field of American history and American thought, has given deep and sympathetic attention to the subject of children's literature, and that he took immediate interest in what this undertaking was trying to do. His natural part has been to write a preface which takes briefer survey, with his own original findings of that development traced in detail in the body of the book.

Doris Patee, who from the beginning has made the juvenile department of Macmillan the able vehicle for carrying the project through, also contributed much in firm and rapid judgment born of her wide editorial experience and her intelligent study of all that has to do with children's books. Thus each person brought to the task a different approach and an individual point of view, resulting also in five-fold variety of literary style. In such a study as this, more than in any other, a pooling of opinion and a safe balance of judgment was of high importance. In one matter alone, the difficult question of what was to be stressed and what was to be discarded, there was so much temptation for an individual to be guided by affectionate remembrance, by single taste, even by tender but unreasonable association, that the decision of several was far wiser than the decision of one. The whole shape and form, the proportion, and emphasis were evolved in frequent consultations, so that all had part in the framing of the whole.

For Doris Patee it was a method which greatly multiplied her work as publisher, with meetings to arrange for busy people living far apart, with a multiple set of correspondences to carry on, with galley proofs to be read by four instead of one. Finally it was her anxious duty to transmit the galleys to Henry Commager, that he might know what he was introducing, galleys which followed him to Oxford, to Italy, finally to Sweden where he had momentarily found resting place at Uppsala. With such a myriad of matters to be attended to, such a host of details to be settled, that the book, complete at last, went to press at the 11th hour and 59th minute that would allow for its appearance in time for the American Library Meeting in June. There were some last frantic additions to the index, some long distance calls to verify footnote references or spelling of names.

A piece of work like this, begun, continued, and ended, brings to light for the writers much more than merely that toward which the general research was aimed. It reveals how, in spite of a certain number of excellent collections of early children's books in some of the great libraries of the country, there is otherwise, and in general, a baffling elusiveness of juvenile literary material. In the Rosenbach Collection, now the property of the Philadelphia Free Library, the custodian will take out a morocco and gold-tooled case, fit repository for some precious family jewel, and reveal a battered little paper volume of a few pages and a few inches square, so old and frail that it seems one touch of the most careful fingers will make it fall to pieces. Yet here may be the only existent copy of some publication that embodies all the warm and generous spirit of John Newbery, or all the suppressed imagination and tightly drawn severity of Puritan thought, in the form that it first came, new, into children's hands. The American Antiquarian Society in Worcester, Massachusetts, has, in the publications of Isaiah Thomas, preserved by him and given to the society which he founded, a fine record of what young New Englanders and others could finally turn to when they rose up against "Fox's Book of Martyrs" and the "New England Primer." But for the most part, early books for children, in minor libraries or among even the careful purveyors of old books to collectors, are relegated, unlisted, to dusty shelves.

The study reveals, too, how few and far between, really, are the college courses in children's literature, knowledge of which should be an essential part of the mental equipment which arms young teachers as they set forth to guide the minds of the young. It makes clear, also, how seldom busy parents know what they are doing when they essay to direct the reading of their offspring who can consume a volume a day and cry rapidly for more. "Don't read that," or "I loved this when I was your age," are not satisfying expressions by which to stress the danger of forming taste on trash, or the impulse to seek action and excitement with the least mental effort. Thinking people should know more of children's literature as a whole.

"MY FATHER SAYS TO GET A CLASSIC"*

Phyllis Fenner

I don't know how many times through the years a child has said to me, "My father (or mother, or grandmother) says to get a classic." Sometimes it has annoyed me very much because the child has needed just good reading to make her equal to the classics. And once I remember retorting a bit impertinently, I am afraid, "Ask your father what a classic is."

What is a classic? I consulted a dictionary. It says something like this: "A literary or art work of acknowledged excellence." It doesn't say that it has to be fifteenth century, eighteenth century, or even old. Of course, the fact that a book is still in print, still read by some people, is pretty sure proof that it is good, or at least has been liked by a lot of people through the ages. On the other hand, just as with many things that we accept without question because we have not stopped to reconsider, some of the classics have lost their usefulness, but because once we considered them good we have kept right on thinking so.

What the father mentioned above would have suggested for his little girl I have no way of knowing, but I'll bet he would have been stumped. The trouble with us old ones in regard to children's classics is that we left off being children a long time ago, and for us the classics ended then. The fact that 20 or 30 or 40 years have passed and newer books have begun to become classics does not enter our heads.

How long does it take to make a classic? As Josette Frank says in her admirable book, "Your Child's Reading Today," some books may just be long-lived, not classic. That may prove true of many of the books today that are of "acknowledged excellence": but some of them surely will be in the top ranks for generations, and are far better than some of those we so fondly cherish in our remembrance.

Of course we want our children to read the good old books that have meant so much to so many generations. They have much to offer that modern books do not seem to have. The old books give continuity to our lives, books that have run through several generations and are known by grandparents, parents, and children.

The classics are melodramatic, often sentimental, sad. Nowadays authors are almost afraid to make their stories sad, even though children are noted for loving sad tales, because parents don't want their children to face the facts of life. No modern book for children would have a death like Little Nell's.

If we want our children to read the old books, timing is very important. We give our children things before they are ready for them, so eager are we to have them get the things we love. The electric train father gives his son for Christmas is not appreciated until years later. Father plays with it. In the same way, we often give books to children before they are ready. Donald's aunt wanted so for him to love books that she began building up a library for him the minute he started in school. What did she buy? The classics, of course, in nice bindings. Donald not only could not appreciate them then, but he was slow in learning to read. Had she given him *Little Eddie* it would have been better. He would have been more interested and would have learned to read by reading. How often we hear people say, "I think I must have read that book when I was too young to understand it." And so often the books we had before we were ready we never go back to; we only remember that we thought them dull because we did not understand. Even if we could read the words they meant little. We did not "get" the thing that has made the book live all these years.

When an older person goes to a bookshop, and he has not kept up on what is new and good, he looks around. A familiar title catches his eye. (How we love and feel secure with familiar things!) He doesn't recognize *The Moffats,* or *Homer Price,* or even *Mary Poppins.* His eye lights on *Heidi.* He has heard of it (so has the clerk). And doesn't it say on the bottom of the back strip "Children's Classics"? It must be good. It is likely to be in a more attractive edition at a lower price than new books, partly because it is royalty-free. He buys it. It may be entirely too old or for the wrong person.

A mother told me she was reading *Hans Brinker or The Silver Skates* aloud to her youngster. She made a wry face. "It seems rather dull," she said. We ourselves cannot always tell when a thing is dated. I read *The Princess and the Goblins* aloud to a group of nine-year-olds. I was quite conscious of the unusual sentence structure and words and the "talking down." The children adored it. It had no date as far as they were concerned. Some books don't have the story appeal to carry them beyond the datedness.

A word should be said about abridged and adapted versions of the classics. The theory is that a young person might better read *Lorna Doone* cut and simplified, than not to read it at all. The opposite side says a child might better miss the story than not to have it the way the author wrote it. The answer, I think, is in how good the abridgment is, and of what book. *The Three Musketeers,* so far as I know, is always "abridged" for young people. Chapters have been removed without influencing the story whatsoever. But where a book has been entirely rewritten for youngsters I would be suspicious. Is it necessary for a child to read *Robinson Crusoe* before he is really old enough? Can't he wait? He has the rest of his life for an adult story like that. The fact that a child does like the main, exciting part of the story, the shipwreck, does not mean he has to read it when he is eight. A young mother told me she had read *Huckleberry Finn* to her small daughter. But she added, "I admit I changed

some of the words because I didn't want Mary to hear them."
The mother should have waited for her daughter to grow
old enough to read Mark Twain's words. If you are eager to
have your children know *Treasure Island* or *Tom Sawyer,* read
them aloud. They will love them. Later they will read them to
themselves.

We have some books coming out each year that we speak of
as "new" classics because we are sure they will be long-lived.
They have already been tested by the children, reviewed favorably by the adults. Some, if times change as rapidly in the next
30 years as they have in the past 30 will later become out of
date. Time alone will tell.

Below is a list of some of the classics old and new that children really read and enjoy. But remember . . . it is important to
get *the right book at the right time.*

Classics for the Youngest

JOHNNY CROW'S GARDEN. Written and illustrated by Leslie
Brooke. (Warne.) A classic picture book with nonsense rhymes.
Ages 2–5.

THE TALE OF PETER RABBIT. Written and illustrated by Beatrix Potter. (Warne.) A necessity for every child to have in its
original edition.

A little boy was trying to tell his mother what the Sunday
School lesson was about. He began, "Peter said to Jesus," and
he then couldn't remember. Later he tried again but got no
further. Finally he said, "Well , what would a rabbit say?" Peter
to children is Peter Rabbit. Ages 2–6.

THE STORY OF LITTLE BLACK SAMBO. Written and illustrated
by Helen Bannerman. (Lippincott.) In spite of the controversy
about it, it is one of the favorite books with children. They
love to "play" it and hear it again and again. Ages 4–6.

PELLE'S NEW SUIT. Written and illustrated by Elsa Beskow.
(Harper.) Lovely pictures tell how Pelle earned his new suit by
raking hay, doing errands. Swedish. Ages 5–7.

Books Well on Their Way to Being Classics

A B C BUNNY. Written and illustrated by Wanda Gág. (Coward.) Beautiful lithographs showing the bunny hopping from A
to Z. Ages 1–5.

MILLIONS OF CATS. Written and illustrated by Wanda Gág.
(Coward.) Bound to be demanded by children for generations to
come. Ages 4–7.

THE STORY ABOUT PING. Marjorie Flack. Illustrated by Kurt Wiese. A favorite story with the 5–7-year-olds.

MIKE MULLIGAN AND HIS STEAM SHOVEL. Written and illustrated by Virginia Burton. (Houghton.) Mike and Mary Ann are favorites. Ages 4–8.

FIVE CHINESE BROTHERS. Claire Huchet Bishop. Illustrated by Kurt Wiese. (Coward.) Forever popular. Ages 5–10.

ANDY AND THE LION. Written and illustrated by James Daugherty. (Viking.) An old story retold with vigorous illustrations. Ages 6–10.

Tried and True for the Slightly Older Child

GRIMM'S FAIRY TALES. Many editions. All the old favorites are here. Ages 8–12.

ANDERSEN'S FAIRY TALES. Many editions. Ages 10–12.

THE PRINCESS AND THE GOBLINS. George Macdonald. Illustrated by Nora Unwin. (Macmillan.) The Princess and Curdie, the miner's son, overcome the wicked goblins. Ages 9–12.

HEIDI. Johanna Spyri. Illustrated by Agnes Tait. (Lippincott.) Most children adore this old story. It is full of Heidi's fondness for her grandfather, her Swiss mountain home, and her goats. There is both humor and sadness in it. Ages 9–12.

THE ADVENTURES OF PINOCCHIO. C. Collodi (pseud). Illustrated after Attilio Mussino. (Macmillan.) An Italian classic for children. The pranks and adventures of a wooden marionette. Ages 9–12.

BAMBI. Felix Salten. (Grosset.) The life story of a fawn poetically told. Ages 10–15.

BLACK BEAUTY. Anna Sewell. Many editions. People can say until Doomsday that this is a sentimental story full of moralizing but children still vote it their favorite book. Ages 8–12.

THE BIRD'S CHRISTMAS CAROL. Kate Douglas Wiggin. Illustrated by Jessie Gillespie. (Houghton.) Children love the sentimentality and humor in this story of the rich little girl who invited the poor Ruggleses for Christmas dinner. Ages 8–12.

THE MAGIC FISHBONE. Charles Dickens. Illustrated by Louis Slobodkin. (Vanguard.) The trials and rewards of the Princess Alicia in taking care of her 18 brothers and sisters. Ages 9–12.

THE WIND IN THE WILLOWS. Kenneth Grahame. Illustrated by Ernest Shepard. (Scribner.) Many other editions too. "One does not argue about *The Wind in the Willows*. The young man gives it to the girl with whom he is in love, and if she does not like it, asks her to return his letters. The older man tries it on his nephew, and alters his will accordingly. The book is a test of character. We can't criticize it because it is criticizing us. When you sit down to it, don't be so ridiculous as to suppose that you are sitting in judgment on my taste or on the art of Kenneth Grahame. You are merely sitting in judgment on yourself. You may be worthy. I don't know. But it is you who are on trial." Thus wrote A. A. Milne in his introduction to the Heritage Press edition. It is a book you love. It becomes an enduring possession. Ages 10 and up.

THE JUST SO STORIES. Rudyard Kipling. Illustrated by Rojankovsky. (Doubleday.) The most famous stories: "Elephant's Child," "How the Leopard Got His Spots," "How the Rhinoceros Got His Skin," "How the Camel Got His Hump." These are in separate volumes also. Children should have these read to them. The language is perfect. Ages 6–10.

ALICE'S ADVENTURES IN WONDERLAND. Lewis Carroll. Illustrated by John Tenniel. (Macmillan.) Many other editions. Not all children like this. Some will like it younger than others. Worth trying, and later coming back to it. It is said that Ethel Barrymore reads it every year to help her imagination. 9 to any age.

THE SWISS FAMILY ROBINSON. Johann D. Wyss. Illustrated by Harry Rountree. (Macmillan.) Many other editions. Children love this improbable tale. A Swiss family shipwrecked on a desert island find many incongruous things that children accept. And as someone said, "Why shouldn't they?" Nothing is impossible to children. Ages 8–12.

TREASURE ISLAND. Robert Louis Stevenson. Illustrated by N. C. Wyeth. (Scribner.) One of the best-loved stories. Quite young children love it read aloud. As one youngster said so wisely, "Stevenson made it a point to be exciting." Ages 9–15.

THE ADVENTURES OF TOM SAWYER. Mark Twain. (Harper.) One of the most popular books of all times. Ages 10–14.

THE ADVENTURES OF HUCKLEBERRY FINN. Mark Twain. (Harper.) Someone was asked what American book would be alive in two hundred years. The reply was *Huckleberry Finn.* Ages 12–16.

TWENTY THOUSAND LEAGUES UNDER THE SEA. Jules Verne. Illustrated by N. C. Wyeth. (Scribner.) Unfortunately because of the movie many children too young for it are wanting to read this story of Captain Nemo and his submarine. Boys and girls of 12 and up will find it an absorbing tale.

MYSTERIOUS ISLAND is another popular story by the same author.

LITTLE WOMEN. Louisa May Alcott. The story of Meg, Jo, Beth, and Amy. Illustrated by Jessie Willcox Smith. (Little.)

Many men writers have given this book credit for influencing them. When the first movie of it came out, many boys read it with brown paper covers over the title. Girls still enjoy it. It is amazingly fresh and undated. Ages 10–15.

ROBINSON CRUSOE. Daniel Defoe. Illustrated by E. Boyd Smith. (Houghton.) Many editions. A great story. Children especially like the saving of the things from the wreck, the building of his house, and the daily scrabbling for a living. The beginning of the book is hard going and has been taken out from some editions. Every child should know this book, but there is no hurry. Ages 12–16.

RIP VAN WINKLE AND THE LEGEND OF SLEEPY HOLLOW. Washington Irving. Illustrated by Maude and Miska Petersham. (Macmillan.) Not easy to read, but children enjoy having it read to them. Ages 10–15.

THE JUNGLE BOOK. Rudyard Kipling. Illustrated by Kurt Wiese. (Doubleday.) Especially should children know the Mowgli stories and "Rikki Tikki Tavi." Ages 8–14.

THE MERRY ADVENTURES OF ROBIN HOOD. Written and illustrated by Howard Pyle. (Scribner.) The very finest edition of the Robin Hood stories; belongs in every teenage boy's library. Ages 10–15.

THE STORY OF KING ARTHUR AND HIS KNIGHTS. Written and illustrated by Howard Pyle. (Scribner.) The finest King Arthur. Not easy to read but a book to own for the rest of your life. Ages 12–16.

THE THREE MUSKETEERS. Alexandre Dumas. Illustrated. (Dodd.) A favorite with children in their teens. Swashbuckling and exciting. Ages 14–18.

THE COUNT OF MONTE CRISTO. Alexandre Dumas. Illustrated by Mead Schaeffer. (Dodd.) A dramatic story for all time. Ages 14–18.

THE PETERKIN PAPERS. Lucretia Hale. Illustrated by Harold Brett. (Houghton.) One of the funniest books that will be enjoyed by the whole family. Ages 10 and up.

More Recent Books That No Doubt Will Make the "Classic" List

WINNIE THE POOH. A. A. Milne. Illustrated by Ernest Shepard. (Dutton.) Story of Christopher Robin and his teddy bear. Ages 8–10.

THE STORY OF DOCTOR DOLITTLE. Written and illustrated by Hugh Lofting. (Lippincott.) An unusual Doctor who knows the language of animals goes to Africa to vaccinate the monkeys and is given an animal called a pushmipullyu as his reward. Wonderful. Ages 7–10.

MARY POPPINS. P. L. Travers. Illustrated by Mary Shepard. (Harcourt.) A story of the remarkable things that happened after Mary Poppins arrived on an east wind to look after the Banks children. Delightful nonsense that children from 6 to 12 love.

HOMER PRICE. Written and illustrated by Robert McCloskey. (Viking.) Six stories about that unusual boy, Homer. Not difficult to read, and loved by all children. Ages 7–12.

THE STREET OF LITTLE SHOPS. Margery Bianco. Illustrated by Grace Paull. (Doubleday.) Little stories about little shops in a little town. Children find them delightful and easy to read. Ages 7–10.

THE MOFFATS. Eleanor Estes. Illustrated by Louis Slobodkin. (Harcourt.) A charming family story with four interesting children, but especially Jane and Rufus. Ages 10–14.

MR. POPPER'S PENGUINS. Richard and Florence Atwater. Illustrated by Robert Lawson. (Little.) The amusing adventures of the Poppers and their penguins. Ages 7–12.

RABBIT HILL. Written and illustrated by Robert Lawson. (Viking.) The little animals watch anxiously for the new people who move into the house on the hill. They find them most considerate. A beautiful story with lovely pictures. Ages 6–12.

THE LITTLE HOUSE IN THE BIG WOODS, and others of same series. Laura Ingalls Wilder. Illustrated by Garth Williams. (Harper.) These stories by their very reality will live for a long, long time. The children know the characters so well. Ages 8–14.

CALL IT COURAGE. Written and illustrated by Armstrong Sperry. (Macmillan.) A great story of a Polynesian boy who sets out to prove his courage and goes through terrific adventures. Children love it best when it is read to them. Ages 10–14.

THE WONDER CLOCK AND PEPPER AND SALT. Written and illustrated by Howard Pyle. (Harper.) Stories based on old folk tale plots. Wonderful for the story hour and for children to read for themselves. Ages 8–12.

MEN OF IRON. Written and illustrated by Howard Pyle. (Harper.) A terrific story of the training of a knight in the Middle Ages. Beautifully written. Ages 12–16.

THE DARK FRIGATE. Charles Hawes. Illustrated by A. O. Fischer. (Little.) The story of Philip Marsham who lived in time of King Charles. An excellent sea story. As one boy said of it,

"If you like suspense, adventure, and pirates, I recommend this book." Ages 13–16.

CADDIE WOODLAWN. Carol Ryrie Brink. Illustrated by Kate Seredy. (Macmillan.) A story of Wisconsin in the early days and a girl who was allowed to be a tomboy. Her adventures are both exciting and humorous. Ages 10–14.

THE GOOD MASTER. Written and illustrated by Kate Seredy. (Viking.) The kind of book that is read and reread. How can it but become a classic? Kate and her cousin Jansci have many adventures on the Hungarian Plains. Ages 8–14.

SHIP'S PARROT. Honoré Morrow and William Swartzman. Illustrated by Gordon Grant. (Morrow.) A lovely story of a boy who takes his parrot to sea. The parrot helps solve a mystery. Ages 8–10.

JIM DAVIS. John Masefield. (Lippincott.) A tale of smugglers on the English coast. Ages 10–14.

CHILDREN'S BOOKS OF 1930-1960 THAT HAVE BECOME MODERN CLASSICS*

Mary Elisabeth Edes

The last three decades have produced an extraordinary number of books which can properly be called modern children's classics. Because so many of these fine books are not always recognized as classics, PW has been conducting an informal survey of children's librarians in the largest cities throughout the country, of reviewers of children's books in New York, Chicago, and San Francisco, and of booksellers with notable juvenile departments, in an attempt to find out just which books of the post-Winnie-

* [Mary Elisabeth Edes] "Children's Books of 1930–1960 That Have Become Modern Classics," *Publisher's Weekly,* 178 (November 14, 1960), 12–16. Reprinted by permission of the R. R. Bowker Company.

the-Pooh era—that is, the past 30 years—have proved to be so popular with children that they deserve to be called classics. It has proved to be a matter of great interest to everyone. We have seldom had a more gratifying response to a PW questionnaire. The replies show great unanimity of opinion. The same titles appeared over and over on the lists we received.

THE FAVORITE IS "CHARLOTTE'S WEB"

The overwhelming favorite is a fairly recent book, E. B. White's *Charlotte's Web,* published by Harper in 1952. This story of a spider who saved the life of her friend, the pig, was mentioned almost twice as many times as the second two favorites, *Mary Poppins* by P. L. Travers (Harcourt, Brace) and *The Little House in the Big Woods* by Laura Ingalls Wilder (Harper), both of which appeared in 1932.

Following closely the above-mentioned books, according to our survey are *Homer Price* by Robert McCloskey, published by Viking in 1943; *Johnny Tremain* by Esther Forbes, published by Houghton Mifflin, also in 1943; Mr. McCloskey's picture book, *Make Way for Ducklings* (Viking), published in 1953; *Mr. Popper's Penguins* by Richard and Florence Atwater, published by Little, Brown in 1938; E. B. White's *Stuart Little* (Harper), which appeared in 1945; *The Moffats* by Eleanor Estes (Harcourt, Brace), a 1941 publication; Ludwig Bemelmans' *Madeline,* first published by Simon and Schuster in 1939 and now on the Viking list; and *The Little Prince* by Antoine de St.-Exupery, which was published by Reynal and Hitchcock in 1943 and is now on the Harcourt, Brace list.

Other books which were suggested by a considerable percentage of our correspondents are *The 500 Hats of Bartholomew Cubbins* by Dr. Seuss (Vanguard, 1950), *Caddie Wodlawn* by Carol Ryrie Brink (Macmillan, 1935), *King of the Wind* by Marguerite Henry (Rand McNally, 1948), *The Yearling* by Marjorie Kinnan Rawlings (Scribners, 1952), *Curious George* by H. A. Rey (Houghton Mifflin, 1940), *Paddle to the Sea* by Holling C. Holling (Houghton Mifflin, 1941), *Mike Mulligan and His Steam Shovel* by Virginia Lee Burton (Houghton Mifflin, 1942), *Lassie Come Home* by Eric Knight (Winston, 1940), *Five Chinese Brothers* by Claire H. Bishop (Coward, McCann, 1938). A good many correspondents felt that all the books in a series like those about Curious George, Madeline, Elizabeth Enright's Melendy Family and the Moffats are classics.

How Many Books Make a Classic?

The sale of just how many books does it take to make a classic? Well, to be utterly crass about it, the answer seems to be at least 100,000 copies and, more likely, 175,000. There must be a yearly sale of somewhere between 5000 and 10,000, though the most popular books sell closer to 20,000 a year. Some books which have attained these heights in a mere two or three years do not seem to have quite established themselves in many minds as full-fledged classics, probably because of their recent vintage. Perhaps a book has to have a certain nostalgia about it before we think of it as classic. Moreover, very recent books have been introduced to a market much larger than that reached by the books of the 1930's. It will be interesting to see if *Mary Poppins,* for example, eventually catches up with, say. *The Cat in the Hat.* Books of the past three years which are obviously going to be classics very, very soon (and there are those who think they are already) include *The Cat in the Hat* by Dr. Seuss (Random House, 1957), which has sold more than 200,000 copies, *The Witch of Blackbird Pond* by Elizabeth George Speare (Houghton Mifflin, 1958) and Joan Walsh Anglund's *Love is a Special Way of Feeling* (Harcourt, Brace, 1959) and her *A Friend Is Someone Who Likes You,* which has sold more than 107,000 copies since Harcourt, Brace published it in 1958, and Beverly Cleary's *Henry Huggins* (Morrow, 1950).

Sales Do Not Tell the Whole Story

Figures on many books which appear on our lists as runners-up, are, in fact, about equal to those of the most-mentioned titles. For example, Robert McCloskey's *Homer Price* and his *Make Way for Ducklings* both appeared on most of our correspondents' lists, but Viking reports that *Make Way for Ducklings* sells about 16,000 a year and *Homer Price* has an annual sale of about 10,000. But so does *The Story About Ping* by Marjorie Flack (Viking, 1933) sell 10,000 a year. It was mentioned on the lists that came in, but not nearly so often as Mr. McCloskey's books. It is a picture book, as is *Make Way for Ducklings.* Every one of these books, Viking reports, is "selling more copies each year. The trend is up." This is also true of Viking's *Madeline* by Ludwig Bemelmans, *Rabbit Hill* by Robert Lawson, *The Story of Ferdinand* by Munro Leaf, *Andy and the Lion* by James Daugherty, *The Good Master* by Kate Seredy, and *Blue Willow* by Doris Gates, all of which had some champions among our correspondents.

SALES OF "CADDIE WOODLAWN" INCREASE EACH YEAR

Macmillan reports that this is true of Carol Ryrie Brink's *Caddie Woodlawn,* a story of a tomboy girl in the Wisconsin of the 1860's, a story which won the Newbery Medal in 1936. More than 350,000 copies of *Caddie Woodlawn* have been sold since the book appeared 25 years ago. Last year's sales were 9772 copies. In 1959 the book sold 8956 and in 1958, 7716.

Houghton Mifflin says that sales of *Mike Mulligan and His Steam Shovel* are about the same as those of Virginia Lee Burton's Caldecott Medal winner, *The Little House,* about 10,000 copies a year with a total of close to 175,000 each. However the rate of sale of *Mike Mulligan* is somewhat higher. *Paddle to the Sea* has sold about 175,000, too, but its rate of sale now is less, about 5500 a year. *Curious George,* on the other hand, has sold a total of 109,000, but it is climbing at a rate of 11,000 annually.

Marguerite Henry's Newbery Medal winner, *King of the Wind,* published in 1948, has sold more than 350,000 copies to date, and it continues to sell 15,000 to 20,000 a year regularly. Mrs. Henry's *Misty of Chincoteague,* however, published two years earlier, had settled down to an annual sale of about 15,000 until about three years ago, when they climbed to more than 20,000. Since Rand McNally has been running a contest in which young readers are asked to suggest a name for Misty's foal, however, sales have shown a further increase. The forthcoming Twentieth Century-Fox movie based on the book will, undoubtedly, spur them further. At present, the total sale stands at about 175,000 copies.

It is interesting to observe that about half of the books mentioned by our correspondents were winners of the Newbery or Caldecott Medals or runners-up for these awards. Some, of course, are books of English origin and therefore never were eligible. The authors of the books are about equally divided between those whose usual business it is to write children's books and have produced a great many of them, and those authors who have written very few juveniles. In the first category, of course, are Robert Lawson, Marguerite Henry, Eleanor Estes, Margaret Wise Brown, Munro Leaf, Dr. Seuss, and Carol Ryrie Brink. Mr. McCloskey and Mr. Bemelmans have done a good many books, but they are slow to produce and are essentially artists rather than author-illustrators. Some are writers who seldom venture into the juvenile field. E. B. White, whose two books for children have sold more than 200,000 copies each, is probably best known for his thoughtful essays and articles written for *The New Yorker*. His *Charlotte's Web* still sells 20,000 copies a year. Esther Forbes is famous as a historical novelist. *Johnny Tremain* is her only book for children. It has sold 344,000 copies, including an educational edition, and it sells 10,000 copies a year in the trade edition and probably as many more in the educational edition. Antoine de St.-Exupery, adventurer, aviator, and author of *Night Flight* and *Wind, Sand and Stars*, whose *The Little Prince* has sold 172,000 copies, wrote no other book for children. Mary Norton, whose book *The Borrowers* has sold 76,000 copies since publication seven years ago, has written one other juvenile in addition to her three books about the Borrowers. She started her career as an actress and has written plays. She is now at work on the script of a movie based on *The Borrowers*. Laura Ingalls Wilder wrote only her books in the Little House series. *The Little House in the Big Woods* alone has sold more than 200,000 copies.

Eric Knight wrote adult novels including the wartime bestseller, *This Above All*. *Lassie Come Home* first appeared as a short story in *The Saturday Evening Post*. Winston's alert editors urged him to expand it to make a book for children, and *Lassie Come Home*, published in 1940, was the result. The original trade edition has sold 100,000 copies just in the past decade, and there have been various reprint and movie tie-in editions.

Richard and Florence Atwater, both of whom were schoolteachers, wrote *Mr. Popper's Penguins* (Little, Brown) in 1938 while Mr. Atwater was suffering from a lengthy illness. He has since died. *Mr. Popper's Penguins* was his only book, and his wife has done no further writing. It is the leading title on Little, Brown's juvenile backlist. Total sales stand at about 175,000 copies, and it sells between 6000 and 9000 copies a year. Pamela Travers, an Australian who has spent much of her life in England, has written no books other than those about that wonderful nanny, Mary Poppins. The first book alone has a total sale of almost 200,000 copies.

In addition to the books discussed above, there are other which were mentioned by our correspondents. A list of these titles follows.

The Rooster Crows by Maud and Miska Petersham (Macmillan, 1945), *The Courage of Sarah Noble* by Alice Dalgliesh (Scribners, 1953), *Ben and Me* by Robert Lawson (Little, Brown, 1939),

Seventeenth Summer by Maureen Daly (Dodd, Mead, 1942), *The Door in the Wall* by Marguerite de Angeli (Doubleday, 1950), *Pat the Bunny* by Dorothy Kunhardt (Golden Press, 1940), *Goodnight Moon* by Margaret Wise Brown (Harper, 1947), *The Hobbit* by J.R. Tolkien (Houghton Mifflin, 1938), *Andy and the Lion* by James Daugherty (Viking, 1938), *And to Think That I Saw It on Mulberry Street* by Dr. Seuss (Vanguard, 1939), *The Melendy Family* by Elizabeth Enright (Holt, 1947), *The Good Master* by Kate Seredy (Viking, 1935), *My Father's Dragon* by Ruth Gannett (Random House, 1947), *Blue Willow* by Doris Gates (Viking, 1940), *Pippi Longstocking* by Astrid Lindgren (Viking, 1950), *Strawberry Girl* by Lois Lenski (Lippincott, 1945), *The Matchlock Gun* by Walter D. Edmonds (Dodd, Mead, 1941), *Mrs. Piggle-Wiggle* by Betty MacDonald (Lippincott, 1947), *Horton Hatches the Egg* by Dr. Seuss (Random House, 1940), *A Hole Is to Dig* by Ruth Krauss (Harper 1952), *The Lion, the Witch and the Wardrobe* by C. S. Lewis (Macmillan, 1950), *Loretta Mason Potts* by Mary Chase (Lippincott, 1958), *The Biggest Bear* by Lynd Ward (Houghton Mifflin, 1952) and the stories about the Black Stallion by Walter Farley, all published by Random House. Still others are: *Roller Skates* by Ruth Sawyer (Viking, 1936), *Timothy Turtle* by Al Graham (Viking, 1949), *Little Eddie* by Carolyn Haywood (Morrow, 1947), *The Story of Babar* by Jean de Brunhoff (Random House, 1933), *The Country Bunny* by DuBose Heywood and Marjorie Flack (Houghton Mifflin, 1939), *Ballet Shoes* by Noel Streatfeild (Random House, 1937), *National Velvet* by Enid Bagnold (Morrow, 1935), *The Ark* by Margot Benary-Isbert (Harcourt, Brace, 1953), *My Friend, Flicka* by Mary O'Hara (Lippincott, 1941), *The Enormous Egg* by Oliver Butterworth (Little, Brown, 1956), *Little Toot* by Hardie Gramatky (Putnam, 1939), *Call It Courage* by Armstrong Sperry (Macmillan, 1940), *One Hundred and One Dalmations* by Dodie Smith (Viking, 1956), *Big Tiger and Christian* by Fritz Muhlenberg (Pantheon, 1952), *Street Rod* by Henry Felsen (Random House, 1953) and *Katy No-Pocket* by Emmy Payne (Houghton Mifflin, 1944).

FREDERIC MELCHER
AND CHILDREN'S BOOKS*

Ruth Gagliardo

With the death of Frederic G. Melcher on March 9, 1963, in his 84th year, the children's book world lost its most devoted friend and champion. For in all his 68 active years as bookseller, collector, editor, publisher, lecturer, initiator, exhorter, and defender, Frederic Melcher, who loved books and people with a passion, was happiest when planning with some of his countless friends— preferably children's or school librarians—how to make children's books better and more readily available. Such a glow of enthusiasm he brought to these contacts! His contagious response to everything concerning books reached out in every direction and to all kinds of people.

His cheers reached out to Kansas when a children's book review column was begun in the *Kansas Teacher* as a regular feature over twenty years ago. His interest deepened when the Children's Traveling Book Exhibit began touring the state a year later, taking to children and their parents and teachers the books all were eager to see. Bookstores were few in Kansas, public libraries inadequate, elementary school libraries practically non-existent, book fairs unknown—twenty years ago.

When Mr. Melcher heard that a few foreign miniature paper editions of children's books had been added to the exhibit to show Kansas children what was happening to books in war-torn England, he increased the number at once, just as later he sent to the Kansas exhibit translations of favorite American children's books which were being distributed and read by children in many other countries. Books, Mr. Melcher knew, could be a great international force to bring people, both children and adults, together.

* Ruth Gagliardo, "Frederic Melcher and Children's Books," *ALA Bulletin* 57 (June, 1963), 549–52. Reprinted by permission of the American Library Association, and the author.

In the late thirties, when Children's Book Week in our small university town became a Community Book Week with 37 organizations participating in window displays in the business district, from school and youth groups to the Flower Club, the American Legion, and the County Historical Society, Frederic Melcher in faraway New York (the distance was greater then) encouraged and applauded.

These examples are not mentioned here because they happened in my state but because Frederic Melcher *knew* they were happening. The chairman of the R. R. Bowker Company was no more bound to New York than he was held to his editorial desk. He was up and away, finding book news or making it—for Frederic Melcher was always the mover and shaker. All great editors are and Frederic Melcher was a great editor.

LIBRARIES AND CHILDREN'S BOOKS

Especially was he sensitive to children and to children's books. He discovered the joy of books early. A special smell of ink, he said, would sometimes hit his nostrils with a twinge of homesickness for his grandmother's front room with its deep window seats where, as a long-legged boy, he used to curl up for a good read, or for the old brown stuffed chair at home, over the arm of which he could comfortably fling a leg and nestle back with a book for hours.

Fred Melcher was not far from those youthful reading days when he went from Newton High School in 1895 to Lauriat's Bookstore in Boston. Working first in the mailing and receiving rooms, he came finally to serve as a salesman where his influence, a colleague recalled fifty years later, was like that of a popular book reviewer. He took charge of children's books "because no one else seemed interested" and, with the help of review lists prepared by Caroline Hewins, a remarkable New England librarian, he advised his patrons about children's books and reading. So the life-long cooperation began that was to make Fred Melcher himself "half librarian."

This interest in libraries and librarians continued with his move to Indianapolis where for 5 years he managed the W. K. Stewart Bookstore. Then, in 1918, with his growing family, Frederic Melcher went to New York to join the R. R. Bowker Company. How the morning stars must have sung together! For if ever there is one right moment, that was the moment for Frederic Melcher and children's books.

Already there were significant stirrings in the children's book field. Bertha Mahony's Bookshop for Boys and Girls had opened in Boston; she had gone to Indianapolis to advise with Mr. Melcher and he had taken her to her first Booksellers Convention in Chicago. Anne Carroll Moore was writing her omnibus children's book reviews, the first, for *The Bookman,* Louise Seaman was heading the first children's book department for the Macmillan Company.

Then, in 1919, Frederic Melcher, with Franklin K. Mathiews, librarian of the Boy Scouts of America, founded Children's Book Week. The idea, sparked by Mr. Melcher's characteristic zest and enthusiasm, caught on all over the country. Here surely was genius at work, for from the very beginning the interest of many national organizations, among them the National Education Association and the National Congress of Parents and Teachers, was enlisted, remaining active to this day. It was Book Week, U.S.A., and it still is, carrying annually into thousands of cities, towns, and hamlets its imperative message: "Children's books are important."

Years later Mr. Melcher's efforts were to assist in the formation of the Children's Book Council with its year-round promotion of children's books. A joint committee today, made up of the Children's Book Council and the Children's Services Division of the American Library Association, is typical of the growing cooperation among organizations and institutions working with books.

The Newbery and Caldecott Medals

In 1921, Mr. Melcher as Book Week national chairman was asked to be one of a panel of three to speak at the Children's Librarians Section of the ALA meeting at Swampscott, Massachusetts. The theme was Children's Book Week—a National Movement. Irene Smith, author of *A History of the Newbery and Caldecott Medals,* in writing of this meeting says:

> Mr. Melcher years later wrote, "As I looked down . . . at the three or four hundred people, I thought of the power they could have in encouraging the joy of reading among children. I could see that I was sure of having the librarians' cooperation in Children's Book Week, but I wanted to go further and secure their interest in the whole process of *creating* books for children, producing them and bringing them to children."

Mr. Melcher went away from the meeting longing for some plan that would enable the librarians to "help encourage the creation of more worthwhile books by outstanding writers." Suddenly he thought of an award and, because he had only recently been reading Charles Knight's *Shadows of Old Booksellers* with its lively impressions of John Newbery, he even had the name! He asked the chairman, Alice I. Hazeltine, if he might speak again at the next day's session. This he did, proposing the John Newbery Award to be given annually to the "most distinguished contribution to American children's literature," with the winner to be selected by children's librarians. The proposal was accepted, to be put into effect the next year, and was then taken to the Executive Committee of the American Library Association for approval.

In talking to the sculptor, René Paul Chambellan, about the casting of the medal which Mr. Melcher was to provide, Mr. Melcher said, "What we want to reward is 'genius giving of its best to the child.'" Always he believed with Walter De La Mare that "only the rarest kind of best in anything can be good enough for the young." It is satisfying now to know that these words are engraved on the Regina Medal which was presented to Mr. Melcher in 1962 by the Catholic Library Association in recognition of a lifetime contribution to children's literature.

The first Newbery Medal was awarded to *The Story of Mankind* in Detroit in 1922. Before putting the medal into the hands of Hendrik Van Loon, the winner, the chairman, Clara Hunt, said to Mr. Melcher, "We feel strong and powerful because you believe in us and are putting in our hands a weapon, one of the most potent of our times—publicity of the best kind."

A month later Frederic Melcher himself wrote in *Publishers' Weekly*, "We should not forget that by creating a greater audience, we are also creating literature itself, for the creator of literature is drawn out by the appreciation of literature; the author needs the audience as much as the audience needs the author."

In 1938, Mr. Melcher established the Randolph Caldecott Medal for the "most distinguished American picture book." This second medal was given for the first time at the Kansas City Conference to Dorothy P. Lathrop for *Animals of the Bible*. In proposing the name of the famous nineteenth century English artist for the second medal, Mr. Melcher said, "It supplies us with a name that has pleasant memories—memories connected with the joyousness of picture books as well as with their beauty. Whatever direction new books may take, I think that joyous and happy approach is one thing we should be gently reminded of." Frederic Melcher had again performed his act of faith.

The Newbery-Caldecott Awards have grown steadily in stature and significance. Mr. Melcher's dream that children's books be recognized as an integral part of our general art and literature was being realized. There were also many signs that parents and the general public were coming to recognize the wonder and the joy, the understanding and the stimulus that books of integrity can bring to the hearts and minds of boys and girls. In 1950, at the 50th anniversary of its founding, the Children's Library Association presented Mr. Melcher with a gold plaque in honor of "his distinguished contribution to the advancement and encouragement of outstanding literature and art in children's books."

Yet Frederic Melcher knew in 1950 how much still remained to be done. In a letter written about this time, he said: "I think all of us, in the areas we are most interested in, realize as perhaps we didn't twenty-five years ago, that the 'progress of mankind onward and upward' hasn't exactly happened. But with doubts and confusion all around, it becomes the more necessary that we build within ourselves a kind of confidence in the things we do know that will enable us to step out and speak out affirmatively." This courage to step out and speak affirmatively Frederic Melcher always demonstrated. Speak out he did, simply, yet with infectious conviction. His belief in the high office of books was implanted in all who knew him.

THE MELCHER LEGEND

It is impossible to measure Mr. Melcher's influence, particularly in the publishing and distribution of books for children, so tremendous has it been. Nor is it easy to name the secret of his success. In part, it was surely his honesty of mind. It was also a complete absence of any kind of self-seeking; that "Kilroy was here" never concerned Frederic Melcher. It was in great part due to his creative imagination and his unique gift of inspiring all kinds of people to take an idea and run with it. His enthusiasm gave wings to ordinary mortals.

Ambassador Winant said to Mr. Melcher in London one day as the two parted after a spirited discussion, "Melcher, don't ever lose your enthusiasm." And he never did. The boy in Lauriat's had found his own course and he never turned from it.

> They would not find me changed from him they knew—
> Only more sure of all I thought was true.

In 1946, when the American Library Association made Mr. Melcher an Honorary Member in recognition of his 50 years of service to libraries and to books, he was already being called a legend. In 1956, the Children's Services Division established the Frederic G. Melcher Scholarship to be awarded annually in honor of its great and good friend. Robert Frost, in expressing his pleasure at this scholarship honoring his friend of 40 years, called Fred Melcher a wonder.

Wonder, legend, bookman-extraordinary—Frederic Melcher was all these and more. One remembers these lines by Frost:

> O Star (the fairest one in sight),
> . . . .
> Say something to us we can learn
> By heart and when alone repeat.
> Say something! And it says, "I burn."
> But say with what degree of heat.
> Talk Fahrenheit, talk Centigrade.
> Use language we can comprehend.
> Tell us what elements you blend.
> It gives us strangely little aid,
> But does tell something in the end.
> And steadfast as Keats' Eremite,
> Not even stooping from its sphere,
> It asks a little of us here.
> It asks of us a certain height,
> So when at times the mob is swayed
> To carry praise or blame too far,
> We may choose something like a star
> To stay our minds on and be staid.[1]

[1] From "Choose Something Like a Star" from *Complete Poems of Robert Frost.* Copyright 1949 by Holt, Rinehart and Winston, Inc., and reprinted with the publisher's permission.

For some of us, these words, "We may choose something like a star / To stay our minds on and be staid," will forever speak of a tall, loved bookman, friend of blessed memory, Frederic Gershom Melcher, whose resolute steadfastness and lively imagination have brought to children for generations to come books of beauty and joy and enduring worth.

THE NEWBERY-CALDECOTT MEDALS: LEGACY TO CHILDREN'S LITERATURE*

Irene Smith Green

Many have attempted to describe the human personality of Frederic Melcher, and spoken words of truth. One with inner knowledge of his multiform components was Christopher Morley. "The number of books, schemes, ideas, transactions, ceremonies, speeches, promotions, dinners, awards, conferences, editorials, articles that have passed through his [Melcher's] mind, leaving, apparently, no trace of erosion or corrugations on his brow," wrote Morley, "staggers me to contemplate."

This bewildering inventory reminds children's librarians that Fred Melcher was spreading his energy in numberless directions all the time; and it is a measure of the size of the man that to us he was the person fervently concerned with fine achievement in children's books. We took it with easy assurance that the Newbery and Caldecott medals were his primary concern, just as they were his invention. Not one of us who worked with him in the annual exercise ever doubted that we had his undivided interest. And indeed we know from his own accounts that the awards he established in our domain had a warm and wonderful place in

* Irene Smith Green, "The Newbery-Caldecott Medals: Legacy to Children's Literature," *Top of the News*, 20 (March, 1964), 191-95. Reprinted by permission of the American Library Association, and the author.

his busy life. There was plenty of room left for a thousand other enthusiasms, but they did not seem to dim his feeling for our enterprise, or deprive us of our special claim to his attention.

The alliance began at Swampscott, Massachusetts, in 1921. This was the first ALA Conference that Mr. Melcher, three years co-editor of *Publishers' Weekly,* attended. He had been occupied with finding ways to encourage a liaison between publishers, booksellers and librarians. As secretary of the American Book-sellers' Association during his first year in New York, it had fallen to him to organize a nationwide observance of Children's Book Week. His concern about children's books stemmed from his own avid reading as a boy, and his bookselling experience at Lauriat's in Boston as a young man. Now his keenly practical perspective sensed the opening of new vistas. He had commenced in 1920 to devote special issues of *Publishers' Weekly* to children's books, and had complimented Macmillan and Doubleday for appointing gifted editors, ready to specialize in the interests of young read-ers. The awards that followed were but further evidence of Fred-eric Melcher's imaginative support of current writing for children.

Alice I. Hazeltine of the St. Louis Public Library, chairman of the Children's Librarians' Secton in 1921, presided at her group's first meeting on June 21, at the New Ocean House in Swampscott. The hotel lacked a large auditorium, so its freshly completed garage was used by the Section. Frederic Melcher, Clara Whitehill Hunt, and Bertha Mahony were on the morning program, to discuss "Children's Book Week—a National Movement," from the respective viewpoints of the National Association of Book Publishers, the children's librarians, and, finally, booksellers.

THE IDEA IS BORN

"It was a great opportunity for Book Week's promotion," Mr. Melcher reflected more than thirty years later. He observed that children's librarians were inclined toward the movement, which fitted into their own framework, but were still somewhat sus-picious of its commercial taint. "As I looked down from the platform at three or four hundred people, I thought of the power they would have in encouraging the joy of reading among chil-dren. I wanted to go further [than Children's Book Week] and secure their interest in the whole process of creating books for children, producing them, and bringing them to the children."

Between the morning and afternoon sessions that same day, the idea of an award, as a means of involving children's librarians in the whole general scheme, occurred to Fred Melcher. Miss Hazeltine gave him time to speak again, and he offered them the Newbery medal, to encourage more worthwhile books for young people, by writers of recognizable talent. Mr. Melcher had just finished reading *Shadows of Old Booksellers* by Charles Knight, and had been stirred by the activities of one John Newbery, the first bookseller who understood what was essential in making books for children. For such an award, Mr. Melcher saw these children's librarians as the proper jury, because their own work brought together every kind of reader and all age levels, on equal footing. The audience responded enthusiastically to his proposition, and voted to put it into effect the following year.

Thus began an enduring partnership between the donor of the Newbery medal and children's librarians, who were charged with responsibility for its function. Forty-two years did not alter the affection between these partners. Succeeding decades of chairmen found the same heartiness in Fred Melcher that warmed his first audience at Swampscott. He imbued every award with his own belief that a constancy of high standards mattered, year in and year out.

Clara Whitehill Hunt, who was in charge of work with children in the Brooklyn Public Library, was the Section's incoming chairman in 1921, and to her fell the organization of a process for selecting the honor book of the year. She and her fellow officers were earnest in purpose, and their foresight helped establish the medal in a position of prestige. Mr. Melcher wrote Miss Hunt in December, when bylaws were being drafted to guide the new undertaking, "I think you will permit me to write my name a little smaller into the plan and to let it stand more specifically as an ALA function. I made the suggestion as a member of the American Library Association, interested that the full potential value of its professional standards should be available in every possible way... I have been talking with a sculptor...."

The sculptor selected by Mr. Melcher to design the medal was René Paul Chambellan, already prominent for his work on several buildings in New York. He engraved a central figure and two children on the medal's face, representing creative talent giving its best to children. The donor put in writing for the records of the Section (which later, of course, became the Children's Library Association and then the Children's Services Division) his agreement to have the Newbery medal struck off in bronze each year, with the understanding that full responsibility was always to be in the hands of the American Library Association.

At once, the awarding of this medal became a Conference highlight. Some early wrinkles were soon smoothed away, as methods of voting, eligibility of authors, and responsibility of librarians were clarified in a series of thoughtful rulings. School librarians were permanently included in the award committee, beginning in 1937.

Reading back through the files of letters that were in Fred Melcher's office, one wonders how he could possibly have found time to write so many sympathetic, judicious answers to the worried chairmen in those early years. He rendered the decision when a point of law was questioned, and as the time of the annual meeting drew near, accepted his share of the hosts' duties, so that the author about to be honored would remember a glowing occasion.

The increased fame and influence of the Newbery medal kindled ideas of a companion award for picture books in Frederic Melcher's mind. He observed that works for older children usually won the Newbery medal, and felt that similar attention was owed young readers, and certainly the artists who were giving them books with excellent pictures. Incoming Section officers and committee members in 1937 adopted the proposal with unanimous consent, and the membership voted enthusiastically for the new award, named by its donor for the artist Randolph Caldecott.

"I gave the sculptor, René Chambellan, a collection of Caldecott's books, not specifying that a Caldecott design should be used, but wishing him to understand the spirit of Caldecott and the reasons for his continuing value. Mr. Chambellan became so delighted with Caldecott's draftsmanship that he immediately said he could do nothing better than put a few typical scenes on the medal, and this he had done."

The beauty of the Caldecott medal delighted everyone. John Gilpin's ride, and the king's pie with four-and-twenty blackbirds, paid eloquent tribute to the artist who, with Walter Crane and Kate Greenaway, brought in the new age of the picture book.

With two awards to create drama during ALA Conference week, the annual ceremony and banquet drew immense throngs. Fred Melcher enjoyed every bit of the excitement, year after year, and his place on the platform became the great tradition of Section occasions. His feature role of toastmaster at the banquets gave continuity to their gala atmosphere. His stories and improvisations, wit, sentiment, and enthusiasm bound our membership in hundreds of recollections. By popular demand in later years he read the poem always to be associated with Frederic Melcher: "The King's Breakfast," by A. A. Milne. Behind the scenes he was always consulted on technical difficulties concerning the awards, but he remained completely ignorant of the voting until it was finished. Perhaps he bestowed medals on books for which he felt little personal admiration, but of this he gave no sign.

ANNOUNCEMENT DATE CHANGED

After 1949 a procedural change brought announcement of the winners early in March, soon after voting was finished. It had become nearly impossible to guard their secret until the summer Conference, which supposedly awaited the announcement in great suspense. Thereafter, Mr. Melcher was host to a small gathering in his office, who saw the medals presented to their winners —temporarily—then taken back into custody until the official ceremony at the ALA Conference. On these March afternoons the donor was in his element, recalling anecdotes and personalities of earlier years connected with the lengthening history of the medals. Facing his desk from one of his bookshelves stood the plaque presented by children's librarians in 1950, thanking him "for his distinguished contribution to the advancement and encouragement of outstanding literature and art in children's books."

It was on such a March occasion in 1963 that we were met at the door by his secretary and told of his death, the day before. No one present will ever forget the great dignity of Daniel Melcher that day, taking charge of the program in his father's place.

The vitality and humor of the medals' donor, which were at their best in the great auditoriums on Award Day, will remain historic. But Frederic Melcher was more than a beloved personality, and more than a generous benefactor. Behind these qualities was the solid, sober conception of value in the awards that will keep us most in his debt. He knew that their existence had raised children's books to a place beside other literature in the public mind; that they had led librarians to give more careful study to the new books; and that they had enlisted those working with children in a most particular responsibility.

SALUTE TO CHILDREN'S LITERATURE AND ITS CREATORS: 21ST BIRTHDAY FOR CARNEGIE MEDAL *

Marcus Crouch

In November, 1957, British librarians met under their President, Dr. J. Bronowski, and in the company of the Parliamentary Secretary for Education, the President of the Publishers' Association, and other notables, to honor the winners of the Carnegie Medal. The occasion would not have caused comment in countries where grand gestures come naturally. The British, however, and, in particular, British librarians, take their pleasures sadly and make a virtue of understatement. The Carnegie luncheon was, in consequence, an event of major importance, an unprecedented salute to children's literature and its creators.

The excuse for this professional junketing was the 21st birthday of the Carnegie Medal. Instituted to commemorate the centenary of Andrew Carnegie's birth, it has remained the only official recognition of good standards in British books for children. The award is made by the Library Association, on the advice of a subcommittee, which considers recommendations of librarians from all parts of the United Kingdom. The medal is presented at the opening session of the annual conference of the Library Association, held in September. It is the occasion of some modest celebrations, although the association, with characteristic

* Marcus Crouch, "Salute to Children's Literature and Its Creators: 21st Birthday for Carnegie Medal," *Top of the News*, 14 (May, 1958), 7–10. Reprinted by permission of the Children's Services Division of the American Library Association, and the author.

distaste of publicity, seldom achieves a notice of the award in the national press.

The Carnegie Medal is comparable in intention with the Newbery, but falls far short of it in impact on authors, publishers, and the world at large. This is a pity, for the association has been remarkably successful in the consistent application of exacting standards, and the list of medal winners incorporates much of the best in British publishing since 1936. Only rarely has the medal gone to a book of meretricious quality, or to one of merely topical interest, although it is clear that the judges have sometimes been puzzled to distinguish between literary quality and originality (or apparent originality) of treatment or subject. In 19 books (for in 2 of the lean years of the war no book came up to standard), it is difficult to fault the selectors more than 4 times, a fair achievement when one remembers how often the personnel of the selecting committee has changed and that their choice has to be made before time has shown the vast output of British publications in perspective. It would perhaps have been better on occasion if the selectors had steeled their hearts and withheld the award. Sometimes, too, they must have longed to strike additional medals in recognition of an *annus mirabilis*.

The English genius in writing for children was first manifested, and still reveals itself, in fantasy. The selectors, perhaps understandably, have fought shy of the more delicate and intangible examples of this elusive art, and the undeniable quality of such stories as *The Children of Green Knowe* and *The River Boy* has gone unrecognized. BB's more robust *Little Grey Men,* however, won a deserved medal in 1942 (but was this really a fantasy or rather an essay in the observation of nature?). Linklater's *Wind on the Moon* was in the English tradition, with its high spirits, its rational nonsense, and its sudden turn from the absurd to the deeply serious. *The Little White Horse* belonged to an earlier tradition than that of Carroll; it harked back to the Victorian (and earlier) moral tales. Elizabeth Goudge dressed her sentiments in delightful language, and her own delight in the grotesque and picturesque characters and the lovely Devon country in which they played their parts was highly infectious.

In *The Borrowers,* the Carnegie Medal recognized that rarest of all books, one which is firmly in its tradition and at the same time highly original in theme and treatment. The minute world of the Borrowers was conceived in exquisite detail and worked out in terms of dispassionate naturalism. Of all the winners of the Carnegie Medal, it is the one book of unquestioned, timeless genius.

The latest award went to C. S. Lewis for the last of the annals of Narnia, *The Last Battle*. In idea this owed something to Dr. Lewis's colleague J. R. R. Tolkien, whose *Hobbit* the selectors unaccountably missed in 1937. It harked back, too, to E. Nesbit and George Macdonald; but in execution, in splendor of vision, in humor, and in occasional triteness of expression, it was highly characteristic of its author.

The naturalistic tradition, which had its abortive beginnings in *Bevis,* came to fine flower in Arthur Ransome, and it was appropriate that the first Carnegie Medal should be awarded to that fine writer, adventurer, and sportsman. Ransome's integrity, his intense interest in practical things, and his respect for children are all illustrated in *Pigeon Post,* which in 1936 set the standard for all subsequent awards of the medal. *The Family from One End Street* in 1937 showed a different aspect of naturalism. It was one of the few books for children written successfully with a purpose. It was, and remains, unique in drawing an attractive and convincing picture of British working-class life, for, although the social conditions which moved Eve Garnett as a young art student to write this protest have largely disappeared, the Ruggles are, fortunately, always with us and may be met today in Miss Garnett's little Sussex town. Noel Streatfeild, Richard Armstrong, and Elfrida Vipont, in very different ways, showed children facing up to the difficult problems of growing up and the demands of an adult world. The Carnegie Medal was a recognition of their integrity. Elfrida Vipont, in *The Lark on the Wing* tackled an even more difficult problem, that of introducing spiritual values into a story without mawkishness or a trace of humbug. Two wartime winners of the medal, Kitty Barne and Mary Treadgold, treated topical events, one with humor, the other in terms of the adventure story.

Since the war there has been a notable revival of the historical novel for children, and two books which won the medal illustrate well the two principal schools. Cynthia Harnett's *The Woolpack* is social and economic history in novel form, an absorbing and scholarly study of life in the Cotswolds at the end of the Middle Ages. Miss Harnett writes quietly, without emphasis. Her effects are gained through a multitude of small details. Ronald Welch is a more dynamic, extrovert writer. *Knight Crusader* is political and military history; a work of scholarship, too, but easily acceptable to children because of its delight in strong colors and violent actions.

The Carnegie Medal has commonly been awarded for a work of the imagination; reasonably so, for a book of outstanding merit can only be recognized by comparison with its peers, and imaginative and informative works are in their natures not comparable. The three nonfictional books which received the medal were all, in a broad sense, historical, and were distinguished by the imaginative treatment of factual material. Eleanor Doorly's sensitive life of Madame Curie, Agnes Allen's study of domestic life and architecture, and, above all, Edward Osmond's recreation of the history of an imaginary valley in word, line, and color, are all essays in the imaginative reconstruction of the past.

I have left the best until last. Two writers of the past forty years have been outstanding in the richness, warmth, and eloquence of their writing. They go together naturally, for they were great friends, both poets, both lovers—without sentimentality—of children, and respectors of the worth and integrity of childhood. The Carnegie Medal was awarded to Walter De La Mare for his book of *Collected Stories,* which incorporated a lifetime of writing. In 1955 Eleanor Farjeon delighted her innumerable friends with *The Little Bookroom,* another collection of tales, matchless in their ripeness, gaiety, poetry, and wisdom. No award of the medal since its inception gave more universal delight.

The land of Carroll and Kenneth Grahame is also that of Caldecott, Greenaway, Beatrix Potter, and Leslie Brooke, and for a long time, the need for an award to honor high quality in illustration was obvious. A new medal was instituted in 1955, the Kate Greenaway Medal, and this was awarded for the first time in the following year. The winner was Edward Ardizzone, most individual and delightful of illustrators, who twenty years earlier had given new life to the English picture book with *Little Tim and the Brave Sea Captain. Tim All Alone* was characteristic of his best work, with its vitality, its fine and restrained use of color, and its masterly prose, which is exactly complemented by the drawings.

The Carnegie Medal has now come of age. On the whole, and remembering the difficulties in the way of making a wise selection so close in time to the subject, the work of the selecting committee has been well done. What has been less than good has been the follow-up. Few members of the British reading public, few children, few booksellers or even publishers, few (dare I say it?) librarians know much about the medal and what its purpose is. There is no publicity for the award in newspapers or on the radio. Not all the publishers bother to mark the prize-winning books in any way. This is a measure of failure, if the medal is intended to set standards and to be recognized as a criterion of excellence.

The medal has had some effect (it is perhaps more than coincidence that the history of the Carnegie Medal is also the history of "Junior Bookshelf," the best of British reviews of children's books, founded in 1936). The general standard of writing for children is much higher now than it was in 1936, and the quality of selection for public and school libraries is proportionately higher. At least six British publishers have a recognizable policy in the children's book department; of how many could this have been said in 1936? In these improvements, the medal has played some part. Its influence is, nevertheless, infinitely less effective than that of the Newbery; and this, I believe, is due to lack of confidence on the part of the Library Association and lack of enterprise on the part of publishers and booksellers.

CARNEGIE MEDAL WINNERS

1936	Ransome, Arthur	*Pigeon Post*
1937	Garnett, Eve	*The Family from One End Street*
1938	Streatfeild, Noel	*The Circus Is Coming*
1939	Doorly, Eleanor	*Radium Woman*
1940	Barne, Kitty	*Visitors from London*
1941	Treadgold, Mary	*We Couldn't Leave Dinah*
1942	BB (D. J. Watkins-Pitchford)	*The Little Grey Men*
1943	Prize Withheld	
1944	Linklater, Eric	*The Wind on the Moon*
1945	Prize Withheld	
1946	Goudge, Elizabeth	*The Little White Horse*
1947	De La Mare, Walter	*Collected Stories for Children*
1948	Armstrong, Richard	*Sea Change*
1949	Allen, Agnes	*The Story of Your Home*
1950	Vipont, Elfrida	*The Lark on the Wing*
1951	Harnett, Cynthia	*The Woolpack*
1952	Norton, Mary	*The Borrowers*

1953	Osmond, Edward	*A Valley Grows Up*
1954	Felton, Ronald	
	(Ronald Welch)	*Knight Crusader*
1955	Farjeon, Eleanor	*The Little Bookroom*
1956	Lewis, C. S.	*The Last Battle*
1957	Mayne, W.	*A Grass Rope*
1958	Pearce, Ann Phillipa	*Tom's Midnight Garden*
1959	Sutcliff, Rosemary	*The Lantern Bearers*
1960	Cornwall, Dr. I. W.	*The Making of Man*
1961	Boston, Lucy	*A Stranger at Green Knowe*
1962	Clarke, Pauline	*The Twelve and the Genii*
1963	Burton, Hester	*Time of Trial* [1]

[1] 1957–1963 Titles added by author by request.

A BRIEF HISTORY OF NATIONAL CHILDREN'S BOOK WEEK *

In a small library on a November afternoon in 1919, a stiff-lipped lady was busy with her scissors, shearing off the bottom third of Jessie Willcox Smith's poster for the first Children's Book Week. A poster showing books scattered in joyous abandon on the floor was more than she could bear to display.

Since that day, our attitude toward children and their enjoyment of reading has undergone a considerable change. Along with that transformation has come the development of National Children's Book Week which each year reminds adults of children's need for good books and their delight in discovering them.

In 1912, the first seed was sown for the creation of Book Week at the American Booksellers Association convention. E. W. Mumford, of the Penn Publishing Company, a man greatly interested in the possibilities of better books for children, delivered a paper entitled "Juvenile Readers as an Asset." This address, a strong indictment of the harm of trashy books for children, was sum-

* The Children's Book Council, Inc. "A Brief History of National Children's Book Week," (pamphlet). Reprinted by permission of The Children's Book Council, Inc.

marized in *The New York Times,* where it caught the attention of James West, Director of the Boy Scouts of America. Mr. West asked the recently appointed librarian of the Scouts, Franklin K. Mathiews, to consider the possibility of the Scout organization taking an initiative in giving new direction to boys' reading. This led to the appearance of Mr. Mathiews at the 1915 Booksellers Convention, where he delivered a fiery speech warning publishers and booksellers about their responsibilities. The idea of Children's Book Week was conceived, and agencies throughout the nation, who would be interested in such a proposal, were asked to support it. Although World War I delayed concrete developments, an increasing number of librarians, Scout leaders, and booksellers continued their efforts to encourage the publishing and enjoyment of fine books for children.

A book list, "Books Boys Like Best," was issued by the Scouts, but Frederic Melcher of the R. R. Bowker Company and members of the American Library Association saw no reason to exclude girls from the program; therefore, a general catalog called "The Bookshelf for Boys and Girls" was prepared under the supervision of Clara Whitehill Hunt of the Brooklyn Public Library.

In 1919, Mr. Melcher, who was Secretary of the Booksellers Association, asked librarians to be guests and speakers at the annual meeting. He also asked Mr. Mathiews to present his plan for a Children's Book Week, and at the end of the convention a resolution was passed, committing the Association to the organization of a Book Week in November. A few months later, the official approval of the American Library Association was also secured during its first Children's Librarians session.

Mr. Melcher formed the first Book Week Committee which included publishers, booksellers, librarians, and Scout leaders. This committee, as is still the case, met to select the first slogan ("More Books in the Home"), create the first poster, and prepare other forms of publicity for the celebration of Book Week.

In the second year of Book Week, the National Association of Book Publishers took over the promotion of the observance. When this organization went out of existence in 1934, the R. R. Bowker Company assumed the administrative responsibilities. As the years passed, more and more schools and libraries joined in the festivities. Eventually Bowker found it could no longer handle the volume of promotional detail, bookkeeping, and mailing involved.

Just as a need for good books for children inspired Children's Book Week, so the continual demand for the celebration itself was responsible for the formation of the Children's Book Council in 1945. Since then, the Council has served both as Book Week headquarters and as a year-round promotion and information center for children's books.

Each Book Week celebration involves more libraries, bookstores, schools, and parents than the one before and, therefore, more children. Librarians, educators, and publishers in other countries have been inspired by our Book Week to undertake similar events.

Librarians like the one who snipped the first poster have now faded into obscurity, but the need for Book Week continues. Mr. Melcher's vision of it is as true today as it was when he said, "Book Week brings us together to talk about books and reading and, out of our knowledge and love of books, to put the cause of children's reading squarely before the whole community and, community by community, across the whole nation. For a great nation is a reading nation, and in this broad country of ours books should be freely available for every boy and girl. Until they are freely available we have a great task."

BOOK WEEK SLOGANS AND POSTER ARTISTS

1919–23	More Books in the Home Jessie Willcox Smith
1924	More Books in the Home, Let's Read Together—Smith
1925–26	After All, There's Nothing Like a Good Book—Brubaker
1927–28	Books—Romance, History, Travel—Wyeth
1929	More Books in the Home—Gellert
1930	More Books in the Home—Smith
1931	Round the World Book Fair—The Petershams
1932	Young America's Book Parade—Cole
1933	Grow Up With Books: Add a Shelf a Year—Nichols
1934	Ride the Book Trail to Knowledge and Adventure—Paull
1935	Reading for Fun—Floethe
1936	Books to Grow On—The Modern World for Young Readers—Reibel
1937	Reading—The Magic Highway to Adventure—Fagg

1938	New Books, New Worlds—Binder
1939	Books Around the World—Fuller
1940	Good Books, Good Friends—The Petershams
1941	Forward with Books—Sewell
1942	Forward with Books—Haase
1943	Build the Future with Books—Jones
1944	United Through Books—Walker
1945	United Through Books—Howe
1946	Books are Bridges—The Petershams
1947	Books for the World of Tomorrow—d'Aulaire
1948	Books Tell the Story—de Angeli
1949	Make Friends with Books—Wolcott
1950	Make Friends with Books—duBois
1951	New Horizons with Books—Brown
1952	Reading is Fun—Duvoisin
1953	Reading is Fun—Balet
1954	Let's Read—Ward
1955	Let's Read More—Williams
1956	It's Always Book Time—Weisgard
1957	Explore with Books—Provensen
1958	Explore with Books—Rand
1959	Go Exploring in Books—Rojankovsky
1960	Hurray for Books—Sendak
1961	Hurray for Books—Burchard
1962	I like Books—Seredy
1963	Three Cheers for Books—Adams
1964	Swing into Books—Munari

Part Five

ILLUSTRATIONS AND CHILDREN'S BOOKS

ILLUSTRATING BOOKS
FOR CHILDREN *

Anne Carroll Moore

"What is the use of a book," thought Alice, "without
pictures or conversations?"

Lewis Carroll

The greatest artists are none too good to make drawings for children's books," wrote Rockwell Kent from Alaska in 1918. He
tells of reading from a book of King Arthur stories to his nine-
year-old son. "I don't think the pictures in the book are half
nice enough," said Rockwell. "I think of a wonderful picture
when you read the story, and when I see the one in the book I'm
disappointed."

No wonder the boy who watched the making of the drawings
for *Wilderness* was disappointed by a conventionalized illustration for a King Arthur story. The names of the artists are not
given in the list of books mentioned in Rockwell Kent's delightful journal of a winter spent in the wilds of Alaska, but I am
quite ready to believe there wasn't a breath of life in the King
Arthur pictures and that the illustrations for Andersen's *Fairy
Tales* were also a disappointment.

Every time I've opened *Wilderness* I have been tempted to slip
in a short list of books whose illustrations live in the memory
and which I think would light up a cabin in Alaska or elsewhere
for a boy like young Rockwell Kent. Since his father clearly
states that imagination and romance in pictures and stories are
what a child wants above everything else and that those qualities
in illustration are the rarest, he may like to be reminded of a
few books whose pictures possess them to a degree which sets
them apart from all others.

Without any hesitation at all, I should make room for the
Ruskin Grimm—*German Popular Stories* is the title under which
the first selection and translation of Grimm's *Fairy Tales* into
the English language was reprinted, at Ruskin's request, in 1868.

* Anne Carroll Moore, "Illustrating Books for Children," *My Roads to
Childhood*, The Horn Book, Inc., 1961, pp. 127–34. Reprinted by permission
of The Horn Book, Inc.

The book was edited by Edgar Taylor, who made the original translation just a hundred years ago in 1823. Of the original etchings by George Cruikshank, Ruskin says they were unrivaled in masterfulness of touch since Rembrandt, which to Gleeson White, after days spent in hunting up children's books of the period, they appeared as masterpieces of design, justifying for the first time the great popularity of Cruikshank and giving almost the first glimpse of the modern ideal in illustration.

In its present form the book is not attractive to children without introduction, but I have never known a child who did not respond to the inimitable drawing for the *Elves and the Shoemaker* and, once discovered, turn back to it again and again. Of the versions of Grimm this is the most satisfactory to read aloud. Ruskin's introduction in defense of children's rights to their inheritance of fairy tales as the remnant of a tradition possessing historical value is even more needed today than at the time it was written, for on both sides of the water there has been far too much careless editing and rewriting of old fairy and folk tales to accompany new illustrations.

And after I had put the Ruskin Grimm on the Alaska bookshelf, I would place beside it the *Nonsense Books* of that prince of travelers and painter of mountains, Edward Lear. The first of these books appeared in 1846, the fourth and last in 1877. Thackeray's Christmas pantomime, the *Rose and the Ring*, with his own matchless drawings, published in 1850 would come next and then Tenniel's *Alice* in the order of chronological sequence. The first volume appeared in 1865, the second in 1871.

To share the approach to any one of these books through the pictures and the artist's personality as revealed by his contemporaries is a delightful experience. If the text has seemed silly or has bored anybody, M. H. Spielmann's *History of Punch* and the bound volumes of the magazine itself will send that person to look at the pictures in *Alice* and *Through the Looking Glass* with a new sense of wonder and admiration for the artist who took so much out of his own head. It is thrilling to boys and girls to know that Sir John Tenniel never forgot anything he had ever seen, and that he could reproduce it to the life. "I have a wonderful memory of observation," he says, "not for dates but anything I see I remember." When Lewis Carroll wanted him to use models for the illustrations of *Alice* he flatly refused and declared he needed none, any more than the author—a mathematician—"needed a multiplication table to work a mathematical problem." It has been said of Tenniel that his pictorial memory surpassed his imagination, but to *Alice* he brought both. "It is a curious fact," he wrote some years later to Lewis Carroll, when asked to illustrate another of his books, "that with *Through the Looking Glass* the faculty of making drawings for book illustrations departed from me, and notwithstanding all sorts of tempting inducements, I have done nothing in that direction since."

I know of only one other artist who so perfectly realizes the conception of the author while communicating his own essential spirit. In his introduction to the new edition of *Uncle Remus: His Songs and His Sayings,* published in 1895, Joel Chandler Harris wrote of A. B. Frost's illustrations: "You have breathed the breath of life into these amiable brethren of wood and field. By a stroke here and a touch there you have conveyed into their quaint antics the illumination of your own inimitable humor which is as true to our sun and soil as it is to the spirit and essence of the matter set forth."

Gleeson White had said of Frost in *Children's Books and Their Illustrators:* "By his cosmopolitan fun he has probably aroused more hearty laughs by his inimitable books than even Caldecott himself."

The pity is that Frost has done no series of picture books corresponding to the Caldecott picture books of which *John Gilpin,* published in 1878, was the first, and *The Great Panjandrum,* appearing in 1885, the last. The proposal to illustrate these books to be printed in colors was made to Caldecott by Edmund Evans, who had begun printing the Walter Crane toy books more than ten years before. It is interesting to learn from Walter Crane's *Reminiscences* that while Caldecott arranged for the drawings of his toy books on a royalty basis, Walter Crane was never able to make a similar business arrangement for himself. Whether Caldecott's motto, "the fewer the lines the less error committed," had anything to do with it is difficult to affirm, but we like to think it may have. There are far too many lines drawn which mean nothing in books designed for children.

Caldecott's love for animals and knowledge of them, his interest in everything connected with farming, markets, and country life in general, his lively humor and sense of beauty make of each of his picture books a pictorial record of England, looking from the nineteenth century back to the eighteenth.

Randolph Caldecott is bound to America by many ties and by none more securely than those fastened upon him by the children of the public libraries. His illustrations for Washington Irving's *Old Christmas* brought the book to life, and it is amusing to find that these illustrations were considered "inartistic, flippant, vulgar, and unworthy of the author" by one of the leading publishers of London when the drawings were submitted. *Old Christmas* was published in 1876.

Caldecott met Mrs. Ewing while the story of *Jackanapes* was simmering in her brain, and at her request made a colored sketch of a fair-haired boy on a red-haired pony. At this time he designed a cover for *Aunt Judy's Magazine* and arranged to illustrate other stories of Mrs. Ewing, who had unbounded admiration for his work. After years of ill health, Randolph Caldecott died in St. Augustine, Florida, in 1885.

Kate Greenaway gives two or three charming glimpses of her friendship for Caldecott in the letters included in her Life and her correspondence with Ruskin, edited with rare interpretation of the artist and the child in *Kate Greenaway* by M. H. Spielmann and G. S. Layard. I do not suggest this book to take to Alaska, although I could be quite happy in rereading both text and drawings any time, anywhere.

It is next to being in England in springtime to look at these drawings of old cottages and farmhouses set in fields or gardens where flowers bloom more naturally than in any book I know and children dance and play with a grace and gravity and charm that Kate Greenaway alone knew how to give. *Marigold Garden, The Pied Piper* (of which 150,000 copies were sold), *A Day in a Child's Life,* will be looked at with new eyes after reading what the critics of her own and other nations, notably the French, have said in praise of her art and her love of childhood for its own sake. The publication of *Under the Window* in 1878 gave Kate Greenaway a place of her own in the world and doubtless was a determining influence in Boutet de Monvel's decision to make picture books of and for the children of France, for it was in that very year that he made the drawings for a French edition of *St. Nicholas* by which he became known as an illustrator. Delagrave, who asked Boutet de Monvel to make the illustrations for a child's history of France, published this French *St. Nicholas.* Between 1883 and 1897 Boutet de Monvel, a portrait and genre painter, was painting the children of France, creating and naming characters so true to life that no one who has met them in his books will fail to recognize them in the Luxembourg Gardens or on their way to a village school in the Aisne. Many of Boutet de Monvel's pictures are true portraits of his own children, or of his brothers and sisters as he remembered them. *Nos Enfants, Filles et Garcons, La Civilite, Vieilles Chansons,* and *Chansons de France* all record children playing, singing, and dancing under French skies.

Jeanne d'Arc was published in 1897 and became deservedly popular among American children as soon as it was given a place in the children's room of a public library as well as in its art department. I would take a copy to Alaska by all means, and preferably in the French language, to fix the authenticity of the book in the boy's mind and stimulate a spontaneous desire to read the simple text which accompanies the pictures. It is now possible to include two or three of Beatrix Potter's little books which are as true to nature and art in the French language as in their native English.

Pierre Lapin or *Jeannot Lapin,* accompanied by Beatrix Potter's Christmas story, *The Tailor of Gloucester,* in English, would make a child or grown-up feel at home anywhere.

Two books I should want to take to Alaska for their remarkable pictorial impressions of the North and the folk interest are: Snorre Sturlason's *Kongesagaer,* which is illustrated by six of the leading artists of Norway, and *Norske Folkeeventyr* illustrated by Erik Werenskiold. The illustrations in both books are unique in their power to reincarnate the old sagas and invest the life of both animals and people of the North with the racial inheritance which belongs to them. Since neither of these books is readily obtainable for a journey I would make a point of asking a boy to go see them wherever they could be found. Asking boys to look at certain special books in libraries or bookshops is a most interesting thing to do. If I could find a volume of *St. Nicholas* between the date of its first publication, 1873, and 1883, I would certainly add it to the Alaskan collection, for among the pictures the drawings of the best artists of the day would be reprinted. Mary Mapes Dodge did not hesitate to ask anyone, writer or artist, to do his best work for children. The reason why so many of the pictures in *St. Nicholas* are remembered is for the simple reason that the drawings were good and the subjects interesting. Howard Pyle was a contributor to *St. Nicholas* years before his illustrations for *Robin Hood, Pepper and Salt,* and *The Wonder Clock* gave him his own place among American illustrators of

children's books. Palmer Cox, whose "Brownie Books" are still
the favorite picture books in American libraries after more than
forty years, made his first drawings for *St. Nicholas.*

The good art of this American magazine stands out in constructive testimony of what could be done in a period when
aesthetic movements of one sort or another were playing, as they
are still, with all sorts of things which had no bearing on the
illustration of books for children.

Young Rockwell Kent came back from Alaska at the end of
six months, but that bookshelf still intrigues my imagination,
and I should like to add to it two books of Lovat Fraser, *Nursery Rhymes* and *Pirates,* both of which have been received with
enthusiasm by big boys and little ones in the children's rooms of
the libraries in the holidays of 1922. "Nursery lore remains with
us, whether we would or not, for all our lives," he says in his
introduction to *Pirates,* published in 1913; "and generations of
ourselves, as schoolboys and preschool boys, have tricked out
Piracy in so resplendent a dress that she has fairly ousted on
our affections, not only her sister profession of 'High Toby and
the Road,' but every other splendid and villainous vocation."

The untimely death of Lovat Fraser in 1921 is as great a loss
to children's books as to the dramatic world, which he enriched
by his *Beggar's Opera.*

To place the *Velveteen Rabbit* at the end of a bookshelf which
spans a century of illustration of children's books may seem a
strange thing to do to those who have not seen William Nicholson's pictures for it, and who are unacquainted with the artist's
remarkable character portraits which appeared about twenty-five
years ago.

Mr. Nicholson has always been thought of as the painter of
what he sees. His character portrait of Queen Victoria with
her dog done from life anticipated Lytton Strachey's book by
many years and surpasses it for those pictorially minded. He has
painted some remarkable portraits of children.

Why should he be interested in bringing a velveteen rabbit—
a child's nursery toy—to life? I wanted to know so I went to
Appletree Yard to ask him. The story touched him, he said, and
he had taken it away with him on a holiday at the request of
Sydney Pawling, who had fallen in love with the story, believed
it a classic for children, and wanted to give it the best form he
could devise.

Mr. Nicholson had worked from models to some extent—I

found the velveteen rabbit on the chimney piece in the studio; the old skin horse had been in the family for many years—but it is his imaginative understanding of the past—the reality of children and their interests in his own life which enabled him to give personality to a velveteen rabbit in a nursery and place him in the open fields and woods with his wild brothers with a certainty of record that admits of no challenge by child or grown-up.

The children say of the pictures, "You can almost see the Velveteen Rabbit changing."

THE SHAPE OF MUSIC*

Maurice Sendak

Vivify, quicken, and *vitalize*—of these three synonyms, *quicken,* I think, best suggests the genuine spirit of animation, the breathing to life, the surging swing into action, that I consider an essential quality in pictures for children's books. *To quicken* means, for the illustrator, the task first of deeply comprehending the nature of his text and then of giving life to that comprehension in his own medium, the picture.

The conventional techniques of graphic animation are related to this intention only in that they provide an instrument with which the artist can begin his work. Sequential scenes that tell a story in pictures, as in the comic strip, are an example of one technique of animation. In terms of technique, it is no difficult matter for an artist to simulate action, but it is something else to *quicken,* to create an inner life that draws breath from the artist's deepest perception.

The word *quicken* has other, more subjective associations for me. It suggests something musical, something rhythmic and impulsive. It suggests a beat—a heartbeat, a musical beat, the beginning of a dance. This association proclaims music as one source from which my own pictures take life. To conceive musi-

* Maurice Sendak, "The Shape of Music," *New York Herald Tribune,* Book Week Fall Children's Issue, November 1, 1964, pp. 1, 4–5. Reprinted by permission of the New York Herald Tribune and the author.

cally for me means to quicken the life of the illustrated book. All of my pictures are created against a background of music. More often than not, my instinctive choice of composer or musical form for the day has the galvanizing effect of making me conscious of my direction. I find something uncanny in the way a musical phrase, a sensuous vocal line, or a patch of Wagnerian color will clarify an entire approach or style for a new work. A favorite occupation of mine is sitting in front of the record player as though possessed by a *dybbuk,* and allowing the music to provoke an automatic, stream-of-consciousness kind of drawing. Sometimes the pictures that result are merely choreographed episodes, imagined figures dancing imagined ballets. More interesting to me, and much more useful for my work, are the childhood fantasies that are reactivated by the music and explored uninhibitedly by the pen.

Music's peculiar power of releasing fantasy has always fascinated me. An inseparable part of my memories of childhood, music was the inevitable, animating accompaniment to the make-believe. No childhood fantasy of mine was complete without the restless, ceaseless sound of impromptu humming, the din of unconscious music-making that conjured up just the right fantastical atmosphere. All children seem to know what the mysterious, the-riding-fiercely-across-the-plains (accompanied by hearty, staccato thigh slaps), and the plaintive conventionally sound like; and I have no doubt that this kind of musical contribution is necessary to the enrichment of the going fantasy. The spontaneous breaking into song and dance seems so natural and instinctive a part of childhood. It is perhaps the medium through which children best express the inexpressible; fantasy and feeling lie deeper than words—beyond the words yet available to a child—and both demand a more profound, more biological expression, the primitive expression of music. Recently I watched a mother tell her little boy a familiar, ritualistic story while he embellished the tale with an original hummed score. He kept up a swinging motion "in time" to the story, then punctuated the end with a series of sharp, imitation bugle sounds, and a wild jungle jump.

My intention is not to prove music the sole enlivening force behind the creation of pictures for children. But music is the impulse that most stimulates my own work and is the quality I eagerly look for in the work of the picture-book artists I admire, those artists who, in my opinion, achieve the authentic liveliness that is the essence of the picture book, a movement that is never still, and that children, I am convinced, comprehend and enjoy as something familiar to themselves.

M. Boutet de Monvel's illustrations for La Fontaine (*Fables Choisies pour les Enfants*) beautifully exemplify this quality of authentic liveliness. His subtle and exquisitely animated pictures have, to an astonishing degree, an inner life of their own. Every aspect of individual character seems to have been explored, and the result is complete truthfulness of gesture and a synthesis of movement that is a triumph of genuine animation. The continuous flow of movement across each page is comparable to a sustained and subtly shaded melodic line.

The lamb in Monvel's delicate rendering of *Le Loup et L'agneau* performs, before meeting an unjust fate, a sequence of linear arabesques, a superb dance of death that painfully conveys and dramatically enlarges the fable's grim meaning. The eye follows from picture to picture the swift development of the story—the fatalistic "folding up," the quiet inevitability of the lamb's movements, ending in a dying-swan gesture of hopeless resignation. And then the limp, no longer living form hanging from the raging wolf's mouth. One can scarcely fail to be moved by the terrible poignancy of Monvel's interpretation. I think of these fine, softly colored, and economically conceived drawings as a musical accompaniment to the La Fontaine fable, harmonic inventions that color and give fresh meaning in much the same way that a Hugo Wolf setting illuminates a Goethe poem.

Relating genuine animation to musical expression might appear too personal an identification for it to have any validity in the analysis of another artist's work. It is, of course, impossible to know whether Monvel related his own work to music, but it is difficult for me not to think so. Certainly in the case of Randolph Caldecott it is impossible to imagine his not being conscious, at least to some extent, of his musical sympathies. His pictures abound in musical imagery; his characters are forever dancing and singing and playing instruments. More to the point is his refinement of a graphic counterpart to the musical form of theme and variations, his delightful compounding of a simple visual theme into a fantastically various interplay of images.

Caldecott's pictures for *The Queen of Hearts* are an instance of his extraordinary development of this lively form. He takes off sedately enough by illustrating his theme ("The Queen of Hearts, she made some tarts") simply and straightforwardly. Then begin the purely Caldecottian inventions, the variations that enrich and build up the nursery rhyme into an uproar of elaborate and comical complications. He accomplishes this not with flowing, sequential drawings across each page, but with tremendously animated scenes that rush from page to page. The crescendo reached at the line "And beat the Knave full sore" is worth describing for its delightful musical content: in the background Caldecott pictures the Knave being soundly beaten by the King to the rhythm of a minuet danced gracefully in the foreground by a lady and gentleman of the court. Another Caldecott book, *The Three Jovial Huntsmen,* is a veritable song-and-dance fest with its syncopated back-and-forthing between words and pictures. It has a galloping rhythmic beat that suggests a full musical score.

The sympathy I feel between the visual and the musical accounts for my liking to think of myself as setting a text to pictures, much as a composer sets a poem to music, and I have found that telling a story by means of related, sequential pictures allows me to "compose" with assurance and freedom. I do not, however, equate the musical approach to sequential drawings. George Cruikshank's pictures for the first English Grimm definitely qualify as self-contained, full-page illustrations—the very opposite of the animated sequence and, as far as I am concerned, the most difficult of forms to bring alive. But there is nothing inanimate about the Cruikshank pictures. They have a restlessness and noisiness that are true qualities of childhood and the life's blood of the Grimm tales.

In our own day, Andre Francois is expert at achieving liveliness within the full-page picture; his subtle arrangements of shape and size on the page make for an original and zany sense of animation. His illustrations for John Symonds' *Tom and Tabby* have a massive grandeur that yet contains an infinity of lively detail. These pictures—so typically Francois in their singular interpretation—are painted in modulated tones of sepia, and to my musically oriented eye, they have the rich sonority of organ music.

Tomi Ungerer, in his illustrations for *Flat Stanley* by Jeff Brown, cleverly avoids the inert full-page picture. He solves the problem through a sequence of movement, not within each individual page, but from page to page. Imaginative manipulation of space and deft use of color give the happy effect of pictures fairly dancing through the book.

In considering the little colored-picture books William Blake intended for children, I can touch only superficially on aspects of these masterpieces, which are set apart by Blake's incomparable genius. How beautifully his *Songs of Innocence and of Experience* could be set to music, and how beautifully Blake did set them. The intensely personal images seem the very embodiment of his mystical poetry. His ingenious and wonderfully ornamental interweavings of illustrations, lettering, and color visually animate the spirit of the poetry and create a lyrical vision of otherworldliness. And it is all expressed with an economy only the masters achieved.

The musical analogy and its relevance to my own work is nowhere more apparent than in my illustrations for the picture books of Ruth Krauss. Her lovely and original poetry has a flexibility that allowed me the maximum space to execute my fantasy variations on a Kraussian theme, and perhaps the last page from *I'll Be You and You Be Me* is the simplest expression of my devotion to the matter of music.

CHILDREN'S PREFERENCES FOR COLOR VERSUS OTHER QUALITIES IN ILLUSTRATIONS *

Mabel Rudisill

Professional educators and laymen alike place a high valuation on color in pictures for children regardless of the other characteristics of the pictures. Since illustrations are assuming a large proportion of space in children's books and since color is an important factor determining the cost of illustrations, it is im-

* "Children's Preferences for Color Versus Other Qualities in Illustrations," by Mabel Rudisill. *Elementary School Journal* 52 (April, 1952), 444–51. Reprinted by permission of The University of Chicago Press. Copyright April, 1952.

portant to investigate the validity of this opinion. The results of the investigation here reported give some indication of the importance which children themselves place on color and on other qualities which give illustrations an appearance of realism (lifelikeness) or the reverse.

THE PROCEDURE

Materials Used in the Study.—Five types of illustrations which occur in books written for children were selected for experimental testing. They were chosen to represent differences among illustrations in amount of color, and in degree of realism (or lifelikeness) in the form and in the color. They were:

1. The uncolored photograph
2. The colored photograph
3. The colored drawing, realistic in form and in color
4. The outline drawing, realistic in form but outlined in color without regard for realistic effect
5. The colored drawing, conventionalized in form, decorative but unrealistic in color

To insure that the type of illustration rather than its content should be the determining factor, the same subject was reproduced in the five art types. First, two copies of a large uncolored photograph (24 by 30 inches) were obtained, one of which was colored by an artist. These constituted Types 1 and 2—the uncolored and the colored photograph. The same artist made watercolor drawings, reproducing the exact size and content of the photograph in three different types of drawings: the realistic drawing (Type 3), the outline drawing (Type 4), and the conventionalized drawing (Type 5). The same colors—red, blue, yellow, green, and brown—were used in all the colored drawings of the subject.

Three different subjects were used, each being the picture of a child engaged in interesting activity with an animal or a toy. Since each was reproduced in the five different art types, fifteen different pictures were obtained.

The five types of pictures of the same subject were paired in their 10 possible combinations (1–2, 1–3, 1–4, 1–5, 2–3, 2–4, 2–5, 3–4, 3–5, 4–5). For the three subjects (labeled A, B, and C) there resulted a total of 30 different pairs which were arranged in three different series. While the two pictures of a pair were displayed, each child indicated the one he liked better. In order that a particular picture should not appear more than once during a day, each child voted on six different days, only five pairs of a series being presented on any one day. The order of presentation of the three series was rotated in different schools in order to balance any possible carry-over effect of initial choosing (or not choosing) of a given picture.

Each pair of pictures presented a choice between two representations of the same subject which differed in amount of color, in degree of realism in form or in color, or in both.

The Children Who Participated in the Study.—Choices between the pictures in the 30 pairs were obtained from (a) the children of the kindergarten and the first six grades of the Demonstration School of Western Kentucky State College and (b) the children of the first six grades in the public schools in Bowling Green, Kentucky. Four schools were involved, including 6 first grades, 6 second grades, 5 third grades, 6 fourth grades, 5 fifth grades, and 6 sixth grades. There were 27 kindergarten children and from 150 to 200 children in each of the six grades.

Each picture was displayed with a large number in the upper left corner. The children of the first six grades voted between the pictures of a pair by encircling on a ballot the number of the preferred picture. Since the pictures were large enough to be seen clearly from any distance in a classroom, all the children of a room, except kindergarten and the first grade, voted at the same time. No comments were allowed. First graders voted in groups of 10 or fewer. Each kindergarten child voted privately. He was asked to point to the picture of the pair which he liked better.

Adults Who Participated in the Study.—In order to obtain an estimate of the extent to which adult judgment of children's preferences would agree with the children's own choices, a vote was taken in a college assembly composed largely of students distributed among the four classes, some faculty members, and a few townspeople. Seven hundred twenty-five votes were obtained.

Only one series of pictures was used, Subject A, and the series did not include the colored photograph. Therefore, the combinations included Types 1–3, 1–4, 1–5, 3–4, 3–5, and 4–5. These adults marked on a ballot the number of the picture of each pair which they would choose for a child of six or seven years.

QUANTITATIVE RESULTS

Since the children voted on each combination three times—once for each subject used—the number of choices is approximately three times the number of children voting. The word "approximately" is used since absences caused some variation in the number voting at each of the six sessions. Per cents were calculated on the actual number of votes secured.

Table 1 summarizes the choices of the children in each grade for each type of illustration in each of the 10 combinations, the adult votes for certain types when choosing for a child of six or seven years, and the standard error of each majority.

The test of significance for a majority in the given direction was computed for all first grade per cents under 60 and all kindergarten per cents under 70. These are reported in the discussions where they apply.

A study of Table 1 reveals that all per cents higher than 60 in Grades I through VI are statistically reliable majorities, since no standard error exceeds 2.4 and three standard errors could not exceed 7.2. All kindergarten per cents above 70 are statistically reliable majorities, since no standard error exceeds 5.5 and three standard errors could not exceed 16.5.

Colored Vs. Uncolored Photographs.—There was one combination of types (three pairs) in which the pictures were identical except for color—the colored photograph (Type 1) versus the uncolored photograph (Type 2).[1] The preference was for the colored photograph. In the various grades, from 70 to 86 per cent of all the children voted for the colored photograph. All are statistically reliable majorities.

Realistic Vs. Conventionalized.—For the one combination of types (three pairs) in which the pictures—one realistic (Type 3) and the other conventionalized (Type 5) drawn by the same artist—had the same colors in the same amount and intensity; the realistic one was favored in all grades. The vote for the realistic drawing varied from 58 per cent in the kindergarten to 93 per cent in Grade VI. The vote of adults, choosing for a child of six or seven years, agreed with the children's vote. The test of significance of the kindergarten vote yielded a t ratio of 1.46

---

[1] The realistic-colored drawing was rated as less realistic than the uncolored photograph on the basis of the children's comments which were invited after the voting was completed: "It looks more real" (the photographs); "It looks rough," "It looks painted" (the colored drawings).

with a probability value of .072, indicating that a majority of this size could occur 7 times in 100 by chance and therefore would usually not be thought a statistically reliable majority. The standard errors of the differences in per cents for all groups above the kindergarten indicate that the per cents were reliable measures of the probable vote of other similar groups presented with the same choice.

Colorful Realistic Vs. Colored Outline.—There were two combinations of types (2–4 and 3–4, three pairs each) in which the more colorful picture of the pair was also the more realistic.

The colored photographs were preferred above the colored-outline drawings, the per cents varying from 78 in the kindergarten to 97 in Grade VI. The standard errors indicate that these per cents were highly reliable. In this combination the favored picture was much the more realistic and slightly the more colorful of the two.

The realistic-colored drawings were chosen in preference to the colored-outline drawings with per cents ranging from 54 in the kindergarten to 85 in Grades III and V. The adult vote (95 per cent) was still more dominantly for the realistic drawing. The test of significance of the kindergarten per cent yielded a t ratio of 0.73 with a probability value of .23. Hence, the obtained kindergarten majority cannot be considered statistically reliable. All other per cents were highly reliable, as shown by the standard errors. In this combination the favored picture was the more realistic and much more colorful of the two.

Less Colorful and More Realistic Vs. More Colorful But Conventionalized.—There were six combinations of types (1–3, 1–4, 1–5, 2–3, 2–5, 4–5, with 3 pairs each) in which the less colorful picture was the more realistic of the two.

In the choices between the uncolored photographs and the realistic-colored drawings, the uncolored photographs received the majority of the votes in all grades,[2] with per cents from 51 in Grade I to 83 in Grade VI. The kindergarten and the first grade majorities for the uncolored photograph, however, were

---

[2] It seems that the quality of product is a determining factor in this comparison between two realistic types. In a preliminary investigation in which pictures were taken from first grade books, the photographs were of poor quality and 77 per cent of the first grade children (31 children, 87 choices) chose the realistic-colored drawing. In the present investigation the photographs were of high quality, while the colored drawings were less excellent representatives of their type.

TABLE 1

TABLE 1

PER CENTS, AND STANDARD ERRORS OF THE PROPORTIONS, OF CHILDREN OF EACH
GRADE WHO CHOSE PICTURES OF TYPES 1, 2, 3, 4, 5, WHEN PRE-
SENTED IN ALL COMBINATIONS OF PAIRS

Types Presented	Kindergarten	Grade I	Grade II	Grade III	Grade IV	Grade V	Grade VI	Adults Choosing for Child
Number of choices between each pair ..	81	450	440	450	490	390	480	725
1. Uncolored photograph	29	30	21	24	16	14	20	....
2. Colored photograph ..	71	70	79	76	84	86	80	....
S.E. of the proportion .	5.04	2.16	1.94	2.01	1.66	1.76	1.83	....
3. Realistic colored drawing	58	73	84	86	91	91	93	92
5. Conventionalized colored drawing	42	27	16	14	9	9	7	8
S.E. of the proportion .	5.48	2.09	1.75	1.64	1.29	1.45	1.16	1.01
2. Colored photograph ..	78	77	91	93	96	97	97	....
4. Colored outline drawing	22	23	9	7	4	3	3	....
S.E. of the proportion .	4.60	1.98	1.36	1.20	0.88	0.86	0.78	....
3. Realistic colored drawing	54	69	81	85	83	85	84	95
4. Colored outline drawing	46	31	19	15	17	15	16	5
S.E. of the proportion .	5.54	2.18	1.87	1.68	1.70	1.81	1.67	0.81
1. Uncolored photograph	56	51	63	67	74	80	83	14
3. Realistic colored drawing	44	49	37	33	26	20	17	86
S.E. of the proportion .	5.52	2.36	2.30	2.22	1.98	2.03	1.71	1.29
1. Uncolored photograph	64	73	89	93	93	95	96	83
4. Colored outline drawing	36	27	11	7	7	5	4	17
S.E. of the proportion	5.33	2.09	1.49	1.20	1.15	1.10	0.89	1.40
1. Uncolored photograph	64	69	85	86	92	94	97	71
5. Conventionalized colored drawing	36	31	15	14	8	6	3	29
S.E. of the proportion .	5.33	2.18	1.70	1.64	1.23	1.20	0.78	1.69
2. Colored photograph ..	63	62	72	79	87	91	90	....
3. Realistic colored drawing	37	38	28	21	13	9	10	....
S.E. of the proportion .	5.36	2.29	2.14	1.92	1.52	1.45	1.37	....
2. Colored photograph ..	71	72	86	90	95	96	96	....
5. Conventionalized colored drawing	29	28	14	10	5	4	4	....
S.E. of the proportion .	5.04	2.12	1.65	1.41	0.98	0.99	0.89	....
4. Colored outline drawing	35	56	61	67	73	69	76	21
5. Conventionalized colored drawing	65	44	39	33	27	31	24	79
S.E. of the proportion	5.30	2.34	2.33	2.22	2.01	2.34	1.95	1.51

not statistically reliable. From Grades II through VI all majorities for the uncolored photograph were highly reliable as indicated by their standard errors. The majorities consistently
increased with increase in grade level. In this choice between
two pictures of realistic types, children in each grade either were
about equally divided or gave a significant majority to the uncolored but more realistic picture.[3] On the other hand, most
adults believed that first and second grade children would prefer
the richly colored drawing.

The vote between the uncolored photographs and the colored-
outline drawings favored the uncolored photographs in all grades.
The per cents for the uncolored photograph varied from 64 in
the kindergarten to 96 in Grade VI. The kindergarten per cent
was a statistically reliable majority (t = 2.62). In Grades I through
VI the obtained per cents were highly reliable. Here the adult
judgment agreed with the children's. All groups rejected an
unrealistic-colored picture in favor of an uncolored one which
was realistic.

In the vote between the uncolored photographs and the highly
colored, conventionalized drawings, again the uncolored photograph was preferred, per cents varying from 64 in the kindergarten to 97 in Grade VI, with a consistent increase in per cent
with the increase in grade level. All the majorities were statistically reliable (t of kindergarten per cent = 2.62). For the above-
kindergarten levels the obtained per cents were highly reliable.
The adult vote was in the same direction as the children's but
less positive. All groups preferred an uncolored-realistic picture
to a strongly colored unrealistic one.

The vote between the colored photographs and the realistic-
colored drawings favored the colored photographs,[4] varying from
62 per cent in Grade I to 91 per cent in Grade V. The per cents in
kindergarten and Grade I were statistically reliable majorities,
and in other grades the obtained per cents were highly reliable.
In this choice between two realistic types, less color with more
realism was preferred to more color with less realism.

The colored photographs were preferred to the colored-
conventionalized drawings with per cents from 71 in the kindergarten to 96 in Grades V and VI. All per cents were statistically

[3] As noted previously, the uncolored photograph was rated as more realistic
than the colored drawing on the basis of children's comments.

[4] As between these two realistic-colored types, quality of product probably
is a determining factor, as already noted (see footnote 2).

reliable and highly so above the kindergarten. The less colorful but decidedly more realistic of the two pictures was the overwhelming choice.

The colored-outline drawing was preferred above the colored-conventionalized drawing by large majorities in all grades except the kindergarten. The per cents for the outline drawing varied from 35 in the kindergarten to 76 in Grade VI. All were statistically reliable majorities in the given direction. In this choice between two unrealistic types, the less colorful and more realistic of the two was the majority preference of all grades except kindergarten. The adult vote for the first and second grade child was sharply reversed, 79 per cent of the adult vote being for the more colorful but less realistic picture.

Thus, in the case of the six combinations of types in which the less colorful pictures were the more realistic, out of a total of 42 choices by grade groups, all were dominantly for the less colorful and more realistic ones in each combination, and the per cents were highly reliable statistically, with three exceptions: one out of six majorities in the kindergarten and one out of six in Grade I were statistically unreliable; one kindergarten majority was reliable but the majority was in the opposite direction from that in the other grades.

COMPARISON OF CHOICES BY GRADES

There was a general tendency toward greater unanimity of opinion with increase in grade level up to Grade IV. There was little difference in degree of unanimity in Grades IV, V, and VI. In these three grades, out of 30 choices by grade groups, there were only four instances in which the per cents were less than 80. There were 17 instances in which the per cents were 90 or higher.

While the kindergarten vote was not, to a conspicuous extent, more evenly divided than the first grade vote on the various instances of choice, the kindergarten vote was invariably less reliable because fewer children were included.

COMPARISON OF VOTES OF CHILDREN AND ADULTS

The adult vote for the children agreed with the children's own vote in rejecting an unrealistic type of picture in favor of a realistic one in the four instances in which an adult vote was obtained.

The adult vote for the children sharply disagreed with the children's own vote in choosing the more highly colored but less realistic type: (a) in the one instance in which two realistic types were compared (Types 1 and 3) and (b) in the instance in which two unrealistic types were compared (Types 4 and 5).

REASONS FOR CHOOSING OR NOT CHOOSING PICTURES

In each group, after all the voting was done, the children were asked to look at all the pictures and discuss them. About one-fourth of the sixth grade children had recognized the photographs as photographs. Some fifth-graders and a few fourth-graders had recognized them as such. None of the younger children had realized that they were photographs. Therefore, the vote was determined by the appearance of the pictures and not by knowledge of how they were produced.

The reasons which fourth, fifth, and sixth grade children gave for preferring a picture were: "It looks more real." "It shows up better." For most of the children, the best-liked pictures were the colored photographs. For a few, they were the uncolored photographs, and these children gave the same reasons for their preference and argued as stoutly as did those who preferred the colored photographs.

The reasons children gave for not choosing certain pictures were: "You can't tell what it is." "It looks funny." "It looks painted." "It looks rough." "It doesn't look real." Actually they liked all of them except one instance of the conventionalized drawing. Often they said, "They are all pretty," or, "They are all cute."

The younger children were less able than the older children to analyze the reasons for their preference. Almost invariably they said, "It is colored prettier." For example, even when telling why they liked the uncolored photograph (Type 1) better than the conventionalized, colored drawing (Type 5), they would say, "Number 1 is colored prettier." One kindergarten child seemed to express the same idea as the older children when she said, "I can tell what it is better."

CONCLUSION

The findings of this study seem to justify the following conclusions with respect to picture preferences of children of the ages here studied–kindergarten through Grade VI. Since the subject matter of all pictures used in the present study was realistic in character, the present findings and conclusions are not assumed to apply to other than realistic subject matter.

1. If two pictures are identical in all other respects, most children prefer a realistically-colored one to an uncolored one.

2. If different pictures include the same subject matter and the same colors, most children prefer the one which is treated in such manner as to give the truest appearance of realism or lifelikeness.

3. If different pictures include the same subject matter, most children prefer an uncolored one which gives them an impression of reality above a colored one which does not seem to conform to reality.

4. If different colored pictures include the same subject matter, most children prefer a less colorful one which gives a greater appearance of reality above more colorful ones which appear less lifelike.

5. There is an increase in unanimity of these preferences with increase in grade level up to Grade IV. This greater unanimity of preference of older children, as compared with younger children, is believed to be due to the former's greater capacity for discriminating reality.

6. Typical adult opinion overemphasizes the importance of color per se and underemphasizes the importance of other qualities in illustrations for children.

7. Photographs of excellent quality, both colored and uncolored, deserve much wider use than they are at present being given in illustrations for children.

8. These findings do not justify the statement of a general principle as to comparative preference between photographs and realistic-colored drawings because the examples of the two types used in the present study were not of equal quality.

9. Consideration of the first four conclusions above, together with children's stated reasons for choosing or not choosing certain pictures, suggests: (a) In looking at a picture, a child apparently seeks first to recognize the content. (b) Any picture (assuming a certain content) proves satisfying to the child in proportion to its success in making that content appear real or lifelike. Whether it is colored or uncolored is less important than the appearance of realism. (c) A perfect visual representation of realism includes color, and color in pictures proves satisfying to the child in proportion to its success in increasing the impression of realism or lifelikeness.

Part Six

THE YOUNG CHILD
AND HIS BOOKS

RECIPE FOR A MAGIC CHILDHOOD *

Mary Ellen Chase

As I write these words at the kitchen table of an old Connecticut farmhouse above a quiet valley, a January snowstorm is whitening the brown fields beyond the windows and the gray stone walls surrounding them. A gravel road leads from the farmhouse to one of the main Connecticut highways along which cars and trucks are doubtless speeding; but since I can neither see nor hear them, I can be pleasantly unaware of their existence. The red-and-white-checked cloth of this kitchen table, the wood fire burning in the iron range, the smell of a pot roast taking its time in the oven—all these suggest an earlier time and, perhaps, a less confusing and problematical existence. At all events, once I had seated myself at this table and looked out upon the drifting snowflakes, I found the book which I am supposed to review intolerably dull and determined instead to write some desultory paragraphs about other January snowstorms, about another kitchen, and about books not dull at all. For January snowstorms are always indissolubly connected in my mind with those I knew in Maine many years ago, and any kitchen, by comparison or by contrast, is equally closely connected with the one in which I was literally brought up.

In Maine country villages, at the beginning of the present century, the kitchen of all homes was the center of their activities. It was not only the one room in the house sure to be warm, but also the one place where a mother, inevitably dedicated to its never-ending rites and ceremonies, could keep an eye on her children. Country winters in my childhood also added to a mother's responsibilities, for in Maine, at least, there was no school during January and February. Whether this Long Vacation, as we called it, was made necessary by municipal poverty, or whether rural school boards then had more confidence in the educational value of parents than many school boards, rural and urban, entertain at present, I do not know; but, happily for us,

* Mary Ellen Chase, "Recipe for a Magic Childhood," *Ladies' Home Journal* 68 (May, 1951), 205–07, © 1951 by The Curtis Publishing Company. Reprinted by permission of the author.

the situation persisted throughout my childhood. In January and February our village schoolhouse remained closed and frigid and we, when snowstorms or bitter weather made coasting and skating impossible, went to school in our mothers' kitchens.

Our Maine kitchen was large and sunny, with red geraniums in its eastern windows and from its western a wide view of fields and hills. Jutting from its south wall was our huge black wood stove, known by its name in raised iron letters across its oven door as The Rising Sun; and my mother kept it shining by a polish called by the selfsame name. Between the eastern window stood our kitchen table with a red-and-white-checked cloth to match the geraniums, and by one of the windows was a Boston rocker, also painted red and flanked by four small red stools, which were pushed under the table when not in use. The black iron kitchen sink separated the two western windows and held on its right shelf a green pump, which often had to be "caught" by a dipper of water drawn from the water pail on the shelf to the left. Against the north wall, opposite the stove and affording a view from both eastern and western windows, was the piece of furniture which most intimately concerned us children. This was what we termed the "secretary." It was in reality a high and heavy chest of six drawers, with two stout and wide shelves above them. The upper shelf had on either side a stout carved post; the lower, below two smaller drawers, was just the right height from the upper to serve as a perfect footrest for small feet.

My mother was a versatile young woman, as she had need to be with four children before she had reached the age of 30; and she early saw in the old secretary an indispensable ally. Even in a kitchen as large as ours four pairs of feet about the floor could be not only an intolerable nuisance, but a possible source of perils to her and to us; and, long before I can remember, she had solved this problem by elevating us all to the top shelf of the secretary. A roller towel, carefully placed beneath the armpits of the two children on the right and then around the convenient post; a similar securing of the two on the left; and we were proof against any cold drafts across the yellow painted floor, against kettles of hot fat, and, best of all, against the possible boredom of any number of January snowstorms.

I spent innumerable winter mornings on the top of that old secretary with my two sisters and my brother. I can still smell the warm spicy smells of gingersnaps baking in the oven, of apple pies rich with cinnamon, and of countless doughnuts merrily bobbing about on the surface of boiling fat. My mother sang hymns as she went about her work and often encouraged us to sing with her. One of her favorites was "Shall We Gather at the River?" and all of us, joining in the chorus, loved to assure her that we most certainly would gather there. "Yes, we'll gather at the river, the beautiful, the beautiful river," we would all shout together, each, I feel sure, thinking of that river only as some pleasant family picnicking ground on some pleasant, undefined day in the future. When the old clock in our dining room slowly struck eleven, my mother reached up to each of us a fresh cooky and a cup of milk; and we laid aside our spool knitting machines or the books we were reading for this mid-morning excitement.

It is always with books that the old secretary associates itself in my mind, for we read for hours there, sometimes the older of us aloud to the younger while they were still unable to read, sometimes, after we had all learned the magic of words, by ourselves. And we learned this magic very early, not waiting to be taught at school. Without doubt, since we possessed a father who when at home was almost never without a book in his hand, and a mother who somehow found time to read as well as to darn and cook, fashion clothes and refashion them, clean and wash and iron, we absorbed while still very young the wholesome truth that books held manifold riches which we must discover for ourselves. And, since fortunately the four of us were separated by only a few years, we could share this discovery without too much responsibility one for another. There we would sit for hours upon our lofty perch while the snow fell or bitter winds blew across our white fields, not actually upon the secretary at all, but instead in Arabia with Aladdin, or in the dark forest with Hansel and Gretel, with the four ingenious Robinsons on their mysterious island, or with Oliver Twist in the workhouse, with David Copperfield on the Peggotty's houseboat, loving the alluring smell of crabs and lobsters and the blue mug holding a nosegay of seaweed, or with Jim Hawkins, crouching in the apple barrel of the Hispaniola.

My mother usually somehow managed, at eleven, to sit down for half an hour in the red rocking chair by the window. She called this half hour her "respite," a word which early charmed me; and on days when no drafts were blowing across the floor (for even The Rising Sun was not always victorious over the

worst Maine weather) she would help us down from our Parnas-
sus and allow us to sit upon our red stools while, our cookies
and milk consumed, she herself would read aloud to us. Here
was the very doorsill to complete enchantment, for she was seemingly as lost as we in whatever she was reading. The iron tea-
kettle simmered on The Rising Sun; the red geraniums glowed
with life; smells of our approaching dinner filled our noses from
stew-pans or baking dishes; while my mother's voice brought
trooping into our kitchen all those with whom we rejoiced or
suffered, admired or feared, loved or hated.

Nor did she bring them among us only by her voice. Seemingly
she became as distressed as we over their misfortunes, as angry
as we over their misdeeds. "Isn't he a wicked man?" she would
cry when Fagin terrified Oliver in the dark attic; and, suiting her
behavior to her disgust and loathing, she would slap the passage
which chronicled such horrid goings-on. Then nothing would do
but that we should each in turn slap the page, she solemnly
allowing us this expression of righteous indignation.

There was always the excitement of our father's coming home
at noon, stamping the snow from his overshoes, shaking his coat
in the entry, commenting on the storm or cold. He was always
interested, as he lifted us down from the secretary, in our morning, in what we had been reading; and if he was not too en-
cumbered by the ways and means of feeding both our bodies
and our small heads, he would sometimes promise to go on that
evening with an especial book, reading to us himself by the
living-room fire while my mother, as avid a listener as we, should
darn the countless socks and patch the red flannel underwear.

It is not only in tribute to the old secretary that I write of its
blessings, but even more in tribute to two young parents, who
knew well that in opening the wide doors of reading to their
children, they were building for them houses not made with
hands, dwelling places of the mind, which would always furnish
them with food, shelter, and delight. My mother and father, to
be sure, were not faced fifty years ago with the battle of books
against the conflicting forces of the radio, the movies, comics,
and television, and yet had they been, they would not, I think,
have been too dismayed. After all, even in those days, which
often seem so far removed from life as we know it, parents had
to meet other encroachments upon time, to cope with other
intrusions. The endless tasks which faced a woman from dawn
until dark in a house quite without "modern conveniences"

took a vast toll of both time and energy and often resulted in physical weariness almost inconceivable today. Nor were country villages and even their outlying farm districts in any sense places of monastic seclusion. They had their manifold social gatherings, then as now, their church suppers, school exhibitions, village dramatic societies, whist parties, lodge and Grange get-togethers. Even a far greater measure of neighborliness took its toll of hours and of effort. Then as now, in fact, all families were faced with the ever-present problem of the salvaging of time, with the wise saving of hours to be used for the common benefit and the common pleasure. Had my parents been besieged by pleadings for a television set in the living room or seen The Lone Ranger, or Hopalong Cassidy, or Superman in the process of winning the day over the family reading circle, I rather think they would have met these claimants to our attention and devotion with the only possible weapon then as now—the clear and uncompromising example of their own enthusiasms and values.

They were only in their late twenties when we four children were learning, or had learned, to read; and like most young parents today they loved excitement and were eager after all things new and strange, even in their relatively stable world. Recalling how my father invested money which he could not afford in the first bathroom to appear in our small town, and daily hauled in his neighbors to view his new pride and joy, I am sure that he would have bought a television set; and I am equally sure that my mother's Wednesday and Saturday baking of many loaves of bread would have been vastly enlivened by a radio serial. But I am even more certain that hours for the enjoyment of each would have been strictly defined and clearly understood and that neither would ever have been allowed to usurp the place of books and reading in our common life.

For there is no substitute for books in the life of a child; and the first understanding of this simple and irrefutable truth must come from his early perception of his parents' faith in it. They alone can give him this knowledge just as they alone are responsible for the practice of their faith. If they themselves look upon radio programs and the television screen, valuable as certain of their offerings may be, as clearly secondary to the chapter from the bedtime book, and if they good-humoredly insist that neither takes the place of hours spent in quiet reading, the battle for the books is won.

There are many ways in which parents can make clear to

children their own respect and love for good reading. The gift of a book or the buying of one from the family budget can easily be made an event in the life of a child. He should be taken to the bookshop on the momentous day of the purchase and allowed to look about on its bright offerings. Taught by example as well as by precept, he will learn the careful handling of such treasures. Once at home and his hands carefully washed before the parcel is opened, the binding of the new book, its illustrations, even its print should be shared with him and the time for its reading discussed. And if in the shop he has been entranced by a comic, as every child I have known in the past decade *has* been entranced, the wise guardian of his destiny will not become either openly disapproving or inwardly too deeply distressed. Most children read comics with their tongues in their cheeks, knowing them, I am convinced, for what they are far better than their elders know them. Parents, I feel sure, worry too much about their baneful influence. The constructive anxiety which results in the quiet substitution of beautiful books for cheap and ugly ones is far more to the purpose.

I would even go so far as to suggest that we concern ourselves much too seriously with *what* a child reads. *That* he reads early and eagerly should be our first concern; and if good books are placed within his reach and he knows, not that they are "good for him," but that his parents once read and loved them, or even still do, he will eventually form his own tastes. In my childhood and young girlhood I was never forbidden to read any book in our relatively small bookcases. I assume that my parents saw to it that none which might be unwise for my eyes and mind was there; but I was never once told that any book was "bad" for me or "too old" for me. I read most of those we owned, novels, poems, biographies, in a "first fine careless rapture"; and once I had done and there was nothing new that I could find, I read them again with almost equal excitement.

Two young parents whom I now know allow their son and daughter, aged 8 and 10, to read for an hour every night in bed after they are sent there promptly at 8 o'clock. I know of no wiser plan to ensure a love of books and a dependence upon them. The very sight of a book upon his bedside table widens the horizons of a child and affords a spur to his imagination. And a shelf of them of his own, however small in number, kept within reach of his hands, is a possession no child should be without.

The characters in books, as well as those of radio programs, should be household words and their authors should become familiar presences at family tables, a habit which only parents can generate and preserve.

In this connection I can never forget an incident which happened to me in the year 1894 when I was seven years old. In my childhood, Robert Louis Stevenson, or R.L.S. as he was always called, was such a household word, for his stories were read and adored by the parents and children alike of countless American families. My grandmother, who spent much of her time with us and who was herself an avid reader, returned one December morning from a walk to the village. When she entered our kitchen, we saw to our astonishment that she was crying. She sat down in the Boston rocker by the window and to our further amazement covered her face with the black sateen apron which she always wore. "I won't believe it!" she said in response to my mother's questions. "I can't bear it! They say that R.L.S. is dead."

This, I suppose, was the first time in my small life that I had ever realized the devotion which an author can stir within the hearts and minds of his readers, the part that he may forevermore play in their imaginations, the satisfactions he may be capable of granting them. The impression, though perhaps dimly understood, was a lasting one; and I have never forgotten that December day so long ago.

Perhaps I have seemed to speak with undue authority in these paragraphs, written at this kitchen table in this Connecticut farmhouse. For I am still here; the snow still falls on fields now white; the pot roast has long since been eaten and the dishes washed; the short winter day is now, as we say in Maine, "on the edge of darkness"; and the paragraphs have perhaps become far too many.

But I feel that I can speak with more than a little measure of authority, for I have spent 40 years of my life in the teaching of literature to boys and girls of grade school age, to high school students, and, in the past 30 years, to girls in college. I have, in these years, learned a great deal about the minds and imaginations of the young. I know that, if they have been nurtured and nourished by an early love of books, they have far finer and more sensitive minds and imaginations; and I know, too, that girls (and boys, as well) who possess books will live far richer lives than they could otherwise live and will contribute that richness to the communities in which they will become the successful parents of children. I am even convinced that many of the girls whom I teach, or try to teach, have received a better preparation for college in their homes—yes, even in their mothers' kitchens— than they have received at school, provided always that their parents have, even without a massive old secretary as an aid, known how to lift them above what Wordsworth calls "the dreary intercourse of daily life" by leading them early into the paths of books. For through their reading in those most formative years from 7 to 17 they have become all unconsciously the dwellers in many lands, the intelligent and eager associates of all manner of people. Through their early familiarity with words they have gained a facility in speech and in writing which no other source can give. They will never be bored, for they can always seek out a world perhaps at the moment more desirable than the one in which they live and companions often more real than those close at hand. The value of the experiences which they themselves will meet in life can be increased by their knowledge of similar experiences in the realm of books; and the sorrows which they must weather can be made more bearable by the lines of poetry forever in their minds. Every year when they come to me as freshmen I know at once whether or not they come from homes where books have been thought indispensable and where parents have already made their study in college rewarding and delightful.

And now since supper is an hour away and the wood in the cookstove is crackling in preparation, I think I shall fetch my ragged copy of Oliver Twist and imagine myself again on the top of the old secretary.

"Please, sir," said Oliver, "I want some more." He was asking for gruel and got but a blow from the ladle instead; yet his words will continue to be spoken by children and wise parents together concerning that better food which is forever theirs for the taking.

WHAT THEY ARE LIKE:
HOW TO IDENTIFY THEM *

Elizabeth Guilfoile

THEY ANSWER A NEED

The wordless appeal of the six-, seven-, eight-year-old, initiated into reading but laboring with limited vocabulary and rudimentary skills, has long been, "Give me books with good stories, with people like me in them, with interesting happenings, with pictures that help me understand the story, with not too many new words—books that I can read over and over because they are funny, or exciting, or tell me about things; books I-can-read-for-myself."

Perhaps teachers and librarians have been helping to phrase the appeal, in teacher-librarian language: books with memorable characters and situations; stories with action, suspense, and climax; information clearly written, clearly pictured, and often about the children's own here and now; language clear to the reader—sentences generally short and in normal word order; desirable, natural repetition; fine illustrations interpreting the text, not avant-garde art, nor cheap and cluttered color; attractive pages with good spacing, glareless paper, plain but bold type—"seeable" text.

The books anticipating the beginning book movement had come, it would seem, by happy chance, but suddenly publishers were developing whole lines of books for beginning readers. The trickle of these books that appeared in the middle fifties grew to a flood tide after 1957. Realism, fantasy, information, and humor now vie for a place on primary reading tables. For some children in the first year of school, for many in the second, and

* Elizabeth Guilfoile, "What They Are Like: How to Identify Them," *Books for Beginning Readers* (pamphlet) Champaign, Illinois, National Council of Teachers of English, © 1962, pp. 1–7. Reprinted with the permission of the National Council of Teachers of English and Elizabeth Guilfoile.

for multitudes in the third, these books comprise a whole new library for their independent reading.

The teacher's hope of developing real readers lies in stimulating interest, initiating the pupils into the process of reading, and then supplying the materials and the guidance for their further growth. Her goal is to have children delight in books, and to develop in each child as early as possible the desire to read for himself, to read on his own initiative, even though he must seek help. Children whose school reading is limited to class and group work seldom make real readers.

However, teachers who have wished to broaden at once the child's base of reading experience with additional materials have in the past found few books for the purpose other than individual copies of supplementary texts. In schools with library facilities, "easy" books have been available, highly pictured, usually, with small amounts of text, some with much, but typically not having all the requirements of a book planned to be read for himself by the child at a low reading level.

There have been, of course, in the best schools and homes, "read-to-me" books appealing to the interests of young children, with language suited to their listening, with ideas and situations that the adult reader might help to interpret through words and intonation.

Different from both the picture book and the read-to-me book, though it partakes of the qualities of both, is the book that the beginner can read on his own initiative, with maximum aid from the pictures, with minimum vocabulary for the subject treated, with simple sentence structure, and often with much repetition; a book he can read *for* himself, although not necessarily *by* himself.

They Have Definite Earmarks

How do teachers, parents, and others know that a book is a beginning book, that it is suitable for a child of six, seven, or eight with limited skills and vocabulary, and an interest range related to his experience? How do they know that this is something he can read mainly on his own initiative and that he will read it because it appeals?

The beginning books have characteristics, more or less definite, and of course these are shared always in some measure with all books that children like. These books are *written* as are books for older children and adults—not built around vocabulary to be mastered; they have plot, idea, theme; they deal with situations appreciated by young children, with life as they see it, or fancy as they can take it; such books are usually rereadable.

Over and over readers can relive the suspense of *Small Clown* (Nancy Faulkner), *Hurry, Hurry* (Edith Thacher Hurd), or *The Boy Who Couldn't Roar* (Grace Berquist). Often the books lend themselves to dramatization as *It's a Deal* (Poul Stroyer) or *Wanted, a Brother* (Gina Bell). In general the pictures have reality, though one finds such exceptions as *The Cantankerous Crow* (Lennart Hellsing and Poul Stroyer) translated from the Swedish, with its crows that are just of color and lightly appended wings and feet.

Readability at the early levels, of course, depends much on vocabulary control, on repetition, on length and structure of sentences, on the amount, size, and spacing of print on a page, and on the breaking of the text material into paragraphs or brief thought units. Yet story and fact value, manner of telling, and illustration take precedence over language control and physical make-up. What the reader desires must come first.

In fiction, children like books with action, dramatic quality, suspense, even mystery, and satisfying conclusions. They like people and events of the real world, yet they like also to range far and wide in imagination. Their interests range over animals and machines, heroes and fairies, people of now and of long ago, children like themselves and children that are different. In informational books, they like their facts challenging and exciting, but understandable, and with a touch of the familiar. In both story and fact books, children are best able to take off from where they are.

The readers' own emotional needs must be met vicariously. *Little Bear* (Else Holmelund Minarik) must have parents who love and understand him. Jonathan must succeed in getting his trained turtle into the *Pet Parade* (James Ayers); *Small Clown* (Nancy Faulkner) must become a clown like his father; Freddy in *Who Will Be My Friends?* (Syd Hoff) must win acceptance and playmates.

The power of the beginning book, nevertheless, as a learning-to-read book lies not alone in the appeal of the content, but also in the child's growing realization that he can read a book for himself, in his inclination to turn to the library table and seek out a book on his own.

The importance of the small reader's sense of I-can-read-it-myself accounts for the starkness of content and language in books like *A Trip to the Zoo* (Isabelle Groetzinger). *Fun on the Farm* (Gladys McHorne), *I Like Birds* (Dorothy Joslyn), and others of this series.

THEY ARE OF MANY KINDS

Variety is the most marked characteristic of the beginning books. Some, like *Come to the Farm* (Ruth Tensen), use pre-primer-primer style text to give the child the satisfaction of being able to read on his own as in,

> Bow-wow
> We want to play.
> Where are all our friends?
> Will you come and play?

But it is the numberless photographs in this and the companion volumes *Come to the City* (Tensen) and *Come to the Zoo* (Tensen) that really supply the content.

Informational books not only are increasing in number but also are more and more skillfully adapted to the level of younger readers. Straight facts are given in *Time Is When* (Beth Youman Gleick).

> At night you sleep.
> While you are sleeping
> A new day begins.

While this language is of the simplest, it has a winning quality unlike the prosaic style of many factual books. The pictures are appealing, too, and interpret perfectly the spirit of the text. The two lines,

> September is the end of summer
> and the start of fall,

are accompanied by pictures of leaf-burning so entrancing that all young readers will surely burn up their towns come next October.

Successful stories that teach facts through fantasy are rare, but *The Boy Who Got Mailed* (Bill and Rosalie Brown) and *A Bear Is a Bear* (Inez Hogan) do it well. Peter, who got mailed with $3.79 in stamps on his forehead, and a label, *This end up,* to his aunt in Kansas, experiences all the processes of the mail. Usable by second-graders who visit the post office in their study of the mail, the book is not in primary format and appeals to older children as well. *A Bear Is a Bear* tells of a self-important grizzly who learned in his travels that there are many kinds of bears.

Then, as a special kind of approach, there is the complete nonsense of Dr. Seuss, who only by sheer ingenuity overcame the handicap of starting with a word list. Some of his imitators have not overcome it and, though patterning after *The Cat in the Hat,* have produced foolishness instead.

All these approaches serve a purpose, but unless the books are interesting in content, attractive in make-up, and appealing in illustrations, they seldom accomplish other purposes with young readers.

THEY SET SOME CRITERIA

In selecting any books for children, the adult will naturally ask of a science or other factual book, "Will the children use it often?" The answer is in such books as *The Tall Grass Zoo* (Winifred and Cecil Lubbell). Its rhythmic prose and black and white sketches against lightly colored backgrounds give information about frogs, ants, caterpillars, ladybugs, and other denizens of the grass. The youngest can pore over it, identifying the creatures; able second graders can read and reread it; third graders and older children will return to it often for reference.

Of fiction, the question is "Will they read it over and over?" and the answer is in books like the well-known *The Big Snow* (Berta and Elmer Hader) and in *When the Cows Got Out* (Dorothy Koch), which is memorable not only for its direct story and for Tim's sense of responsibility but also for beautiful design and illustrations. Paul Lanz's brushwork, detailed down to the barbs on the wire fence and the knotholes in the barn planks, is set against color brightened or softened to show the hour of the day and the mood.

To the question "Is it playable?" there are Paul Galdone's *The Old Woman and Her Pig, Who Will Be My Friends?* (Syd Hoff), and *The Goings On at Little Wishful* (Warren Miller). "Is it applicable?" many young readers have said. "Sometimes *Nobody Listens to . . . me* either!"

They Have Additional Uses

These books, of course, have uses in addition to primary reading. As books for oral reading, some appeal to preschool children; as easy books for rapid gains in vocabulary and in speed, many are usable in the intermediate grades. Elements of plot and suspense, information and fun in some of the books appeal to older children with slowly developing reading skills. Many pupils, even of junior high school age, need very simple books. For one or two pupils so retarded, or for a remedial reading class, the teacher may find some of these books usable. *I Want to Be an Airline Hostess* (Carla Greene), with simple language, large type, and highly informative pictures, could be interesting reading for older, educationally retarded girls. The hostess is grown up, the information about her work is challenging, and a whole array of splendid uniforms, for different airlines, is pictured. Older slow-to-read children will find the straightforward style of *Christopher Columbus* (Clara Ingram Judson) to their liking and his adventures within their understanding.

Sailor Jack and Bluebell (Selma and Jack Wasserman), with the grown-up sailors, the big ship, the atomic submarine, and the reckless parrot, appeals to older children as well as to first graders. It has, perhaps, its best use in classes for retarded readers and with group procedure. The pictures furnish content and stimulate discussion. Bluebell also appears in Sailor Jack, which is simpler but has less incident.

These two books present the dangers and excitements of today while *Dan Frontier* (William Hurley) and *Dan Frontier Goes Hunting* (Hurley) recreate the adventures of past time in a setting of forest and field. *Bucky Button* (Edith S. McCall) and *The Buttons and the Whirlybird* (McCall) are blue collar family stories. These books are part of the total list that includes the inimitable *Cowboy Sam* (Edna W. Chandler) and *Cowboy Sam and Freddy* (Chandler) among the earliest used by teachers seeking material for the children who make progress slowly in reading. They are usable by the younger children for independent reading.

There Were Early Examples

While the production of beginning books is presently a deliberate movement, good stories have been told for many years to satisfy some of the needs of beginning readers. *Merry Animal*

Tales (Madge A. Bingham), recently reissued with its original pictures, was published first in 1906. The story of the rats and their feud with the fat cook and the fat cat presents Blackie Blackrat, his amiable father, and his anxious mother, and just the kind of situations in which a small boy would find himself.

Cherry Tree Children (Mary Frances Blaisdell) and *Bunny Rabbit's Diary* (Blaisdell), first published in 1915, although they lack the story value of *Merry Animal Tales,* remain readable today. These older books have a quiet, slow-paced charm. The characters behave as people do, but children like such animal stories along with the more realistic ones.

The Little Red Lighthouse and the Great Gray Bridge (Hildegarde Swift and Lynd Ward), classic story of the lighthouse that found it was needed despite the great flashlight turning on top of the new bridge, published in 1942, is just as appealing today. Another classic, *The Five Chinese Brothers* (Claire Huchet Bishop and Kurt Wiese), a simple retelling at about second grade level of an ancient tale, was published in 1938.

Little Toot (Hardie Gramatky) appeared in 1939. Story and pictures were designed for children too young to read, but no child should miss this extravaganza of the river, harbor, and sea, and the frivolous little tugboat that rose to a big occasion. *Creeper's Jeep* (Gramatky), 1948, lends human characteristics to machinery and endows it with reason as well as emotion. The author's own pictures enliven the humor.

Churchmouse Stories (Margot Austin) reprints five of the author-illustrator's books in one volume. *The Three Silly Kittens,* first published in 1950, with its one-page episodes and simple language, suits second-grade reading level while the remaining stories are better for listening.

Bear Twins (Inez Hogan) launched in 1935 Inez Hogan's long list of twin stories. *A Day at School* (Agnes McCready) was published in 1936. *A Puppy for Keeps* (Quail Hawkins), easy and factual, presaged in 1943 a multitude of stories on the theme of a child's desire for a pet.

WHAT SEVEN-YEAR-OLDS
LIKE IN BOOKS*

Agnes G. Gunderson

The literature program for the seven-year-olds in our school includes the sharing of many books and stories. Having read these books to several groups of second graders over a period of years, one becomes accustomed to hearing such comments as: "I like Dr. Dolittle the best of any story I have heard. Will you please read it again?" "Oh Boy, this is a good story! ("Elephant's Child") I have heard it may times but I like to hear it again!" "Are there any more books about Mr. Popper's Penguins?" "Will you read *Princess on the Glass Hill?*" "Miss Wood has her green beads on—Will you read the poem [1] about the green glass beads?" "I wish we had another book about Stuart Little." When teacher had read about half-way through the book, *Mister Penny,* a child was heard to say, "I hope it will turn out all right."

It is the belief of the writer that a teacher can more wisely and effectively guide children in their reading if she knows what are the particular qualities in books which appeal to children at different age levels. A study was made in Grade Two of the University Elementary School in an effort to determine what those qualities are by finding out how seven-year-olds react to certain books and stories.

Some children testify to the truth of the following statement: "Sometimes the best way to react to a story is just to sit and think how good it was," [2] by doing just that. Others like to discuss the book and the characters in it. Among the books and stories read to this group of 21 children, the 12 books used in this study were selected by the teacher for discussion. The usual

---

* Agnes G. Gunderson, "What Seven-Year-Olds Like in Books," *Elementary English*, 30, No. 3 (March, 1953), 163–66. Reprinted by permission of the National Council of Teachers and Agnes Gunderson.

1 "Overheard on a Saltmarsh," by Harold Monro.
2 Dora V. Smith, "Literature and Personal Reading," *National Society for the Study of Education*, 48th yearbook, part 2, 1949, p. 214.

response at the conclusion of a story or book read to these second graders is "I like that book." "That was a good story!"

In an attempt to discover the reasons for such liking, or which qualities in the book were especially liked, the teacher asked, "Why do you like it?" The most frequent responses were, "It's funny," "It's interesting," "It's exciting," "It's scary," "It's magic."

To encourage children to analyze their reactions further, the teacher asked such questions as, "Why do you think it is funny?" "What do you mean by 'funny'?" "What are the scary things in this book?" "Why is it exciting?" "Why is it magic?" In response the children made such comments as, "I liked when Mary Poppins got laughing gas and went up in the air." "It was exciting when the Elephant's Child stepped on the crocodile;" "Dr. Dolittle is interesting because he had so many adventures;" "I like scary stories like when Bartholomew Cubbins was to be pushed off the high tower;" "I liked the part where Maia walked up into the sky like there were invisible steps—that's magic."

During the discussion of the different books following the reading of them to the group, the teacher jotted down the comments given by the various children. Only as long as comments were made spontaneously and rapidly was this discussion carried on. No attempt was made to exhaust *all* the factors that might account for the popularity of the book. The teacher deliberately refrained from asking the children, e.g., to think of *all* the reasons why they liked the book, as this might encourage them to give superficial reasons.

All comments are direct quotations—the child's own words as he gave them in the discussion—and show his evaluation of or reaction to the books. Some are in complete sentences, and many are mere phrases, which is a natural way for young children to talk when discussing or conversing on a topic. The following comments given on two of the books are illustrative.

Comments on the book, *The Story of Dr. Dolittle,* which is a perennial favorite of seven-year-olds, are as follows:

1. (Adventure)
   "I liked it because Dr. Dolittle had so many adventures."
   "He went to Africa to cure sick monkeys."
   "He was chased by pirates."

2. (Excitement)
   "It was so exciting."
   "The soldiers chased Dr. Dolittle and his animals."
   "Dr. Dolittle and his animals were put in jail."

"The sharks go after the pirates."
"Dr. Dolittle talks to sharks and to pirates."
"Dr. Dolittle got away in the pirates' ship."

3. (Humor)
"I like it because it is so funny."
"Polynesia (parrot) got Dr. Dolittle and his animals out of jail."
"Polynesia frightens the king of Jolliginki—she tells him she can give him mumps just by raising her little finger."

4. (Accomplishments)
"I like it because Dr. Dolittle can do so many things."
"Dr. Dolittle is a good doctor."
"He can cure all the sick animals."
"He could tell what the animals need—spectacles for the horse."
"He could talk the animals' language."
"Dr. Dolittle always got out of any trouble he got into."

5. (Justice)
"I liked it because the pirates couldn't catch Dr. Dolittle."
"Dr. Dolittle got away in the pirates' ship."
"He made the pirates be farmers."

6. (Personality of Leading Character)
"I liked it because Dr. Dolittle was kind."
"He was funny, friendly, jolly."
"He always got into funny things."

Rabbit Hill is another favorite. The reasons given for its popularity are:

1. (Kindness to animals)
"I liked the book because the people in it were kind to animals."
"Folks helped Georgie (Rabbit) when he was hurt."
"Folks put out food for animals."
"Folks helped Georgie (Rabbit) when he was hurt."
"Folks put out a sign, 'Drive Slow.' "
"Folks didn't let man put out poison."

2. (Humor)
"I liked the book because it is funny."
"It was funny when the rabbit kicked that cat in the stomach."

"Uncle Analda's house was disorderly—I could keep house better than he could."

"Mother Rabbit worried all the time—Silly to worry all the time."

3. (Frightening or scary incidents)

"I liked the book because it is exciting."

"It was exciting when the old hound chased Georgie."

"It is scary—I liked where Mother was afraid Georgie had been put in the dungeon."

4. (Adventure)

"I liked it because Georgie had so many adventures."

5. (Accomplishments)

"I liked the songs that the rabbit made up."

"I liked Georgie—he jumped Dean Man's Brook."

6. (Satisfaction)

"I liked *Rabbit Hill* because new folks finally came and they were planting folks, so the rabbits got food."

"I liked the book because it is funny," was the reason most frequently given for liking these books. As the comments indicate, children use the term "funny" in a broad sense. They use it to indicate:

(a) The *ridiculous*

"The pelican flew right over the Statue of Liberty and didn't even see it—the Statue of Liberty is about two miles high."

"Funny—had to call the policeman to get Honk (moose) out of the livery stable."

"It's funny—pig not sick, but Mister Penny gave the pig medicine anyway."

"It was funny when the pig snored—I never heard a pig snore."

"It was funny—cat dancing with a fish—imagine a cat dancing with a fish."

(b) The *unbelievable*

"Mary Poppins slid *up* the bannister." "The Wind carried Mary Poppins up over the trees."

"It is funny to have a mouse in the family."

"It is funny for a mouse to make poems."

(c) The *surprising*
"Every time Bartholomew took off his hat another hat was on his head."
"The parrot got Dr. Dolittle and the animals out of jail."

(d) The *imaginative*
"Magic bottle—different kinds of medicine in the same bottle."
"Everyone got laughing gas—table went up in the air—had a tea party up in the air."

(e) The *absurd*
"The king was so angry that the wheels of the carriage shook."
"It's funny that Honk could eat a ton of hay; I have never seen anything that could eat so much hay."

(f) *Other humorous situations*
"It was funny when the fat lady slipped on a banana peel."
"I liked the book about the pelicans—it was funny when the babies ate fish out of the pelican's mouth."
"It was funny when the pig got stuck in the hole in the fence."

Strickland [3] bears out this same tendency regarding the young child's humor:

> The sense of humor of primary children is crude and objective. The child laughs at what he sees and hears; anything amuses him so long as it calls attention—sudden falls, comic faces, and dramatic situations.

Excitement, suspense, and *frightening or scary incidents* are other reasons given for liking books, as seen in these comments: "I liked 'The Elephant's Child' because it is exciting, like when the Elephant's Child stepped on the crocodile;" "it is scary—you don't know what might happen—crocodile might eat him," "I liked the part about Mary Poppins in the zoo—that was exciting."

A satisfactory ending, or the justice of the folk tale—kindness rewarded, evil punished—are standards demanded by the young child as seen by these remarks: "I liked when the elephant's child spanked his relatives who had spanked him;" "The rooster's tail came off—served him right;" "It turned out a happy story because

---

[3] Ruth G. Strickland, "English is Our Language," *Guide for Teaching*, Grades I and II, D. C. Heath, 1950, p. 13.

Mister Penny got rich;" "I liked *Wait for William* because William got a ride on the elephant; the big children were not kind to him, but he was the only one who got a ride on the elephant;" "I like the ending because Peter Churchmouse finally got cheese."

One factor only was singled out for specific attention—that of vocabulary. The teacher asked" Were there any interesting words, or words that you particularly liked in this book?" Here also, only those comments that the children gave quickly and spontaneously were included. It is interesting to note the seven-year-olds' appreciation of Kipling's colorful words in the story, "The Elephant's Child." The following quotations are particularly liked: "Satiable Curiosity; O Best Beloved; Kolokolo Bird; Great-grey-green-greasy Limpopo River all set about with Fever Trees; Scalesome, flailsome tail; Bi-colored-python-rock snake; Armour-plated upper deck." Other words or quotations liked in these books were: "You stupid piece of warm bacon" (from *Dr. Dolittle*), "Well, I'm jig-sawed to a puzzle" (from *Mr. Penny*), "Well, I'll be frost-bitten" (from *Honk the Moose*). Also refrains occurring again and again, such as: "New folks coming. Oh My! Oh My!" (from *Rabbit Hill*), "Fuss, fuss, fuss" (from *Peter Churchmouse*).

Illustrations were sometimes given as reasons for liking the books. *The Little House,* a Caldecott Award Book, was chosen for discussion in order to get the children's reaction to a book distinguished for its illustrations rather than content. Their comments, "I like the book because it has such beautiful pictures. There are many pretty colors—in fall rusty brown, and in winter white snow," "The pond against the green trees and grass is pretty," show that seven-year-olds are sensitive to beautiful colors. Their concern about what happens to the house is seen here: "The house is sad because it cannot see stars—no grass now, no trees;" "The house was happy at last because it was moved back into the country;" "Hooray! It was moved out of the city!" Their feeling of relief when it was finally moved back into the country shows how they endowed it with the human emotion of happiness. Close observation and attention to details in illustrations is revealed in the comment: "Little Georgie looks like Robbut." When teacher told them that the same artist (Robert Lawson) had illustrated both *Robbut* and *Rabbit Hill* it seemed to them natural that they should look alike.

The discussion or evaluation of the various books reveals many items of interest. It is interesting to note that the group pre-

ferred *Rabbit Hill,* which is one of the Newbery Award Books
and written for older children, to *Robbut,* another book about
rabbits by the same author but classified for younger children.
The humor in *Stuart Little* is also on a higher age level than
that of *Peter Churchmouse* (main character in both books is a
mouse) but as the comment, "Stuart Little is smarter than Peter
Churchmouse," indicates, seven-year-olds can appreciate it. This
group distinctly did as Hazard [4] suggests, "Let us revel in nonsense."

Some people feel that young children should not be exposed
to any gruesome or frightening details in books. This group of
seven-year-olds found nothing too frightening in these books—
on the contrary, they liked certain books *because* they are "scary,"
as when Bartholomew's head was to be chopped off or when
Elephant's Child stepped on the crocodile.

In summarizing these comments through which children reveal their reasons for liking these books, the qualities that seem
to account for their popularity are: humor, excitement, suspense, adventure, kindness to animals, an element of magic or
fancy, a leading character able to accomplish the unusual or
unexpected, and an ending in which justice triumphs.

As we select books for children, younger as well as older, let
us keep in mind Robert Lawson's [5] advice:

> We must not give them (children) just a splendid or an in-
> triguing Juvenile List.
> We must give them *books*—books that will become tattered
> and grimy from use, not books too handsome to grovel with.
> Books that will make them weep, books that will rack them
> with hearty laughter. Books that absorb them so they have
> to be shaken loose from them. Books that they will put under
> their pillows at night. Books that give them gooseflesh and
> glimpses of glory.

Books Used in This Study

1. *Story of Dr. Dolittle* by Hugh Lofting, J. B. Lippincott
   Company, Philadelphia, 1920.
2. *Peter Churchmouse* by Margot Austin, E. P. Dutton and
   Company, Inc., New York, 1941.

[4] Paul Hazard, *Books, Children, and Men,* The Horn Book Inc., 1944, p. 137.
[5] Robert Lawson, *The Hornbook Magazine,* 17:283, July 1941.

3. *Stuart Little* by E. B. White, Harper and Brothers, New York, 1945.
4. *Rabbit Hill* by Robert Lawson, Viking Press Inc., New York, 1944.
5. "The Elephant's Child," *Just So Stories Series,* Rudyard Kipling, Garden City Publishing Company, Inc., Garden City, New York, 1942.
6. *Honk the Moose* by Phil Stong, Dodd, Mead and Company, New York, 1935.
7. *Mister Penny* by Marie Hall Ets, Viking Press Inc., New York, 1935.
8. *Mary Poppins* by Pamela L. Travers, Harcourt, Brace and Company, New York, 1940.
9. *Pelican Here, Pelican There* by Leonard Weisgard, Charles Scribner's Sons, New York, 1948.
10. *Wait for William* by Marjorie Flack, Houghton Mifflin Company, Boston, 1935.
11. *The 500 Hats of Bartholomew Cubbins* by Dr. Seuss, Vanguard Press Inc., New York, 1938.
12. *The Little House* by Virginia Lee Burton, Houghton Mifflin Company, Boston, 1942.

MOTHER GOOSE TO HOMER*

Sister Mary Joan Patricia, S.S.J.

Paper read at the joint meeting of the New England Unit and the Metropolitan Catholic College Librarians, Providence, Rhode Island, May 19, 1951.

Mother Goose to Homer! How far apart they seem! Yet someone has truly said, "If you want your child to love Homer, give him Mother Goose."
This flawless literature delights the child, awakens in him

* Sister Mary Joan Patricia, S.S.J., "Mother Goose to Homer," *Catholic Library World* 23 (December, 1951), 75–79.

a responsiveness to rhyme and rhythm, develops his sense of humor through the nonsense surprise jingles, pleases his dramatic sense with verses about Miss Muffet and Little Boy Blue, and gives him a feeling of relationship with these old-fashioned children.

At his mother's knee, he is simply charmed with the irresistible appeal of this age-old, worldwide literature which cultivates ear and taste with rhythmic measure, beautiful sound, and quaint imagery. This pleasure has its roots in some power so deep and fundamental that it defies explanation or imitation.

The child doesn't know or care that many Mother Goose rhymes originated as political lampoons and popular satires about Mary Queen of Scots, Henry VIII, Mary Tudor, and Elizabeth. But when the drama of English history brings these famous personages to the stage, and the college student comes to take a lively interest in the human side of the English monarchs and their courts, he is intrigued to see the annals of their times reveal with caustic wit the comedies, tragedies, and romances of high and low. For the working people, too, used these rhymes as the only means of voicing their complaints, e.g.:

> Baa, Baa, Black Sheep, have you any wool?
> Yes, sir, yes, sir, three bags full;
> One for my master, one for my dame,
> And one for the little boy that cried in the
>   lane

This recounts the spirit of discontent and revolt in the reign of Edward VI, when the king and wealthy nobles demanded so much wool that vast tracts of arable land were turned into sheep folds, resulting in an economic crisis, lack of foodstuffs, and field labor, low wages, and high costs. "The master and the dame" are the king and the rich courtiers. "The little boy that cried in the lane" represents the poor people who were often hanged for crying out against abuse.

Katherine Elwes Thomas, after much scholarly research, also offers, in *The Real Personages in Mother Goose,* interpretations of many other nursery rhymes, some of them attributed to Shakespeare and other literary wits, some even to Queen Elizabeth.

"Mary, Mary, Quite Contrary" and "Little Miss Muffet" refer to Mary, Queen of Scots. "Little Boy Blue" is a jibe at Cardinal

Wolsey who had received the degree of Batcheleur of Arts at 15 and was often called "the Boy Bachelor."

You may recall some of your childhood favorites that have come down to us in variant forms.

"Sing a song of sixpence" alludes to Henry VIII's confiscation of rich abbey lands, his divorce from Catherine of Aragon, his infatuation with Anne Boleyn, her short reign and swift execution:

Sing a song of sixpence,
(Henry's jubilant humming over his stolen riches)
A pocket full of rye,
(rich grain fields Henry had confiscated)
Four and twenty blackbirds
Baked in a pie;
("blackbirds" refers to friars and monks; p y e meant a monk's cowl and hence the monk himself. As in the case of "Little Jack Horner," the monks, to satisfy the avaricious Henry, sent him twenty-four title deeds to monastic property. According to the prevailing custom, these were arranged in the form of a pie.)
When the pie was opened,
The birds began to sing;
Wasn't that a dainty dish
To set before a king?
("dainty dish" because Henry selected choice portions, such as Newstead Abbey, to give to favored friends)
The king was in the counting-house
Counting out his money.
(the holdings he had stolen)
The queen was in the pantry,
Eating bread and honey;
(Catherine of Aragon eating English bread with Spanish assurance that the divorce from Henry could not take place)
The maid was in the garden
(twenty-year-old Anne Boleyn in the garden of Whitehall Palace where Henry first saw her)
Hanging out the clothes,
(beautiful frocks which Anne brought from France to enhance her charms)
When down flew a blackbird
(a cleric, in this case Wolsey, "the royal headsman")
And snipped off her nose.
(beheaded her)

Another special favorite of childhood is "Hey, diddle, diddle":

Hey, diddle, diddle
(the name of an old dance, which suggests Elizabeth's love of dancing, music, and jollity)
  The cat and the fiddle
(Elizabeth was often dubbed "the Cat." She played with her cabinet as if they were mice and outwitted the statesmen of Europe.)
  The cow jumped over the moon;
("The Cow" was another nickname for Elizabeth. Her father had been called "the Dunne Cowe" because of heraldic bearings. "The moon" refers to Walsingham. Elizabeth, herself, playfully spoke of the staid Walsingham as "the moon" when she sent him on a trip to the imprisoned Mary of Scotland, apparently to investigate an alleged plot of Mary against Elizabeth.)
  The little dog laughed
(When Elizabeth tired of her sometime favorite, the Earl of Leicester, she playfully jeered at him by calling him her "lap dog." Once, when he was out of favor with the Queen, he asked to be sent to France on a diplomatic mission. She refused on the ground that when people saw him they would know she was near, and vice versa. "He is like my lap dog," she said.)
  To see such sport
(political sport and tilt yard tournaments with grotesque antics)
  And the dish ran away with the spoon.
(The "dish" was the formal title of the courtier who brought the royal dishes to the queen's dining room. The "spoon" was a beautiful lady-in-waiting who tasted the royal meals as a precaution against poisoning Elizabeth. The "dish" in this case was Edward of Hertford who secretly married the "spoon," Lady Katherine Grey. When the vain and jealous Elizabeth heard of this, she threw them both into prison for the remaining seven years of their life. They had two children in prison.)

Since none of all this underlying meaning has come to the child, he simply revels in the happy, jingling rhymes that add sunshine to his joyous hours.

It is only a step from Mother Goose to simple poetry. By careful guidance, the child can be led to love the best. He already responds to rhyme and rhythm, alliteration and imagery, and through poems about things that fall within his observation, or that appeal to his inherent ideals, mother, teacher, or librarian may lay the foundation of literary appreciation that will normally develop through his school and college years. He may even, in these early years, be introduced to poets who will be his lifelong companions, whom he will not only meet in his college course but cherish long years after.

Stevenson was endeared to the child's heart because he saw through the child's mind and with photographic precision presented what he saw. The very qualities of sincerity, simplicity, understanding, clearness, strength, and musical cadence which occurred in his children's poetry will recur in the books assigned for college reading. Because he early came in contact with poems by a host of authors, including Riley, A. A. Milne, the Brownings, Christina Rosetti, Blake, Lear, Tennyson, Bryant, De La Mare, Teasdale, Meynell, Noyes, Kilmer, and Fyleman, the student will greet these poets as friends in college.

If Wordsworth and Bryant drew him to the woods and fields and made him love nature and nature's God, he may find rare enjoyment in the mature essays of Burroughs or Dallas Lore Sharp. Possibly, he may follow the trail to nature fiction or travel and in worthwhile literature relish a wholesome fare which will make less worthy books pallid and tasteless.

Lessons of courage, heroism, unselfishness, truth, faith, love, and sacrifice abound in beautiful poetry quite within the range of eight to eighty. Some current poems by a little-known author appealed to my class this year. These lines were written by Byron Herbert Reece, a Methodist poet from Georgia. The following is an excerpt:

THE ADORATION

If I but had a little coat,
A coat to fit a no-year old,
I'd button it close about His throat
To cover Him from the cold,
    The cold,
To cover Him from the cold.

. . .

If my heart were a house also,
A house also with room to spare
I never would suffer my Lord to go
Homeless, but house Him there,
    O there,
Homeless, but house Him there!

And in a poem to Our Lady he writes:

MARY

In Nazareth dwelt Mary Mild,
She carded and she spun;
On Christmas Day she bore the child
Of God, His only Son.

No doubt, the imagination cultivated in poetry is further exercised through beautiful folk or fairy tales, beautifully told. Not all folk tales are suitable for children. In fact, we know that folk tales were not originally written for children but were told by simple people around the evening fire to wile away the long hours. Some tales are gory, cruel, immoral, and unfit. But there is such a wealth of lovely lore from which to draw that no child's store should be impoverished. Andersen, Hawthorne, and Padraic Colum with individual and inimitable style have presented a host of deathless favorites to people the child's world. Who better than Colum can throw open the gates of Troy and over land and sea follow Odysseus, making the Greek hero come alive for the boy or girl breathlessly traveling in his wake?

The folk tale does far more than develop the imagination or furnish a means of escape from the commonplace into the magical. In their inherent desire for wish fulfillment, the boy or girl read themselves into the story. With the right book, they broaden and deepen, mentally, emotionally, spiritually. Seeing virtue rewarded and vice punished with poetic justice, they learn valuable lessons of virtue and courtesy. Isn't one secret of the tremendous success of Walt Disney's *Snow White* the artist's remarkable understanding and portrayal of human nature? Isn't this quality of the very essence of the folk or fairy tales? Isn't the sense of humor a delicious quality common to the primitive droll or noodle tale, to *Uncle Remus, Alice in Wonderland,* Kipling's *Just So Stories* and Stockton's charmingly absurd fiction? What a delight for the college student who renews acquaintance with Stockton when he picks up a copy of *The Casting Away of Mrs. Lecks and Mrs. Aleshine!* What more effective counter-irritant to modern sophistication, what better introduction to poetry or mythology or romance?

Because, as a child, he loved the stories of Grimm, the college student with scientific archeological bent may care to delve into the past as did those scholarly brothers Grimm, who recorded by folk tale the religious and social ideals of primitive peoples.

Simultaneously or successively, the child may call for fairy tale or myth, for they have elements in common. Without a knowledge of myths, the student is handicapped in college when he meets mythological allusions in Greek or Latin, in classical poetry or other literature, and sometimes in other fields, science, for example. One of the newest elements discovered has been called Promethium, an energy produce liberated during current work on the atomic bomb. To a chemistry student who knows the story of Prometheus Unbound the suitability of the name is evident.

Historically, myths have an antiquarian value, for we are interested in the religious beliefs and the tales by which primitive man explained what was beyond his ken, for example, day and night, as told in the story of Phoebus, and the change of seasons as in the stories of Ceres and Proserpine and of Balder and Hoder.

Exercising great discretion in the choice of myths, the storyteller no doubt presented to the lad's youthful mind those stories suitable for children and probably favored the Norse myths, because they stressed the spiritual ideals rather than the physical, emphasized wisdom rather than craft, and cherished respect for women, family, and home, especially dear to man in a land where cold and hardship taxed moral and physical strength and challenged courage and patient endurance.

Again and again, in college reading of Lagerlöf, Undset, Rölvaag, Gulbranssen, and other Scandinavian writers the student senses the racial characteristics evidenced in the Norse myths.

To know his Aesop, La Fontaine, Lessing, Gay, and Cowper, the college student finds his early acquaintance with myths an asset. In Horace, Chaucer, and Hawthorne he will read literary versions of some old favorites.

When Peter Rabbit hopped into the little boy's friendship, he started him on the alluring trail of nature literature, which included Thornton Burgess and *Uncle Remus,* and, perchance, branched off to Thoreau, Burroughs, and Sharp, or, perhaps, to nature romance or fiction, animal or sea story, which through adolescence and adult life wile away many an hour and tempt the reader further afield into travel or science.

Speakers, writers, artists, and conversationalists make such ready use of the fable that really a college student loses half the meaning of a reference if unacquainted with the fable. "Wolf! Wolf!," "It's a case of sour grapes," or "Who will bell the cat?" occur so often in everyday conversation that one cannot afford to be ignorant of their connotation. Many a time Abraham Lincoln made use of the fable to prove a point or convey an idea.

From the prudential fable the child, no doubt, advanced to another type of symbolic story—the parable—used so frequently and exquisitely by Our Lord, the most perfect of all storytellers. As he grew older, no doubt, the boy came to an awareness of the beauty of the parable and a realization that the Prodigal Son was the best short story ever told. If, in aroused interest, he searched further and came upon Father Meschler's *Life of Our Lord,* he learned that:

> "to speak in parables is a peculiarity of all Oriental wisdom and that if Our Lord wished to be considered a great Master, He must give evidence of proficiency in this mode of instruction ... [which] offered advantages for the speaker as well as the hearers ... learned and unlearned alike. Further ... the method had this advantage ... that [Our Lord's] glorious intellect could reveal itself in all its depths, clearness, delicacy and grace, together with its power of reaching the minds of the people ... Thus He advanced in the esteem and favor not only of the people but also of the teachers of the law ..."

Further study of the Bible or of the life of Our Lord would be a natural consequent. Our college students have been charmed and deeply affected by Archbishop Goodier's *Public Life of Our Lord Jesus Christ* and claim that the graphic details of God's biographer have made Christ live for them.

Among the many lives of Christ, Fulton Oursler's *The Greatest Story Ever Told* has made a strong appeal. J. L. Ross, in the *Library Journal,* says it is "vivid" and "retains intense interest" and that "these scripts" make the story "feel as real and contemporary as a newspaper report." And N. K. Burget of *The New York Times* comments:

"The stories are simply written and can be read as entertainment, as introduction to the Gospel story or as commentary. The important thing is that they present in modern form an account of those dramatic, long past, ... events that have ... changed the world." Monsignor Sheen commended the author "very highly for this contribution to religious literature."

This year, Oursler has published a *Child's Life of Jesus*. Virginia Kirkus calls it "one of the best books of this type we have seen."

During the hero worship stage, the boy's fancy was fired with tales of chivalry, of knightly ideals, and fine, noble living. In romance cycle and legend immortalizing the heroic exploits of Beowulf, Robin Hood, Don Quixote, King Arthur, Roland, the boy laid a foundation for the best in literature and approached the threshold to biography.

With all the concreteness of the new biography which presents real people wrestling with and overcoming real difficulties, the boy meets and loves flesh-and-blood saints like Damien the leper and Don Bosco. He is stimulated by the real experiences of men and women who overcame personal or physical handicap, broke their way through virgin forest, mastered science, discovered new lands, or rose to eminence in statesmanship or profession, army or navy.

Since the best books for the child must hold the interest of the adult, these may well form a part of his permanent private collection.

Though conscientious book selectors sound a warning note to the buyer of science books for children, there are in the recommended lists many charming editions in good format and a variety of subjects in useful and applied arts. For example, the "how-to-do" and "how-to-make" books encourage initiative in the "hand-minded" child and, while serving to lessen the discipline problem, offer illuminating evidence of the child's aptitude.

If the girl and boy get good fiction graded for their years, it is not difficult for the college librarian or teacher to develop a love of good literature with a discriminating reading habit.

Through all the years from childhood to manhood and womanhood, "the gift of reading" brings treasured friends into lives made better and happier and richer by contact with good and great and lofty minds.

Bibliography

Curry, Charles M., and Clippinger, Erle Elsworth.
  Children's Literature. Rand McNally, 1921.
Meschler, Maurice J. *Life of Our Lord Jesus Christ the Son of God*. Herder, 1913.
Reece, Byron Herbert. *Bow Down in Jericho*. Dutton, 1950.
Thomas, Katherine Elwes. *The Real Personages of Mother Goose*.
  Lothrop, Lee & Shepard, 1930.

HOW TO TELL A STORY *

Ruth Sawyer

The ancient challenge for a story has gone unanswered in far too great a measure. This is true especially in small towns and rural districts, where for generations boys and girls have never heard a story told. This need not be so. Wherever there may be a small library, a school, a community center, a scout troop; wherever there may be a librarian, a teacher, a leader, or parents —there can and should be story hours. For example, recently in Maine groups of high school students have been going into isolated districts to tell stories in the small one-room schoolhouses. They have been guided by an experienced storyteller and have discovered for themselves as well as for their listeners the fun and enthusiasm that lie in good stories.

To learn something new is stimulating. To learn by one's own effort, by the older and perhaps the best method in the world— trial and error—is equally stimulating. A beginner need not be

* *Compton's Pictured Encyclopedia*, vol. 13, pp. 463–65. Reprinted from the 1964 edition of *Compton's Pictured Encyclopedia* with permission of copyright owner F. E. Compton Co., Chicago, a Division of Encyclopedia Britannica, Inc.

fainthearted. For the beginner in storytelling here are two primary facts that may provide a springboard. First, everyone is a potential storyteller; everyone receives that racial heritage passed on by the traditional storytellers. Second, whether one be conscious of it or not, nearly everyone has been telling stories since he learned to talk.

Children and adults have continually felt the urge to tell stories about themselves, about the books they have read, about the plays or motion pictures they have seen, about something they have heard over the radio. Both the urge to tell and the ability are ingrained in us. Taking off from here it would be well to mark those factors in storytelling which are of most importance to the beginner.

BUILDING VOICE AND VOCABULARY

Every art requires its own special tools and mediums for expression. For the storytelling art, these are a pleasing voice and a certain skill in using words. The storyteller needs to acquire a listening ear so that he can hear his own voice as well as other voices; he must also learn to mark, to compare, to arrive at some standard by which to judge a voice. Is it well pitched—not so high as to be thin and shrill, not so low as to be mumbling? Is it a flexible voice? We all know how dull and uninteresting a monotonous voice can be. Is there good breath control? This means a voice may be pulled out of the throat and placed on the diaphragm where it belongs. A throaty voice tires easily; it does not carry well. A few simple exercises in breathing, the practice of speaking vowels and words on the breath, can add strength, clarity, and a pleasing tone to voices that may at the start be not too pleasing.

As for the use of words—they are for the storyteller what notes are for the musician or colors for the artist. A good, well-rounded vocabulary is a rich possession. It is out of words that storytellers create those pictures that captivate the listeners; for it is through the medium of pictures that the story is told and gathered in by the listeners. Words should be strong, of simple meaning; they should have color and that quality which arouses the imagination. Children take a peculiar delight in the sound and flavor of words. They enjoy strange words if there are not too many of them. Anything unfamiliar should be explained before the story is begun. Never break the magic by stopping the story to explain.

What Makes a Good Story?

It is important to have some understanding of what makes a good story to tell. Nearly all the stories included in what we call folk literature make for good telling. Nursery and fairy tales, myths, legends, and hero tales hold a universal appeal. They have simple and strong language and their form is closely knit, usually around a single idea or plot. The ones that can be told on the "short breath," as the French say, are the best for the beginner. The introduction in the story should be short, but it should arouse that sense of anticipation which makes the listener eager for what is going to happen. The development, or action, in the story should be logical, step by step. Once the climax is reached the ending, or fulfillment, should come quickly; it should satisfy, and it should seem the right and only ending for that particular story.

In the main a good story should appeal to those emotions that are felt to be both true and desirable in childhood: humor, love of adventure, desire for courage, compassion, a sense of good fellowship, joyfulness, and fresh untrammeled imagination.

How to Prepare a Story

What inevitably concerns the beginner is the best way to memorize a story. To learn word by word is both tedious and difficult. This form of memorizing tends to make the story mechanical; too often it gives the impressions of a recitation. True storytelling should have qualities of spontaneity and freshness. A musician recreates his music each time he plays it. A dancer recreates what she dances. So with the storyteller—the story should be recreated each time it is told; it should come to each listener as a living experience; it should hold the immediacy of something that is just happening. Even a beginner can make what she tells seem spontaneous, newly created if she never allows the story to become mechanically repeated, over and over, while it is being learned.

It has already been stressed that stories come to both the storyteller and the listener in the form of pictures. It is as a series of pictures that a story should be memorized. Let it be read slowly, letting the picture of each character and event be formed naturally in the mind. Close the book and think the story through in terms of those pictures the mind—or imagination—

has made. Then read the story again for the language. With two or three readings it is amazing how words fit themselves to the pictures and the story takes form. We all know what a strong hold pictures take on both imagination and memory. Stories memorized in this way are never forgotten; they belong to the storyteller; she can trust them, tell them with enthusiasm and authority.

That this way of memorizing by pictures may be more readily understood, here is a concrete example. The story used is "The Bremen Town Musicians" taken from the tales of the Brothers Grimm. It is a great favorite with children. Here are the pictures as they form themselves naturally in the mind of any storyteller:

An old ass, or donkey (American children are more familiar with donkeys), is the first character to be introduced. All his life he has worked hard. Now that the donkey is too old to work his master has turned him out.

He takes the road to Bremen. He will become a town musician. On the road he falls in with Growler, the old dog, also abandoned.

Together they travel and meet up with Whiskers, the old cat. No longer able to catch mice, the cat is going to be drowned by her mistress.

They come to a barnyard. Here on a post they hear the old cock bemoaning his fate. He has failed to crow fair weather for Lady's Day, so he is to be served up for the holiday dinner.

The donkey persuades them all to come with him to Bremen and form a band. Their spirits rise. They are no longer outcasts.

That night they take shelter in the woods. The cock and cat go up a tree, the dog and donkey lie down under it. Aloft the cock spies a light. It may offer better shelter.

Making their way through the woods the four find a barn where robbers are hiding. They are feasting around a table.

"Good fare for us," announces the donkey. It is time to start being town musicians. On the donkey in turn mount dog, cat, and cock. Together they bray, bark, caterwaul, and crow.

Terrified, the robbers flee. The four take over the barn. They feast, then settle themselves for the night, each in his accustomed place.

The robbers return. One of them attempts to discover what has happened. While he tries to find his way in the dark the cat scratches him, the dog bites him, the cock claws him, the donkey kicks him. More terrified than before he tells the others that witch or devil has taken over their hiding place. That is the last of the robbers.

The four, left in peace, end their days in comfort and plenty.

"The Bremen Town Musicians" illustrates every point in a good story: it is short; language is simple; introduction is brief; it develops logically; the ending follows quickly upon the climax; and it satisfies. Beginners find it easy to learn and delightful to tell.

SOURCES OF GOOD STORIES

The transition for the beginner from the simple, unified folk tale to the more complex story by a fine author should not be too difficult. Stories should be told from such writers as Rudyard Kipling, Eleanor Farjeon, Elizabeth Coatsworth, Henry Beston, Laura Richards, Beatrix Potter, Parker Fillmore, Seumas MacManus, and Wanda Gág. Such a story as Wanda Gág's "Gone Is Gone" makes a perfect and easy transition from the simple to the more complicated form of story.

Furthermore children's books should be "told from"; to tell just enough from the beginning of a good book whets the appetite for more. It invites those who are poor or slow readers to do more reading on their own account. So often it happens that boys or girls, thus invited to read a book through for themselves, will go to the librarian and ask for another book "just the same kind." Thus will wider reading interest grow; and that is good.

THINGS TO REMEMBER

There is a final point in storytelling that needs emphasis—the matter of timing. This is as important in the art of storytelling as in that of music, dancing, or the theater. Think of what a dreary, stupid performance it would be if a whole symphony were played through at the same tempo; if lines throughout a play were given at the same speed; if a dancer never changed her rhythm, never broke it with a moment's pause.

So with a story. There are moments which call for slow, leisurely telling. As the action grows, as things begin to happen, it is natural to hurry the tempo. Before a moment of awe, of rising wonder, of excitement, a pause can add much to the tang and flavor of a tale, and a storyteller gets far more fun out of the telling when she has learned to use timing effectively.

Here is a summary of those things of value that may lie in the art of the storyteller for the beginner:

To remember that storytelling is a part of our racial heritage.

To remember that nearly everyone is a potential storyteller.

To learn to listen to voices, including one's own, and then to mark what makes a pleasing voice: the right pitch, flexibility, breath control, clear enunciation.

To realize the importance of words—to use them richly, with strength, meaning, and power.

To know what makes a good story for telling: one with a single idea or plot, a short introduction, a logical development, the ending following closely on the climax. A good story uses simple language, holds a universal appeal.

To memorize a story by pictures.

To be conscious of timing and to use it effectively.

Books about Storytelling

The Art of the Storyteller. By Marie L. Shedlock. (Dover.) The clearest and most readable exposition of storytelling as an art. It brings out a good approach to storytelling and to the selection of a story. It has great value in training courses for librarians and teachers. Eighteen stories are given in full. The revised edition includes a foreword by Anne Carroll Moore, and the bibliography has been brought up to date by Eulalie Steinmetz.

The Way of the Storyteller. By Ruth Sawyer. (Viking.) This book combines the philosophy and the rich experiences of one of the best modern storytellers. It includes 11 stories as well as an excellent bibliography.

Books of Stories

Granny's Wonderful Chair. By Frances Browne. (Macmillan.) Eight stories of fairyland told to a little girl by her grandmother's wonderful chair. "The Christmas Cuckoo" and "The Greedy Shepherd" are especially popular.

Big Music. Chosen by Mary Noel Bleecker. (Viking.) An excellent selection by an experienced storyteller of 20 humorous and vigorous folk tales.

A Baker's Dozen. Selected by Mary Gould Davis. (Harcourt.) Thirteen favorite stories of boys and girls with an introductory chapter for storytellers.

The Wonder Clock. By Howard Pyle. (Harper.) Twenty-four stories by a master storyteller and a fine artist. *Pepper and Salt,* a companion volume, is an equally rich source for the storyteller.

Just So Stories. By Rudyard Kipling. (Doubleday.) The choice of words and the good plots of these imaginative "how" stories about an elephant's trunk, a camel's hump, a whale's throat, etc., make them easy to tell and fun to listen to.

The Little Bookroom. By Eleanor Farjeon. (Walck.) A selection by the author of the favorites among her own short stories for children. "The Little Dressmaker" and "The Seventh Princess" appeal especially to older girls.

The Long Christmas. By Ruth Sawyer. (Viking.) A collection of stories to celebrate the birth of the Christ Child. They come from Spain, Italy, Ireland, Austria, the Isle of Man, the gypsies, and France.

The Bold Dragoon and Other Ghostly Tales. By Washington Irving. Edited by Anne Carroll Moore. (Knopf). A fine collection of classic American stories to tell at Halloween or around the campfire at night.

Rhymes and Verses. By Walter De La Mare. (Holt.) Story poems, like "The Isle of Lone," please boys and girls who are sensitive to the sounds of words, while the shorter poems make a good beginning and ending of the story hour.

Rootabaga Stories. By Carl Sandburg. (Harcourt.) These original fairy tales are derived from the American scene and they are full of poetry and nonsense.

The Great Quillow. By James Thurber. (Harcourt.) A humorous fantasy that tells of a toymaker and a giant. The author's *Many Moons* is equally good.

The Spider's Palace. By Richard Hughes. (Random.) The light-hearted nonsense of these modern fairy tales is at its best in "Living in W'ales" and "The Dark Child."

The Street of Little Shops. By Margery Williams Bianco. (Doubleday.) Gay and original stories of village life. "The Baker's Daughter" is a great favorite with the children.

Ting-a-ling Tales. By Frank R. Stockton. (Scribner.) These fanciful stories about a smart young fairy named Ting-a-ling and his giant friend, Tur-il-i-ra, first appeared in *St. Nicholas* magazine.

THE STORY HOUR:
A SIGNIFICANT PROGRAM OF
CHILDREN'S DEPARTMENTS
IN PUBLIC LIBRARIES *

Nora E. Beust

The story hour [1] has long been a significant program of children's departments in public libraries. It is natural that this activity has developed in libraries as the children's rooms are an ideal setting for the story hour. They are stocked with a variety of reading suited to the abilities and interests of children of all ages and are housed in pleasant quarters that are decorated and furnished for children's enjoyment.

These rooms are open to the boys and girls after school hours, on Saturday, and during vacations for reading, browsing, and other activities related to pleasure with books. The work of the children's department is in charge of a librarian whose basic training has stressed the importance of introducing boys and girls to the best of the literature of childhood.

The objectives of the story hour may be briefly stated as: to acquaint children with the best stories in the field of children's literature (folk and fairy tales and modern stories) and to give the children opportunity of listening to well-told stories.

The Children's Department of the Enoch Pratt Free Library

* Nora E. Beust, "The Story Hour: A Significant Program of Children's Departments in Public Libraries," *School Life*, 30 (May, 1948), 26–28. Reprinted by permission of author.

1 Material for this article was furnished by the children's departments in the public libraries of the following cities: Baltimore, Charleston, S.C., Chicago, Cleveland, Denver, Detroit, Indianapolis, Long Beach, Calif., Los Angeles, Minneapolis, New York, Pittsburgh, St. Paul, Seattle, Tacoma, Wash., and Washington, D.C.

expresses its philosophy of the story hour as, ".... that pleasant time when the group and herself (the storyteller) are in absolute accord and sharing with great zest—an adventure."

The story-hour program in the library usually begins in the fall, soon after the opening of school, and continues until spring. In The New York Public Library the "season" begins with the high festival of Halloween. The old Dutch school bell at the Harlem Branch Library "rings in the witches" with all their fascinatingly scary paraphernalia, the fires burn low on the hearths of the Reading Rooms, and "The Boy Who Drew Cats" and "The Hobyahs" and "Baba Yaga" stories are told to the boys and girls all over the boroughs of Manhattan, the Bronx, and Richmond.

In New York Public Library System

Stories are told weekly in all of the branches after Halloween, and monthly in the sub-branches of The New York Public Library System. Story hours last from 45 to 60 minutes and are held in some quiet room in the library set aside for that purpose. The children go to the room in procession. They are greeted by the storyteller who has the books from which she will tell the stories on a table with a bowl of flowers and the story-hour wishing candle. This is blown out at the end of the story hour with a wish going into the candle flame from each child.

There are no interruptions during a story hour, no staged participation, no questioning and quizzing afterward by the storyteller to discover reactions. Children often tell voluntarily what a story has meant to them, and frequently a remark made weeks or months after a story hour reveals what the child took from the story told. A story may, at the moment of telling, have no meaning for a child; but a time may come when an experience will give it meaning for him, and he will draw it from his subconsciousness to fulfill its cultural, spiritual, or humorous role.

The story-hour season closes with the celebration of Marie Shedlock's birthday in May. It was her telling of fairy tales of Hans Andersen that inspired Anne Carroll Moore, then superintendent of work with children in The New York Public Library, to conceive the idea that storytelling is a legitimate and necessary part of library work with children.

The regular story hours are for children from approximately the third to the sixth grade. Folk and fairy lore are the backbone of these story hours. The only mediums used at any of the library story hours consist simply of books and storytellers. The stories told are selected from approved books in their reading room collections. Imaginative stories are told in the words of the author. The essence of the folk tales is preserved in their telling. Stories are told simply, with due regard for authenticity. They are told because a children's librarian wants to share them with her boys and girls. The supervisor of storytelling says, "That liking and the desire to share it is the twofold secret of a successful story hour."

CARNEGIE LIBRARY OF PITTSBURGH

Story hours are also a regular activity of the children's department in the Carnegie Library of Pittsburgh. It is through this means that the literature of the world is introduced. For the first time the child may hear of the wondrous adventures of Ulysses, the ring of Thor's hammer, the bravery of Beowulf, or the friendship of Roland and Oliver. He hears the tales that circled the world before man could write, the stories so old that no one knows their age: Cinderella, Sleeping Beauty, Jack the Giant Killer. Newer innovations are tried from time to time, puppet shows, pictures, plays, each successful in itself, but never taking the place in the child's heart of the story that is told. Always there is someone to remark, after some other form of entertainment. "Now, please tell us a story."

CLEVELAND BRANCHES

In the branch libraries of the Cleveland Public Library, story hours are held once a week from fall until spring for younger children, and for a shorter period another story hour is conducted for older boys and girls. Myths and folk tales which have been told since primitive times, along with some stories of more recent origin, are told to the younger group. A high standard is always maintained in the selection of these stories by the children's librarians. The older children are told idealistic, heroic literature, such as the King Arthur legends, the Volsunga Saga, the Cuchulain saga, stories from the Persian heroes, the adventures of Robin Hood, and heroic tales such as that of Ulysses.

Show methods are avoided and careful preparation is stressed. The storyteller brings to the listeners an interpretation which grows from a sympathetic understanding and background of literary appreciation.

A number of libraries report that they, too, are continuing their programs of telling the best versions of old folk tales and carefully selected modern stories. In Cleveland the story hour was curtailed along with many other activities during the war years. When the stories were resumed, hundreds of children stood patiently in line awaiting their turn to go into the story-hour rooms.

IN OTHER CITIES

Staff and housing shortages requiring adjustment of programs still exist in libraries. Minneapolis and St. Paul have worked out innovations. In Minneapolis the staff of the central children's room, which has no easily accessible place for stories, cooperates in the Saturday morning program of the Science Museum Society throughout the winter months. The program includes films on some aspect of natural science, a story, and a treasure hunt. The attendance sometimes reaches 400 children, but carefully selected, well-told stories hold their interest. In other parts of the library, stories are often read, rather than told, due to the shortages of staff members, because it is, of course, better to have a story well read than poorly prepared and badly told.

St. Paul is using book-browsing hours at both the main library and the branches. A series of these programs is held three or four times a year for the period of a week. Minnesota authors are featured. The young people meet them and hear them talk or tell stories. Junior books of authors and the works of illustrators are featured as well as folk tales. The book-browsing groups range in age from the third grade through junior high school. The children's department turned over the space formerly used as a story-hour room and auditorium to the development of work with adolescents, because the library staff felt the importance of providing this service, and it was impossible to carry on story hours regularly because of staff shortages.

The preschool story hours are a comparatively recent development in libraries and are still thought of as experimental in some instances. The staff of the Long Beach (Calif.) Public Library believe that the discussion groups carried on with parents at the time of the preschool story are as important as the work with little children. Books on child care, books of general interest, and children's reading are stressed. Pittsburgh began its preschool story hour in 1947. Mothers bring their children (ages 3–5) for a half-hour story hour every other Wednesday. While the children are enjoying their own stories, the mothers in an adjoining room are having a program planned and executed by the librarians from the adult department.

Tacoma, Washington, resumed its story program in 1947 with the preschool age group, as it was felt that there was an immediate need to interest adults in the library and its use. The small children are in many cases accompanied by their parents. Stories for the picture book hours also require less preparation in the matter of learning than stories for older children, and with an insufficient staff any time-consuming efforts were avoided.

Detroit began preschool story hours approximately 15 years ago. The form it takes depends upon the experience, personality, and philosophy of the individual who conducts it. Chicago, Cleveland, Los Angeles, Minneapolis, New York, and Washington, D.C., are also including some separate programs for young children.

Indianapolis has a radio library story hour once a week over a local station. This is given on Thursday afternoons from 1:30 to 1:45, and is part of the Indianapolis Public School Radio Program. The children listen in the classroom during school time. The radio story hour has been carried on since 1936. The estimated audience is 7,000 children.

An effective radio story hour is one activity in the cooperative program with the Board of Public Education and the Carnegie Library of Pittsburgh. Two mornings a week their storyteller goes to a school classroom to make a wire recording of the story that is to be broadcast later in the day to each school in the city. The school children have a chance to see the broadcast made and to participate with songs and and verses. In this manner each child in the primary grades throughout the city has an opportunity to hear and see a library storyteller. In all cases the children's librarian at the local branch accompanies the storyteller so that the children link "their" library to the radio storyteller. Most of the parochial school pupils, as well as many in the county schools, also listen to the broadcasts.

Minneapolis, Tacoma, and Seattle also use the radio.

The puppet show is another medium that children enjoy. Denver, St. Paul, Los Angeles, Chicago, and Washington, D.C., tell of effective "shows." Records are used to supplement the story in Seattle, Chicago, Minneapolis, Indianapolis, Washington, D.C., Long Beach, and Los Angeles. Slides, motion pictures, and children's own dramatizations are used in Chicago, though the motion picture programs based on popular children's books at the main library children's room have been temporarily discontinued due to lack of facilities. Slides were also listed as being used in Minneapolis. A magic show and at times children dressed in native costume of countries when the stories have a foreign setting give children an opportunity to contribute to the story hour in Seattle. Dramatization and magic shows are also used at times in Los Angeles.

Many of the libraries cooperate with the recreational departments in conducting summer story hours or reading groups on the playgrounds. Stories are also told to such groups as Boy Scouts, Girl Scouts, and church summer schools. In all the libraries the close cooperation between public library and school library indicates the importance that teachers place on the contribution which children's librarians are making to boys and girls in their appreciation of literature.

Part Seven

TRADITIONAL AND MODERN
IMAGINATIVE TALES
FOR CHILDREN

FAIRY TALES AND THEIR EFFECT UPON CHILDREN PART I *

Ruth C. Horrell

WHAT IS A FAIRY TALE

In order to identify a fairly tale in the literature of twentieth century children, we must understand it first in its broader sense. This will necessitate a brief knowledge of the origin of the fairy tales and their development into their present connotation. Bess Proctor Adams does this when she says:

> The word "fairy" has undergone gradual modification in meaning. Originally from the French, faerie or feeree denoted a mysterious abode of certain supernatural creatures called fees. Women who knew the power of herbs and incantation, who had to do with charms, spells and enchantments, were called fees (fays). In England the word fairy was eventually applied to the mysterious inhabitants of the elfin kingdom as well as to the country itself. The term is now loosely applied to many stories in which there are no fairies. The fairy tale is one form of folk literature, and the two terms (fairy and folk) are not finely differentiated.[1]

These were also known as "household tales" because they were told around the fires of the household for the entertainment principally of the adults. Blanche Weekes prefers this title, for she says:

> This seems to be a better name as many of the so called fairy tales bear no relation to the fairies and fairyland; nor is

* Ruth C. Horrell, "Fairy Tales and Their Effect Upon Children," Part I. *Illinois Libraries*, 38 (September, 1956), 235–39. Reprinted by permission of the *Illinois Libraries* and the author.

[1] Bess Proctor Adams, *About Books and Children* (New York: Henry Holt & Co., 1953), p. 312.

there always present a supernatural or more than natural force at work to cause events to happen. The term fairy seems to have come to mean something extraordinary. The term fairy tale, however has a hold on people's thinking because of the glamorous connotation of the word. The term "household tale" gives a cue as to the original purpose of these stories.[2]

Time seems to have pruned these tales and preserved their style and pattern until modern writers have subconsciously imitated them in what is known as "modern fairy tales" of an imaginative nature with no roots in a folk tradition. Dorothy White recognizes this development, for she says:

> The traditional folk tale has always exerted a healthy influence on the modern fairy story and many successful writers have observed some of the folk forms and conventions.[3]

In order to further define a fairy tale and to show its growth from the folk roots let us consider the characteristics of both the old and the new. Folk tales proper are impersonal, embodying the dreams and emotions of a whole people, sometimes a whole race. This quality of universal appeal, along with an unsurpassed literary style has affected its preservation. "The fact that folk tales have lived through the centuries proves that they have intrinsic merit." [4] May Hill Arbuthnot agrees with this in the following statement:

> Folk tale themes are not only strong but objective and understandable. They have to do with winning security, earning a living, or a place in the world, accomplishing impossible tasks, escaping from powerful enemies, outwitting wicked schemes and schemers and succeeding with nonchalance. These strong themes are the background of these old tales and largely account for their vigor.[5]

The modern literary fairy tale differs from the traditional in that it is the artistic imaginative work of one author bearing the

2 Blanche E. Weekes, *Literature and the Child* (New York: Silver Burdett, 1935), p. 99.
3 Dorothy Neal White, *About Books and Children* (New York: Oxford University Press, 1949), p. 53.
4 Lillian Hollowell, *A Book of Children's Literature* (New York: Rinehart, 1950), p. 45.
5 May Hill Arbuthnot, *Children and Books* (Chicago: Scott Foresman and Company, 1947), p. 225.

stamp of his individuality. The reader is aware of a greater subjectivity in the modern stories. Adams compares the two by saying:

> Pathos is practically unknown in the older tales. The story is told objectively; one is not taken into the confidence of the hero whose emotions are treated so casually that the reader views his efforts with curiosity and a certain suspense, but rarely with complete empathy.[6]

However, "The modern fairy tale ... in the hands of a writer of near genius ... can scale the heights with its triumphant imagination." [7] In all modern fairy tales the same process is at work as is in the traditional folk tale in that the allegory relates to a whole people's emotions.

In the traditional tales the characters are stereotypes and few in number. These few are types which are common to the human race. Character contrast is common in each tale. The plots vary but the actors are the same in each, representing some universal emotion based upon human facts and situations instead of fancy. The plot is cohesive, simple, direct, and swift. Many of the tales seem to be outline pictures only, as though the mere framework is given on which the reader can hang his imagination. Certain conventions are followed—three wishes, three sons, three tasks, three suitors, three gifts, three sisters, or three riddles. Even the repetition of phrasing is often a pattern of threes. Arbuthnot accounts for their popularity by defending these characteristics:

> The vigorous plots of the folk tales, full of suspense and strong action, appeal strongly to young readers. The heroes do things. ... The plot that unfolds their doings has logic, unity and economy. ... Suspense is built up and maintained until it reaches a peak in the climax, after which it declines and the action ends with a flourish.[8]

The form of the fairy tales along with the content reveals four distinct types: the accumulative or repetitive tale, the comic or droll, the beast tale, and the märchen or nursery tale.

The accumulative or repetitive tale is the one which grows by the addition of several episodes, such as "The Old Woman

6 Adams, *op. cit.,* p. 314.

7 White, *op. cit.,* p. 66.

8 Arbuthnot, *op. cit.,* p. 227.

and Her Pig," "The House that Jack Built," or "The Straw Ox."
A refrain of poetry is repeated in many tales of this type which
enhances its literary quality in content as well as in form. "This
use of repetition with variation provides mounting interest and
expectation on the part of the reader or listener." [9]

The droll or comic is one inspired by foolish blunders of human beings. The humor is ridiculous, primitive, and absurd,
but not coarse. We find this type in "The Three Sillies," "Hans-
in-Luck," and "The Husband who Minded the House."

In the beast tale we find some people as characters, but it is
definitely the animals who hold the stage and who contribute to
the interest. Examples of this type are: "The Bremen Town
Musicians," "Chicken Licken," and "The Three Pigs." The latter two are also part repetitive tales. The fable with its human-
ized beast suggests the folk fairy tale classified as a beast tale.
The fabulist uses the characters as a means to an end. A human
weakness is portrayed to influence politics, society, and religion,
but is not a product of the folk mind.

The märchen or nursery tale is a term used to cover all stories
of the "Once upon a time" or "Far, far away" type. In its strict
sense, this is the true fairy tale—the type to which major criticisms are directed. As Weekes puts it:

> They are the tales that have come to be regarded as the fairy
> tale or the tale in which the kind fairy, the wicked fairy, the
> terrible giant, or ogre, the magic wand, the wishing cap, the
> shoe of swiftness, the invisible clock, and of course, the beau-
> tiful maiden and the prince charming are found.[10]

Let us examine the form of these original fairy tales. We find
in these folk tales a pattern that is as clear cut and definite as
that of the old drama that it so closely resembles. Weekes defends the form of these tales when she says:

> Criticism of the fairy tales is directed against the content
> rather than the form, for the latter is accepted as being so per-
> fect that modern writers do well to imitate it.[11]

The folk-tale pattern always provides for three easily discernible
parts: the introduction, the development, and the conclusion.

[9] Lillian H. Smith. *The Unreluctant Years; A Critical Approach to Children's Literature* (Chicago: American Library Association, 1953), p. 54.

[10] Weekes, *op. cit.*, p. 101.

[11] *Ibid.*, p. 163.

Time is effectively accounted for by conventional phrases that carry the reader at once to a dream world where anything is possible. Brevity of introduction is an important phase of the charm of these folk tales. The scene is also briefly sketched on a mere framework that must be filled in by the imagination of the reader. The plot development is rapid and vigorous; the suspense is relieved in a direct satisfying conclusion.

* * *

WHY ARE THEY CRITICIZED

There are those literary critics who would have us believe that there are elements in these old tales that have a bad psychological effect upon children. Since they are a record of primitive philosophy, religion, customs, standards, and taboos, some critics contend that they are beyond the comprehension of the child. It is also feared that the author or narrator will be unable to interpret and account for the harshness and the vindictive cruelty, the unethical conduct, and the vicious jealousy of the fairy-tale people, all of which may prove a shock to the sensitive child or stimulate his acceptance of such as typical adult conduct. The fear-inspiring elements may yield unfortunate returns in emotionally disturbed children. Dorothy Baruch feels that this is the case, for she says:

> We avoid tales of threatening punishment. We steer clear of the gruesome and the cruel. We admit that stories which have an element of tragedy or horror should not be read or told to very young children.
> It is also feared that the child will confuse the fantastic with the real and thereby lose his sense of security; that false values will evolve which may throw his understanding askew; that he may accept fiction as fact.
> The harm is not in pretending, but in the believing that what we pretend is true.[12]

These realistic critics would permit us to use the beast tale, the comic or droll tale even with small children, but would have

12 Dorothy Baruch, "This Question of Fairy Tales," *Progressive Education,* IX (May, 1932), p. 364.

us leave the märchen or any tale possessing supernatural or vicious pretending elements for the eight or nine year olds, at
which time the critics feel that an orientation with parallel reality has been thoroughly established within the child. It seems to
be recognized that adventuring into this fantastic world should
be brief and gradual when introduced to the child for fear that
he may reject the responsibilities of the world of reality. There
is support for the conclusion that earliest reading should be more
realistic and less fanciful. "It would be ideal to build a sort of
ladder whereby children might travel from the real to the fanciful," [13] says Baruch.

Stories to come under the ban as first literature would include
"Jack the Giant Killer," "Bluebeard," "Snow White and the
Seven Dwarfs," "Hansel and Gretel," "Cinderella," "Puss in
Boots," and "Jack and the Beanstalk." Hollowell brings out the
opinion of critics in this matter:

> Didactic writers disapprove of the tales for moral and reli-
> gious reasons, asserting that they would hinder, rather than
> aid in developing worthy ideals, since craft and cunning too
> often help win the reward.[14]

One of these didactic critics says:

> These stories are not didactic in intent. . . . In some instances
> they are completely unethical . . . The reader, if he must have
> a moral in his stories, will have to read it into them himself.
> He will not find a consistent, sustained, moral concept. . . .
> Very few references are made to prayer or Deity or any of the
> things we associate with religion. . . . The main character may
> lie, break his word, . . . Kill, or rob in order to make his
> fortune.[15]

The cause of these so-called "twisted ethical concepts" is attributed to the fact that a simple childish primitive people produced them, whose standards of right and wrong were not well
developed; that these stories represent mass thinking which is

---

13 *Ibid.*, p. 366.
14 Hollowell, *op. cit.*, p. 45.
15 Pauline Byrd Taylor, "Ethics in Fairy and Household Tales," *Elementary English Review*, XVII (May, 1940), p. 190.

always on a lower plane. Taylor concludes by admitting that they do, however, have value:

> Since we cannot use them consistently in pointing out the road to perdition or the pathway to paradise, perhaps we should accept them for what they are—entertaining stories to while away the hours of childhood.[16]

16 *Ibid.*, p. 191.

FAIRY TALES AND THEIR EFFECT UPON CHILDREN PART II *

Ruth C. Horrell

A LITERARY HERITAGE

Some of the arguments in favor of the fairy tales are to the effect that undue alarm is expressed over the vices in these tales and that children accept these as make-believe episodes in which evil receives due punishment. The proponents of these tales point out that a great many fairy tales contain no vicious elements whatsoever; that the value of right conduct is strongly emphasized in that the doer of kind deeds receives the favor of the fairy while the villains are satisfyingly punished. "These conclusions satisfy the child's eye-for-an-eye code of ethics and apparently leave his imagination untroubled," [1] says Arbuthnot.

* Ruth C. Horrell, "Fairy Tales and Their Effect Upon Children," Part II. *Illinois Libraries*, 38 (November, 1956), 278–82. Reprinted by permission of *Illinois Libraries* and the author.

1 May Hill Arbuthnot, *Children and Books* (Chicago: Scott Foresman and Company, 1947), p. 227.

She also believes that the fairy tales are so predominantly constructive in their moral lessons that they leave an "indelible impression of virtue invariably rewarded and evil unfailingly punished." [2] She asks a pointed rhetorical question at this point. "Can this world and this code hurt a child?" [3]

A comparison has been made to the Old Testament stories that these didactic critics would have children read, such as that of Jacob tricking his brother, Esau, out of his birthright, or the terrors of Daniel in the lion's den. It is advocated by these proponents that these Bible stories are definitely not protective of children's emotions, and contain as much horror as the most criticized fairy tale.

Ella Cummings quotes Walter Taylor Field as saying in "Finger Post to Child's Reading" that "To most children the fairy tale brings the first real distinction between good and evil and thus is effective in awakening and developing the moral sense." [4] Therefore she feels that the fairy tale can justify its popularity with educational results. She further says:

> Elemental truth of the moral law and general types of human experiences are presented in fairy tales ... The fairy tale is the literary heritage of every child. "The House in the Wood," "Little Daylight," "Snow White and Rose Red," "Briar Rose," "The Elves and the Shoemaker," "The Story of Midas" all leave children better off ethically than before they heard them.[5]

Another proponent would like to defend them against the frequent criticism that they are too fantastic for today's children, by calling our attention to some of the evidences of today's miracles. "Today's man flies through space more swiftly than sound in something more comfortable." [6] Gates also speaks of the magic eye, the x-ray machine, television, intercommunication systems where voices come from the wall, and electronic "Open Sesame" doors that at one time would have been fantastic also, but to

---

2 *Ibid.*, p. 227.

3 *Ibid.*, p. 227.

4 Ella Cummings, "Should We Believe in Fairy Tales," *Grade Teacher*, LXXI (February, 1954), 47.

5 *Ibid.*, p. 47.

6 Doris Gates, "Six Impossible Things," condensed in *Education Digest*, XIV (March 1949), 27.

today's children, they are very real. She defends the fairy tales further by saying:

> Another frequent criticism of fanciful literature is that it is too gruesome for children. To such critics I suggest a careful reading of the daily newspaper, and the popular pictorial magazines, an evening at the movies or before the radio. The only difference between the gruesomeness of the one over the other lies in the fact that the horror of our everyday world is more vivid and dreadful ... without reason and without justification of any kind ...
>
> In the land of "once upon a time," issues are never clouded. Good triumphs always and evil is punished. No confusion, no bewilderment, and as neat a little sermon on moral virtues, without sermonizing, as any earnest grown-up could desire.
>
> The witch in "Hansel and Gretel" was evil enough to lure children into her grasp by tempting them with a house built of cookies. When the children succeeded in outwitting that evil and dealing with it in forthright fashion, the reader feels only satisfaction; that justice has been meted out. There is no shock.[7]

Ollie Depew respects the opinion of a noted author in regard to this subject when she says:

> Concerning the value of fairy stories in cultivating the child's imagination, Samuel Taylor Coleridge wrote: "Should children be permitted to read romances, and stories of giants, magicians, and genii? I know all that has been said against it, but I have formed my faith in the affirmative." [8]

These proponents of the fairy tales bring out a justifiable number of values that lie in this type of children's literature. These values coincide with the basic needs of children and seem to do much toward meeting these needs. Smith says:

> That fairy tales have a permanent place in children's literature may be assumed, since a story which has lived for hundreds of years must possess a vitality which is imperishable and immutable. . . . The child who listens to or reads these tales

---

[7] *Ibid.*, p. 28.

[8] Ollie Depew, *Children's Literature by Grades and Types* (Chicago: Ginn, 1938), p. 35.

has had the pleasure of suspense which heightens the satisfaction of an appropriate conclusion. He has had, as well, though he may not know it, the aesthetic pleasure which pattern, form, and proportion give, and the moral pleasure of seeing good overcome evil.[9]

She quotes Walter De La Mare as saying in his introduction to *Animal Stories* (N.Y., Scribner, 1940, p. 38), that:

"A sorrowful, a tragic, even a terrifying tale, picture, or poem ... may feed the imagination, enlighten the mind, strengthen the heart, show us ourselves. It may grieve, alarm, or even shock us and still remain intensely interesting ... Much depends upon how they have been told and with what reason and intention.

"Even in my youngest days I could easily manage to stare into Bluebeard's silent and dreadful cupboard, could watch the nail pierced barrel containing the wicked queen go rolling down a steep place into the sea, and Great Claus's execution with his club ... I enjoyed these stories, knowing them to be stories, and I am certain as can be that they did me not the least harm." [10]

Smith says also that beauty and poetry are to be found in fairy tales in both form and the content. This unconsciously satisfies a child's aesthetic need. She also says that it deepens and broadens emotional sympathy. Adams also speaks of emotional security in these tales:

It carries the reader along into genuine, if vicarious, experience; it stirs his emotions, arouses his curiosity, stimulates his mind, gives him a measuring stick for living.[11]

Arbuthnot says concerning the value of these tales:

These old fairy tales contain in their "picture language" the symbols of some of the deepest human feelings, and satisfy in fantasy, human desires for beauty, sincerity, achievement, and love ... The castle speaks of achievement and the little hut of peace and security, ... love fortifying the weak, the misunderstood and the oppressed giving them sanctuary in peril and

9 Smith, *op. cit.*, p. 45.
10 *Ibid.*, p. 45.
11 Adams, *op. cit.*, preface.

reinforcement in their weakness and rewarding their courageous struggles.

Whether children are conscious of it or not, these stories may become sources of moral strength—a strength which is part faith and part courage, and is wholly unshakable.[12]

Their moral and spiritual security is reassured in the preface to a book of Andersen's fairy tales:

> Isn't it true, that dragons and serpents are always conquered in fairy tales, that generosity is always rewarded, and sincerity always triumphant, and goodness always a source of joy? [13]

This same writer emphasizes the fact that fairy tales meet a child's need to achieve when he says, "They worship heroes and heroism, because they feel the need of heroism and want to be heroes themselves." [14]

Another general statement concerning the values of these tales was given as a tribute to Hans Christian Andersen on the 150th anniversary of his birthday in a recent metropolitan newspaper:

> The virtues that the fairy tale recognizes and glorifies are many—kindness, sweetness, love, courage, endurance, loyalty— but, except where it has been put into a sort of didactic harshness by much later and less happy moralists, they are all virtues out of an Eden so innocent that one cannot conceive of its harboring evil.[15]

All lovers of fairy tales seem to agree upon the fact that they afford escape, change, and enjoyment; that the strange quietness and the old word pictures of these stories afford relaxation as well as create a strong mood that only music or poetry can approach.

Jean Betzner feels that they have a recreatory value, for she says:

> If this form of literature suggests playing with the affairs of life, it should be encouraged as a means of securing what real

12 Arbuthnot, *op. cit.*, p. 233.

13 Francis Hackett, preface to *Fairy Tales and Stories,* by Hans Christian Andersen, edited by Signe Toksvig, New York: Macmillan, 1953.

14 *Ibid.*, preface.

15 Sean O'Faolian, "For the Child and the Wise Man," *The New York Times Magazine* (March 27, 1955), p. 9.

play can always contribute—perspective and renewed vigor which can be secured in no better way.[16]

Weekes emphasized their entertaining and relaxing qualities when she says:

> After the age of three the imagination becomes more creative and is characterized by flights of fancy of the fairy-tale type. The contention is that the fairy tale thus plays its part in making the life of reality more bearable, thereby contributing to adjustment.[17]

It is thought that children live too much amid pressure and obstacle of fact to want a world of "bland insipidity." While they are in this imaginative world where obstacle and pressure have been removed, they are developing the ability to think in terms of the fanciful and the abstract. "Dreamers become builders; a nation of unimaginative realists would produce no artists, poets, authors, musicians, inventors, or scientists." [18]

A good summary of the values for children found in fairy tales is given by Hollowell:

> What then, can fairy tales do for children? First, they develop the imagination and deepen emotional experience; second, they satisfy a child's need for self-expression; third, they cultivate a wholesome sense of humor; fourth, without sermonizing, they supply effective moral teaching; fifth, they are valuable as a preparation for an appreciation of literature in later life; and sixth, they broaden a child's mental horizon and offer an opportunity to absorb the flavor and atmosphere of other countries.[19]

CONCLUSION

After learning of the characteristics of the various types of fairy tales and of their criticisms and values as given by some of the literary critics in the field of children's literature, I have reached the following conclusions as to their effect upon children.

They do have a definite place in the literature for children.

---

[16] Jean Betzner, *Exploring Literature with Children in the Elementary School* (New York: Little & Ives, 1943), p. 56.

[17] Weekes, *op. cit.*, p. 165.

[18] Adams, *op. cit.*, p. 178.

[19] Hollowell, *op. cit.*, p. 46.

Their versatile values make their use profitable with children from three years of age to early adolescence and in some cases even beyond. I agree that the height of their appeal is reached with the seven, eight, and nine year old, but that the simpler animal stories can and should be used with even the preschool child.

A mother who realizes the value of time spent reading to her preschool child is not going to pick any of the tales containing cruelty which would frighten a child because of immaturity or improper use. For, in my opinion, these two abuses of the fairy tales are the only manner in which they can bring harm to children. It was never intended that these tales should be used in any manner which would frighten any reader or listener, and only when oral tradition misuses them in this way will they be harmful.

The skillful first grade teacher will realize that realistic stories of pets and toys are vital in the literary development of her pupils, and that the fairy tales containing giants, witches, or cruelty should be reserved for grade two and three, when the child can perceive them in their proper perspective. The second and third grade teacher must still intersperse realistic stories into her literary program in order to maintain a balance between the real and the fanciful.

Since these stories have stood the literary test of time and have been emulated by modern writers, they are worthy of preservation. They have within them hidden qualities that many readers do not recognize, but merely realize the fact that children like them and continue to ask for them.

After studying the qualities of these tales and matching them with the needs of children, we find the reason for their continued popularity. All seven of the recognized needs of a child are met to a varied degree, vicariously or otherwise, in the reading of fairy tales, namely: emotional security, moral stability, achievement, aesthetic pleasures, loving and being loved, escape and change brought about through imagination, and the need to know. Even the need to belong to the group is vicariously satisfied in many of the tales.

Knowing and thoroughly understanding the fairy tales enriches the life of the child and even of the adult who attempts to pass them on to the next generation. I agree with Hans Christian Andersen when he said that they are "our dream,—the hem of our garment of immortality."

Bibliography

BOOKS

Adams, Bess Porter. *About Books and Children.* New York: Henry Holt & Co., 1953.

Arbuthnot, May Hill. *Children and Books.* Chicago: Scott, Foresman and Company, 1947.

Betzner, Jean. *Exploring Literature with Children in the Elementary School.* New York: Little & Ives, 1943.

Depew, Ollie. *Children's Literature by Grades and Types.* Boston: Ginn, 1938.

Hollowell, Lillian. *A Book of Children's Literature.* New York: Rinehart & Co., Inc., 1950.

Smith, Lillian H. *The Unreluctant Years; A Critical Approach to Children's Literature.* Chicago: American Library Association, 1953.

Toksvig, Signe. *Fairy Tales and Stories by Hans Christian Andersen.* New York: Macmillan Co., 1953.

Weekes, Blanche E., *Literature and the Child.* New York: Silver, Burdett and Co., 1935.

White, Dorothy Neal. *About Books and Children.* New York: Oxford University Press, 1949.

ARTICLES

Baruch, Dorothy. "This Question of Fairy Tales." *Progressive Education,* IX (May, 1932), 364.

Cummings, Ella. "Should We Believe in Fairy Tales," *Grade Teacher,* LXXI (February, 1954), 47.

Gates, Doris, "Six Impossible Things," condensed in *Education Digest,* XIV (March, 1949), 27.

O'Faolian, Sean. "For the Child and the Wise Man," *The New York Times Magazine* (March 27, 1955), 9.

Taylor, Pauline Byrd. "Ethics in Fairy and Household Tales," *Elementary English Review,* XVII (May, 1940), 190.

FOLK-TALE COLLECTIONS*

Eulalie Steinmetz Ross

In the nineteenth century the folk tale appeared as a joyous reading form for the child. The first folk-tale collections were by eminent scholars—the Grimm Brothers, Asbjörnsen and Moe —who went directly to the source for their material: the people themselves. They wrote the stories down as they heard them, preserving the stark, characteristic form of the folk tale as well as its peculiar, individual turns of speech. Joseph Jacobs used printed sources also, but by training and instinct produced English, Celtic, and Indian folk tales faithful in every respect to the distinctive traits of this literary form.

Later on storytellers produced collections of folk tales from their own national backgrounds, thus giving them a two-fold authenticity. Such are the Irish folk-tale collections of Seumas MacManus and the versions of the Asbjörnsen and Moe stories done by Gudrun Thorne-Thomsen. Other storytellers gathered folk tales from various peoples, told the stories themselves to children, and then put their versions in books. Ruth Sawyer did this for her Spanish stories and her Irish ones; Richard Chase collected and told—and then wrote—folk tales from our southern mountain states.

In recent years Harold Courlander used the methods of the earliest folklorists when he gathered stories from the peoples of Africa, Haiti, and countries of the Middle East.

There have also been editors, through the years, who have dipped into this collection and that collection to gather stories for their own thick volumes. Andrew Lang did this and produced his rainbow series; Kate Douglas Wiggin and Nora Archibald Smith did it too for their "Tales" titles. There were no less than 140 stories in *Tales of Laughter*. Here was enchantment for many a long hour's reading!

* Eulalie Steinmetz Ross, "Folk-Tale Collections," *The Horn Book Magazine*, 39 (October, 1963), 490–91. Reprinted by permission of The Horn Book, Inc., and the author.

Recently there has been a fresh burgeoning of folk-tale collections. Most of these are "researched," as their dust jackets have it, from printed sources. They vary in degree of excellence, depending on whether the writer has a natural affinity for the country of his research, an understanding of the folk-tale form, and the ability to discipline his writing to achieve the necessary simplicity of style.

Frances Carpenter has been working in the field of the folk tale for so many years that she has come to terms with its restrictions and peculiarities. In *African Wonder Tales* (Doubleday, 216 pp.), illustrated by Joseph Escourido, she tells with practiced ease 24 stories of people and animals from the various parts of Africa. "Who Can Break a Bad Habit?" is clearly the African antecedent of "Brer Rabbit and the Mosquitoes"; "The Monkeys and the Little Red Hats" is a version, from the Egyptian Soudan, of the monkey-see, monkey-do theme; "Omar's Big Lie" is the Celtic "Jack and the King Who Was a Gentleman"—as told in Algeria. These stories should tell easily, especially to the younger children who are sometimes at a loss to understand the more cryptic wit of Courlander's African stories.

For years Joseph Jacobs' folk tales have been alone in their excellence on the Putnam list. Now the publisher proposes to include these in a series, Folk and Fairy Tales from Many Lands, along with new publications in the field. This is an intrepid venture indeed, for any folk-tale collection so equated with the Jacobs ones will receive hard scrutiny. Four titles have been published in the United States this year after earlier English editions: *Russian Folk and Fairy Tales* by E. M. Almedingen (192 pp.), illustrated by Simon Jeruchim; *Chinese Folk and Fairy Tales* by Leslie Bonnet (191 pp.), illustrated by Maurice Brevannes; *German Folk and Fairy Tales* by Maurice and Pamela Michael (189 pp.), illustrated by Anne Marie Jauss; and *French Folk and Fairy Tales* by Roland Gant (192 pp.), illustrated by Portia Takakjian. The last two titles are indifferent, but the Russian one is splendid and the Chinese one, too, has merit. The writers of the collections acknowledge the source of their material—and they are honorable sources—and both have lived in the lands where their stories originated. They are at home with their material and their delight in the stories communicates itself to the reader. Neither writer is of Jacobs' stature, but they are in his mold. It is hoped that the format of the books in this series will improve as the series grows.

The attractive format of the Favorite Fairy Tales series (Little, Brown) is one of its most engaging characteristics: readable type face, excellent page layout, and lively illustrations by recognized artists. This fall Virginia Haviland has edited three more titles for the series: *Told in Poland* (90 pp.), illustrated by Felix Hoffmann; *Told in Scotland* (92 pp.), illustrated by Adrienne Adams; and *Told in Spain* (87 pp.), illustrated by Barbara Cooney. These books, like their six predecessors, offer the young child or the slow reader a friendly, easy-reading entrance into the world of the folk tale. Children, however, tend to become attached to series publications and sometimes will refuse to read anything else. There is some danger then that the Favorite Fairy Tales series may, by its very nature, defeat Miss Haviland's purpose: to make it serve as a springboard to the robust and full-bodied collections of folk tales from which she retells the stories in her volumes. Miss Haviland's books are invitations to the feast, hors d'oeuvres if you will, to whet the appetite for the collections of such folklorists and storytellers as Joseph Jacobs, Wanda Gág, Seumas MacManus, Ruth Sawyer, Richard Chase, and Harold Courlander. Here are the roast beef and mashed potatoes of the folk-tale banquet, for children and storytellers alike.

TRADITIONAL SCANDINAVIAN LITERATURE FOR CHILDREN *

Siri Andrews

There are two groups of children to whom the traditional literature of the Scandinavian countries should be of value and interest: first, those who are of Scandinavian descent and to whom it should be an inherited possession, and second, those who are not, and to whom it is strange and foreign. The Americanization

* Siri Andrews, "Traditional Scandinavian Literature for Children," *Reading and The School Library*, I (October, 1934), 13–15, 44–45. Reprinted by permission of the author.

of foreign peoples will take care of itself in time, but the preservation of their older cultures and literatures in America must be carefully fostered. American civilization and tradition are not endangered by this broader background; on the contrary the civilization and tradition of other nations can only enrich and enlarge our own. The literature of their forefathers, as well as that of other nations, should be known to the children of Scandinavian ancestry, while it should add richness and strength to the imagination and emotional life of children with other literary and racial backgrounds.

In speaking of traditional literature for children, it is perhaps natural first to mention folk tales, and in folk tales the Scandinavian countries are singularly rich. Among the best editions for children are those selected from the great collections made by two young Norwegians early in the nineteenth century. Inspired by the brothers Grimm of Germany, whose work led to the modern interest in folklore as a science, Peter Asbjörnsen and Jörgen Moe began collecting the tales of Norway, the former as a naturalist who wandered into far parts of the country in the interests of his work, the latter as a clergyman and poet, who spent his summers in the mountains or among the fisherfolk in the coast hamlets, both collecting the unwritten stories current among the unlettered. Their first collection appeared in 1842–1843, and several other volumes followed. They were translated into English about 1850 by Sir George Dasent, an Englishman whose sojourn as a diplomat in Stockholm aroused an intense interest in the Scandinavian literature which led later to a visit to Iceland and to the translation of much traditional literature hitherto unknown in English. Several editions are known to us under Dasent's name, but the original sources were the Asbjörnsen and Moe collections. (See list following the article.)

The stories themselves are fundamentally realistic in spite of the presence of giants and trolls, and the small uncertain creatures of the North. There are no very extravagant flights of the imagination; the life portrayed is hard and simple; the humor is obvious and robust, all of which elements appeal to younger children. The best edition of the Norwegian stories for little children is *East o' the Sun and West o' the Moon* by Mrs. Gudrun Thorne-Thomsen. Mrs. Thorne-Thomsen presents the stories she knew as a child in the words she uses in telling them to American children; the result is an excellent selection of stories and a style of simple grace.

The Swedish stories are best represented, I think, in Nils Gabriel Djurklou's *Fairy Tales from the Swedish*. Djurklou was vitally interested in archeology and in the folklore of his own people, and his collections form a very important part of the whole body of Swedish folklore. Humor is perhaps the outstanding quality of these stories, and humor of a sort which appeals to children, realistic and naïve. The stories are more concrete than fantastic, the situations quite within a child's understanding. The black and white illustrations by Scandinavian artists fit the stories perfectly. Another good collection, for younger children than Djurklou's, is Eva March Tappan's *The Golden Goose*, containing half a dozen of the best liked and most imaginative of the Swedish folk tales.

Perhaps the most popular of the Danish collections of folklore is the one by Jens Christian Bay called *Danish Fairy and Folk Tales*, charming stories simply told. But the most scholarly collection is one for slightly older children, *Danish Fairy Tales* by Svend Grundtvig, a serious student of folklore who has made significant contributions to this science. His collections, as were those of Asbjörnsen, Moe, and Djurklou, were made up of stories current among the people at the time, rather than from secondary sources.

Before leaving the subject of folk tales, one more collection should be mentioned, *Mighty Mikko*, a most interesting group of Finnish folk stories retold by Parker Fillmore. They are simply written, have plots similar to those of many of the familiar European stories, but an atmosphere all their own.

The Norse myths have a ruggedness and directness which make them more suitable for the younger children on the whole than the Greek myths. They have a humor which is lacking in the Greek stories, a vigor of action which contrasts favorably, as far as the children are concerned, with the subtler developments of the more involved and sophisticated situations of the Greek myths. Abbie Farwell Brown's *In the Days of Giants* is no doubt the simplest retelling of these stories of Thor and Odin and Loki, and therefore the best for younger children, in spite of occasional condescensions and moralizing quite out of keeping with the original feeling of the stories. The most literary version is perhaps Mabie's *Norse Stories*, though Colum's *The Children of Odin* is more attractive in make-up and easier reading. The latter contains also the story of the Volsungs.

The Norse myths have been preserved in the two great Eddas

of Iceland, the Poetic and the Prose Eddas. But Iceland has preserved not only the stories of the Norse god and goddesses but also of their heroes, both legendary and semi-historical. Of these, the most appealing is probably Sigurd, known as Siegfried in the German version, the noble warrior, the true and steadfast friend, who was treacherously slain by those whom he had helped. Baldwin's *Story of Siegfried* follows the German version on the whole but includes incidents from the Norse and also stories of the Norse gods. But we have too William Morris' verse translation from the Icelandic, *Sigurd the Volsung,* in two forms suitable for children, one in a somewhat shortened form by Winifred Turner and Helen Scott, and the other Dorothy Hosford's *Sons of the Volsungs* which is a prose retelling of the first part of the poem, through Sigurd's awakening of Brynhild, retaining Morris' dignity of language but avoiding the difficulties of the verse form. These stories should be known to the children while they regard them as good stories, before they come to think of them and study them as literature; they should read these tales when they make their greatest emotional and imaginative appeal. This is the best argument I think, for presenting this literature in versions for children. It seems worthwhile to make these stories available to them in a form which they will find interesting at a time when the tales have a vital meaning.

But Sigurd is not the only hero of the North. There is also Grettir the Outlaw, one of the great semi-historical figures of Iceland, whose story is told by Allen French in *The Story of Grettir the Strong.* His retelling of the Njal saga, which was translated into English first by Sir George Dasent, is entitled *Heroes of Iceland* and is a good shortened form of a very involved story. These two books give an excellent picture of Icelandic (and Norse) life, customs, laws, and beliefs of the tenth to the twelfth centuries. The vigor and uncompromising realism of these stories appeal to the older boys who have something of a reading background.

More than seven centuries ago a great Danish scholar known as Saxo Grammaticus wrote in 15 books, a history of Denmark from legendary times until the year 1185; his work contained much that was legendary, much that was semi-historical, and some truth, the whole being in fact a series of biographies of the Danish kings. A few years ago some of these stories were made accessible to children in a book by Julia Adams, called *The Swords of the Vikings.* Mrs. Adams has selected some of the stories which would appeal to children because of their action or their romantic qualities, and has presented them in their original strength and directness.

One national epic remains to be mentioned, and that is the *Kalevala* of Finland. This is really a series of ballads which were gathered from all corners of Finland and first committed to paper about 1835 by the Swedish scholar Elias Lönnrot. Lönnrot had been aided by the work of earlier collectors, among them Zakarias Topelius who had gathered and published a few cantos, and himself added to his first edition later, working the many disconnected fragments into one whole. The *Kalevala* is full of folk superstitions and is more poetic and less realistic than other epics; it is written in the meter Longfellow found so musical in a German translation of the *Kalevala,* and used in his "Hiawatha." The best known version for children is Baldwin's *The Sampo,* which retells practically the whole story without distortion. Parker Fillmore's *Wizard of the North* is a more attractive looking book, and as it is much shorter and simpler would appeal to somewhat younger children.

Although I had meant to limit myself to traditional literature, it seems hardly possible to omit mention of the two Scandinavian writers for children who are the most famous in this country, namely Hans Christian Andersen, the Danish author whose fairy tales created a new form of writing for children nearly one hundred years ago, and Selma Lagerlöf, whose textbook on Swedish geography and history became a fairy tale in the form of *The Wonderful Adventures of Nils,* wherein Nils as an elf travels with a flock of wild geese over Sweden, learning its flora and fauna, its legends and stories, its topography and history. But perhaps both do properly belong here, for some of Andersen's stories were based on folklore or had folklore themes, and the rest have become classics, and therefore *almost* "traditional," or at least universal possessions, and many of the stories Miss Lagerlöf retells are folk beliefs and anecdotes. Having gone thus far, we might go one step further and include Zakarias Topelius, the son of that Topelius who was a pioneer in collecting the cantos which now make up the *Kalevala.* He was a poet, a novelist, and dramatist who also wrote tales for children which were among the most widely read in the Scandinavian countries for several generations and which still have their following. He was a Finn

who wrote in Swedish a great many stories which are partly realistic and somewhat moralizing, partly fantastic and poetic. *Canute
Whistlewinks* is an excellent selection from his tales. Others appear in Mrs. Thorne-Thomsen's *The Birch and the Star* and in
Emilie Poulssen's *Top-of-the-World Stories.*

This brief discussion does not by any means exhaust the field
of Scandinavian literature for children; it is meant merely to suggest the value and interest which the traditional literature of the
Scandinavian countries may have for American children of the
present day, whatever their ancestry.

FINNISH TALES

Mighty Mikko by Parker Fillmore, illustrated by Jan Van Everen
(Harcourt, Grades 4–5).

NORWEGIAN FOLK TALES

East o' the Sun and West o' the Moon by Peter Asbjörnsen and
Jörgen Moe, translated by G. W. Dasent (McKay, Grades 4–6).
East of the Sun and West of the Moon by Peter Asbjörnsen and
Jörgen Moe, illustrated by Hedwig Collin (Macmillan, Grades
4–6).
East of the Sun and West of the Moon by Peter Asbjörnsen and
Jörgen Moe, illustrated by Kay Nielsen (Garden City, Grades
4–6).
Fairy Tales from the Far North by Peter Asbjörnsen and Jörgen
Moe, translated by H. L. Braekstad (Burt, Grades 4–6).
Tales from the Fjeld by Peter Asbjörnsen and Jörgen Moe, trans-
lated by G. W. Dasent (Putnam, Grades 5–6).
Norwegian Fairy Book edited by Clara Stroebe, translated by
Frederick Martens (Stokes, Grades 4–6).
East o' the Sun and West o' the Moon by Mrs. Gudrun Thorne-
Thomsen (Row, Grades 2–5).

SWEDISH FOLK TALES

Fairy Tales from the Swedish by Nils Gabriel Djurklou, trans-
lated by H. L. Braekstad (Stokes, Grades 4–6).
Swedish Fairy Book edited by Clara Stroebe, translated by Fred-
erick Martens (Stokes, Grades 5–7).
Golden Goose and Other Fairy Tales translated by Eva March
Tappan (Houghton, Grades 3–4).

DANISH FOLK TALES

Danish Fairy and Folk Tales by Jens Christian Bay (Harper, Grades 3–5).

Danish Fairy Tales by Svend Grundtvig, translated by Gustav Hein (Crowell, Grades 4–5).

Danish Fairy Book edited by Clara Stroebe, translated by Frederick Martens (Stokes, Grades 5–7).

NORSE MYTHS

In the Days of Giants by Abbie Farwell Brown (Houghton, Grades 4–5).

Norse Stories Retold from the Eddas by Hamilton Wright Mabie (Rand, Grades 5–8).

Children of Odin by Padraic Colum, illustrated by Willy Pogany (Macmillan, Grades 5–7).

Myths of Northern Lands by Helene Guerber (Amer. Bk., Grades 7–8).

Tales from Norse Mythology by Katherine Pyle (Lippincott, Grades 4–6).

NORSE HERO TALES

Story of Siegfried by James Baldwin, illustrated by Howard Pyle (Scribner, Grades 5–7).

Siegfried by Edith Heal, illustrated by Milo Winter (Follett, Grades 5–7).

Story of Sigurd the Volsung by William Morris, edited by Winifred Turner and Helen Scott (Longmans, Grades 7–8).

Sons of the Volsungs by Dorothy Hosford, illustrated by Frank Dobias (Macmillan, Grades 7–8).

Heroes of Iceland by Allen French (Little, Grades 5–8).

The Story of Grettir the Strong by Allen French (Dutton, Grades 5–7).

Swords of the Vikings by Julia Adams, illustrated by Suzanne Lassen (Dutton, Grades 6–8).

Sampo: Hero Adventures from the Finnish Kalevala by James Baldwin (Scribner, Grades 5–7).

Wizard of the North by Parker Fillmore, illustrated by Jan Van Everen (Harcourt, Grades 4–6).

MODERN FAIRY TALES

Fairy Tales by Hans Christian Andersen, illustrated by Gordon Brown (Stokes, Grades 4–6).

Fairy Tales by Hans Christian Andersen, illustrated by Charles Thomas and William Robinson (Dutton, Grades 4–6).

Wonderful Adventures of Nils by Selma Lagerlöf (Doubleday, Educ. ed., Grades 4–6).

Further Adventures of Nils by Selma Lagerlöf (Doubleday, Grades 4–6).

Canute Whistlewinks by Zakarias Topelius, illustrated by Frank McIntosh (Longmans, Grades 4–5).

The Birch and the Star edited by Gudrun Thorne-Thomsen (Row, Grades 3–4).

Top-of-the-World Stories translated by Emilie and Laura Poulsson (Lothrop, Grades 4–7).

MEMORIES OF MY FATHER, JOSEPH JACOBS *

May Bradshaw Hays

Until I was nearly eight, I thought that all fathers wrote fairy tales to earn a living for their families. As matter of course every morning I would watch my father, Joseph Jacobs, take his bowler hat from the hall-stand, place the crook of his umbrella over his left arm, and start out for the British Museum "to find more stories to put in the fairy books."

With the end of each week, came the fun. We three children would go into Father's library, where the red damask curtains would be drawn to shut out the heavy, greenish London fog which pressed against the windows, and a cheerful fire glowed

* May Bradshaw Hays, "Memories of My Father, Joseph Jacobs," *The Horn Book Magazine*, 28 (December, 1952), 385–92. Reprinted by permission of The Horn Book, Inc., Boston, Massachusetts and the author.

behind the bars of the high English grate. Father sat in his scuffed and worn old black leather chair, I was perched on his lap, and Sydney and Philip were curled up on the floor on either side. Impatiently we would watch while Father filled his pipe, tamped the tobacco down with his little finger, lit it with a match, blew out a couple of puffs, and then, in his hearty voice with an undercurrent of laughter in it, he would begin: "Once upon a time, though it wasn't in my time or in your time, or in any-body else's time"—and the room was filled with magic for the three of us. We didn't know, of course, that he was "trying it on the dog"; that he was using us as a trio of child critics. If we sat entranced during the telling of a tale, that particular story would be included in the current volume of fairy tales he was plan-ning to publish—*English Fairy Tales, More English, Celtic, More Celtic,* or *Indian Fairy Tales.* If we fidgeted, or if our attention wandered during the telling, that story was not used. We had re-jected it, unknowingly, and he accepted our judgment.

Sometimes, when he was tired from a hard week of research and writing, he would try to play a trick on us. He would sud-denly say, "And the little prince, who was very tired, went into a nearby wood, lay down, closed his eyes and went to sleep like this..." He would shut his eyes but at once we would be on him, tickling, biting, and punching, with cries of "No you don't! You stop that! It isn't fair!" and then thoroughly awake from the tussle, and with a shout of laughter, Father would continue, "but the little prince found a big bear in the wood, and he came running out and went on his way..." and we would settle down again, satisfied that we were going to have the whole story, then and there.

One of the delights of his homecoming each day was his pock-ets. In them, we were allowed to rummage, and there was al-ways something for us—generally sweets, bull's-eyes in the winter, lemon drops in the summer. I imagine he had been calmly munching some of them out of a paper bag in the sacred confines of the Library of the British Museum and under the outraged eyes of the attendants, but Father never worried about what other people thought of him. Sometimes, on cold winter evenings, he would buy two hot baked potatoes or some baked chestnuts from the old man on the corner near the Museum, and use them to warm his hands in his pockets on the way home. We children would then open and eat them on the clean, scrubbed kitchen table, while the cook grumbled that she was trying to get the dinner; but we had our treat, and loved Father for having such enchanting ideas.

My father came from a very new country, Australia, in 1872, after he had received a degree from the University of Sydney. He planned to go on with his education at St. John's College, Cambridge, to become a lawyer, and then return to his native land to practice. But literature was in the air at Cambridge and, after matriculating, he decided to go to London and become a writer. There he met Miss Georgina Horne and married her, and as we children came along and the needs of his family grew, he had to turn his pen toward any source of income which offered. He told me once, with a rueful smile, that his first published book was a piece of ghost-writing he did for a dentist, titled *Dental Bridges and Crowns;* but in a few years his book reviews —which always presented a fresh and ingenious point of view— began to make literary London aware of him. It was his enthusiastic review of George Eliot's *Daniel Deronda* which brought him an invitation to one of her Sunday afternoon receptions at The Priory, 21 North Bank, Regent's Park. The delighted young reviewer was presented to the great novelist by her "life's companion," George Lewes. Blushing hard, Joseph Jacobs said he hoped she liked his review of her new book, but was met with the quiet parry, "I never read criticisms of my own works." He had a very expressive face, and his confusion and disappointment must have been apparent to George Eliot, because she was very kind to him on his subsequent visits, and made an especial effort to introduce him to many of the great writers and artists who became his friends.

These men were rebels and innovators—Edward Burne-Jones, who rebelled against the smug complacency of Victorian art as shown by the Royal Academy, Dante Gabriel Rossetti, William Morris, and the others who formed the Pre-Raphaelite Brotherhood. In such a group as this, my father felt much at home. Proudly he hung reproductions of Burne-Jones paintings on our walls, and bought William Morris wallpapers for our rooms. Although this was the era of embossed velvet on walls, and elaborate and puffy Victorian furniture, our house was furnished in the manner of which Morris approved—the lines of our furniture were simple, the walls were light and the woodwork white.

Another innovator whom my father admired greatly was Dr. F. J. Furnivall, acknowledged authority on Chaucer and Shakespeare—and firm believer in Woman's Rights. He was the man who founded the first Rowing Club for Working Girls, and who hounded the owners of the ABC tea-shops until they provided chairs for the waitresses to sit down on when they were not working. Rowing was his relaxation and greatest source of enjoyment. Every Sunday he would arrange trips up the Thames for parties of his friends. Many a time we rowed from Hammersmith to Richmond, where we disembarked on a little island and, having eaten the invariable lunch of cold roast lamb, tea, bread and butter, bottled gooseberries, and custard, we children would play hide-and-seek round the island while the grown-ups discussed art and literature, speaking with the quiet authority to which their reputations entitled them.

Dear Dr. Furnivall—I can see him now, gallantly doing his share of rowing, although he was 77. I remember his blowing white beard and hair; his gray flannels and the tie made of pink ribbon which he always wore. I remember, too, the string bag of oranges which he always brought for us children and which he insisted on our eating on the train—much to our embarrassment. It was this mixture of learning and simplicity that my father shared with all these great Mid-Victorians and he had the same lack of self-consciousness. Father used to take us regularly to museums and art galleries, and afterwards we would go to a pastry-shop where we had a choice of either creampuffs or chocolate eclairs. These we would eat in the shop, then lick our fingers and wipe them on Father's large white silk handkerchief. We felt it wasn't quite the right thing to do but, looking back, I know it was the knowledge of the treat-to-come which took my dragging feet from picture to picture in the Tate Gallery. How well my father knew the heart of a child!

Joseph Jacobs could make friends with any child at once. He never used the trite questions, "How old are you?" or "Where do you go to school?" but began an absurd little quarrel with the child, on any subject which popped into his head. Then, when they were both stamping their feet at each other he would suddenly say, "What's this in my pocket; have a look, will you?" and there was always some little present which made the child his friend for always. When he went out to dinner, the children in the family were waiting for him on the stairs, with cries, through the banisters, of "Tell us about Tom Tit Tot, Uncle Joe!" or "We want to hear 'The King o' the Cats,' Mr. Jacobs!" In his white tie and tails, Father would sit among their little nightgowned figures until the tale was told, and then he would go and make apologies to his hostess for his lateness. He was always a Pied Piper. One look into his brilliant hazel eyes, and a child was his forever. He loved the nonsensical words which delight children—we had many in the family vocabulary, which would be sheer gibberish to an outsider. I think he would have been perfectly delighted if he knew that Mary Gould Davis, superb storyteller, had included his "Master of all Masters" (from *English Fairy Tales*) in her collection of humorous stories to tell to children, *With Cap and Bells*.

Among my most vivid memories are the Sunday afternoons when Father would take me to Burne-Jones' studio, where pictures of great figures of angels and of beautiful drooping women in blue robes lined the walls. I would sit on William Morris' lap while he held his great handleless bowl of tea in one hand and stroked my pale-gold hair with the other. I didn't enjoy having my head patted, but was consoled by the knowledge that I had on my new green silk Kate Greenaway dress with the yellow smocking at the yoke. Scraps of the conversation going on round me penetrated my childish preoccupation with myself, however, and I remember particularly well one stormy argument between Joseph Jacobs and Andrew Lang. Mr. Lang said, "You folklore people (Father was president of the Folk Lore Society at the time) would refuse to print any stories for children which haven't been handed down from granny to granny, and if you can't trace them right back to their beginnings among the rustic folk of every country." To which my father mildly replied, "Now, Andrew, do me justice, old man. In collecting the stories for my fairy-tale books I have had a cause at heart as sacred as our science of folklore—the filling of our children's imaginations with bright trains of images. If a story will advance that cause I have always used it whether I knew its derivation or not. I simply want to make children feel that reading is the greatest fun in the world; so that they will want to get to books for themselves at the earliest possible moment." There spoke the young innovator from Australia, rebelling against folklore traditions!

Then there was that other Sunday, when Rudyard Kipling (who was Lady Burne-Jones' nephew) tramped up and down the studio inveighing against the way in which history was taught in the schools. He declared that history could be told in a way which would make it as exciting as any fairy tale, and then children would never forget it. I like to think that this was the hour in which he conceived the idea of writing those superb historical tales in *Puck of Pook's Hill* and *Rewards and Fairies.*

At the end of each of his fairy books, Dr. Jacobs always appended the sources and parallels for the stories, and his illustrator, John D. Batten, would draw a final picture warning little children not to read these notes "or they would fall asleep an hundred years." In these appendices, or in his prefaces, the author explained that he "called them all fairy tales, although few of them speak of fairies ... the words 'fairy tales' must accordingly be taken to include tales in which occurs something 'fairy,' something extraordinary—fairies, giants, dwarfs, speaking animals ... Every collection of fairy tales is made up of folk tales proper, of legends, droll or comic anecdotes, cumulative stories, beast tales, or merely ingenious nonsense tales put together in such a form as to amuse children ... and generally speaking it has been my ambition to write as a good old nurse will speak when she tells fairy tales."

Years spent in tracing the exact derivations of fairy tales convinced my father that many of the European folk tales have their source in India. He never felt, as other folklorists did, that the tales were brought to Europe by the Crusaders, but rather that they traveled in the most natural way, from father to son. In his notes appended to *Indian Fairy Tales* he tells how he has "edited an English version of an Italian adaptation, of a Spanish translation of a Latin version, of a Hebrew translation of an Arabic translation of the Indian original!" He calculated that the original Indian tales have been translated into 38 languages, in 112 different versions. In one of the *Jatakas,* or Birth Stories of Buddha, he was of the opinion that he had traced in the story called "The Demon with the Matted Hair" (*Indian Fairy Tales,* p. 194) the source of the Tar-Baby incident in *Uncle Remus!*

It was in 1896 that Dr. Jacobs was invited to come to America to deliver a series of lectures on "English Style and Composition" at Johns Hopkins University. On his return he told us, "I've found the country I want you children to grow up in." And so, his library of 12,000 books was packed into strong wooden boxes and swung into the hold of a Cunarder and, at the turn of the century, we began life in a new country. Father put down strong roots at his second transplanting, and always loved the United States "next to Australia." He had a book-lined library overlooking the Hudson in his house in Yonkers in which he would contentedly play innumerable games of chess with my husband, David Hays. He never needed to look at the chessboard but would play "blindfold," as they call it, sitting on the other side of the room with not even a glance at the chessmen. Dave always said, "He could beat me with both eyes tied behind his back."

Father fully intended to collect and retell the rich treasure trove of the folk tales of New England, but this was a dream which never came true. However, when his granddaughter, Margaret Hays, was born, he said, "Peggy must have a book of her own, just as you children have," and so he set to work and gathered together the sixth and last volume—*Europa's Fairy Tales.* In his amazing, scholarly fashion he found and noted on the dedication page all the variants of the name Margaret, over twenty of them!

People grow old in different ways. Some begin with a hardening at the heart which spreads outward until no trace of childhood is left. Others, the lucky ones, age only on the surface and keep the sensitive core of childhood within. In such a happy company did Joseph Jacobs belong.

After his death, letters and tributes came to us from all over the world. Best of all, we liked the editorial which was headed, "That fountain of fun frozen—impossible!" Those words described him exactly. My father was a fountain of fun which sparkled for all who knew him—young or old.

AMERICAN FOLK TALES *

Mary Gould Davis

Before explorers from other countries stepped on the shores of the continent of North America, there existed here a folk literature. Like the myths and legends of Asia and Europe, the American Indian folk tales were an expression of faith as well as a literature. Many of them tell of the spirits the Indians wor-

* Mary Gould Davis, "American Folk Tales," *The Horn Book Magazine,* 28 (February, 1952), 55–62. Reprinted with the permission of The Horn Book, Inc., Boston, Massachusetts.

shiped—the sun, the moon, the rain, the fertile earth. The Indian characterization of animals is quite different from that of the French Reynard and the Russian "little humpbacked horse." The relationship to man is closer. In her version of the epic tale of Raven, the "giver of light," Fran Martin shows that the early Indians of the Northwest had the power to change from men to animals and from animals to men. There is often a touch of humor in the Indian folk tales. They are subtle and ingenious and sometimes cruel.

In the tales of the Pueblo Indians there is a curious likeness to the stories brought from Africa by the Negro slaves in colonial times. Among the Zuni Indians of New Mexico, Frank Hamilton Cushing found the almost universal theme of "Cinderella" in a story called "The Turkey Girl." In "The Legend of Scarface" from the Blackfoot tribe the Hero's journey in search of "the abiding place of the Above Person, the Sun" foretells the coming of the pioneers and fur traders who crossed the western plains and the Great Divide and saw, finally, the shores of the Pacific. We owe George Bird Grinnell a debt of gratitude for the dignity and beauty of his wording of this legend.

With the coming of the pioneers, men and women from Europe who found in North America the freedom and the fertile land they sought, a new and an entirely *American* hero began to emerge in songs and stories. He is like the hero of no other country. His dominant qualities are uniquely American. Many years after the deeds of Paul Bunyan and Pecos Bill were sung and told in lumber camps and on the western plains Rudyard Kipling wrote a poem called "The American." It is not a complimentary poem, but he redeems the picture in three lines:

> But, while reproof around him rings,
> He turns a keen, untroubled face
> Home to the instant need of things.

It is this consciousness of the "instant need of things" that stands out in the American hero. He had a wilderness to tame; so Paul Bunyan emerged from the pioneers who cleared the forests, Pecos Bill from the cowboys who tamed the wild horses, John Henry from the workers in the cotton fields and on the railroads, Joe Magarac from the steel mills. Their theme is work and their hallmark is humor. In his introduction to *The Legends of Paul Bunyan* Harold Felton says, "The voices are American.

They sing American words and they sing with the American spirit." Even when this American hero became a statesman, like Daniel Webster, he retained this spirit and spoke in this idiom. Children instantly recognize the difference between the American hero and the heroes of the older European epics. They admire Siegfried when he kills the dragon, Fafnir, in the Volsunga Saga. They love, intimately and warmly, Pecos Bill and Slue-foot Sue, Paul Bunyan and Babe, the Blue Ox.

The American hero appears, too, in sea stories. There are Stormalong, and Ichabod Padduck whose encounter with the mermaid "in the belly of a whale" is as fantastic in plot and setting as are some of the European folk tales; but Ichabod himself remains an American—resourceful, practical, salty, and humorous. Nothing could be more fantastic, or funnier, than Stephen Vincent Benét's tale of Samanthy, the lovesick sea serpent who followed Daniel Webster from New England down the Atlantic coast and up the Potomac to Washington, and embarrassed that famous statesman mightily by hooting through the night her longing for his company.

When America entered the industrial age, there was Joe Magarac fighting for his "U. S. A. citizen papers." When pirates beset our coast there were Captain Kidd and Blackbeard and Jean Lafitte. In them all are the self-confidence, the boastful spirit that Kipling found in his American; but in them all are also vigor, intelligence, resourcefulness, and humor. In their speech is a rhythm unlike the rhythm of any other language.

We know that in other countries the folk tales were preserved for centuries through the human voice rather than through written records. This is true, too, in America. When Richard Chase went into the Southern Highlands to record the stories that had never been written, he found that many of them had been told by an almost legendary storyteller, Council Harmon. Some of them owed their plot, and often their heroes, to European folk tales; but in every case the hero and the plot were "localized."

I once told "The Brave Little Tailor" from Grimm's fairy tales to a group of boys and girls in a remote secton of the Cumberlands. Afterwards one of the boys said to me, "We have that story here, but he wasn't a tailor. He was a boy named Jack who lived down the road a piece."

Knowledge of their songs and stories is an "Open Sesame" to the people of the Cumberlands and the Great Smokies. When Richard Chase and I went into the rural schools in North Carolina to tell stories to the children they were puzzled, doubtful. Who were these strangers and what had they come for? But when he took out his recorder and played the air of "The Riddle Song," they instantly relaxed.

I brought my love a cher—ry that has no stone,

I brought my love a chick—en that has no bone,

I told my love a story that has no end,

I brought my love a ba—by and no cry—en.

> How can there be a cherry that has no stone?
> How can there be a chicken that has no bone?
> How can there be a story that has no end?
> How can there be a baby and no cryen?

> A cherry when it's blooming it has no stone,
> A chicken in the egg, it has no bone,
> The story of our love will have no end,
> A baby when it's sleepin', there's no cryen.

The riddle in the second verse with its answer in the third is as familiar to the children as are their own names. It opened a door into their minds. Humor runs all through the folk tales of the Southern Highlands—the humor that understates wildly exaggerated action. This same kind of humor is the outstanding characteristic of a creative American writer, Frank R. Stockton.

On the seacoast of the Carolinas there is a "creation" cycle that owes its origin, as far as we can learn, to no other country.

It is told by the Gullah Negroes. One of the most amusing and original scenes in it is the story of Sis Nannygoat and the tails. At that time the animals had no tails and the Serpent persuaded them that tails would be an asset. So Sis Nannygoat was elected to go to the Lord and ask for them. She returned with "a great coil of tail," a work basket, and a paint box. She lined the animals up in front of her and selected, sewed on, combed, brushed, and painted tails for all of them. The rabbit, who was jealous of Sis Nannygoat, refused to take part in the ceremony until the coil of tail was all gone. When he saw how proud the animals were, and how useful they found the tails, he demanded one for himself. Poor Sis Nannygoat had to cut off a piece of her own to satisfy him. That is why the rabbit's tail today is so short and the goat's tail so homely.

In character, neither Sis Nannygoat nor the rabbit is like Brer Rabbit or Brer Fox of the Uncle Remus stories. Uncle Remus, we are fairly sure, told the tales that were brought from Africa in colonial times. Some of them, in both plot and characters, can be traced to the Buganda folk tales. We are fortunate to have had a writer like Joel Chandler Harris and an illustrator like A. B. Frost to make these tales immortal. Like the Negro spirituals they have become a part of the American heritage.

In the Carolinas, too, are the tales of the Negro hero, Big Roadwalker, and his tiny wife, Hokey. They were told to Mrs. Eula Duncan by her Negro cook, Alice. They were told to her father by *his* father, and beyond that, are lost in the past.

Down in the bayous of Louisiana the folklore has a French flavor because of the Acadians who came there from Canada. And in the Southwest, notably in California and New Mexico, the folk tales and the folk music stem from Spain. Monica Shannon's "The Bean Boy" is American, but in it the Spanish influence is unmistakable. Many of the Southwest legends show the influence of the Catholic Church, as the Jesuits lived and worked among the native Indians. F. G. Applegate calls one of these stories, "San Christobal's Sheep," in his *Native Tales of New Mexico*. There is a beautiful legend of the Virgin in Willa Cather's *Death Comes for the Archbishop*.

In Delaware the Swedes and in Pennsylvania the Dutch brought their folk tales and folk art to America, where it is still preserved. Katherine Milhous' *The Egg Tree* pictures an example of an art and a custom that have been made a part of American life. The Moravians, too, bringing their faith and its historic background to Pennsylvania and North Carolina, have given America a fine example of the "good life" and beautiful religious music.

In New York State, Washington Irving's "Rip Van Winkle" and "The Legend of Sleepy Hollow," and his stories of the early Dutchmen on Manhattan and along the Hudson, have become American classics. Robust and humorous, they form an enduring record of the folk legends that still haunt the Hudson River and the Catskill Mountains. Old local tales, still preserved by word of mouth, are found in Carl Carmer's *Listen for a Lonesome Drum* and in Dr. Jagendorf's *The Marvelous Adventures of Johnny Darling*, the Munchausen of American folklore. His are the tall tales of the traveler, not of the worker.

In New England the tales of the sea captains who sailed the clipper ships round the world are legion. Here, too, are the witch stories, from the purely legendary to the historical accounts of the persecution of women who were supposed by the Pilgrims to be witches. To New Hampshire belongs the matchless story, written by a famous poet, of the court scene when Daniel Webster called up the spirits of the great American dead to bear witness and refute the claims of the Devil. In some New England folk tales the Devil is outwitted by a woman as he is in the "devil" tales of Czechoslovakia and Spain. In New Hampshire, too, is the ghost of Ocean-born Mary, who was born in a sailing ship off the New England coast in 1720 and given her name by a famous pirate, Don Pedro. New England folk tales, remembered and still told, can be found in Dr. Jagendorf's *New England Bean Pot* and in Marion Lowndes' *Ghosts That Still Walk*. The stories by Mary E. Wilkins Freeman in her *The Pot of Gold* are not strictly folk tales, but they reflect the New England spirit and are often based upon New England customs. Her indomitable old lady in "The Silver Hen" is a typical New Englander, and even the "Pumpkin Giant," fantastic though it is, is as New England as pumpkin pie.

America loves her heroes who are half historical, half legendary —Johnny Appleseed, that gentle, courageous man making his way through the wilderness, leaving behind him the seeds of our great American apple orchards; Kit Carson, David Crockett, and Daniel Boone. It took a poet to weave legends around Daniel Webster and a dramatist to bring to the American people the humor and simplicity of Abraham Lincoln.

In the recordings of the actual voices of those who tell the folk tales and sing the folk songs the Library of Congress is preserving today our folk heritage. From this splendid reservoir will come some day poems and stories, songs and operas that are purely American. Already the theater of today has felt its influence. In the meantime the growth of folklore in published books by gifted writers or devoted students is encouraging. As long as America can laugh at and with its heroes the American spirit will remain strong.

Bibliography

Native Tales of New Mexico, by F. G. Applegate (Lippincott)
"Daniel Webster and the Sea Serpent," by Stephen Vincent Bénet. In his *Thirteen O'Clock* (Farrar and Rinehart)
The Devil and Daniel Webster, by Stephen Vincent Bénet (Rinehart)
John Henry. Pecos Bill, by James Cloyd Bowman (Whitman)
America Sings, by Carl Carmer (Knopf)
Listen for a Lonesome Drum, by Carl Carmer (Sloane)
Death Comes for the Archbishop, by Willa Cather (Knopf)
Grandfather Tales. Jack and the Three Sillies. The Jack Tales. Wicked John and the Devil, by Richard Chase (Houghton)
Zuni Folk Tales, by Frank Hamilton Cushing (Putnam)
Big Road Walker, by Eula G. Duncan (Lippincott)
Legends of Paul Bunyan, by Harold W. Felton (Knopf)
The Pot of Gold, by Mary E. Wilkins Freeman (Lothrop)
Blackfoot Lodge Tales, by George Bird Grinnell (Scribner)
The Favorite Uncle Remus, by Joel Chandler Harris (Houghton)
The Bold Dragoon and Other Ghostly Tales, by Washington Irving; edited by Anne Carroll Moore (Knopf)
Rip Van Winkle and The Legend of Sleepy Hollow, by Washington Irving (Macmillan)
The Marvelous Adventures of Johnny Darling. New England Bean Pot, by Moritz Jagendorf (Vanguard)
Ocean-born Mary, by Lois Lenski (Lippincott)
Ghosts That Still Walk, by Marion Lowndes (Knopf)
Yankee Doodle's Cousins, by Anne Malcolmson (Houghton)
Nine Tales of Coyote. Nine Tales of Raven, by Fran Martin (Harper)
The Egg Tree, by Katherine Milhous (Scribner)
Black Genesis, by S. G. Stoney and G. M. Selby (Macmillan)
How Old Stormalong Captured Mocha Dick. Joe Magarac and His U.S.A. Citizens Papers, by Irwin Shapiro (Messner)

CHILDREN OF WORLD COLLECT PENNIES TO ERECT PINOCCHIO STATUE IN ITALY *

Virginia Bright

Youngsters around the globe this past week have been collecting "Pennies for Pinocchio." And a Boston University professor, Mr. Camillo P. Merlino, is responsible for putting this voluntary drive on an official, national scale in America.

The purpose of the penny saving is to erect a statue to the lovable little puppet that has become a literary classic on a par with Alice in Wonderland, for example, or Don Quixote.

Over in Pescia, Italy, in the town of Collodi, home of the author of *Adventures of Pinocchio,* is a veritable fairyland garden, a kind of Pinocchio Park, for little people where the statue is to be erected.

On a visit to the park back in 1950, Prof. Merlino, though captivated by the whimsical layout of the garden, noticed a glaring oversight. There was no statue to the perenially popular Pinocchio known to children around the world! He casually suggested to his guide, Rolando Anzilotti, a fellow professor at the University of Florence, that Pescia should erect such a monument.

Last August Prof. Anzilotti was elected Mayor of Pescia over the sturdy opposition of the Communists. Somewhat facetiously, omitting reference to the possibilities of incoming tourists' dollars, he incorporated Mr. Merlino's suggestion into one of his political planks advocating the erection of a statue to Pinocchio. Before his Communist opponent could learn the official party

* Virginia Bright, "Children of World Collect Pennies to Erect Pinocchio Statue in Italy," *The Boston Daily Globe,* January 27, 1953. Reprinted by permission of The Boston Daily Globe, and the author.

stand on puppets, the newspapers were hailing Anzillotti's victory with headlines, "Pinocchio Routs Reds By a Nose."

As Mayor, he presented the idea to the Ministry of Public Instruction and got their permission to form an Italian committee to raise lire among Italy's schoolchildren for a Pinocchio monument. Honorary committee members include the President of the Republic and Premier de Gasperi.

Associated Press wires picked up the story and transmitted it around the world. Soon, from Sicily to Seattle, South America to Sweden, token contributions began to pour in to the Mayor of Pescia. Caught by the humor of the situation, adults as well as children responded—all because of their love for the wooden marionette of timeless, universal appeal.

When he heard last summer of his friend's entry into the politics and his campaign for a Pinocchio monument, Prof. Merlino thought if a "Pennies for Pinocchio" drive could be put on a national, but modest and efficient scale it might become a gesture of international goodwill among children. He consulted B.U.'s library committee which in turn referred him to Miss Evelyn R. Robinson at the State Department of Education, 200 Newbury St. Her official title is Consultant for School Libraries and Library Work with Children and Young People.

It happened that the American Library Association's annual convention was due to convene the following week in New York. Miss Robinson volunteered to present to the Association the idea of American boys and girls raising "Pennies for Pinocchio." The plan met with immediate approval. And a national committee was formed with Miss Robinson as chairman; Prof. Merlino, consultant; and Miss Eleanor Kidder, of Chicago, president.

November was selected as the month for the first official drive since it was the birthday month of Carlo Lorenzini, Pinocchio's creator. A former newspaperman, Lorenzini wrote under the pseudonym of Carlo Collodi, using the name of the Italian town, his mother's birthplace. Christmas marked the second drive. Final plans for the windup drive will be discussed when the American Library Association meets again between Feb. 2 and 7 in Chicago.

The committee of the American Library Association Division for Children and Young People left details of the actual methods for collecting children's pennies entirely up to the children's librarians in each state.

Local libraries in Malden, Beverly, Concord, to mention a few, set aside a corner in the children's section with a box welcoming "Pennies for Pinocchio."

Miss Marian Miller, children's librarian in Concord, was one of the first locally to recognize the significance of honoring a child's storybook hero. In keeping with the modest scale on which the campaign is being conducted, she sent a check representing her own small contribution and that of Concord's schoolchildren direct to Mayor Anzilotti. Just emerging from the stress of helping to stage Concord's renowned theatrical production of *Little Women,* she added a note that she hoped, however, Pescia would not reciprocate with a drive to erect a monument to the four little women!

Pescia's mayor quickly replied expressing his gratitude to her and the children of Concord, whose generosity will make possible the erection of a Pinocchio monument by the end of 1953.

In Italy, a contest is already being conducted to find the best architect and sculptor to design the statue. Any funds remaining in excess of the cost of the monument will be set aside for the establishment of an International Library for Young People in Italy.

Mayor Anzilotti has forwarded Prof. Merlino photostat copies of letters from contributors from Kansas, Oklahoma, Indianapolis, New York, West Virginia, Montana, Kentucky, New Jersey, and Arizona.

Many of the letters were written by adults who recalled happy childhood hours spent reading *Pinocchio* or who remembered seeing the antics of the wooden puppet back in 1939 in Walt Disney's famous fantasy.

A newspaper editor from Maryland even enclosed a small personal contribution to Pescia's Mayor requesting that he forward a certificate, duly signed, to the editor's four children entitling the holders therof to tell one tiny fib a week "without their noses growing any longer!"

HOMAGE TO PINOCCHIO *

Ida Schroeder

In the city of Florence, Italy, a plaque on a modest house in a narrow street bears the following legend:

In this house was born
In 1826
Carlo Lorenzini Collodi
Father of Pinocchio

About an hour's bus ride from Florence in the tiny Tuscan town of Collodi, a 15-foot bronze monument weighing 4,400 pounds has been dedicated to Pinocchio, the wooden puppet whose fibs made his nose grow. It was here that the brainchild of Carlo Lorenzini Collodi was born.

How the monument happened to be built is a story in itself. In 1951, Rolando Anzilotti, a college professor with a liking for children, ran for the office of Mayor of Pinocchio's home town and, like all good politicians, he carried a slogan: "Elect me, and I will see that a big monument is built to Pinocchio."

He won the election by a tremendous majority and promptly set out to fulfill his campaign promise. He appealed to the Government and to the mayors of other towns for contributions. Then he asked the schoolchildren of Italy each to send five lire, which is less than one cent, promising that all contributors would receive a Pinocchio certificate signed by the Mayor and entitling them to tell one fib a week without having their noses grow.

The response was overwhelming! Pennies, pennies, pennies came rolling in, not only from the schoolchildren of Italy, but from children all over the world. From many countries adults also joined in with contributions great and small. Among these was the Division of Libraries for Children and Young People of

* Ida Schroeder, "Homage to Pinocchio," *The Horn Book Magazine,* 35 (October, 1959), 368–73. Reprinted by permission of The Horn Book, Inc., Boston, Massachusetts, and the author.

the American Library Association, and Walt Disney who made a Pinocchio movie.

Thus in 1956, with a statue created by the sculptor Emilio Greco, a promise became a reality.

Built in a spiral suggesting the Big Oak in the book, and binding together the group of figures—Pinocchio rising out of the tree and looking up into the serene face of the Blue Fairy, and above her the Falcon who was sent to release the puppet—the monument epitomizes the many trials and tribulations that went into the eventual transformation of Pinocchio from rogue to good boy.

The old Village Piazza in which the monument stands is surrounded by an uneven wall that is nowhere too wide or too high for small limbs to climb, and having climbed it, a scene that is full of surprise and delight greets the young climbers.

Extending along the inner wall four colorful mosaics by Venturino Venturi, in gold and the rarest of marble, depict the adventures of Pinocchio. At the left stands the open door through which Pinocchio ran away; next, the gendarme near the prison in which the puppet will land; the tree of spangles which lures him; the man broader than he is tall who leads Pinocchio and his friend Lamp-Wick to the Land of Toys.

On the right Geppetto is seen carving the piece of wood; close by, the Talking Cricket, and then the Fox and the Cat at the Inn of the Red Crawfish where the Cat, feeling seriously indisposed, could eat only 35 mullet in tomato sauce and four portions of tripe with Parmesan cheese; and just beyond, the Fox and the Cat now reduced to begging.

Then, there is the dog Alidoro who rescues the puppet, with the Carabineers in pursuit; and finally, the Green Fisherman, and all the rest of the unbelievable friends in the story who have contrived to change the name of the centuries-old Village Piazza to Miracle Square.

To round out the "places" in the book and to accommodate the thousands of visitors, big and little, who come to Collodi each year, the "Inn of the Red Crawfish" is about to be built.

Rising light and airy on the green hillside which faces Miracle Square is the historic seventeenth century Garzoni Castle with its grand staircase leading up to a marble façade and overlooking one of the finest Renaissance gardens in Italy, replete with cascades and fountains and statuary and, amidst picturesque thickets, a labyrinth which was made famous in the poetry of that romantic period.

It was in the kitchen of the Garzoni Castle, where his mother was employed as a seamstress, that a penniless newspaperman, Carlo Lorenzini, began the tale of Pinocchio and, while writing it, adopted the pen name of Collodi after the town where his mother was born. The 200-year-old house in which she first saw the light of day still stands, and the guide conducting groups of tourists through the Castle indicates it on descending the hill.

Few children's stories have had so universal an appeal as that of Pinocchio. Since its first publication in book form in 1883, millions of copies have been printed and distributed all over the world. Certain it is that Pinocchio is one of the most widely translated of books. Fifty-two translations line the shelves of the Library-Museum at the entrance to Pinocchio Park, where Miracle Square is located, and Mr. Anzilotti states that 75 translations are known to exist.

A Latin translation has recently been made by Enrico Mafficini, a teacher in a Boys' School, who insists that he has found another facet of usefulness to mankind in the wooden puppet. "For," says this educator who wanted to offer beginners a Latin reader, "boys love Pinocchio. They may even pardon his Latin!"

ALICE LIDDELL OF WONDERLAND *

Mary Elisabeth Edes

July 4 marks the centenary of what is undoubtedly the most famous picnic in literary history. On that day in 1862, a shy, stiff Oxford don, the Rev. Charles L. Dodgson, his friend, Canon Robinson Duckworth, and their three child guests, Lorina, Alice,

* Mary Elisabeth Edes, "Alice Liddell of Wonderland," *Publishers' Weekly*, 182 (July 2, 1962), 112–15. Reprinted by permission of R. R. Bowker Company.

and Edith Liddell hired a boat and rowed three miles up the Isis from Oxford to Godstow, where they ate their picnic supper in the shade of a haycock.

As they traveled along under a summer sun, Dodgson told the children a story in which his acknowledged favorite, 10-year-old Alice, was the heroine. It was filled with private jokes and references to life in the Liddell family which delighted the girls and made them forget their fear of the swans on the river. Later she begged him to write it down for her, and he did. His book, of course, became *Alice's Adventures in Wonderland,* published under the pseudonym Lewis Carroll. It is one of the juvenile bestsellers of all time, and one which shows little sign of going out of fashion. There are at this moment 20 different editions of the book available in this country alone.

Who was Alice, and what became of her? She was, as Dodgson's many photographs of her show, an enchanting child, and though he saw her less and less after she was 12 or 13, Dodgson never forgot her. When she was a middle-aged matron, he wrote to her: "I have had scores of child-friends since your time, but they were quite a different thing."

Alice Pleasance Liddell was born on May 4, 1852, in London, in the house next door to Westminster Abbey. Her father, Henry George Liddell, who had previously been chaplain to Prince Albert, was then head of Westminster School. Alice was christened in Westminster Abbey. Her mother was Lorina Reeve Liddell, a handsome woman from whom the Liddells' many attractive children are said to have inherited their good looks. When Alice, the third of eight children, was four, the family moved to Oxford where her father had been made Dean of Christ Church College, a position which he held for the next 36 years. He was coauthor of a standard Greek Lexicon, and when he moved his family into the deanery at Christ Church, he installed a stately staircase paid for with earnings from his book. Dean Liddell was interested in architecture and was responsible for various changes in Christ Church buildings during his time. He was also something of an innovator in education, and the Rev. Mr. Dodgson did not always agree with him.

It was at Christ Church that Alice and her family met Dodgson. He had gone there as an undergraduate in 1851, and remained to teach mathematics almost all his life. He met Alice on April 25, 1856, when he was at the deanery photographing the Cathedral. Alice and her numerous brothers and sisters led a life that was probably typical of upper-class Victorian children. They played croquet in the deanery garden. They enjoyed card games. They played with their cat, Dinah, a creature that, Dodgson noted in his diary, "was nearly as well known in Christ Church as the Dean himself." The three oldest daughters were put in charge of a governess, Miss Prickett, with whom they took a great many long walks, singly or together. Dodgson's diary is so filled with references to meeting them on these walks that one cannot help wondering whether, even within the confines of a college community, these meetings were all accidental. Miss Prickett was not especially well educated, and her duties were more like those of a nurse. She later married a Mr. Foster and ended her days a proprietress of the famous Oxford hotel, the Mitre. Alice believed that Miss Prickett disliked her and that Lorina was her favorite.

The Liddell girls had masters who taught them French, German, Italian, and music at home. They also had lessons in dancing and cooking, and they went to an art school where John Ruskin taught them to draw. In the summer, they went to Llandudno, on the coast of Wales.

They were quiet, well-bred, polite, and obedient, qualities which, in addition to their good looks, made them ideal subjects for Dodgson's camera. Alice told her son, when she was an old woman, that they were willing to put up with the boring business of posing for him, often in fussy costumes, because they so enjoyed the thrill of watching him develop the pictures in his darkroom. Before he took the pictures, he often told them stories which he illustrated with drawings as he went along. Perhaps he was the inventor of the "chalk talk."

"He told us many stories," Alice recalled in later life, before the picnic at Godstow. "Much of *Through the Looking Glass* is made up of them, particularly the ones to do with chessmen, which are dated by the period when we were excitedly learning chess." She also said that some material from stories predating the picnic was used to make up the difference between "Alice's Adventures Underground," the first version of the book, which Dodgson wrote out and illustrated at her request, and the finished version of *Alice's Adventures in Wonderland,* which was not published until three years later.

Encouraged by his friend George MacDonald and others, and, more important, by the MacDonald children, to publish his book, Dodgson decided not to attempt the pictures himself but was delighted to have Sir John Tenniel do them. Dodgson also decided that Tenniel's Alice should not resemble Alice Liddell. Perhaps he feared the wrath of Mrs. Liddell if she did. He showed Tenniel a photograph of Mary Hilton Badcock, daughter of another clergyman, but there is doubt as to whether Tenniel actually sketched this child or simply used the photograph as a guide. She did look much more like the familiar illustrations than Alice Liddell.

THE AMERICAN EDITION IS THE FIRST EDITION

Dodgson was the kind of fussy, fidgety author who drives publishers mad, and it is, perhaps, significant, that Tenniel never did another children's book. But when the first edition was off the presses, Tenniel decided that it wouldn't do. Dodgson had it all reprinted, and the actual first edition was finally sold to Appleton in New York.

Dodgson also sent Alice illustrated letters, which her mother made her tear up after they had been read. In later life, she had no recollection of what was in them. Biographers of Dodgson have been very harsh with Mrs. Liddell for doing this, and she has been accused of being a snob who thought him a social inferior, a narrow creature unable to appreciate genius and a proud woman resentful of his criticisms of her husband's work. Still, as every parent knows, some of the things children accumulate have to be dispensed with. To a woman with a busy social schedule and a large family, Dodgson's constant requests to take pictures, which had to be fitted into the schedule, must have been a nuisance. Furthermore, even in those innocent pre-Freudian days, the constant attentions of a 30-year-old man to three little girls looked rather odd. It was much gossiped about in the college community, and Mrs. Liddell was, undoubtedly, a conventional woman. In any event, she does not appear to have encouraged the friendship, which continued sporadically for many years, though she was polite and gracious to Dodgson. Once Alice broke her leg in a fall from her pony, but though she was in bed for six weeks, Dodgson did not visit her. When she wrote asking him to be godfather to her first child, a boy, he did not bother to answer her letter.

Dodgson's last photograph of Alice was taken when she was about 22. It shows a young woman of slight build and medium height, with a sweet, grave face. She had very dark hair and grey-blue eyes, and her voice is reported to have been soft and low.

He seems to have seen her last in 1891 when she was in Oxford visiting her mother. She told her son that this was her last sight of him, and she is not mentioned thereafter in his diaries. She was always gracious to people writing about Dodgson, and when asked how it felt to be *Alice in Wonderland* she would reply "very amusing." But it seems to have been a mixed blessing. She told Arthur Houghton, Jr., in 1932 that she had had to keep her manuscript of "Alice's Adventures Underground" out of sight in her home because it caused so much comment. She had to make a firm rule never to autograph copies of *Alice,* though she broke this rule once to sign one for the present Queen Elizabeth when she was an infant princess. She also found that she had to refuse all interviews and requests to photograph her.

Some Suggested That Dodgson Was in Love With Alice

On September 15, 1880, in Westminster Abbey, Alice married Reginald Gervis Hargreaves, a wealthy sportsman. He had attended Eton and had been at Christ Church from 1872 to 1878. It seems likely that she met him during his studies there. They seem to have had a rather prolonged courtship, and the wedding may have been postponed at least once because of Alice's deep grief at the sudden death, from complications following measles, of her sister Edith, who was very near to her in age, and to whom she was very much attached. Edith had been engaged to marry Aubrey Harcourt at the time of her death. She was only 22. Lorina had already married in 1874, W. B. Skene, another Christ Church scholar.

There have been suggestions that Dodgson was actually in love with Alice Liddell, though most authorities today doubt this. In any case, Reginald Hargreaves was everything that Dodgson was not—a good shot, a cricketer who played for Hampshire, and an enthusiastic fisherman. He took Alice to live at Cuffnells, an estate he had inherited at Lynnhurst, Hants. He was very much interested in gardens and especially in trees, and his private arboretum was famous all over England.

The Hargreaves had three sons. Alan was killed in France in 1915. Leopold Reginald fell in the battle of the Somme in 1917. Caryl, the youngest, also served in World War I, but he survived. His unusual name, incidentally, has nothing to do with Lewis Carroll's, but was the name of a character in a book that one of his aunts happened to be reading at the time of his birth. Caryl Hargreaves tried to persuade his mother to write out her recollections of Dodgson and the telling of his stories, but she always resisted his pleading. However, she did tell him a great deal about her youth, which he wrote down, and this has been a valuable source to students of *Alice*. She read *Alice's Adventures in Wonderland* to him when he was a child, but like many another woman with her children, she found that he did not like it much.

In 1928, two years after her husband's death, Alice decided to sell her original manuscript. Immediately, there was protest in England. Sir Stanley Unwin, for example, wrote a letter to *The* (London) *Times*, arguing that so valuable a bit of English literature must not be allowed to leave England. Alice, however, stood firm. The manuscript was sold to A. S. W. Rosenbach in a historic sale at Sotheby's, bringing $75,000, at that time the highest price ever realized for an English book. There was and is some doubt as to whether she really needed the money. She insisted that she did, and probably by her rather high standards she was considerably poorer after her husband died than she had been.

CARROLL TERCENTENARY EXHIBIT OPENED BY ALICE

When the Lewis Carroll tercentenary was held in 1932, Alice opened a vast Carroll exhibition in London, and in the spring of that year, accompanied by her son and her sister, Rhoda, she came to this country where Columbia University had a Carroll celebration and gave her an honorary Litt. D. As soon as her trip was announced, she was besieged with mail from children wanting autographs. She refused to comply, as usual, but she did make a radio broadcast to American children. Her arrival caused a great stir in the American press, though she had been in New York previously without causing any comment whatever. Those who met her in 1932 recall that she still retained her old charm, and photographs of her show that she still had the unusual heart-shaped face that looks out from Dodgson's pictures taken some 70 years before.

"She was very spry—mentally," John Fleming, the well-known rare book dealer, recalls, "and very beautiful for a woman of her age. She was gentle and kind, but very reticent. It was hard to draw her out." Mr. Fleming says that she did not appear to be in the least sentimental or emotional about being Alice or about having parted with the copy she had kept so long. "She met the new owner, Eldridge R. Johnson," he says, "and she took it in her stride, like a professional bookseller."

ALICE HARGREAVES DIED IN NOVEMBER 1934

Arthur Houghton, Jr., who has been a Carroll collector for many years, has much the same kind of memories of her. "She was entrancing," he says, "and as one would have wished Alice to be when she grew old." She was very modest, and felt that she was being acclaimed for something that the author, not she, had accomplished. She was still rather embarrassed at the manner in which, some seventy years before, she had shamelessly "pestered" Dodgson to write out his book. "What a nuisance I must have made of myself," she said. "Still I am glad I did it now, and so was Mr. Dodgson—afterwards." She was rather fearful lest Americans think her "stand-offish" because she was compelled to decline so many invitations. She could be rather sharp with reporters, too. When asked if she were really Alice, she said, "It has been told so much in the past six months, there is no need of telling it again." When asked what Dodgson looked like she replied briskly, "Like his pictures." She said that her favorite character in the book was not Alice at all, but the Cheshire Cat ("I don't know why, but he was so funny"), and her favorite poem was "Soup of the Evening, Beautiful Soup." She retained her interest in card games all her life, though she never took up bridge, and she gave up chess.

Early in November, 1934, she suffered a stroke while out driving with C. W. Odell, who had been her chauffeur for 38 years. She died at the home of her sister Rhoda in Westerham, November 16. She had outlived all who attended the famous picnic, and her elder brother, Harry, and her younger sister, Violet, as well. In addition to Rhoda, she was survived by her son, Caryl, and two brothers, Lionel, who had retired, and Sir Frederick Liddell, who was speaker of the House of Commons. Her last years were cheered by the presence of her first grandchild, a dark-haired little girl named Alice Hargreaves, who looked very much like the young Alice Liddell.

Part Eight

FICTION FOR CHILDREN
AND YOUNG PEOPLE

LITERATURE OF HUMAN UNDERSTANDING *

Josette Frank

> Excerpts from one of two talks given by Miss Frank at a workshop "Parents, Children and Books," held on the University of Washington campus at Seattle, under the sponsorship of the Graduate School of Librarianship and the National Book Committee, Inc. Complete proceedings of the workshop will be published this spring by the University of Washington Press.

You have certainly given me a large subject to discuss! "Literature of human understanding" might be any literature! The scope of this topic is so vast that I hardly know where to begin.

We have always believed that literature has the power to broaden and deepen human understanding. Especially we expect it to do this for our children and young people. We believe—in fact, we think we know—that reading will give our children greater insight into themselves and help them grow in appreciation of other people.

What we do not know, however, is just what kind of reading will do this for any given child. Which particular book, what special kinds of reading will be, for any individual boy or girl, the "open sesame" to understanding? Children are unpredictable, and so are the effects of reading. We have no studies that search deep in the inner child for this answer. We have only our hopes and our hunches.

You are asking me to pinpoint for discussion here a special *kind* of literature; a literature, I take it, whose primary goal or purpose is to help children and young people understand themselves and others. This includes, of course, understanding the world they live in, and the forces which operate to make people think, feel, and behave as they do—especially the effect of these forces upon themselves.

There is a large and growing literature for children of all

* Josette Frank, "Literature of Human Understanding," *Top of the News* 15, no. 2 (December, 1958), 7–11. Reprinted with permission of the Children's Services Division of the American Library Association and the author.

313

ages which strives to do just this. We have had books and books and books! Some of them have been consciously geared to one "problem" or another in human interrelationships, aimed at furthering the brotherhood of man. Others have been concerned with the young reader's inner emotional life. Some have tried to clarify conflicts within family living: problems of broken homes, of divorce, and death and step-parents, or of the normal differences in outlook between parents and children. Many of these books, I fear, have bogged down under the weight of their own good intentions. But there have been a few which have done their job extremely well, shedding light in dark places and managing to be good literature as well. It takes courage and insight—not to mention writing skill—to write such a book, and these are all scarce commodities in the literary market.

Only a writer with the skill of Pearl Buck could reconcile children to the inexorable facts of catastrophe and death, as she does in *The Big Wave,* and still offer them, in poetic prose yet in terms a 10-year-old can grasp, a philosophy of the on-goingness of life. Again she comes to grips with life in another little book, *The Beech Tree,* when she tenderly explains to her young reader what it means to grow old—the difficulties and compensations of old age. In a culture which has not learned how to treat its old people, this is surely a matter which must puzzle and concern many a 10-year-old whose grampa has come to be a burden in the household.

For younger children, Taro Yashima's *Crow Boy* makes very clear to five- or six-year-olds how lonely a little boy can be when the other children find him, "different" and how even that different little boy can blossom, nurtured by the warmth and friendliness of his school fellows. All this deep lesson in beautiful pictures and simple narrative—without a line of preaching.

But to understand others, we must, of course, understand ourselves, and books may be a child's richest source for self-discovery. All great fiction, perhaps, may be said to hold up a mirror to its readers. But for boys and girls certain books especially reflect back an image they recognize as themselves.

This brings me to a kind of book of which we are finding a growing number, addressed to the very young. I am frankly puzzled by such books as Ruth Kraus's *I'll be You and You be Me.* I wonder if children, even quite young children, want to have their innermost thoughts and feelings, their secret fantasies, so thoroughly explored by a playful adult. Here, we say to them, in effect, "I know just how you feel, just what you're thinking. With my all-seeing eyes, I can look right inside you!" To me this seems a sort of adult intrusion into the child's privacy. I say this without certainty, however, for I really do not know whether children resent, as much as I do for them, having their thoughts and feelings so publicly aired. On the other hand, this same author, in a winsome picture story, *The Bundle Book*, invites the youngest listener to join in a gentle game with mother, but without psychoanalyzing him!

I sometimes wonder if the old fairy tales, and perhaps some of the newer ones, too, don't offer children a more acceptable picture of themselves and their own feelings—more acceptable because so disguised. In the wishful thinking of *Cinderella*, in *Hansel and Gretel's* triumphant outwitting of the parents who rejected them, in the boastful prowess of *The Brave Little Tailor*, in the brazen chicanery of the fradulent weavers in *The Emperor's New Clothes* (who, by the way, got away with it!) our boys and girls may find reflections of their own deep feelings, hopes, and fears. As a rule in these stories, the moral is plain, even if the morality is not exactly in line with the standards we set for our children. But the young reader's identification with characters in the tale is screened by the remoteness of the locale and circumstances. A little girl who feels "put upon" by her mother or an older sister is vindicated by the triumph of her prototype in many fairy tales. A boy who might have loved to be one of those scoundrel weavers who hoodwinked the emperor doesn't have to admit it, even to himself.

Next to understanding oneself comes the necessity of understanding one's family, especially one's parents. Here we are not so rich in books which come to grips with reality, perhaps because of the taboos that attach to writing for children. We have many, many books about families. They abound in cookie-baking mothers and fun-loving fathers. Occasionally the mother has died before the story begins, and the father and the girls are carrying on bravely. Sometimes father blusters a bit, but he's essentially all that a father should be. Few indeed are the books which dare to suggest that a family may not be an altogether happy unit. Nora Benjamin Kubie, in her sensitive book, *Remember the Valley*, pictures the stress and turmoil that comes to young people when their loyalties hang suspended in their parents' divorce. That a daughter can love and comfort a father who is an alcoholic is the theme of Mina Lewiton's story, *A Cup of Courage*. In Florence Musgrave's *Marged*, a little girl's parents are drowned in a flood—and the child's agony turns into anger at her grandmother, whose stubborn refusal to leave her home caused the tragedy. Too early in life this child has to learn that even good people can make dreadful mistakes, and the tragic ending is softened by the reconciliation between these two survivors, who learn to understand one another's silent suffering.

With our large divorce rate today, the stepmother is not just a fairy-tale character. Divorced or widowed parents often remarry, and for many children a stepmother or stepfather is a reality they must come to grips with. In her two books about the Davenport family, Alice Dalgliesh helps young people recognize some of the problems confronting both the children and the new mother who has come to preside in their family.

The question which arises for those of us who guide the choices of young readers is whether and when to suggest such books to children whose living situations parallel those of the book. There is a good chance that they will reject and possibly resent our too obvious intrusion into their deeply personal problem. I have seen this happen with a book which opened with a girl's agonized refusal to attend her father's funeral. This most sensitive and comforting book, Margueritte Harmon Bro's *Sarah*, was given by a sympathizing adult to a young girl whose father had just died. She simply couldn't read that book—not then, at any rate. Perhaps months later, when the sharpness of her grief had softened, she would be able to find comfort in the story of this little girl who was suffering as she had. The special value of such books often lies, it seems to me, in sharpening perception and deepening understanding in children who are not themselves in similar situations, but whose friends or classmates may be. I remember that the late Jerrald Beim, when he was taxed with the question whether the smallest boy in the class might not resent being given a book called *The Smallest Boy in the Class,* replied that he had written that book not for that boy but for his classmates, to help them help him overcome his difficulties.

Even more urgent is our need to bridge the gap which sets apart children in minority groups: There have been several books about Puerto Rican children in New York, but we are still waiting for a really good one. Perhaps the best so far has been, oddly enough, a little story by Doris Plenn called *The Green Song,* wherein the adventurous journey of a little tree toad from his island home in Puerto Rico to the jungles of New York draws a parallel any child can recognize. Questions are often raised about stereotypes in long-accepted books. However, of the many books that have been written hoping to give the Negro child status with his white schoolmates, most have been, it seems to me, too obviously pleading. Empathy and understanding grow best in subtle ways.

I must speak of one more great category of books on which we have always leaned heavily as a literature of human understanding: biography. Among the many truly fine biographies we have had in recent years, presenting many kinds of people and addressed to a wide range of ages, it would be hard to choose which will provide that special ingredient that reaches deep into the soul of any one child. Would it be the life story of Schweitzer, or Lincoln, or perhaps Babe Ruth or Wyatt Earp? Would it be a life of Madame Curie or of Elizabeth Barrett Browning or of the famous actress, Mrs. Siddons? We are told that Napoleon drew his inspiration from reading about Caesar. Yet most of us have read about Caesar and have not felt impelled to emulate him. Could it be that something within the boy Napoleon directed his choice of reading? And would his character and military ambitions have been altered if someone had placed in his hands a biography of Savonarola? There is little doubt that fine biography, self-chosen, can be a rich source of inspiration. But we adults must guard against overoptimism. We cannot count on biography to raise our children in the way we would have them go.

One mother, who came to me for advice about her 11-year-old daughter's reading asked for a biography of Florence Nightingale. "Is she especially fond of biography?" I asked, thinking I might substitute another title for one I didn't have. "Well," she replied, "I found her reading a biography of Nijinsky. She's crazy to be a dancer! And I don't want her to go on with any such idea. And besides, she's a pretty selfish little girl, and I thought reading about such an unselfish character as Florence Nightingale might cure her of that!" Don't we all wish it were as easy as that!

Please understand I mean in no way to disparage biography, my own favorite kind of reading, and, to judge by the vast numbers of them being published, also the favorites of many young readers. The thrill and revelation of a meaningful life is nowhere more contagious than in authentic, well-written biography.

Now, I have been able to mention only a sampling of the many books which might be called a literature of human understanding. I'm sure each of you will think of many excellent titles that might have been included. But I can hardly close a discussion of such a literature without reminding you of the greatest book of them all: the *Bible*. Whatever special place this great work may have in a child's religious life, the human values in its stories are rich beyond comparison. Here are stories about people that plainly reveal the workings of their minds and hearts. Children can have some of these stories read to them directly from a well-edited edition of the *Bible* itself—not a watered-down version.

I suppose it is unnecessary to raise again the question of how effective any reading may be in changing the attitudes or deepening the insights of any young reader. We hope and believe reading will open the minds and hearts of our children. I want only to add this warning: books alone won't do the job. The young reader doesn't just read; he lives in a family, works in a classroom, plays in a neighborhood. Everything he hears and sees and feels in the people around him will register, too.

An old Puerto Rican friend once recited to me a little Spanish verse which she said her mother had given to her. Freely translated, it goes:

> Daughter you are,
> Mother you will be
> That which you do,
> That you will see.

MAKING THE WORLD SAFE
FOR THE JANEY LARKINS *

Julia L. Sauer

It is incredible that anyone can be alive and engaged in any kind of work in the world today without questioning the value of that work in relation to a world at war. As the conflict and the horror spread on every front, as our protecting oceans shrink to

* Julia L. Sauer, "Making the World Safe for the Janey Larkins," Reprinted from *Library Journal,* 66 (January 15, 1941), 49–53, copyright R. R. Bowker Company, 1941.

moats before our eyes, each of us longs for the steadying conviction that what he is doing *counts* in some measure. Counts, that is, against the forces at large in the world today that threaten those values that we believe make life worth living.

In so far as children's librarians have consciously formulated a philosophy of their work, it has been a simple one. They have been made strong by their faith in the power of books to influence the child. They have bent their energies toward bringing the child and fine literature, both classic and modern, together; and they have, with the cooperation of publishers, done much toward the further development of a literature for children and toward putting that literature in suitable and artistic form to attract the readers for whom it is intended.

Is this work important in the face of world crisis? No children's librarian would question it. Never was there greater need in the world to foster and preserve the cultural heritage that literature hands on to succeeding generations. That cultural heritage is as much the right of European children as of our own. No doubt there are weary grandmothers and despairing mothers still trying to quiet terrified children in bomb-shelters and behind the eight-foot wall of Warsaw with the telling, through white lips, of gay folk tales. But at the moment, America must shoulder the responsibility for the preservation of that cultural heritage of children's literature.

There is more than a touch of magnificence in the thought. Children's librarians may easily feel that, in an unassuming way, perhaps, they are helping to hold steady the life line in a heaving world. There is truth in it, and there is reassurance; and in that reassurance lies the danger—danger of the long perspective. The long perspective gives us faith that the fine things of a crumbling civilization will survive. But it somehow overshoots the present. It soothes us into calm acceptance of our present. Is it tempting us to overlook another kind of need that today's children may have? Are we, in bringing children and fine literature together, doing *all* that can be done? Twenty-two years have elapsed since the close of the World War. Children who were 8 then are men and women of 30 today. Thinking of the span of a children's room as covering the years from 8 to 14, we work with one child but 6 years. In the last 22 years nearly four generations of children have had access to all we have to offer. Have we accomplished, with those of America's children whom we have reached, what we wanted to accomplish? Have we sent them on knowing all they should know? Are they ready for the next 10 years, or at least as ready as we can make them? We want America's children to see life "steadily and to see it whole." The classic literature can give them the capacity to see it steadily. They must rely on the books of the present to see it whole.

Children of today need more books about the present. Selfishly, as well as protectively, we want for our children the happiest possible childhood. In that spirit we would spare them, if we could, all knowledge of the tragedy and suffering rampant in the world. But when children in other parts of the world are sacrificing their lives, their health, their security, is it asking too much that America's children should sacrifice something of their carefree childhood? Children can be given some of the materials with which to *think* without being made, axiomatically, to *suffer*. Thinking and suffering are not necessarily synonymous. Sometimes we seem to be carrying the "happy childhood" theory to absurd lengths. "The evasion of grim facts has become an unconscious procedure. . . . We are still close enough to our frontier life to wish for our children the carefree youth and educational opportunities which our forefathers did not have." [1] comments one woman returning to America and seeing us again in a new light. And Dorothy Thompson in her column raises the question, "Are we not producing a people unable to face the most ruthless fact of life, namely, the certainty of death?" There is a possibility that the child of tomorrow may not thank our generation for his carefree childhood. There is a possibility that today's child when confronted with tomorrow's chaos will ask simply, "Why wasn't I told?"

It is not the present in Europe or the Far East with which I should wish to see children concerned. Nor, for that matter, do I believe that material on present-day conditions in any country of the other hemisphere, at war or at peace, is of paramount importance to our children at the moment. We have worked for 22 years on the belief that we could build some sort of international friendship through children's books. It has stimulated the production of an enormous supply of "background" books on other lands. We are surfeited with them. For some few we are grateful. Far too many are unsuccessful in that the plot or story and the life of the people are completely unfused. They will never reach children's hearts. The manners and customs are

---

1 Princess Paul Sapieha in *Harper's Bazaar*, Dec., 1940.

taken out and shown to the reader much as the dentist exhibits an extracted nerve, the nerve which becomes so suddenly impotent and pathetic the instant its relation to vital living is severed. Our faith in the possibility of stimulating sympathetic understanding of peoples of other lands in our children through the books they read was an idealistic theory of which we are proud. What it has accomplished we should soon be able to judge. At the moment we can hope to do little more there. That case must rest. It is on the present in our own country that attention needs to be focused.

A child can read in the excellent books of nonfiction everything he need possibly know about his mechanical present and his scientific present. Transportation, aviation, fire fighting, deep sea diving, construction, engineering are all covered thoroughly and at various reading levels. But his history stops at a discreet distance from current affairs and to hear his disappointed query, "Aren't there any 'right now' stories in?" is to be convinced that the supply is in no way adequate to the demand. In children's fiction, few periods in our history are overlooked but the present. Every librarian knows how easy it is to make a supplementary reading list for the social sciences prior to 1914. To be sure there are the modern vocational stories for the young people which came in response to a demand. And, too, the books for the preschool child have for the most part a background as streamlined as his family car. The world in which the preschool child lives, to judge from his literature, is prosperous.

When educators formulated their theory that the little child must be thoroughly oriented in his own environment, suitable preschool books began to appear. We had had all too few books whose subject matter was sufficiently restrained to fit into the narrow circle of his experience. With the supply now available some of us are wondering if the very quantity has not become that dangerous thing, the by-product of a virtue. Previously, when the easiest books were finished a child was tempted to listen to something more difficult. He was encouraged to grow in his interests. Now he can be supplied and satisfied indefinitely with books that touch his world alone. It may be that Jonathan Daniels was right in his column when he deplored the complete preoccupation of the small child with his scooter and his Scottie. It meant, he says, "that the early training of the child as part of a nation and a civilization extending beyond his scooter was discarded. He was no longer one who shared the mythology of little George beside the cherry tree or the little boy who saved Holland with a finger in a hole. I think he lost something important when he lost contact with them and swapped them for a story about a Scottie puppy." [2] The small child may not need stories which will help him to see himself as part of the nation. The educators may know best about that. But certainly the greatest need of today of the child from 8 to 14 is for books that will make him see, make him think, and help him to relate facts.

It has been said that there are at the moment only two kinds of people in the country—those who are conscious of the world and its problems and those who are not. And it is not difficult to believe when we see how loathe we are to face the possibility of any kind of sacrifice for social reform. There is no age limit to the need for building sympathetic understanding of the lives and problems of all the groups within the country. For children, and possibly for many adults, the surest way is through the medium of good fiction, "human history" as Conrad called it, that makes its appeal first to the emotions and then to the mind.

It is startling to find how few modern books we can offer a child that have any social significance whatever. Actually I can list less than a dozen. It cannot be entirely because these are the books that are most difficult to write. The artist and the adult author find inspiration in the present scene. Is it because there is no demand for that type of book? Do such manuscripts exist and have they been refused because publishers question their need? Or question their appeal to children, or to the adults who choose books for children? Think what pictures of this country we could have if all our talented writers of children's books were to stay at home and write honestly of their own environments as they are today. The books we cherish as classics, such as *Water-babies* and the novels of Dickens, were in many instances stories that touched daringly on the current problems of their day. Some of the accepted titles with foreign backgrounds for children, *Flaxen Braids* by Turngren, for example, make no effort to avoid social conditions in those countries. We have, and rightfully, cast out as outmoded or scorned altogether many old stories because they were emotional and sentimental. But certain of those very stories had the power of setting up in us, in our childhood, an overwhelming compassion for the underprivileged in our midst. The beautifully written and exquisitely made books we have to-

2 *The Nation*, Oct. 19, 1940.

day, with their relatively trivial subject matter, are not clear gain. Perhaps, if in place of the lovely books that a child *looks* at idly as he *listens* to the radio, there were some that touched his life more closely he might be tempted to *read*. Why does the preschool child alone need complete orientation in his environment? Miss Moore herself has given us the encouragement, "Tragedy lies, I think, not in knowing too much, but rather in not knowing enough to think things through." Children cannot possibly know enough to think straight or to think things through solely on what they learn in school and from the books we can now put in their way. We are afraid, no doubt, that the charge of propaganda will be hurled at us. But propaganda is nothing more or less than the scheme or plan for the propagation of a doctrine or system of principles. We should be propagating no doctrine in putting into children's hands stories that give them as realistic pictures of their own land as we are willing to show them of other lands.

Exactly what subjects should I like to see woven into fiction? Here are a few. Any social worker could round out the list. There is the question of living conditions, of housing. Men and women working in our cities today on housing boards and housing commissions are appalled at the attitude of our best citizens. Opposition is to be expected where their incomes are affected; but more serious still is the apathy which comes from complete ignorance of the facts. There is only one children's book that I can find in which housing plays a part. A widow and two children who lose their fortune decide to live in an apartment in their own tenement, all that remains of their extensive real estate. There is one black iron sink for each floor. They learn what it means to keep clean, to bathe, when water must be carried to fill and empty a portable tub. The one fact leaves a vivid impression long after the second-rate story is forgotten.

Why not a story of a mining town—any one of the drab towns we leave behind so gratefuly on a motor trip? Children live there. True, it would be well-nigh impossible to write such a story without some tragedy, because tragedy stalks each family. But children study mining and coal and its uses. Why not the miner as well? And there is a place for many more stories about our migratory population in all parts of the country and at various reading levels.

Think what it would mean to have children growing up who sensed something of the complicated world of business. Far too many of them know at first hand the results of unemployment, and, if they think at all, they attribute them all to an evil employer. But business itself might be dramatized in contrast. A story with its setting in the home of a little businessman, showing his problems as he struggles to adjust to new conditions and as his children feel them, would be pertinent. This is a situation that must affect thousands of families all over the country. There would be the danger of over-simplification to avoid, as in all stories dealing with complex economic conditions, but some cool-headed author might succeed in doing it.

In a book now little read, H. G. Wells defined the "aristocratic" life.

> This life is not good enough for me. I know that there is a better life than this muddle about us ... Now this better life is what I mean when I talk of Aristocracy ... Only by the conquest of four natural limitations is the aristocratic life to be achieved—fear, physical indulgence (desire), jealousy, and prejudice. ... To subdue fear, desire, and jealousy is the aristocrat's personal affair; it is his ritual and discipline, like a knight watching his arms; but the destruction of prejudice and all its forms and establishments is his real task, that is the common work of knighthood.[3]

Prejudice and all its forms and establishments—class, racial, religious—could be combated in children's books. It is not enough to turn down books that show prejudice. We need a positive approach. And no child is too young to need it—not even the very small girl who refused, in a slightly superior tone, *The Dog, the Brownie and the Bramble Patch* with its illustrations in silhouette because "she wouldn't want to read a book about colored people." We need more and more stories about the Negro—not necessarily in relation to the white man—but pictures of him as he lives and works and studies; his dreams and aspirations, and the possibilities of their realization. We have had some that are excellent. *The Great Tradition* handled a real situation with power and delicacy. And *Shuttered Windows* was a satisfying book. Incidentally, it has had unusual success. Its publishers tell us that its sales for the second year far exceeded the first and that the third-year sales will equal, if not exceed, those of the second. Is this because it is so good a story that readers forget its heroine

[3] H. G. Wells, *The Research Magnificent* (New York: Macmillan, 1915).

is a Negro? Or is it because it is a living, honest picture of a phase of American life? *Key Corner* for younger children contrasts the Negro schools with those for the white children, unresentfully and without apparent intent, but the impression remains.

Soon we will need stories of the refugee just as in another period we needed Mary Antin's *Promised Land* to understand the immigrant. Our present compassion is all too apt to fade once the immediate stimulation is removed. The facts about this problem will help to keep it alive. Even now we could use stories to build up distinctions between the Japanese people and their war lords before the rising prejudice gains headway. And what of anti-Semitism? Beginning with very little children, before the seeds so carelessly planted, so casually fed by catch phrases can grow to ugly size, there could be stories that would make little Protestants and little Catholics proud to have Jewish friends and playmates, proud to be asked to their homes to share as guests the beauty of their ageless ceremonies—ceremonies through which the Christian child can come closer to the life of Christ than he does in his Sunday school. The author of *The Boy of the Lost Crusade* created a magnificent Jew for young minds to admire and to grow strong on, but it is a story of hundreds of years ago. In *Toplofty* a group of Girl Scouts visit the Jewish home of one of their Jewish members. It is the only present day story I know that even mentions such relationship.

We talk glibly about wanting for our children greater freedom. What freedom is more desirable than the freedom from cramped minds, from the petty processes of thinking that develop from the crippling prejudices foisted on children in the safety of their own homes? The father who declaims over his coffee, "I don't like Italians," the mother who says, "I couldn't quite trust Mrs. S——. She is a——, you know," might far better bind their children's feet or tie their heads to a board. Yet this kind of training goes on so constantly that we are barely conscious of it.

Organized charity has taken out of children's lives the experience of having their sympathies directed toward less fortunate children. From the point of view of the "objects of charity" it is a humanitarian advance, but the privileged child is the loser. He may meet the child of the family on relief as an equal, but any quickening of sympathy for that family is all too apt to be crushed by his father who says cynically, "Don't worry about them. They know where their next meal is coming from. Better worry about your father who has to pay for it." Why not some poignant stories that will show something of the hundreds of families on relief whose underlying tragedy is their losing fight to keep their self-respect? These families are no less common, no less natural than those of the "chiseler." If our economists cannot foresee the time when this problem will not be ours to face, we cannot begin too soon to build for it a humanitarian understanding that will see *all* its implications.

Books on such subjects should not attempt to solve these problems; they cannot *solve* them. Our generation has made spectacular demonstration of its incapacity to do so either in reality or fiction. But it can at least present them so that children may be turning them over in their minds and hearts. As they grow in understanding with these pictures before them, answers and solutions may come.

We have believed it worth our best effort to try to build a foundation for international friendship through better understanding of each other on the part of little children. The need is even more urgent to do what we can to build a national understanding while there is still time. When the crest of the wave that is coming reaches us, it is difficult to see what can save us but complete unity and solidarity. To act alike is to think alike. "Each of us," says Dr. Cabot, "does his thinking with material which he does not create." If we all had a common basis of facts on which to base our moral judgments—a common material for our thinking—our future would look more secure. How on earth can we better build such an understanding than through a wealth of books streaming out to America's children?

We have been told until we have accepted it that hero tales breed heroism. It has come to be a cornerstone in a children's librarian's faith. Even now, I think, we do not doubt that it is basically true, but we do question whether children or adults are altogether able to apply to the confusion of their daily living the heroism that may be in their souls. Someone has said that "every tale is true so long as the telling lasts." Every one reading a hero tale is a hero within the covers of the book. But does he know Grendel when he meets him on his Main Street? Is he even beginning to see in present conditions situations that call for the same stuff that heroes used? The phrase "two-step thinking" has been added to our modern patter, referring to the mental process necessary to apply accepted facts. More books that give an honest picture of our land today should help in developing two-step thinking.

This need for modern realism does not negate the need for the classics and imaginative literature. Both are important; both have their place. Neither is it a question of imaginative and feminine authorship versus red-blooded realism and the masculine touch. Thus far authors (Mr. Pease, who touched a question of national honor in *Highroad to Adventure*, is one of the few exceptions) who have dared to mention any subject of current social import, successfully or otherwise, have been women. The men have been content to give us virile tales of danger at safe distances in place or time. To depict the far more dangerous present requires the courage of the commonplace, and it requires caution. The following extract from an editorial by Amy Loveman, at the time of the Children's Crusade for the Children, sounds a warning:

> There is, to be sure, in any movement to direct the sympathies of children constant need for caution. It is so easy on the part of teacher or parent to slip from conviction to propaganda, to let detachment yield to strength of feeling. It is so difficult for even the most well-intentioned person to steer a safe course between preaching righteous wrath against cruelty and tyranny and ruthlessness and giving vent to an indignation that will sow hatred and rancor.[4]

Can unimpassioned books that depict social conditions be written? Two months ago we should have said, "We hope so." Now we can say "Yes," because it has been done. In *Blue Willow*, Doris Gates has written a story of our migratory population. Janey Larkin is an American child with a longing in her heart to stay somewhere, to settle, so that her roots may go down deep in our American soil and draw from it strength and nourishment. She is as real an American as Tom Sawyer or Jo March. We need many more books about the Janey Larkins in our literature for children. And when we get them we will need the courage to give them to our children. Our taste, our choice of the literature upon which we would wish our children to grow is not changed. Our values may remain the same to the last grain. But the glass is reversed through no doing of ours. The sands are running the other way. And before a world can be made safe even for nightingales, it must be made safe for the Janey Larkins.

---

[4] *Saturday Review of Literature*, April 20, 1940.

REGIONAL CHILDREN'S LITERATURE *

Lois Lenski **

[From a speech to the New York State Library Association, 1946.]

We are grateful to Wendell Willkie for giving us the phrase "One World." He meant, as we all know, that we must learn to live as brothers to make the world "one." We have now many separate worlds, little worlds with fences between, fences so high we cannot see over them. Each of us thinks that *our* world is the only one. We do not know or understand other people's worlds, beyond our own fence. Before we can hope to understand foreign nations and live at peace with them, we must understand our own country and the different kinds of people who live in it.

Regional art, painting, and literature is, basically speaking, the presentation of a *way of life* in a certain region which has developed or preserved in itself a certain homogeneous individuality. Because of the great diversity of setting and of types of people in our country, it is practically impossible to write of it as a whole, as a national entity. We have our New England, our South, our Middle West, our Far West, and under these divisions, many more subdivisions and groups. And so any sound understanding of our country as a whole becomes an understanding of its component parts.

Regional art in America is a fairly recent development. Only a generation ago it was considered necessary for an artist to study painting in Paris. American art schools were not good enough; or, if an artist started in them, he had to finish in Paris. He had to paint European landscapes, he had to paint in a European manner. Certain subjects were considered "artistic," other

* Lois Lenski, "Regional Children's Literature," *Wilson Library Bulletin*, 21 (December, 1946), 289–92. Reprinted by courtesy of The H. W. Wilson Company, New York with permission of the author.
** Author, winner of the Newbery Medal, 1946, for *Strawberry Girl*.

subjects were taboo, among them, machinery or locomotives, mechanical or industrial subjects, ugly and sordid subjects, especially anything that smacked of realism. Art in the Paris tradition was romantic, sentimental to varying degrees, artistic, but it had little relation to real life.

It took considerable courage for a few men to break away and to find America worth painting. Outstanding examples are three—Grant Wood of Iowa, John Steuart Curry of Kansas, and Thomas Hart Benton of Missouri. Along with their choice of American subject matter, these men developed also a more forthright technique, painting with directness, simplicity and vividness.

At the same time that this regional American art was developing, American literature was doing the same thing. Theodore Dreiser, Erskine Caldwell, Willa Cather, and others were finding America worth writing about and writing of it simply, directly, and vividly.

Regional art, painting or literature, can be produced by a native son or daughter, or by an outsider.

The native son, who has his roots there, should be by all means the best interpreter of his own region. There are many fine examples of authors who have done this. I think particularly of Sara Orne Jewett and her fine stories of New England and New England character. Among our juvenile books we have Marguerite de Angeli of Pennsylvania, May Justus of Tennessee, Will James of the Cow Country, Laura Ingalls Wilder of the Prairie Country, and many others.

But often the native son has limitations. He is too close to the scene, he "cannot see the forest for the trees." Sometimes too he is ashamed of his own background and beginnings. He wants to go *somewhere else* to find something to paint or write about. The native son may know the scene so well he cannot get outside of it and see it with perspective. For example, Grant Wood had to go to France and Italy first and learn that they held nothing for him, before he was ready to come back to Iowa and see what his own state offered him. One's own autobiography is always the hardest book to write, because the details are all too personal and it hurts too much to write objectively of them.

ADVANTAGES OF THE OUTSIDER

The outsider, coming into a region new to him, has the great advantage of having "eyes to see," he has a greater receptivity because of the newness of the scene—it has never had a chance to grow stale to him.

It was, of course, as an outsider that I gathered the material for my three regional books, *Strawberry Girl, Bayou Suzette,* and *Blue Ridge Billy.* I did not deliberately set out to travel in search of book material, but I have always found material, crying out to be recorded. Those who have "eyes to see" never run out of subject matter for creative expression.

Some fifteen years ago, I, Ohio born and bred, went to live in Connecticut in an old 1790 farmhouse. Before I consciously realized what was happening, I was learning Connecticut history from my neighbors and I was starting a series of books for children with Connecticut and New England historical backgrounds. Incidentally I also started to paint a series of portraits of my rural Connecticut neighbors—a gallery of "Connecticut Yankees" —but my books soon began to absorb all my time, and this ambitious project had to be abandoned! The writing of these books was forced upon me, the material was lying there on my doorstep—"treasure for the taking." I could not sidestep it, although outwardly this little Connecticut town was no different from any other and not spectacular in any way. Many authors or artists might have passed it by and said there was nothing there.

But the experience of writing teaches us over and over again one important lesson, that there is a story in every human being. How many stories then can a small town offer—if we have the time to pause, the eyes to see, and the hearts to understand.

Later, it so happened that because of ill health, my doctor advised my spending my winters in a warmer climate. I went first to Louisiana and spent a winter in New Orleans, where I was confronted with stories on all sides. There was the exciting history of old New Orleans, the charm of the French Quarter, the fascination of the colored children—a thing to be constantly resisted—and there was the real life I saw being lived by French-speaking people in the rural regions along the bayous, especially the life of the children there. I had to put it into a book, I couldn't help myself. It was there waiting for me.

When I found out what an exciting life the Louisiana children live, I wanted to go right home to Connecticut and tell the children there about it. Then I went to Florida and learned that children live still different lives in that land of sunshine and orange trees and strawberries. Why don't we know more about our own country? Why shouldn't the children of Louisiana and Florida and Connecticut and other parts of the country get to know each other? Why haven't Louisiana writers told us how

Louisiana people live? Why haven't Florida writers told us how Florida people live? If the native sons and daughters have not "eyes to see," why should not an outsider do it?

And so I found myself writing regional books for children, and through the process, I have developed an insatiable curiosity about how other people live.

To write these books, I went to live with the people in these regions, to really get to know them firsthand. I talked with them, ate and drank with them, sat in their kitchens and on their porches, and always I listened as they told their experiences. The children told me a great deal and so did their parents. I took my sketchbook with me, and made drawings of the people, their houses, their furnishings, and many details of their surroundings. If anyone was suspicious of me as an outsider, I did not know it. My drawings helped me, as nothing else could, to make friends of complete strangers. Children crowded round me like flies, eager to watch a drawing grow on a sheet of paper, devoted friends after the first stroke. Knowing the children was but a step toward knowing the adults, who accepted me without question and gave me many of my best stories.

It is easy to win the confidence of people if your approach is fundamentally sympathetic, if you show a kindness that is real, not affected, and if you can forget your own life, your own background, and put yourself wholeheartedly into their point of view in all their trials and experiences. Most people like to talk of themselves and talk best under the stimulus of a sympathetic audience. I am the best listener in the world: I never interrupt!

It is a wearing and an exhausting experience, both physically and spiritually, to become "one of them," to live in imagination with people who are different from any you have seen or known before, but it is a rewarding experience as only creative activity can be.

Children often ask me if my stories are true, and my characters real. I call these regional books "true to life," because for most of the characters in them, I had living persons in mind. Birdie Boyer in *Strawberry Girl* is a real little girl I saw plowing in a sandy field in Florida. Little did I dream when I snapped her photograph and talked to her, that she would make friends for me all over the country and return to me nearly three years later, bearing the Newbery Medal in her hand! So when I am asked if my characters are real, I feel I can honestly say yes.

Regional Literature A Challenge

Because of its very nature, regional literature for children becomes a challenge, a challenge to authors to interpret our regions with insight and understanding, and a challenge to those of us who use books, to understand the fundamental purpose and thus help in the important task of widening understanding among different groups.

A regional book shows how a way of life is controlled by an environment. It shows how people live in a certain region and why they live as they do and how outward circumstances have made them live as they do. It will emphasize unimportant outward differences, but it will also emphasize the inward universal likenesses in behavior.

A book is always a vicarious experience. This is particularly true for a child, who identifies himself with the hero of a book in an astonishing way, because of the tremendous power of his imagination. In a book about a horse, the child *becomes* the horse. In a book about a dog, he *is* the dog. In the same way, an adult or child lives with the hero or heroine of a novel, thinks with him, suffers and rejoices with him, speaks and acts like him, understands and loves him.

Surely we all realize the inadequacy of personal experience. Two people, standing face to face, can be as remote as the north and south poles. How often, standing before him, you have not the slightest clue to what the other person is thinking. Faced with a strange person, a strange scene or situation, an unfamiliar experience, we are apt to be suspicious or to laugh defensively. After we get to know the strange person, we are surprised to learn that he has two eyes, two ears as we have. He has two arms, two legs, even a heart, and a mind. He is no longer a misunderstood monster, but a human being like ourselves, with faults and frailties, similar to our own, but also with our feeble goodness, our own faith in the right, in justice, and in truth. How can this metamorphosis come about? How can this unfamiliar monster be changed into a human being?

One of the best ways is through books. This is about the only way that children—or adults—can get a vivid glimpse into the inner life and thought processes of a strange person—by sharing it in a book. This is made possible because the author has studied, sympathized with, and loved these people, shared their life, become "one of them," and by his gifts of creation and imagination has laid the strange person's thoughts, emotions, motives, and intentions bare before the reader—*and they are not very different from the reader's own.*

I believe that children should be constructively taught a sympathetic approach to the strange person, and by the phrase "strange person" I mean any person different from themselves in race, color, creed, or background. Without such teaching, children are apt to follow the crowd like sheep; they think in herds, because they haven't the courage for independent thinking and action. They are thoughtless—they can torture a newcomer in their group who is different in speech, in clothing, or in habits. But I do not believe for a minute that they have basically cruel or barbaric tendencies. When they perpetrate cruelties, it is either the result of adult example, or they do it out of thoughtlessness or lack of imagination. They do not realize how it hurts the other person. They have never learned to put themselves in the other person's place. This shows their great need of guidance, of books which stress the inward thinking of different kinds of people.

Children need to be told that we want to keep differences in speech, in habits, in personality. Why should we all dress alike, talk alike, think alike, act alike? The world would be a stupid place if we did. It is all these racial and regional differences that make our country unique. Our country has always stood for the widest kind of cosmopolitanism.

LOCAL PRIDE

We want to encourage a pride in our own locality, a pride in our own local, colorful use of the American language, and a pride in the particular cultural heritage which our group has contributed. Instead of emphasizing these differences between groups deliberately to separate and bring hostility between them, we want to look upon them as a valuable heritage. We want to encourage also a pride in those universal qualities which are common to all groups and which can help us to live harmoniously together. The magnificent thing is that out of so many backgrounds and heritages, there exist so many similarities and likenesses if we will only look for and acknowledge them.

We must never forget that among all men there exists a response to the beautiful, the love of home and family, the fear of insecurity, the appreciation of sacrifice, the desire for personal achievement, and the longing to be at one with the universe.

These are universal experiences, these are the bonds which hold men together.

There used to be a time, not so long ago, when the little home, the little farm in this country was self-sufficient and self-contained, a safe little world in itself. But the automobile and enlarged means of communication have changed all that. People now leave their own backyards and, in the family car, travel thousands of miles into other regions than their own. They see people living in all sorts of different ways they never thought possible before. Southerners come north, northerners go south, easterners go west, westerners come east. The traveler comes home, and he remembers those other regions, those other homes so different from his own, that other people love just as dearly as he loves his own. He becomes a new person, a person with a wider vision. He comes to only one conclusion: here is our great, wide, beautiful country, with room enough for all, for many kinds of people. We need not all be alike, we must not all be alike. We must hold fast to our individuality, but our local patriotisms can be cherished without any conflict between them. And so, loving my own little corner, where my roots are put down, becomes a part of loving the whole, a part of a true tolerance for all those other people in their backyards.

In regional books for children, then, we stress a particular environment and the way of life which it has brought into being. By understanding this environment, we learn *why* the people speak, think, and act as they do. We realize that under the same circumstances, we would speak, think, and act the same as they do. And so we come to understand a basic concept behind all experience—the universality of human behavior. The most important lesson that any child—or adult—has to learn is the ability to put himself in the other person's place.

And so we need to hold our banner high, the banner of unselfishness, of genuine love for others, and of faith in our fellowmen. This may be a dark and a confused and a complicated age through which we are passing, but there are certain eternal verities as true today as they have always been. Let us hold them up as a lighted candle in a dark place. Fortunate indeed, are we who work with children. In their world, there is always joy, beauty, and hope. There is constant faith, trust, and respect for all. Work with and for children is always constructive, building for the future—building One World.

BOOKS ABOUT NEGROES FOR CHILDREN *

Charlemae Rollins

> Books which avoid stereotypes and present Negro life objectively make an important contribution to better human relations. Their number has been growing in recent years.

The first edition of the pamphlet *We Build Together,* published in 1941 by the National Council of Teachers of English, listed only 72 titles of acceptable books about Negroes for children of elementary school age. In 1948 a second edition included 90 children's books, dealing with Negro life.

In 1949 Mrs. Augusta Baker, assistant coordinator of work with children and supervisor of storytelling in the New York Public Library, published a pamphlet, *Books about Negro Life for Children,* which included 95 books about American Negroes for children. Her latest pamphlet, published in 1957 with the assistance of a Dutton-Macrae Award, critically evaluates more than two hundred excellent books about American Negroes for children.

The purpose of this article is to point up the progress that has been made in the field of writing, illustrating, and publishing books about Negroes for children in the last ten years. In addition, it is hoped that librarians, teachers, parents, and others interested in selecting books to meet a specific need will also find some help here.

For those who are unaware of the sensitive areas in writing about Negroes for children, a brief summary of the criteria used in the pamphlets cited above may be helpful.

*Charlemae Rollins, "Books About Negroes for Children," *ALA Bulletin,* 53 (April, 1959), 306–8. Reprinted by permission of the American Library Association and the author.

1. Books with illustrations that stereotype or ridicule the Negro child are objectionable. These are known as "pickaninny pictures."

2. Books that use *terms of derision* such as "nigger," "darkey," "coon," "spook," "Rastus," "Sambo," and "Pickaninny."

There are exceptions to this. In historical fiction for older children where the characters are known to have used these terms, this is accepted. An author who tries to present an honest portrayal of a period must of necessity set down the words as they were naturally used. In order to recreate certain scenes in a particular setting he must try to give a faithful presentation. Examples of this may be found in *Railroad to Freedom,* by Hildegarde Swift (Harcourt, Brace) and the more recent Newbery Award winner *Rifles for Watie* by Harold Keith (Crowell).

The real objection to these terms arises when the author uses them in referring to his characters. Examples of this unconscious stereotyping are: "The ancient darkey scratched his kinky head." "The fat black cook waddled into the kitchen." "An engaging pickaninny rolled on the dirty cabin floor." "The terrified coons scuttled for cover." The home of a poor Negro is a "cabin." The Negro minor character never smiles or laughs, he "grins widely." All Negroes have "pearly white teeth."

3. The use of *heavy dialect* in children's books has been discussed widely. No honest author of children's books uses it simply as a handy gimmick to delineate a character, whether he is a villain, a Negro, or any minor character.

Recently a supervisor of children's work in a large midwestern city wrote to the publisher of the Doctor Dolittle books when a member of her staff questioned the value of replacing them because of the objectionable language. The reply happily brought out the fact that the latest edition of the Doctor Dolittle books no longer includes the words she referred to. The publisher deplored their use as much as others did, but revision, especially of books by an author who is no longer living, presents difficult problems.

Publishers are reconsidering their older books in the light of such inquiries, and alert librarians in reevaluation for replacement have a fine opportunity to make certain that in considering older books for repurchase the book collection keeps pace with the present-day interpretation of human relations.

We Build Together made a plea for heroes for Negro children —books about real people. This need is now being adequately met by a yearly output of at least a half-dozen individual biographies of eminent Negroes, past and present. There are also useful special collections of biographies, such as *Famous Negro Music Makers* by Hughes (Dodd, Mead) and general biography collections notable for their inclusion of all the important persons in a particular field regardless of race. An example is *Giants of Jazz* by Terkel (Crowell).

Elizabeth Yates was awarded the Newbery Medal in 1951 for *Amos Fortune: Free Man* (Aladdin), a splended hero story for any child above the fourth grade.

Several good books have been written, both nonfiction and fiction, about Harriet Tubman, the slave woman who led more than two hundred of her people to freedom. Mary McCleod Bethune and Marian Anderson are also popular subjects.

A really notable book of 1958 was *Captain of the Planter* by Sterling (Doubleday). This is a thrilling and fully documented account of the unlettered slave boy who boldly sailed the *Planter,* a Confederate ship, into the hands of the Union Army.

In poetry and in fiction Negro children are encouraged when they see reflections of themselves. Gwendolyn Books' *Bronzeville Boys and Girls* (Harper) and the merry folk rhymes and games of Margaret Taylor's *Did You Feed My Cow?* (Crowell) are especially cherished by Negro children, although they are enjoyed by all boys and girls.

For older girls, Florence Means, well known for her earlier pioneering in the field, has written *Reach for a Star* (Houghton Mifflin), significant because it is the only story which gives a picture of life at a large coeducational Negro university. It is a warm and wholesome love story as well. Miriam Blanton has written a girl's story, *Hold Fast to Your Dreams* (Messner), about the trials faced by a Negro girl who longed to be a ballet dancer. This story also touches the problem of school integration in the Midwest. *Julie's Heritage* by Catherine Marshall (Longmans) is a story of the problems that beset a Negro girl in a northern city. Hope Newell has written two popular stories about Mary Ellis, a Negro student nurse who trained in a white hospital. *A Cap for Mary Ellis* and *Mary Ellis Student Nurse* (Harper). *The Barred Road* (Macmillan) by DeLeeuw is a story of the friendship between a white and Negro girl that withstood the pressures of a hostile community.

Writers of books on sports, both fiction and nonfiction, have kept pace with the gains that have been made by Negroes in the major sports fields—baseball, football, basketball, boxing, and track. Among the many successful writers of sports books are John Tunis, Gregor Felsen, Duane Decker, Jesse Jackson, and C. H. Frick. Gilbert Douglas in *Hard to Tackle,* a football story, successfully combines the sports element with a community problem.

A bold venture in the field of stories for junior high school boys and girls is *New Dreams for Old* by Person (Longmans), a present-day story of youth in the Deep South which provides an easily understood view of the economic as well as the cultural changes there. Equally courageous is *South Town* by Graham (Follett), a story of the hardships faced by an ambitious Negro boy in a small southern community. The important message of this moving story is one of hope for the future when there will be greater understanding between the two races in the South.

The progress of the past ten years reported here is a real tribute to the conscious effort that has been made by hundreds of workers with children and children's books.

Scores of selective lists have been prepared. Among the many now available are:

Books about Negro Life for Children, Augusta Baker, New York Public Library, 1957.
Books Are Bridges, The American Friends Service Committee and the Anti-Defamation League of B'nai B'rith, 1957.
Brotherhood Lists, The National Conference of Christians and Jews.
Reading Ladders for Human Understanding, by Margaret Heaton, Washington, American Council on Education, 1955.

FOREIGN BOOKS FOR CHILDREN*

Clara J. Kircher

> What books are available, their contribution to the
> life of the foreign-born children, how and where to buy
> them.

This article could not have been written without the help of
Mrs. Maria Teresa Braga, children's librarian of the Van Buren
Branch, and Norma Grosken, children's librarian of the main
library, who work directly with our foreign-language speaking
children.

When, as an aftermath of World War II, a number of DP families moved into the city, the Newark Public Library became
aware of the need to provide them with books in their native
tongue as well as in the language of their adoption. This presented a challenge, especially in the area of juvenile books, since
the children's department of the library owned few books in
foreign languages except picture books and we realized that such
a book collection was not suited to our needs. The picture books
had been used for display purposes and for loans to parents and
teachers. We needed a collection of books suitable for the elementary school child.

The reading ability of the French- and German-speaking children who started to use our foreign book collection at that time
was far above the picture book level. In many cases it was above
that of Newark's native-born children. We had to find suitable
books for these children as well as for children of families from
Puerto Rico, Spain, Portugal, and Cuba who by 1954 were moving into Newark in great numbers.

To serve as a bridge from their old language to their new one,

* Clara J. Kircher, "Foreign Books for Children," *Library Journal,* 83
(March 15, 1958), 947–51. Reprinted by permission of R. R. Bowker Company and the author.

and to do what we could in a small way to see that these children would retain an interest in and respect for their old language, a number of books in Spanish, German, and French were purchased for our main children's room and our Van Buren Branch to supplement what we already had in these and other languages. The titles chosen were not picture books but rather stories such as *Pinocchio* and the Andersen and Grimm fairy tales, loved by children everywhere without regard to language or national origin. In addition to titles such as these, we were careful to see that representative authors like Charles Perrault, Johanna Spyri, Erich Kastner, and Maria Morales were represented in their original language. Finally, we bought a number of typical English and American classics like *Mary Poppins, Little Women, King Arthur,* and *Treasure Island,* and modern stories like Helen Boylston's *Sue Barton,* Adele De Leeuw's *Linda Marsh,* Miriam Schlein's *A Day in the Park,* and Wesley Dennis' *Flip and the Cows.* To these we added a number of titles from the Little Golden Books and Landmark Books. Thus, the Spanish-speaking child will see on our shelves today not only books already familiar to him, but also, to mention just a few, Samuel Hopkins Adams' *El Expres Pony,* Pearl Buck's *Los Chinatos de la Casa de al Lado,* and Kathryn Jackson's *El Occupado Tom.* The same is true for the child whose native language is French or German.

USING THE BOOKS

No sooner were the new titles purchased and the books added to our shelves, than they were snatched from the shelves, borrowed by children like the Puerto Rican child, typical of the many who could speak little or no English. Upon obtaining her library card, she left the children's room beaming and clasping tightly in her arms a reader in English plus *Pinocho* and *Goldilocks y los Tres Osos.* The word spread like wildfire, one child telling another and bringing him in to see the *library*—that newly-discovered place where books that he could read in his own language were to be found. Thus a first step was taken to do what we could lest foreign-born children, in their anxiety to be American, become ashamed of their old language and traditions and fail to retain an appreciation of their old culture as they began to feel at home in the new.

Our program for these children does not end with merely supplying foreign language books to be borrowed. During the summer the foreign-speaking children are encouraged to join our summer reading club, Robin Hood's Merry Band. Through the means of this club we not only learn to know the children better, but as the members read and report on the books they have read they get a great deal of personal satisfaction from the reading itself, from the feeling of belonging that comes with membership in such a club, and from earning a Certificate of Award. Mrs. Maria T. Braga, the children's librarian at the Van Buren Branch who is equally at home in English, Spanish, and Portuguese, says of their interest in membership in the club and of its great value to them: "We feel that the reporting on books, which is given in English mixed with much Spanish, is the result of real effort on the part of the children and will be a means of helping them to learn English more quickly than they might without this goal as an incentive, and that it will help in their adjustment to a new environment." Little seven-year-old Rafael who came up to Mrs. Braga exclaiming in accented English, "Today, I hit the bull's-eye, oh yes!" is a concrete example of the truth of this statement.

Last summer a boy joined the summer reading club and read the 10 books necessary to qualify him to receive a certificate. Then he had to return to Puerto Rico with his family. But before he did so, he came to the library to say good-bye to Mrs. Braga, leaving with her his address and a six-cent stamp with instructions that his certificate be mailed to him at the end of the summer. Many non-English-speaking parents visit Mrs. Braga, also, saying that they wish to see the library that has given their children so much help and pleasure.

During the school year Mrs. Braga visits the two public schools in the city where there are Americanization classes for children with a Latin background. Arrangements are then made for the children to visit the library as a group to listen to stories in Spanish and Portuguese and to become library users. A typical comment after such a visit was that made by a little nine-year-old girl from Spain who said to Mrs. Braga upon leaving, "It is beautiful to visit the library." The parochial school closest to our main children's room has many Puerto Rican children enrolled. When Norma Grosken visits this school, she extends a special invitation to the Puerto Rican children to join the library. They generally swarm into the main children's room after her visit and wipe out our small foreign book collection in one day.

The language barrier created by non-English-speaking borrowers is not insurmountable since the Puerto Rican children are willing interpreters and a Hungarian mother and child brought their own interpreter when they came to register at the library. Paperback interlanguage grammars are a help to staff as well as public in these cases. At one of our branches when the desk assistant ran into difficulty in trying to explain to an Italian mother the intricacies of signing an application, she turned to *Say It in Italian* and managed to write a note to the parent explaining what to do. Then, too, any difficulty soon disappears, for the children make the transition from one language to another very quickly. A frequent visitor to our main children's room is a small boy who only a short time ago was living and attending school in France. Two months ago he knew no English. Now he speaks English better than Miss Grosken does French and has become an ardent recruiter of borrowers, bringing one or two pals with him each time he visits the library. At the main library the same is true; when Miss Grosken said to a young Puerto Rican boy, in her best Spanish (which she has picked up from the children themselves), *"Tienes que escribir tu nombre acqui,"* he answered in English, "I can write my name!"

Miss Grosken has noticed that many Puerto Ricans are very self-conscious about their speech. In a sixth grade class she asked for help in translating the titles of some of the Spanish books she had brought to show the children.

"The children," she says, "seemed almost ashamed of their language background. It is not hard to account for their feelings. Suddenly they have found themselves in a new country where their language is a disadvantage, where it sets them apart, where they find communication with English-speaking people difficult.

"But they do come to the library. Quite a few know no English at all. Some, though they can understand English, are shy about speaking it. These children usually come with a friend who can act as interpreter to help them register for a card. Though at first I knew no Spanish, I have tried to learn enough to be able to register a borrower without an interpreter. My attempts along this line usually evoke delighted laughter from the new borrowers. For once they find their trying situation reversed. Often this encourages them to try speaking in English, finding that their own English, even though meager, is better than my Spanish.

"The younger children who know no English seem to pick up the language rapidly. Some of the very young ones, first graders, can speak both English and Spanish quite easily. But they are learning to read only in English. They take Spanish books home for their parents to read to them. It is to be hoped that, once reading in English is no longer a difficult new skill, they will learn to read in Spanish as well.

"It is amazing how many easily accepted cliches about bilingual people are just not true. Children of Spanish background, for example, do not toss in a Spanish expression when they are not sure of the English word or phrase. Instead, they talk around it. And no child who could speak one word of English has ever said to me, 'Si, Senorita.' 'Yes' and 'no' greetings and the proper forms of address are among the first expressions they learn.

"The contact with children who speak foreign languages has heightened the interest in language-learning among English-speaking children. One boy who knows no Spanish has taken home an attractive Spanish picture story. He has a friend who can read it to him and tell him what it means. A group of girls is working out an informal exchange teaching setup. One girl who speaks English fluently, although her original language is German, is teaching English to the brother of two of her Spanish-speaking friends. The two friends and their mother are teaching her Spanish. When Spanish and English are mastered, they plan to go on to German.

"I think this is a good sign. In the United States, where one can travel thousands of miles without running into another language area, we take English for granted. Not much effort is made to teach foreign languages as practical speech. Our foreign-born children cannot help but learn English since they are surrounded by it. If they do not lose their original language they will end up with two languages and will have an advantage over the English-speaking student who, in the ninth grade, begins a textbook study of a second language."

PURCHASING BOOKS

Purchasing juvenile books in foreign languages is not a routine or easy task. We have found that because of the poor quality of paper, binding, and illustrations in many books produced outside of the United States it is advisable to see the books before purchasing them. For this reason we have visited book importers in New York and chosen our books personally from their shelves. We have found the largest number of good books in Spanish and Portuguese at the Franz C. Feger Company (17 E. 22 St., New York 10). Mr. Feger has a large and constantly changing selection of books and hopes to issue a catalog some time soon. This should be of great value to those librarians who cannot easily go to New York to do their buying in person.

Foreign books can also be ordered by referring to such lists as *Foreign Children's Books Available in the United States* compiled for the American Library Association in 1954 by a committee of which Helen A. Maston of The New York Public Library was chairman. A supplement to this list appeared in the May 1957 issue of *Top of the News*. This is a good, annotated list arranged by language groups. Pequeno Paquete, S.A. (P.O. Box 817, Coral Gables, Florida) has a catalog of some 90 Spanish books which have been chosen by a librarian and elementary school teacher. Emphasis is on books which are available in both English and Spanish. Many titles are available in buckram as well as in the original bindings, which are generally paper-over-board and very flimsy. A selective sampling or individual titles may be ordered on approval.

We have ordered French books sight unseen by checking the catalog of the French Book Guild (1860 Broadway, New York) but this practice is not advisable except for French books which on the whole have relatively strong and attractive formats.

Little Golden Books having the same format as their English cousins can be purchased from the companies listed above but not from Simon and Schuster.

A list of Landmark Books which have been translated into six different languages is available from Marjorie Currey of Random House. These can be ordered directly from their foreign publishers or from import houses.

Fabio Coen of the Package Library of Foreign Children's Books (69-41 Groton Street, Forest Hills 75, N.Y.) will send his catalog on request. Most of the books on this list are picture books and have been selected by Maria Cimino and Helen Maston of The New York Public Library. Prices of individual titles will be supplied upon request. Ordering need not be restricted to language "packages."

In general, prices of foreign books are higher than American ones of comparable physical quality but not so much as to cause them to be luxury items.

A SPANISH "CHILDREN'S CATALOG"

In 1954 the *Direction General de Archivos y Bibliotecas* of Madrid published the *Cataloge Critico de Libros Para Ninos*. This is a 350-page catalog similar to our American *Children's Catalog*. It was compiled by the *Gabinete de Lectura "Santa Teresa de Jesus,"* a group of women who have opened a children's library in Madrid. (For an interesting account of this library, see "Report on Children's Books in Spain" by Lavinia R. Davis in the Feb. '57 *The Horn Book*.) It has annotations for 2,280 books broken down into age and subject classifications. While the majority of the books are Spanish, books written in other languages are included. The catalog has an author and title index as well as a list of publishers and distributors. The selection is based upon interest and literary, moral, artistic, and psychological values. Although all information is given in Spanish, even the non-Spanish reading librarian will be able to use it without too great difficulty.

We are still searching for more ways of obtaining books that will help children to love and respect their cultures both old and new. We do not feel that we have by any means settled all of our problems. We know that we are reaching only a few of the many children who need our special interest and help. But we have made a start and we have great hopes for the future.

SOME FUNNY BOOKS *

Annis Duff

Some books are funny to some people, other books are funny to other people; and people who find the same books funny can enjoy the interplay of reference, and the subtle sympathy of laughter that gives companionship a special intimacy. Our family has 10 great favorites. It doesn't particularly matter *why* we find

* From *Bequest of Wings* by Annis Duff. Copyright 1944 by Annis Duff. Reprinted by permission from The Viking Press Inc., and the author.

them amusing. The important thing is that we have the most wonderful fun reading them, talking about them, and quoting from them. They prick up points of light in all sorts of ordinary happenings, and, by association, add a peculiar piquancy to our enjoyment of people. Every one of them is known as a child's book, not so much because its appeal is limited to children, as because children can so heartily enjoy it. All of them are service-able books, the kind you read and reread, with a compound interest of pleasure, from the time you are a sprout till you share them—as we hope to do—with your grandchildren.

Winnie-the-Pooh was the first of our favorite funny books that we read to our daughter, and it had a sort of delayed action that made it seem even funnier. She took it all quite seriously at first, listening with wide-eyed enchantment to all the ridiculous, adorable adventures of Pooh and Piglet, Rabbit, Kanga, Eeyore and Owl, and never laughing at all. Then one evening when we two were sitting quietly with our books in the living room, we heard sounds of muffled laughter from upstairs. Curiosity got the better of us after a while, and we went up to ask what the joke was. Our five-year-old was sitting up in bed, with crimson cheeks and dancing eyes, almost speechless with mirth because she had suddenly thought of Pooh, stuck in the doorway of Rabbit's house, with Christopher Robin at the north end of him, reading a Sustaining Book "to help and comfort a Wedged Bear in Great Tightness," and Rabbit hanging his washing on the south end.

After that, when we read *Winnie-the-Pooh* or the *House at Pooh Corner,* she laughed just as much as we did, and to this day we cannot get through some of the stories without dissolving into helpless laughter. We have almost forgotten that there is such a word as "elephant"; an elephant to us is a Horrible Heffalump, or a Herrible Hoffalump, or a Hellible Horralump or a Hoffable Hellerump. People move away uneasily when they meet us in zoos, because we go off into such gales of merriment and talk such a queer jargon. But we know what we mean. Anyone in our family who does a stupid thing is a Bear of No Brain at All; when our daughter went through a phase of patient resignation to being neglected and misunderstood, she was known as Eeyore. Nobody writes "Happy Birthday" any more—it is always "HIPPY PAPY BTHUTHDTH THUTHDA BTHUTHDY." An expedition is always an Expotition, between meal refreshment is "a smackerel of something"; any sort of jollification is

"Merriment, what ho!" *Winnie-the-Pooh* and *The House at Pooh Corner* are *infectious* books. I still resent the reviewer who dismissed them with "Tonstant Weader Fwowed up." Any books that families can have such superior fun with are "the real thing."

Not very long ago my daughter and her father were sitting side by side on the couch, reading *The House at Pooh Corner,* one waiting for the other at the foot of each page, and both chuckling happily. When they came to the end of a chapter our daughter looked up with a grin. "Are you reading a children's book, or am I reading a grown-up book?" she asked. "Both," said her father emphatically.

Ferdinand is another sort of funny book, a mixture of drollery and burlesque that we find very palatable. The pictures are a delightful adjunct to the story, and part of the fun of quoting lies in the fact that words and phrases conjure up the appearance of things that amuse us. We particularly like the picture of Ferdinand sitting under his favorite cork tree. One of the reasons why we are especially enjoying *Ferdinand* just now is that Duff Secundus, who is still too little to share most of our funny books, is having *such* a good time with it. "Smelling the flowers just quietly" is a phrase that he might have made up himself, it is so like the things he says, and we three older ones bubble over every time he uses it. I hope he will say to me one day, as his sister did a year or two ago, "You are a very understanding mother, even though you are a cow."

One doesn't mind such reflections on one's appearance, knowing what they come from. My daughter has a very engaging custom of bringing me little tributes of flowers every now and again, always with a suitably inscribed card enclosed. Once when I had distinguished myself in some mild way, the card bore congratulations, handsomely engraved in silver, and below, in a somewhat wobbly hand, "With love from the Elephant's Child." I don't quite remember how long ago we began to read the *Just So Stories,* but it has been long enough for the language to become thoroughly assimilated into the family idiom. There is a richness of invention about these stories that almost takes your breath away; they are absurdly and hilariously funny, but we do not laugh very much when we read them for fear of missing something. But the flavor remains on the palate, and the words settle so securely into the memory that they keep the stories all alive for thinking about and enjoying afterward. A favorite term of approval in our household is "man-of-infinite-resource-and sagacity"; our children from the time they were fledglings have sent their food down into "the warm dark inside cupboards." A shirker is reproved with "Is it right to be so idle, with the world so new and all?" and we have only to call our daughter "Taffaimai Metallumai" if her manners require correction—she knows that it means "small-person-without-any-manners-who-ought-to-be-spanked." She used to talk at school about her "satiable curiosity," and when one of her companions asked her why she used such long words she stuck to her text and replied, "I always use long words. I'm a grown-up."

The *Just So Stories* are pleasantly associated with the life at our Georgian Bay cottage, because we regularly read them each summer. It is great fun to find how aptly many expressions fit into our conversation there. The woods behind the house we refer to as "the Altogether Uninhabited Interior." Our bay is "all set about with fever-trees," and the turtle who lives under the dock is called "Slow-and-Solid." Once, on a picnic, we cooked a rather peculiar stew over the fire, and when I asked our child how she liked it, she said "Nice—nice but nubbly." That same day when we were on the way home she said that my sunburned face "reflected the rays of the sun with more-than-oriental splendor."

Our funny little boy will be all ready for the *Just So Stories* when he is old enough to enjoy them, for the expressions are so familiar to him. When he occasionally refuses to come along with the rest of us on walks, his sister tells him that he is the "wild, wild cat, waving his tail and walking by his wild lone." If he disturbs her too much when she is busy with something, she threatens to "spank him with her hard, hard claw," for "dancing hornpipes when he shouldn't." What a wonderful book is this book that gives us so much fun when we read it, and goes with us everywhere ever after!

The Three Policemen is a book that lives more between its own covers than our other favorites. We do not quote from it nearly so much as from most, but we read it over and over again, enjoying the distinctive flavor of its nonsense. It is a very restful book; everything is so straightforward, uncomplicated, and business-like. All the work goes through so expeditiously, and Young Botsford, our pet character, is so reliable and efficient. There is one passage that to us is exquisitely funny, the description of the three policemen being awakened punctually at 7:30, by a gramophone record, made by the mayor of Farbe Island.

It had a deep growling bass voice: it went something like this:

> Bong!—out of bed
> Bong!—wash, shave and brush your hair
> Bong!—put on your shirts and socks
> Bong!—trousers, belts and vests
> Bong!—on with boots and gloves
> Pling!—helmets and coats
> Good morning, gentlemen.

Young Botsford of Farbe Island was also wakened by a gramophone record which was set off by an alarm clock. His record was much shorter, however; it simply said: GET UP! GET UP! GET UP!

The Three Policemen was our daughter's introduction to mystery stories. If they were all as bland, as ingenious and as hilarious as this one, what fun they would be!

Mary Poppins and *The Wind in the Willows* are two books that fit into almost any category. Both have moments of real beauty; both have superb fairy-tale quality; both are full of the milk of human kindness, and both are funny, with a humor that is subtle and irresistible. The essential funniness of *The Wind in the Willows* is in the situations and the behavior of the characters; Mary Poppins is her own funniness. Pathos and sweetness are so mixed in with the drollery of the adventures of Ratty, Mole, Toad, and their friends that if you try to separate and analyze the element of laughter you lose the perfect balance of the whole; but Mary Poppins stands aloof from the situations she creates, and you can walk all around her and see why she is so unforgettably comical. We value these books because they both evoke much respect for human personality, and at the same time highlight its foibles and weaknesses with an indulgent humor. A vain person seldom seems wholly contemptible if you know Mary Poppins: a braggart seldom altogether vulgar when you remember that Toad was a little pathetic. We read these books because they are such glorious fun; but their lessons in understanding are as enduring as their laughter.

Our favorite funny families are the Poppers and the Peterkins. In *Mr. Popper's Penguins* you find a family who depart from all the conventional ways of family life and make it seem reasonable. They leave all the windows in the house open so that their penguins will be comfortably cold; they install a freezing

plant in the basement (moving the furnace up to the living room
to make room for it) so that the penguins can raise a family,
and when ten beautiful little penguins hatch out, the Poppers
proceed to train them for a vaudeville act.

The troupe goes on tour, and everything happens! We laughed
so hard when we first read about it that we had to stop reading
to avoid hysterics. Now that we can control ourselves a little, we
go over it slowly, dwelling on each episode, and savoring the
utterly stupendous absurdity of it. The bit we all love the best
is the first penguin's setting up housekeeping in the icebox. What
he took in with him is the most extraordinary list of objects I
know, and we can never read it without howls of laughter:

TWO spools of thread, one white chess bishop, and six parts
of a jigsaw puzzle. . . . A teaspoon and a closed box of safety
matches . . . A radish, two pennies, a nickel, and a golf ball.
Two pencil stubs, one bent playing card, and a small ash
tray.

Five hairpins, an olive, two dominoes, and a sock . . . A nail
file, four buttons of various sizes, a telephone slug, seven mar-
bles, and a tiny doll's chair. . . .

Five checker pieces, a bit of graham cracker, a parchesi cup,
and an eraser. . . . A door key, a buttonhook, and a crumpled
piece of tinfoil. . . . Half of a very old lemon, the head of a
china doll, Mr. Popper's pipe, and a ginger ale cap. . . . An ink-
bottle cork, two screws, and a belt buckle. . . .

Six beads from a child's necklace, five building blocks, a
darning egg, a bone, a small harmonica, and a partly consumed
lollipop. Two toothpaste lids and a small red notebook.

We love our friend Blair, who finds the list as funny as we
do. She arrived at the door one Saturday morning almost hidden
behind a tremendous armful of strangely assorted objects. "I've
brought back some things of yours that we had," she said. "A
flower-bowl and a package of cigarettes and two books and a
bicycle pump and Deirdre's pajamas and some cookies and a pie
plate—and half of a very old lemon!"

The Peterkins *would* be sane and orderly if they *could* be, but
they have an inspired gift of dimwittedness. " 'If,' said Mrs. Peterkin, 'we could only be more wise as a family.' " It would be our
loss if they were, for the remembrance of every ludicrous episode
strikes a chord in this family. No matter how badly we manage
anything, nor however many mishaps occur, we can settle our

nerves and calm our agitation by reflecting that we are no worse
than the Peterkins, and things always turned out well for them.
I am told that I play the alternating roles of Mrs. Peterkin and
the Lady from Philadelphia, which is a comfortable balance;
somebody has got to straighten things out, but it's rather fun to
help to tangle them too.

Every single episode in the chronicles of the Peterkin family
is the essence of pure "loopiness": Mrs. Peterkin's cup of coffee;
the horse that wouldn't go; the piano that couldn't be played in
cold weather; the Christmas tree that didn't fit; Elizabeth Eliza
and her trunk; the mad Fourth of July celebration; the confusion
that modern improvements created, and the Peterkins at the
poorhouse—these are only the cream of the jest, and we read
them over and over again, almost with awe of the brain that
could devise such beautiful nonsense.

The Peterkins are wonderfully quotable. If there is a loud
crash in the house, somebody is sure to say "Is anybody killed?"
If we go off to a picnic place that someone has recommended,
and find it quite impossible, we say "No strawberries and no
nook, but there's a good place to tie the horses." If we oversleep
in the morning, and have to scramble to get everybody off to
school, we excuse ourselves with "It is a very good thing to learn
not to get up any earlier than is necessary."

Life would fall short of perfection without *The Peterkin Papers,* and still farther short without our other funny books. We
wonder what could possibly be an adequate substitute for this
partnership in merriment, in families who do not read together.

THE GLITTER AND THE GOLD *

Richard S. Alm

The last twenty years have seen not only the coming of age of
the novel for the adolescent but also a flood of slick, patterned,
rather inconsequential stories written to capitalize on a rapidly

* Richard S. Alm, "The Glitter and the Gold," *The English Journal*, 44
(September, 1955), 315–22, 350. Reprinted with the permission of the National
Council of Teachers of English and Richard S. Alm.

expanding market. Earlier, the reading available to the teen-ager was limited to literature written for adults, an occasional story of merit involving an adolescent hero or heroine, and a great many series stories patterned on the adventures or exploits of a young super hero.

Today, however, there is coming from the presses a steady stream of junior novels and novels written for adults but taken over by young readers. Writers, perhaps noting the heightened attention given to adolescents and their problems by psychologists, educators, and librarians, have turned to the personal concerns of the teen-ager as the focus of their novels. In the main, these authors deal with an adolescent's relationships with others his own age, with his parents and other adults, and with such worries as deciding upon and preparing for a job, "going steady," marrying, and facing the responsibilities of adulthood.

In writing about these problems, most novelists present a sugar-puff story of what adolescents should do and should believe rather than what adolescents may or will do and believe. Such stories reveal the novelists' lack of knowledge or insight into adolescent behavior as well as a lack of writing ability. These writers do not penetrate beneath the surface of the situation they create. Their stories are superficial, often distorted, sometimes completely false representations of adolescence. Instead of art, they produce artifice. They may not, it is true, intend to produce art, but they fail to breathe *any* life into their characters or to create stories with any substance. The reader of the inferior novel can often, from the very first page, predict with accuracy and perhaps with detail the plot, the characterization, and the outcome.

In writing for young people, the novelist is ordinarily concerned with an adolescent beset with a problem or series of problems. In the inferior novel, the teen-ager solves his problems with a minimum of effort. If he meets rebuff, they serve only to display his exaggerated talents. He is, frequently, the all-wise person in the story, instructing and directing the adults around him. Usually he is a model of virtue—the more-than-kind, noble hero who sacrifices whatever is necessary to make others happy. The young heroine of Janet Lambert's *Candy Kane* is a classic example of such a paragon. Candy is invariably completely unselfish. When Barton protests that she does too much and suggests that the other young people in the community should reciprocate her many kindnesses, Candy says, "I like to do things for people." Jane, the young girl who works at the Officers' Club, pictures Candy as a noble influence in her life: "Whenever I'm tired or low or am thinking, oh, what's the use, you [Candy] come popping in.... Oh, Candy honey.... You're such a dear little girl."

Candy displays none of the normal reactions of a 14-year-old. When all her friends go to the Junior Hop, Candy is neither lonely nor unhappy. Without any feeling of jealousy or of being left out, she goes to the scene of the dance to sit on the ground outside and listen to the music. She thinks about Anne, who is inside, and wonders "... what Anne would say if she could see her spreading her coat on the ground beneath a pine tree, laying out a wilted bar of chocolate and a package of chewing gum. Not for all the world would she have changed places with Anne." Such saccharine sentiments are typical of this heroine who is literally, too good to be true.

Candy's friends are voluble in their praise of her direction and advice. Dirk, for example, is delighted that Candy has resolved his problems: "I think someday you will become one of our most eminent psychologists. You snapped us both out of a complex mighty quick." At the end of the story, Candy herself summarizes her accomplishments with pride: "... she thought how pleasant life was. Jane and Corp were to be married; Leigh was out with Chris; her mother and father were laughing together in the kitchen...." With, presumably, the greatest of ease, Candy has settled all questions.

Oversimplification is reflected, too, in the way in which major changes in the personality of a character are quickly effected. In Helen Boylston's *Sue Barton, Neighborhood Nurse,* what seem to be deep-rooted problems and frustrations of the adolescent Cal are satisfactorily disposed of within eight days by the guiding angel of the neighborhood, former nurse Sue Barton Barry. In Janet Lambert's *Star Spangled Summer,* an eloquent teen-ager, Penny Parrish, influences Langdon Houghton to change life-long habits of reticence to an openness and geniality that make him not only his daughter's companion and confidant but also a favorite of her new friends. The process is a simple one for Penny —writing a letter aimed directly at the man's cold heart and prescribing for him a few days' observation of what the "average American family" is like.

The motivation of such characters is reduced to a single factor. For Penny Parrish, it is her frequently expressed desire to make all others happy. For Sue Barton Barry, it is to be the all-sacrificing, perfect nurse, who, after marriage, which becomes a working partnership with her doctor husband in directing a clinic and caring for three children, still feels remiss by not being on active nursing duty.

In the inferior novel nothing is impossible for the adolescent. He sets his own goal and, armed with great determination, always reaches it. This is especially true in the so-called career stories which too frequently glamorize and misrepresent a vocation, instead of giving the young reader some real understanding of a worker on a job. For example, in the widely-read *Peggy Covers the News* by Emma Bugbee, young Peggy Foster prizes a job on a metropolitan daily and, despite million-to-one odds, wins one. Furthermore, though Kate Morrison, an older woman on the staff, repeatedly underscores the drudgery of a reporter's life, Peggy herself rides always on a crest of excitement. Even the assignments that would have been thought dull by other staff members fascinate her: "... to Peggy they were the very stuff of adventure." She says over and over that hers is a thrilling job:

> This was much more fun, really, than any other job in the world. You never knew from one moment to the next what you would be doing.
>
> School teachers, poor things, always had the same old Caesar or the same old algebra, year in and year out. Librarians, saleswomen, almost all professional women did their work without much change of scene or material. Doctors, of course, lived under an always shifting schedule; but, after all, they must find measles and dyspepsia and sore throats rather monotonous, and their big adventures with victims of automobile accidents were not numerous.
>
> Peggy's mind raced along merrily, comparing her lot with that of all other unfortunate groups of wretched womanhood, doomed never to be reporters.

With little experience and a limited background but with the equanimity of a Pulitzer prize-winning by-line reporter, Peggy has established herself in the newspaper world.

Especially significant in the weakest of these novels is the writer's approach to the idea of *maturity*. These stories give little indication of the *development* of maturity, since so many of the

heroes and heroines, even those 14 and 15, are already perform-
ing on an adult level. They make their own plans, they work
out their own destinies, they assist or direct everyone around
them, including the adults.

Inconsistencies in characterization also mark the lesser adolescent novels. In Mary Wolfe Thompson's *The Steadfast Heart*,
heroine Jo, on first meeting her foster parents, is unusually perceptive about their reactions. Later, however, she seems almost
dull-witted. Even with many clues to the nature of the Bentleys'
sorrow (the loss of a young son), she is, presumably, never aware
of what is troubling them. Furthermore, in spite of a number
of situations which might pique her curiosity, she never seems
curious. Although she is supposed to be primarily concerned with
the improvement of the relationship between her and her sister
and the Bentleys, she misses most of the opportunities to bring
about such improvement.

Another inconsistency in Jo involves her status at the Bentleys
and in the community. At the beginning of the story, she is
embarrassed and self-conscious about being a state ward; she
worries about the reactions of her classmates and of the townspeople toward her. However, in two incidents in which this embarrassment might have been heightened, she displays no feeling
at all about her status. To earn spending money, she goes from
door to door in town selling nuts she has gathered from the
woods near the Bentleys' farm and never once is embarrassed. In
the other situation, Mrs. Preston, the mother of Jo's boyfriend
Marc, volunteers to write her niece for clothes for Jo; the latter
is delighted and shows not the slightest discomfiture. Despite
evidences of Jo's growing maturity in some respects, there is
nothing in the story to prepare the reader for so great a change.
Therefore, Jo is, at many points, an unconvincing character, one
whose reason for being is to force consideration of such problems
as dealing with a drunken father, becoming emotionally independent of others, "going steady," but as someone apart from the
problem and not herself emotionally involved.

That these poorly written stories are highly popular with
young readers indicates that adolescents have little regard for the
disdain or reservations of adults. Thus, these books and others
like them—the series, certain sanctimonious religious stories, the
patently false love story, and the monotonous, patterned Western—endure.

But not all novels written for or read widely by teen-agers

are—from a literary point of view—trivial. Of those which focus on problems common to adolescents, a number are rather well-told stories about credible adolescents, working out, in credible situations, these problems. A few are works of real stature. The hero of these stories is a more complex individual whose actions are carefully motivated. He meets rebuffs, learns certain limitations about himself, develops a sense of responsibility, and makes adjustments regarding his basic problem; in short, he becomes a more mature person.

In Anne Emery, the teen-aged reader has a novelist of considerable merit. Though some of her characters may seem too *nice* and her stories too pat, she shows in her teen-agers a growing maturity, not contrived nor unexpected but rather clearly developed. Sally in *Senior Year,* for example, learns gradually that she is merely a carbon copy of the girls she chooses as her best friends and that she must learn to respect her own individuality. Sally and Scotty, in *Going Steady,* discover that marriage will not mean the end of their problems but the beginning of other, more complex ones. In a third novel, *Sorority Girl,* Emery tells the story of Jean, Sally Burnaby's younger sister, and her relationship to a high school sorority. Here Emery deals with a common enough problem but somehow is less deft in handling the situation. In none of these novels does the problem get out of hand; it serves as the focal point of the story, but the emphasis is on the characters and their reactions.

Betty Cavanna, too, is a writer of some importance. In Rette Larkin, the heroine of *A Girl Can Dream,* she creates a tom-boy whose unconventional behavior and ambitions make her a conspicuous member of the senior class. Unfortunately, the characterization is not carefully sustained, and the story ends too neatly with all *i*'s dotted and all *t*'s crossed. In *Going on Sixteen,* an earlier story, the shy, withdrawn Julie Ferguson develops into a more self-confident, poised adolescent. This heroine is a convincing figure throughout the story. Changes in Julie are carefully prepared for and are neither abrupt nor exaggerated. The one opportunity for giving the story a fairy-tale twist—Julie's attempting to sell her sketches of puppies to an art editor to earn enough money to buy Sonny, the thoroughbred Collie—Cavanna turns instead into an experience that helps Julie to grow up. Betty Cavanna is sensitive to the happiness as well as to the pain of adolescence, and her stories of teen-agers reflect both.

Another good story from a prolific writer for the teen-aged audience is *Street Rod* by H. Gregor Felsen. Though somewhat similar in theme to his earlier *Hot Rod,* this novel is a more carefully written account of the despair of a sixteen-year-old who wants desperately to own a "souped-up" rod. The young hero, Ricky Madison, is a remarkably vivid figure in contrast to the rather superficially-drawn hero of *Hot Rod.* Felsen's delineation of the boy is a careful one. There is no magic alteration of his behavior; his values change slowly. Despite a growing sense of responsibility, however, Ricky finally races his rival—to his own death. This ending is a shock to the reader, not because Felsen's characterization is inconsistent but because he departs from what the typical writer for teen-agers would do in winding up the story.

A second story of Felsen which has caused a considerable stir in recent years is *Two and the Town.* In treating a subject which is ordinarily taboo—the pregnancy of a high school girl and a marriage forced upon two teen-agers—Felson does an excellent job in creating plausible situations and what seem natural reactions on the part of the adolescents. The story has flaws: Buff's mother makes an abrupt about-face in her reactions toward Elaine—an unconvincing change; Buff's redemption and return to his family are too neatly accomplished to be credible. But flaws notwithstanding, Felsen tells frankly and rather well this story for teen-agers in their own idiom and with real insight into the way they sometimes become involved in complex situations which change their entire lives.

Most of the stories dealing with the adolescent's personal problems interest principally girls. Certainly of the novels which are outstanding, most are for girls. Undoubtedly, the most widely talked about and most praised of all contemporary novels for the adolescent is Maureen Daly's *Seventeenth Summer.* Burton believe that it "captures better than any other novel the spirit of adolescence." [1] Edwards declares that with the appearance of *Seventeenth Summer* in 1942 "the new field of writing for teen-agers became established.... This tender story of a young girl's first awakening to love bids fair to become a classic for the teen-agers as did Little Women for younger girls." [2]

[1] Dwight L. Burton, "The Novel for the Adolescent," *The English Journal,* 40 (September 1951), p. 363.
[2] Margaret A. Edwards, "The Rise of Teen-Age Reading," *Saturday Review,* 37 (November 13, 1954), p. 88.

Novelists themselves have recognized the significance of *Seventeenth Summer*. Rette, the heroine of Cavanna's *A Girl Can Dream*, senses what is great about the Daly novel when she reads it in preparation for a writing task of her own. "No other book that she had ever read ... had quite the quality of *Seventeenth Summer*. There was a homeliness, a deep-rooted honesty, a youthfulness about it that made Loretta catch her breath. She didn't live in the sort of town Angie Morrow lived in; she didn't have that sort of family; she had yet to have a love affair. Yet the story was so real and so fresh that Rette *became* Angie. She shared every feeling, every impulse, every hope, and every thrill and every disappointment."

This sense of immediacy which Rette feels in reading *Seventeenth Summer* is the result of Daly's telling the story from Angie's point of view and capturing the excitement of a young girl bursting with happiness she wants to share with intimate friends. The story is a simple one of commonplace events, day-by-day life in a small Wisconsin town; yet it is an engrossing story because the reader is able to identify himself so closely with the reactions of the heroine. What might be sensational—Lorraine's affair with Martin—is played down, and the reader's attention is drawn, not to Lorraine's affair, but to Angie's reactions toward her sister. Angie's is a superb characterization. She is introduced as a rather naive seventeen-year-old, but during one summer she learns a great deal about boys, about her own emotions, and about growing up to face new problems and decisions. That the story does not end in a Hollywood manner with Jack and Angie walking off into the sunset together is a credit to Maureen Daly who does not compromise a characterization in order to make *all* her readers happy.

In the wake of Maureen Daly but not in imitation have come other significant contributors to the field of literature for the adolescent. Mary Stolz, surely the most versatile and most skilled of that group, writes not for the masses who worship Sue Barton Barry but for the rarer adolescent who sees in Anne Armacost (*To Tell Your Love*) a girl of warmth and charm, in love unfortunately with a boy who is afraid to return her love. In a summer of endless days with a telephone which does not ring, Anne slowly understands what has driven Doug away. The poignancy of her losing this first, intense love is a bitter-sweet experience which makes her a little sadder, but a good deal more perceptive of the emotions and reactions of those around her.

The other characters, too, in *To Tell Your Love* are individuals, not types. In shifting her point of view from one to another and giving an intimate glimpse of the feelings and thoughts of each one, Stolz reveals a talent that few writers have. The reader can sympathize with Johnny who at 14 wants to be husky and scorns his own long, bony frame. He enjoys Mrs. Armacost's discomfiture when her son learns the secret of her baking successes. He is impressed by the dignity of Theo's quiet romance and senses that an older Anne will probably be the same thoughtful kind of person. Stolz' other novels—*In a Mirror, The Seagulls Woke Me, Pray Love, Remember,* and *Organdy Cupcakes*—are significant contributions, too, to fiction for the adolescent. In all of them, she tells an engrossing story but, equally important, she presents characters who emerge as sensitively-drawn individuals.

Other novels of stature with appeal especially for older girls are Mildred Walker's *Winter Wheat,* Rumer Godden's *A Candle for St. Jude,* and Margueritte Harmon Bro's *Sarah.* In each, the heroine faces problems of love, career, and complex relationships with others. Mildred Walker, in telling the story of Ellen Webb, gives the reader a sense of the vastness of the Montana country and of Ellen's changing perspective toward it. Her college romance with Gil ends because she feels that they, like her parents, are too different from each other ever to be happy. When he is killed in the war, however, she realizes how much she had loved him. Out of her sorrow comes a closer relationship with her parents. When Ellen says at the end of the story, "I had not always been glad that I was their child, but today I had a kind of pride in being born to them," her words reflect her new understanding of the two people whose relationship to each other had always baffled her.

Rumer Godden, in *A Candle for St. Jude,* lifts the curtain in the theater of ballet to reveal the struggles and the glamor of the disciples of that art. Among the many facets of a beautifully written novel is the story of a young genius almost lost in a tangle of fiery temperaments and a hierarchy of jealously guarded positions of prestige. Hilda, earlier regarded as only a mediocre dancer, creates music and choreography which amaze even the great Mme. Holbein with their brilliance. Hilda grows up in the tradition and discipline of the art and appears destined for greatness under Mme. Holbein's direction. Rumer Godden's prose, dramatic with the excitement of the theater, serves further to distinguish this novel.

Bro's *Sarah* is the story of a young girl faced with the problem of choosing between two careers for which she seems to have special gifts. Despite much help and encouragement by friends who smooth her path, Sarah is nagged by self-doubts and frustrated by unrealized dreams. The fascination of the story lies in its Cinderella-like quality, but this is no pedestrian romance; Bro's skill as a storyteller makes it a superior novel.

Although there are more teen-age problem novels for girls than for boys, there are several notable stories, intended initially for adults, which have particular appeal for boys: *Hie to the Hunters, The Folded Leaf,* and *Walk Like a Mortal.* The audience for each of these, however, is limited in that the stories are not of universal interest.

Jesse Stuart, among his many accounts of the Kentucky hill people, has written a novel which focuses on an adolescent's need for independence from his family and the shift in values which such an achievement involves. In *Hie to the Hunters,* young Didway Hargis leaves his parents to join the hill people and comes to know a life different from his own. Later, a somewhat maturer Did returns to his own people in town, but having been accepted by the hill folk, he knows in the future he can move freely among both groups. Stuart, who as a regional writer is important on the American scene, illuminates the problems of a young boy against the background he knows so intimately. The reader gains a sense of not only the individual but also the contrast and conflict between the ways of two groups.

The Folded Leaf by William Maxwell, a novel of rare beauty, will be read primarily by the mature adolescent. In it, the author contrasts the gentle, bookish Lymie Peters and the handsome, athletic extrovert, Spud Latham. In delineating the relationship of two boys growing into manhood, he probes into their backgrounds, noting carefully the psychological influences on them. With great insight he reveals the forces which pull them together and those which eventually drive them apart. Despite the melodramatic denouement, the story is a unique study of a friendship.

In the third novel, *Walk Like a Mortal,* Dan Wickenden writes with rare perception the story of Gabe Mackenzie who, at 17, sees his parents' marriage disintegrate. Though a rather mature boy at the outset, Gabe is torn between conflicting loyalties and an inability to translate the actions of his mother and father into terms he can understand. As he adjusts to a new life without his mother, he comes to understand her better. When she returns, however, he discovers that his reliance upon her has been superseded by a more mature relationship with his father.

This story of an adolescent's response to the breakup of his home is told with extraordinary skill; no contemporary writer has matched Wickenden's treatment of the subject.

Among stories read widely by teen-agers are two by outstanding contemporary writers who have heretofore been concerned with adult fiction or biography. Though not ordinarily called *problem novels* for the adolescent, *The Yearling* and *Johnny Tremain* do center in the development of an adolescent's personality. *Johnny Tremain,* though set in American Revolutionary days, is a timeless story. Esther Forbes writes of a teen-ager's dilemma when circumstances alter his life. As the arrogant young genius in Latham's silvershop, Johnny's future seems secure. But an accident maims his left hand and forces him to abandon his dream of becoming a silversmith. Sensitive about the appearance of his hand, scorned by his former co-workers, confused because he does not know where to turn, Johnny exists aimlessly until he meets Rab and becomes imbued with the spirit of the colonist's cause. Inspired by Rab's devotion to the Revolution, Johnny loses his self-consciousness, takes on greater responsibilities, and finally, finds himself a part in the Revolution. Esther Forbes captures the spirit of the times and of the people. Her novel is an important social document as well as a powerful narrative.

Marjorie Kinnan Rawlings, in *The Yearling,* tells the story of Jody and his fawn, which to him represents a friend and a kind of security. Eventually, his relationship with Flag is the bridge whereby he moves from childhood to greater maturity. Rawlings writes with compassion for the Baxters who live near the soil and work desperately for a living. The reader sees Jody, growing up in an isolated spot, dependent upon an understanding father and a stern mother. Through the storyteller's omniscient eye, the reader senses the complex nature of their family relationships and the feelings they hold about each other but do not openly reveal.

Two other significant stories which are concerned with a boy's closeness to nature are James Street's *Goodbye, My Lady* and Paul Annixter's *Swiftwater.* Each is a moving portrayal of a boy struggling with the world that encroaches upon his own rather limited sphere and the influence of that struggle upon him.

All the novels discussed here have one element in common: the young hero or heroine is attempting to cope with a personal problem. Each is concerned about his family or his friends or his own individuality and usually his future. Each novel concentrates, to some degree, on the question of the maturity of the central character. To distinguish between the superior and the inferior story, one must consider the novel both as a literary piece and as a vehicle for the presentation of a problem. Such questions as the following may help the reader to make such a distinction: Is the story one of credible people in a credible situation? Does the story have unique qualities, or is it a repetition of an often-used pattern? Do the characters grope somehow in dealing with their problems, or are their reactions formalized and pat? Is the problem of the adolescent in proper perspective in the novel, or does it loom so large that neither story nor characters emerge clearly? Is the stage of maturity of the central character developed naturally, a measure at a time, or is it a magic process accomplished mechanically? Is the reader given some insight into the characters' lives, or must he rely upon superficial sketches? These questions are not easy for the reader to answer, but they suggest approaches by which adolescent fiction may be more adequately judged. To the extent that a novel meets these criteria the writer reveals his ability to deal with the personal problems of an adolescent within the context of literary art.

"WE DON'T EVEN CALL THOSE BOOKS!" *

Esther Millett

Recently, in a developmental reading class of ninth and tenth grade students, I asked the girls to name some of their favorite books. With scarcely a pause, the titles came tumbling over one another: *The Good Earth, Jane Eyre, Hawaii, The Bridge at Andau, Wuthering Heights, Kontiki, The Jungle, The King Must Die, A Separate Peace, To Kill a Mockingbird, Travels With Charlie, To Catch an Angel.* Since these students were slow readers—and some of them reluctant ones—I asked them if

* Esther Millett, "We Don't Even Call Those Books!" *Top of the News,* 20 (October, 1963), 45–47. Reprinted with the permission of the Children's Services Division of the American Library Association and the author.

they were sure that they weren't trying to impress me. Didn't they secretly like some of the many teen-age novels published today? And almost in chorus came the answer, "Oh, Miss Millett, we don't even call those books!"

This experience was one of many that has convinced me over the years that we—librarians, teachers, parents—are not offering enough challenging reading to the high school student of today. We are constantly being reminded of the gifted child and his ability to read and study in great depth and of the modern curriculum, with its increased demands, but we tend to forget that the average reader, and even the slow reader, also needs to be given books which appeal to the adult in him.

Even my 13-year-old neighbor surprised me this year. I have always given him books as gifts, and his thanks have often been lukewarm. So last Christmas I chose a different gift, and as I offered it said, "I know you don't like books much, Bobby, so here is something I hope you will like better." He replied, "Thanks, but I *like* to read now. I just finished *The Townsman*. Gee, it was great."

In my own library—serving grades 9 to 12—I have never stocked any but adult titles. Most of the girls read much voluntarily; in the words of one, "It is the fashion to read at Westover." All students are encouraged to buy as well as borrow books, and even with almost unlimited choice of books at their disposal, there are relatively few who own and enjoy made-to-order teen-age novels.

For years, when I showed some of our reading lists to other librarians, I was told that the students in my school were "special," that in public libraries and public schools one could not aim so high. As editor for a number of years of the *Senior Booklist* and the *Junior Booklist* of the Independent School Education Board (now called the National Association of Independent Schools), I was told that our lists were good but, of course, many of the books were too mature for the average high school reader. As a consultant for *The Standard Catalog for High School Libraries*, my plea that we include more adult books, and leave those labeled "14 to 18" or "14 and up" for the *Children's Catalog*, went unheeded. As I talked to many parents, they were concerned that their children were not ready for the mature reading I recommended.

We expect more and more responsibility from young people today, and I contend that we should expect more maturity in their reading tastes than heretofore. Perhaps they will not get as much meaning from a book as an adult, but who is to say what is the right age to read and enjoy *War and Peace* or *Huckleberry Finn?* The former is a great tale of adventure and a study in philosophy. The latter has been called both a children's book and one of the greatest of American novels. At different ages one finds different values in books. If a book is honest, is well written, is in good taste, is timely, it will appeal to a wide range, and that includes the teen-ager.

Not long ago I heard a college professor state that he was impatient with those who thought that some books should not be studied in high school, but should be saved for study in college. College courses, he said, can certainly deal with the same books in greater depth. If a book is a good one, if it can stand the test of time, it can be read again and again and new meaning found with each rereading.

Happily, of late, I notice many signs that the high school reader is coming into his own, that he is at last being considered, not as being in a sort of no-man's-land between child and man, but as a person who is more adult than child. The *Senior Booklist* is now not one of few, but one of many, book lists for young people that aim high. Publishers send out more and more lists of "adult books for young people"; The New York Public Library's annual *Books for the Teen Age* has in each succeeding issue had a larger and larger percentage of adult books; the *New York Herald Tribune Books* has been printing excellent short reviews of adult books for young people under the heading "For Teenagers." Teachers and librarians in courses which I have taught in library schools have been more and more vocal in their requests for basic and current lists of adult books for high school libraries.

And finally, the H. W. Wilson Company's *Standard Catalog for High School Libraries* is embarking on a general upgrading of its selections. In the preface to the 1963 supplement, the publishers state, "An increasing number of serious articles ... have voiced concern that many high school library collections have failed to keep pace with the more advanced or upgraded curricula now in effect in high schools generally ... It is hoped that a better balance will be found in the present Supplement as the result of this procedure, which will be continued in future Supplements."

I am glad to say that in checking the 1963 supplement against my own collection, I have found a much closer correlation than in the past. I am further assured, moreover, that this new policy will be incorporated in future editions of the basic catalog.

Such changes in approach to teen-age reading are encouraging. They are long overdue, and all of us in the book business must not only rejoice but continue as individuals to provide the best and the most challenging reading within our power for today's young people. High school students will continue to be bombarded with ideas from movies, television, radio. Increasing demands will continue to be made on students—and on libraries for them. Ideas from books have more permanence than all other media, for they are not flashed before us or heard only once but are in such a form that they may be referred to at will.

If the aim of education is to teach the student to think, then we must do all we can to provide young people not with books that touch only the surface and have contrived situations, but with books that inspire them, excite them, give them lasting food for thought. Let us, as Lawrence Clark Powell says, "speak to the latent bookishness in young people . . . arouse and feed the bookish hunger which God mysteriously goes on putting into a number of human beings in each generation, year after year, from the time of the first clay tablet and papyrus roll to the day of doom."

SCIENCE FICTION WRITERS: PROPHETS OF THE FUTURE *

Hanor A. Webb

Wise men tell us that that next great discoveries to strengthen and extend civilization should be—indeed, *must* be—in the realms of human self-control. Perhaps the methods by which so much of man's control of nature has been achieved may contribute to

* Hanor A. Webb, "Science Fiction Writers: Prophets of the Future." Reprinted from *Library Journal,* 80 (December 15, 1955), 2884–85. Published by R. R. Bowker. Used with permission of publisher and author.

man's control of man for the benefit of society. The truly philosophical science fiction writers are thinking along these lines. They write of decades ahead because their plans would have no chance of adoption in the present.

No science fiction writer expects to live to see the day when his ideas will be accepted by society. He hopes, therefore, that the seedlings he plants in society's ground will be nurtured by the next generation of writers and readers and, if his ideas grow and have vigor, by generation after generation until they bear fruit. Such has been the history of every established social principle, although centuries may have been required for a harvest to appear.

SCIENCE FICTION TODAY

John W. Campbell, Jr., editor of *Astounding Science Fiction,* tells us that "the interest in science fiction stories is not economic, not romantic, but technical-philosophical... the hopes and dreams and fears (for some dreams are nightmares!) of a technically based society."

Isaac Asimov, author of some 75 science fiction books, informs us that "science fiction is that branch of literature which deals with a fictitious society, differing from our own chiefly in the nature and extent of its technological development."

Gerald Heard, serious writer on social philosophy but author, also, of many titles of science fiction and mystery, almost frightens us with his claim that "science-fiction is the prophetic—a better term, the apocalyptic—literature of our particular and culminating epoch of crisis."

There are many definitions but each stresses science fiction—as the term understood by the writing craft—to be (a) prophetic, (b) descriptive of the social impacts of science, (c) set in a novel, imaginative, possibly fantastic, situation.

Many, perhaps most, of the authors of today's science fiction have full-time jobs in industrial or college laboratories, and write as moderately profitable sidelines. Well trained as scientists, they prefer to stimulate the imaginations of young adults interested in technology rather than to excite youthful readers.

The readers of modern science fiction are chiefly technically trained, philosophically inclined, imaginative men aged 20 to 25. This from editor John W. Campbell's analysis of his own magazine's circulation.

HISTORY OF SCIENCE FICTION

A venerable science fiction story is *The Lost Atlantis* by Plato (427?–347 B.C.). Other tales of the same type that have lived are Sir Thomas More's *Utopia* (1516); *Gargantua and Pantagruel* by Francois Rabelais (1545); *Gulliver's Travels* by Jonathan Swift (1726). Each of these—and others that have passed into oblivion—were satires on contemporary society, using some science and adventure as a frame on which to drape the satire. Modern science fiction can readily find the explanation for its social slant in its literary heredity.

As science and invention made progress through the decades of the nineteenth and twentieth centuries, science fiction embraced everything new. Jules Verne of France (1828–1905) set a pattern of meticulous exactness in his imaginative science and believed that "what one man can imagine, another man can do." A striking number of modern inventors received inspiration from Verne's more than one hundred books. (See "Mr. Imagination," George Kent, *Saturday Review*, June 5, '54, p. 9.) Following the Verne pattern (a good one, for his works have lived), the science fiction up to 1945 largely explored the possibilities of the physical world.

Then came the atomic bomb, and nothing remains the same!

What do the explosions from 1945 to the present force on science fiction? (Indeed science fiction writers predicted the A-bomb as early as 1935 in their stories.) No one can think of the A-bomb and the H-bomb as merely scientific devices. The social consequences of atomic fission and atomic fusion are inescapable, for evil or for good. Science fiction in its prophecies cannot possibly leave the bomb out or ignore a society either hiding from the devastating atom or enjoying its benefits as a source of electric power. The social slant of science fiction has not crystallized; our present imaginations cannot envision a new technology that of itself, with no social implications, can interest us.

RAY GUNS AND ROCKET SHIPS *

Robert A. Heinlein

> Know something of the sciences yourself or enlist compe-
> tent advisers to assist you when selecting science fiction

"When I make a word do a lot of work like that," said Humpty
Dumpty, "I always pay it extra."

"Science Fiction" is a portmanteau term, and many and varied
are the things that have been stuffed into it. Just as the term
"historical fiction" includes in its broad scope *Quo Vadis,* nickel
thrillers about the James Boys or Buffalo Bill, and *Forever Am-
ber,* so does the tag "science fiction" apply both to Alley Oop
and to Aldous Huxley's *After Many a Summer Dies the Swan.*
It would be more nearly correctly descriptive to call the whole
field "speculative fiction" and to limit the name "science fiction" to a sub-class—in which case some of the other sub-classes
would be: undisguised fantasy (Thorne Smith, the Oz books),
pseudo-scientific fantasy (C. S. Lewis's fine novel *Out of the Silent
Planet,* Buck Rogers, Bradbury's delightful Martian stories),
sociological speculation (More's *Utopia,* Michael Arlen's *Man's
Mortality,* H. G. Wells' *World Set Free,* Plato's *Republic*), adventure stories with exotic and nonexistent locale (Flash Gordon,
Burroughs' Martian stories, the *Odyssey, Tom Sawyer Abroad*).
Many other classes will occur to you, since the term "speculative
fiction" may be defined negatively as being fiction about things
that have not happened.

One can see that the name "science fiction" is too Procrustean
a bed, too tight a corset, to fit the whole field comfortably. Nevertheless, since language is how we talk, not how we might talk,
it seems likely that the term "science fiction" will continue to be
applied to the whole field; we are stuck with it, as the American
aborigines are stuck with the preposterous name "Indian."

* Robert A. Heinlein, "Ray Guns and Rocket Ships." Reprinted from the
Library Journal 78 (July, 1953) 1188–91. Published by R. R. Bowker Company. Article used with permission of publisher and author.

A Definition

But what, under rational definition, is *science* fiction? There is an easy touchstone: science fiction is speculative fiction in which the author takes as his first postulate the real world as we know it, including all established facts and natural laws. The result can be extremely fantastic in content, but it is not fantasy; it is legitimate—and often very tightly reasoned—speculation about the possibilities of the real world. This category excludes the Land of Oz; it also excludes rocket ships that make U-turns, serpent men of Neptune that lust after human maidens, and stories by authors who flunked their Boy Scout merit badge tests in descriptive astronomy.

But the category includes such mind stretchers as Olaf Stapledon's *Last and First Men,* William Sloan's *To Walk the Night,* Dr. Asimov's *The Stars, Like Dust,* even though these stories are stranger than most outright fantasies.

But how is one to distinguish between legitimate science fiction and ridiculous junk? Place of original publication is no guide; some of the best have appeared in half-cent-a-word pulp magazines, with the bug-eyed monsters on their covers; some of the silliest have appeared in high-pay slicks or in the "prestige" quality group.

"The Pretzel Men of Pthark"—that one we can skip over; the contents are probably like the title. Almost as easy to spot is the Graustark school of space opera. This is the one in which the dashing Nordic hero comes to the aid of the rightful Martian Princess and kicks out the villainous usurper through superscience and sheer grit. It is not being written very often these days although it still achieves book publication occasionally, sometimes with old and respectable trade book houses. But it does not take a Ph.D. in physics to recognize it for what it is.

But do not be too quick to apply as a test to science fiction what are merely the conventions of better known fields of literature. I once heard a librarian say that she could not stand the unpronounceable names given by science-fiction writers to extra-terrestrials. Have a heart, friend! These strings of consonants are honest attempts to give unearthly names to unearthly creatures. As Shaw pointed out, the customs of our tribe are not laws of nature. You would not expect a Martian to be named "Smith." (Say—how about a story about a Martian named "Smith?" Ought to make a good short. Hmmm—)

CRITERIA

But are there reliable criteria by which science fiction can be judged by one who is not well acquainted with the field? In my opinion, there are. Simply the criteria which apply to all fields of fiction, no more, no less.

First of all, an item of science fiction should be a story, i.e., its entertainment value should be as high as that which you expect from other types of stories. It should be entertaining to almost anyone, whether he habitually reads the stuff or not. Second, the degree of literacy should be as high as that expected in other fields. I will not labor this point, since we are simply applying an old rule to a new field, but there is no more excuse here than elsewhere for split infinitives, dangling participles, and similar untidiness, nor for obscurity and double-talk.

The same may be said for plotting, characterization, motivation, and the rest. If a science-fiction writer can't *write,* let him go back to being a fry cook or whatever he was doing before he gave up honest work.

I want to make separate mention of the author's evaluations. Granted that not all stories need be morally edifying, nevertheless I would demand of science-fiction writers as much exercise of moral sense as I would of other writers. I have in mind one immensely popular series which does not hold my own interest very well because the protagonist seems to be guided only by expediency. Neither the writer nor his puppet seems to be aware of good and evil. For my taste this is a defect in any story, nor is the defect mitigated by the wonderful and gaudy trappings of science fiction. In my opinion, such abstractions as honor, loyalty, fortitude, self-sacrifice, bravery, honesty, and integrity will be as important in the far reaches of the Galaxy as they are in Iowa or Korea. I believe that you are entitled to apply your own evaluating standards to science fiction quite as rigorously as you apply them in other fiction.

AUTHENTICITY

The criteria outlined above take care of every aspect of science fiction but one—the *science* part. But even here no new criterion is needed. Suppose you were called on to purchase or to refuse to purchase a novel about a Mexican boy growing up on a Mexican cattle ranch; suppose that you knew no Spanish, had never been to Mexico and were unacquainted with its history and customs, and were unsure of the competence of the author? What would you do?

I suspect that you would farm out the decision to someone who was competent to judge the authenticity of the work. It might be a high school Spanish teacher, it might be a friend or neighbor who was well acquainted with our neighboring culture, it might be the local Mexican consul. If the expert told you that the background material of the book was nonsense, you would not give the book shelf room.

The same procedure applies to science fiction. No one can be expected to be expert in everything. If you do not happen to know what makes a rocket go when there is no air to push against, you need not necessarily read Willy Ley's *Rockets, Missiles, and Space Travel*—although it is a fine book, a "must" for every library, desirable for any home. You may instead consult any one of your acquaintance who does know about rocket ships —say an Air Force or Artillery officer, a physics teacher, or almost any 14-year-old boy, especially boys who are active in high school science clubs. If the novel being judged concerns cybernetics, nuclear physics, genetics, chemistry, relativity, it is necessary only to enlist the appropriate helper.

You would do the same, would you not, with a novel based on the life of Simon Bolivar?

Of course, there is the alternate, equivalent method of testing the authenticity of any book by checking up on the author. If the Simon Bolivar novel was written by a distinguished scholar of South American history, you need concern yourself only with the literary merit of the book. If a book about space travel is written by a world famous astronomer (as in the case of the one who writes under the pen name of "Philip Latham"), you can put your mind at rest about the correctness of the science therein. In many cases science-fiction writers have more than adequate professional background in the sciences they use as background material and their publishers are careful to let you know this through catalog and dustjacket blurb. I happen to be personally aware of and can vouch for the scientific training of Sprague de Camp, George O. Smith, "John Taine," John W. Campbell, Jr., "Philip Latham" Will Jenkins, Jack Williamson, Isaac Asimov, Arthur C. Clarke, E. E. Smith, Philip Wylie, Olaf Stapledon, H. G. Wells, Damon Knight, Harry Stine, and "J. J. Coupling." This listing refers to qualifications in science only and is necessarily incomplete, nor do I mean to slight the many fine writers without formal scientific training who are well read in science and most careful in their research.

But some means of checking on a writer of alleged science fiction is desirable. Most writers of historical fiction appear to go to quite a lot of trouble to get the facts of their historical scenes correct, but some people seem to feel that all that is necessary to write science fiction is an unashamed imagination and a sprinkling of words like "ray gun," "rocket tube," "mutant," and "space warp." In some cases the offense is as blatant as it would be in the case of an author of alleged historical fiction who founded a book on the premise that Simon Bolivar was a Chinese monk! It follows that, in order to spot these literary fakers it is necessary to know that Bolivar was not a Chinese monk— know something of the sciences yourself or enlist competent advisers.

Part Nine

*NONFICTION FOR CHILDREN
AND YOUNG PEOPLE*

INFORMATIONAL BOOKS—TONIC AND TOOL FOR THE ELEMENTARY CLASSROOM*

Herbert S. Zim [1]

There is no single panacea for all our educational ills, yet the new informational books which are appearing more and more in classrooms all over the country have the lure of such a promising cure-all. The publishers do not ballyhoo them as "good for man or beast," but several years of school experience show they are good for teachers as well as for pupils. These books are prying us loose from some of our firm convictions about grade placement. They are offering a new challenge to the slow learner. They even imply questions about cherished concepts of curriculum and classroom management. And with the challenge and the questions comes the clear indication that while these are not the educational equivalent of "Old Dr. Souses Herb Compound," they are a spring tonic for the classroom and all who reside therein.

WHAT ARE "INFORMATIONAL" BOOKS?

Informational books are hard to describe or define. In essence all books, from Shakespeare's *Sonnets* to the local telephone directory, are informational. But the books that have caught the attention of children, teachers, and librarians in recent years are a more narrowly defined group. They are obviously nonfiction; however, biographies, histories, and similar books are not usually classified in the informational category. The term does not usually refer to textbooks either—and certainly not to the readers, spellers, and arithmetic books that crowd a pupil's desk, if not

* Herbert S. Zim, "Informational Books—Tonic and Tool for the Elementary Classroom," *Elementary English* 29 (March, 1952), 129–35. Reprinted with the permission of the National Council of Teachers of English, and Professor Zim.

1 Professor Zim, of the University of Illinois, is himself a well-known author of such informational books as *Birds, Stars, Owls, Thunder and Lightning,* and more than a score of others.

his mind. Yet, textbooks have been *used* as informational books in many modern classrooms. Informational books are more than "how-to" books, though this branch of the family cannot be completely disowned. One has the feeling that the term, while ill-defined, is best suited to the scores of well-written, well-illustrated books on factual subjects for young readers; books which children voluntarily choose for hobby and recreational reading though they may often use them in the classroom as well.

Informational books are not restricted to any subject or group of subjects. However, if science is broadly defined, one can say with reasonable justification that the majority of informational books are scientific. Perhaps this is a reflection of my own myopic viewpoint, since I am more interested in science education. Perhaps it reflects the many books on nature study and such naive volumes as the "Boy's Home Book of Chemical Experiments" and their ilk which were the precursors of those we now use. At any rate, the mushroom growth in the number and popularity of informational books has mycelial threads penetrating back into time for twenty-five years and more. Some of these early books set a pattern and suggested standards which have done much to make present-day books as good as they are. Frank M. Chapman's *The Travels of Birds* (Appleton-Century-Crofts, 1916) was an expert's attempt to explain bird migration to children. Dr. Chapman did the job accurately and directly, rightfully assuming that something as interesting as his subject did not require window dressing or sugar-coating. Other books of this period (mostly nature study) did about as good a job as Chapman, though the period itself is characterized by sentimental, anthropomorphic animal stories. But it was not until the '30's with books like Reed's *The Stars for Sam* (Harcourt, 1931), Baruch and Reiss' *My Body and How It Works* (Harper, 1934), and Ilin's *What Time Is it?* and *100,000 Whys* (Lippincott, 1932, 1933) that the real development of informational books began.

A systematic survey of informational books is not a chore to take on lightly. One difficulty lies in the fact that a goodly number do not fit the usual pigeonholes of school subjects. Is a book like Schneider's *Let's Look Under the City* (Scott, 1950) to be considered social studies or science—or both? How about Vera Edelstat's prose-poem *Oceans in the Sky* (Knopf, 1946)? It's certainly science —but it's a good deal more besides. This difficulty is in itself a hopeful sign. It indicates that some authors are less concerned with writing science, industrial arts, or social studies books than in tackling a specific, significant idea for children and and doing their best with it. They stake their bet on a child wanting to have and use an attractive book about something that interests him, in contrast to offering him a general book on an artificial school subject. Another difficulty in appraisal of these books is that they are coming off the press faster and faster. My own home-made list notes 68 published in 1951—and by the time the count is complete and totalled it is likely to be well over a hundred. There are probably over five hundred informational books in print and at least half that number are worthy of teachers' special attention.

Perhaps of more value than a survey is a further look at the characteristics of the informational books that are appearing today. These characteristics may help teachers recognize the books appearing in 1952 or '53, or '54, though, in all fairness, the teacher is not likely to need a checklist to help her. She will probably look at the book and have it reasonably appraised by the time she has thumbed through it. But since informational books, as a group, may be of more than usual importance in modern education, this detailed inspection is justified. If it is to be a glimpse, it is fair to begin with what first strikes the eye—the outstanding illustrations in many, if not most informational books.

THE ROLE OF ILLUSTRATIONS

The best of the informational books have that happy blend of text and illustration that fully supplement each other. The illustrations are not pictures added to the text, but an integral part of the book. The reader does not scurry from text to illustrations, so the second will clarify the first or vice versa. The content and placement of the illustration both complements and supplements the text. In books like Bronson's *Turtles* (Harcourt, 1945), the illustrations add considerably to the factual story and the reader learns from both. Some books make admirable use of full color, like Jannette May Lucas' *Where did your Garden Grow* and *First the Flower, Then the Fruit* (Lippincott, 1939, 1943). Others do equally well without color (Dorothy Hogner, *The Animal Book* and *Farm Animals;* Oxford, 1942, 1945) and some go in between, doing yeoman's work with a single or two colors—H. and N. Schneider, *You Among the Stars* (Scott, 1950) and most of Irma Webber's books, especially *Up Above and Down Below* (Scott, 1943). When photographs are used, authors like Stack (*Asbestos, Radium, Aluminum etc.*—Harpers, 1941, 1940, 1942) and Kane *(Wild World Tales*—Knopf, 1949) have used their cameras well. Even the books that are not outstanding are often marked by good illustrations and some, especially those for older children, have done a good job with a minimum of graphic treatment.

It may sound presumptive to assert that most informational books are well written, but they are. Since many are short books, the author has had to choose each word for maximum effect. It is surprising how much information can be packed into a text that is only three to five thousand words long. Robert McClung has done well in *Wings in the Woods, Sphinx, Ruby Throat,* and *Stripe* (Wm. Morrow, 1948, 1949, 1950, 1951). So has Jeanne Bendick in *How Much and How Many* (Whittlesey, 1947) and in all her other books. Many more examples might be added. Good informational writing for children is an art. On the whole the authors of modern informational books have done well.

The advances which they have made can only be appreciated by comparing these newer books with those more common a generation ago. A common device in those benighted days was to use some nondescript characters like Johnny and the Old Professor or little Tim and his uncle the aviator, to tell whatever facts needed telling. The erudite expert and his juvenile straight man are gone forever. Nowadays the facts are presented for what they are worth and if they are not interesting, it will take more than testimony by the Old Professor to turn the trick. Another device which is fast disappearing involves wild animals whose family life and habits resemble closely those of the normal middle class American citizens of unblemished reputation. Such anthropomorphisms are no longer considered necessary or even "cute." They are recognized for what they really are, distortions of the animal's life history which often cover up our ignorance of how the animal really lives. They have no place in informational books.

THE CONTENT OF INFORMATIONAL BOOKS

It goes without saying that most modern informational books are accurate—scientifically accurate. But is accuracy needed? What does accuracy mean in books like these? Certainly it is not the same level of accuracy that the scientist uses, where the recording of every detail is important so others can verify his experiments. The accuracy toward which most informational books are directed is a level of accuracy to meet—or perhaps slightly exceed

—the needs of the reader. Accuracy, then, is closely correlated to the purpose the information will serve. To this end, unnecessary details are omitted, but at the same time the subject is not reduced to a mass of ambiguous generalities. If anything is slighted, it is the generalities. The writer of informational books always uses specific facts to make his story clear and precise. This judicious selection of factual material, avoiding both unnecessary detail and uninteresting generalities, has been the touchstone of these books. They are, without a doubt, more accurate than books for children have ever been—and more functional too.

There is difficulty in separating the matter of accuracy from the specific contents of informational books. But it is important to stress that *specificity* is a characteristic of them. Not only are they specific, but modern informational books cover a wide range of subjects. Fewer general and encyclopedic volumes appear. Children's interests are specific and specific books on wheels, alligators, snakes, or ants are more accepted than an animal omnibus. Books are now written for children on topics that not so long ago no one would have dreamed of touching below the college level. The surprising and important fact is that such information is wanted, accepted, and used by youngsters.

Leaving for a while the implications of this for the school, it is worth noting the availability of such books as John B. Lewellen's *You and Atomic Energy* and his *You and Space Travel* (Children's Press, 1949, 1950). Jeanne Bendick has explained about television and so has Kingdon Tyler (*Telecasting and Color;* Harcourt, 1946). Ethel Berkeley's *Ups and Downs* (Scott, 1951) is a first book about space. There are, in informational books for children, facts on human reproduction and genetics, atomic structure, weather forecasting, conservation of wild-life, volcanoes and earthquakes, microscopic life, and a dozen other equally erudite topics—each, in these cases, made explicitly clear to children on a level they can understand and use. The success of these books dealing with such a wide variety of topics has helped deal a death-blow to the naive idea that children are interested only in simple, common, easy-to-understand, everyday things.

EXPERIMENTS AND ACTIVITIES

Finally, many of the informational books suggest experiments and activities for the reader. These are not mere gestures to provide busywork in the classroom. In the case of the science books at least, they open the way for individual pupil participation, so that Henry's entire experience in finding out about chemicals becomes a rounded educational whole. The combination of activity and purposeful reading that the informational books supply is hard to beat as a method of learning. Some informational books are devoted almost entirely to activities. Mae and Ira Freeman's *Fun with Science* and *Fun with Chemistry* (Random, 1943, 1944) are best known of this type of book. Beeler and Branley's *Experiments in Science, Experiments with Electricity,* and *Experiments in Optical Illusion* (Crowell, 1947, 1949, 1951) are worth using too. Other good examples are Millicent Selsam's *Play with Plants, Play with Trees* and *Play with Vines* (Morrow, 1948, 1949, 1950). The books which include science or other activities as part of the text are legion. Activities for children are naturally limited in some areas (e.g. disease) but the number of things authors have devised for children to do is astonishing.

If you have read so far without beginning to feel that there is something unique and intriguing in the newer informational books, then my points have been poorly made. Looking over informational books for the past five years or so, a movement seems to be in the making—a movement to give children information they want in a way they can use. It represents a more realistic attempt to meet some of the needs and interests of children than most elementary textbooks have made. The textbooks are written for a captive audience. When the teacher says "open your arithmetic book to page 147," there is little else the class can do. Informational books, on the other hand, stand in open competition with all the other kinds of books a child might use—and with all the other activities that compete for his time. When the child uses them voluntarily in school, or takes them home from the library, the choice itself is not the mean measure of the book's value.

BOOKS AND THE CURRICULUM

All this should imply that informational books have a value in the classroom as well as in the home and library. Their value ties in closely with the newer concepts of the curriculum. In schools today there is a new freedom. Some teachers are using it to develop dynamic programs for their pupils. Many more teachers are somewhat at a loss with this freedom. Some continue teaching as they have taught before. Some teachers, who make an attempt at including new materials and activities, are disappointed because they feel at loose ends and see only meager results. In such situations it is common to find that a teacher has ventured into a new project or unit without adequate preparation. She soon discovers that she has little for the pupils to *do* except sending them to the library on "research." Reading and writing reports as a steady diet soon palls and discipline problems are in the making.

The area of elementary science is one of the newer areas of the curriculum where teachers feel insecure and lacking in their training. Units of work may easily go astray. For some teachers the solution is close dependence on the textbook. Others find they can relax and learn with their pupils. If these teachers have a textbook they use it as a resource book or an informational book, not as a book to be studied page by page. The kinds of information and activities suggested in many of the books previously cited are admirably suited to problems which come up in the classroom or which the group plans to study. Teachers who use their text and these supplementary books together, find them a basis for a program that has a real chance to succeed.

Informational books are not a panacea for the classroom, but they certainly help. Besides giving the program enrichment and activity, the informational books are a boon to the teacher with slow readers. A goodly number of informational books have been written for younger readers and are printed in large type. However, neither the content nor the illustrations is typical of a "baby" book. The slow reader in the middle or upper grades will willingly tackle the simple story of a chipmunk, an airplane, or lightning while he will balk at the primer that seems to repeat "See Susan run" ad infinitum.

Because of their rich specific content, many informational books appeal to a much wider range of readers than one might suspect. And because they are not graded like textbooks, the young boy interested in alligators or in jet planes will pick the best book he can find and will do his darndest to read it. Conversely the older pupil who picks up the same books and who is attracted by the illustrations, will not hesitate to read from cover to cover (usually in 15 minutes) a book set in clear primer type. Even parents are using and enjoying some of the informational books prepared for their young offspring.

The range of material treated in informational books is having its effects on classroom practice also. Teachers broaden their horizons using these books. They see that they can reach the same educational goals through a study of whales as through some more common and less exciting animal. Some of the books dealing with people such as Eva Knox Evans' *All About Us* and *People are Important* (Capitol, 1947, 1951) and Sonia Bleeker's admirable series on Indian tribes (*Indians of the Longhouse, The Apache Indians, The Sea Hunters,* etc., Morrow, 1950, 1951, 1951) are all valuable tools in developing improved human relationships in and out of the classroom. Many of the informational books like those of Schneider or Fenton can enrich the social studies program. A music teacher found James Geralton's *The Story of Sound* (Harcourt, 1948) a real help in explaining to her pupils how instruments worked.

The technique of teachers themselves using children's books is something that should not be overlooked. Teachers are usually busy people. They want to keep abreast of the times and yet may not have the background or ability to cope with material prepared by specialists. By using some of the up-to-date informational books an elementary teacher can quickly, and with relative ease, gain some command of simple data about atomic energy or whatever she will. If she needs a deeper insight, or develops a further interest from what she had read, she will find more advanced books for the intelligent adult reader, which she can sit down and work her way through. There is nothing derogatory in implying that the teacher whose job involves all of elementary education with its own specialized background, should not necessarily want to tackle books on natural history, economics, or chemistry on the same level that she does education or child development. Many a teacher would profit by using these informational books more, and the encyclopedias less. The classroom teacher who wants to use and enjoy the freedom of the modern classroom has to learn to efficiently gather information and materials with which she and her pupils can work. Informational books are a good part of the answer.

CONCLUDING STATEMENT

I cannot conclude this praise of informational books (which seem to offer a grass-roots technique for improving classroom teaching) without striking one blow at a fallacious nine-headed dragon. This blue-nosed creature with an icy breath holds that the widespread use and popularity of informational books and the related interest of the child in the realities of his world are slowly destroying beauty, fantasy, imagination, and poetry. A few educators and critics who should know better have echoed these sentiments. What nonsense! There is no problem of Reality versus Fantasy or Information versus Poetry. No one has to decry the myth, fable, legend, or story of adventure in letting the child discover that the real world around us is also full of wonder, beauty, and things more strange and curious than one can imagine.

Under reasonable guidance, children's choice and use of books usually reach a normal balance. Interest in the comics doesn't last forever. A good story, well told, will have the rapt attention of any boy and girl. The literary diet usually becomes balanced. But in the growing-up process more and more contact with reality is essential. Children who make an early positive contact which helps in the understanding of the machines, tools, and devices, people and other living things around them are taking easier and bigger steps toward maturity. Their vision does not become limited, but becomes wider and deeper. The schools and all teachers have a duty in this regard. The use of informational books in growing numbers makes this duty a happy one.

NATURE WRITING: SCIENTIFIC AND NONSCIENTIFIC *

Millicent E. Selsam

The last ten years have seen the rise of an enormous number of children's books on nature study and science subjects. Many are well written, present information in an easy way, have fine illustrations, and in general are attractive books. Since the subject

* Millicent E. Selsam, "Nature Writing: Scientific and Nonscientific," *School Libraries*, 7 (January, 1958), 13–15. Reprinted by permission of the American Association of School Librarians, a division of the American Library Association, and the author. This article is a revision by the author of the address delivered on the AASL Thursday afternoon program in Kansas City, June 27, 1957.

matter deals with science, one would naturally think that all these books could be classified as scientific. Unfortunately, however, this is not the case. The question I want to deal with is precisely: "What makes a book scientific rather than just about science?"

Science books fill a much needed place in the education of a child not because they give him enough facts to win a prize on a nature quiz program—or just give him a vast store of information. Science books are desirable and necessary when they accomplish other things. One must ask whether a given book contributes to an understanding of the methods of science—observation and experiment; whether it relates its subject matter to appropriate principles of science; whether it helps to build science concepts; and whether it helps to develop desirable scientific attitudes.

A great deal of the vast body of scientific knowledge has been accumulated by the process of *observation*. This observation habit can be encouraged in science books, and often is. A good book on trees, for example, would send a young person out newly aware of all the possible ways trees differ, would encourage him or her to look for flowers, fruit, and seed, to notice differences in bark and branch arrangements.

But knowledge gathered from observation alone is not enough. The best observer might be led merely to identify things in nature and make identification an end in itself, and not a step toward learning more about the thing named. Liberty Hyde Bailey once said, "Nature study does not ask finally, 'What is the thing?'—but 'How does the thing live?'—and 'What does it do?'"

For Darwin, also, observation was a process that led to, and was a part of, extensive experimentation. For young people, observation of natural facts should lead to an interest in discovering the cause of the processes and activities they observe. For example, you can teach children to be observant enough to notice that vines climb in different ways. If they look closely, they will find that some are clinging by roots or tendrils, or leaves, and that others are twined around supports. But this is not enough. By what process do they climb? Can we experiment to find out more? When I started to write *Play with Vines,* I felt exactly the way Darwin did about his book *Climbing Plants.* He said "he found himself so fascinated and perplexed by the revolving movements of tendrils and stems, that he secured seeds of many climbing plants and studied the whole subject." The difference was that I had Darwin to lean on—and his investigations of the subject were the first in the field.

The point is that scientific books should, where the subject matter makes it possible, make simple observations lead to stimulating questions that can be answered by simple experiments. Just watching the tip of a twining vine like the morning glory move around in a circle is exciting and teaches us a lot. But we miss so much if we don't go beyond this observation. Do the stems circle in any definite amount of time? What, if anything, influences the time period? Does the temperature affect it? Does light have anything to do with it? How do we go about finding out? What should our control be? Suppose we find out all we can about this morning glory stem; do we know about all twiners? What is the proper conclusion to be drawn from our experiments?

Even the simplest of experiments can teach the values that only experimentation can give—the kind of thought that goes into the formulation of a problem; the understanding of the need for a control; the necessity for careful observation, and the drawing of proper conclusions from what is observed in the experiment. Experiences of this kind encompass the methods constantly in use in the scientific world and give a young person a glimpse of the processes that have helped to build up the tremendous body of scientific knowledge we now have.

A good science book seeks to relate its subject matter to appropriate *principles of science*. I want to tell you here what I try to accomplish in writing when presented with a book problem. In *See Through The Jungle*, for example, there was a great temptation just to go along and describe the many outstanding and beautiful samples of jungle life—the climbing vines, the orchids perched on the trees, the monkeys, and so on. But when you describe such life, there are opportunities for developing some important principles. In the jungle, where there are many layers of tree life piled one on top of another, there are countless adaptations to climbing. The vines or lianas climb by twining or sending out tendrils or little roots that cling to the bark of the trees and thus wind their way up through a mass of foliage to the light. Other plants get up into the light by the epiphytic habit—the way certain plants have of growing in moist nooks and crannies in forest trees. The animals have many convergent adaptations for arboreal life—such as the sucking discs of tree frogs, the prehensile tail of monkeys, the strong toe nails

that grasp a branch. Pointing out such material helps to illustrate
an important principle—namely, that living things are adapted
to the conditions in which they live. The jungle is alive with
animals that resemble leaves, twigs, or vines, or whose colors
blend in with their background so well that it is difficult to see
them. This gives the opportunity for emphasizing the principle
of "protective resemblance" in nature. There is hardly a science
subject that does not give such opportunity of relating facts to
general principles of science.

A good science book helps to build proper *science concepts*.
One of the most common faults is the tendency to explain everything in nature in terms of purpose (the big name for this is
teleology). It is unfortunately too easy to find examples of this.
I will give you two.

> The squirrel is storing the nut away for future use but it
> may never find it, and then it is just where *Nature* wants it for
> starting a new tree.
> To *Nature*—all plants are important and must go on living.

I submit that such teleological explanations are unscientific.
They keep a young person from asking questions as to how such
things came about. If Darwin or Wallace had been satisfied with
such explanations, we would never have developed the concept
of evolution—one of the most fruitful concepts in the history of
biology.

Every great advance in science has been sparked by the building of concepts that linked phenomena together. Darwin's concept of evolution explained fossils, geologic studies of rocks,
adaptations to environment, comparative anatomical studies, em-
bryology, and lots more. Certainly we can expect our science
books to reveal such big concepts and not to cloud them under
sentences like "To Nature—all plants are important and must go
on living." It happens to be untrue besides, because thousands of
species of plants have died out in the history of the earth's
evolution.

Another common fault is anthropomorphism—ascribing human characteristics to anything from an ant to an elephant. Here
are some examples:

> In a book that discusses earthworms,—"Once the worms
> make up their *minds* that they cannot escape—they will try to
> burrow out of sight." Whether the earthworms escape or not,
> there is one inescapable conclusion one must draw from this

sentence—namely, that earthworms have *minds* to make up—which is untrue.

When I read that a reindeer *knows* that in a few short months his antlers will bud again, it makes me squirm. Reindeers can not *know* in the sense we use the word.

It is time there was recognition of the fact that only man has a brain capable of thought and knowledge. Modern science does its best to stop an anthropomorphic approach and tries to find out how an animal's brain works by studying its behavior.

The better science books encourage a constant use of the methods of science; they encourage an ever-developing, expanding sense of inquiry and wonder about the world around them; encourage a healthy skepticism with regard to prevailing superstitions and prejudices; and accustom young people to solving problems in a scientific way.

Good science books help to produce adults who are aware of the world around them and who can derive pleasure and happiness from maintaining a relationship to nature. They should help to produce adults who have a wide range of interests in the world of nature and natural science—adults for whom the woods, winter, spring, or fall, are not just trees or plants or mosses and lichens, but these particular trees, these identifiable bushes, lichens and so on. They should enable adults to go out at night and see not just stars in the sky above them but familiar stars, recognizing often-seen constellations, an identifiable planet, giving them thence a rich experience of well-known objects associated with previously experienced places and times. Similarly, the study of natural science should enrich chidren's and grownups' lives, whether in city or country, at the seashore, in the desert, or on the mountains, through real acquaintance with and the pleasure of recognition of some little portion of the infinite variety of the things of nature they encounter.

To conclude, children's science books should not only seek to give children a sense of scientific method and a genuine knowledge of some areas of the world we live in, but should also give the human values of "belonging," of feeling at home in the world. We must look to the arts and the social studies for the development of the child's proper relations to his fellows, for the development of attitudes of respect and love for people. But we should turn to the books on the natural sciences for those other values of, let us call it, "at homeness in the world"—a sense of our unity with the totality of nature.

ASTRONOMY BOOKS
FOR CHILDREN *

Donald MacRae
and Elizabeth MacRae

Undoubtedly, the excitement of Sputnik in 1957 and of the more recent space shots has been shared by the children, but it cannot explain all of their current interest in science. The sale of play space suits has fallen off, but the requests for science books continue.

It would seem that most children at a certain age are intuitive scientists and that we adults, in our new enthusiasm for acquainting the children with science—an enthusiasm born sometimes of fear, sometimes of business acumen, but sometimes of a clearer understanding of children's interests—have at last begun to tell our children what children have always wanted to know.

What they want to know in their early school years is everything about the world around them, everything from snakes to stars. They want the old fairy tales, books about prehistoric animals and early man, and books about veteran cars. Time is foreshortened for them. No wonder, then, that children like astronomy, which must look back in time to look out into the universe around.

Although astronomy is itself the oldest of sciences, it beckons the children excitingly into the future. It will be a future of space travel, of course, but, just as appealingly, it will be a future when perhaps the secret of the beginning of things will be unfolded in all its grandeur and orderliness.

Many authors use the historical method of presenting astronomy to children, and this is good. "I want a detective story," said

* Donald MacRae and Elizabeth MacRae, "Astronomy Books for Children," *Top of the News,* 18 (May, 1962), 62–69. Reprinted by permission of the Children's Services Division of the American Library Association and the authors.

an eight-year-old, and he was given one. "No," said he, "I want the important ones about the world and the stars!" The early Greek and Egyptian "detectives" in astronomy must be treated with respect, no matter how erroneous their conclusions. Gallant's *Exploring the Universe* is marred by his scorn for the Greek golden age scientists.

What is a child's first astronomical interest? The constellations used to be considered the primary step but, except possibly for the stories connected with them, this interest comes later. It seems likely that the child's first interest will mirror primitive man's first concern, the sun or lack of it, day and night, and, going on from there, the seasons. Or, taking the sun for granted, he might notice first the moon in the night sky.

Questions about the moon and sun undoubtedly pose themselves to the child long before he can read adequately, if at all. It would seem better to give his parent and him a book they could look at together rather than to offer one of the new picture book controlled vocabulary variety.

The "Let's-read-and-find-out" series is titled optimistically insofar as those books on astronomy are concerned. The choice of subject is good but they are disappointingly written and illustrated. There is a point beyond which simplification leads to smugness if not to absurdity.

Consider *The Moon Seems to Change* by F. M. Branley, illustrated by Helen Borten. (F. M. Branley is the author of the very good book *Mars* written for young adults.) This simple book seems to end in complete confusion, having attempted to explain the size, distance, and particularly the phases of the moon. The time required to reach the moon in a car is estimated and is off by a factor of ten, unless the car were to travel at the rate of a tricycle. The moon appears, in each of its phases, apparently to be seen from the same window. The child is urged to look for himself and see the moon in all of these phases. If he were to try, he would need to stay up until four in the morning to see one of the phases illustrated.

These overly simple books, *What Makes Day and Night, The Moon Seems to Change, The Sun Our Nearest Star,* are neither fish nor fowl. They do not lend themselves to being read aloud by a parent to a very young child. They are foolishly garrulous. They have no information or excitement to offer the alert six-year-old who is beginning to read for himself. At best, then, they are practice reading books, but dull.

The book *Space* by Marian Tellander avoids the dilemma by attempting just enough more than the others to offer something not completely obvious. The illustrations are quieter, more informative, more conventional.

The Role of Illustrations

Illustrations are of prime importance in any science book, and especially in those for the younger readers. If the illustrations in *The Moon Seems to Change* could have been as beautiful and as carefully done as were Helmut Wimmer's for Branley's more mature *The Moon, Earth's Natural Satellite,* the limited text would have been more acceptable. Instead, in an apparent attempt to look childlike, they are sloppy and garish. No matter how bright and unlikely are the colors children use in their own work, there is usually an overall soft-spoken quality about it. The sun in *The Moon Seems to Change* looks like an angry daisy reaching out to envelop the avocado-green moon. The whole thing somehow fails to convey the serene beauty of our moon as she "walks the night." There is little sense of wonder.

In the books intended particularly for young children, the illustrations should convey something of the majesty and vastness of space. Colored charts and diagrams add life and clarity to the text, but there seems little advantage in the almost universal portrayal of Jupiter as a gay beach ball.

One of the accepted conventions is to show the moon upside down, as it appears in the telescope, but it should not be reversed also as on page 16 of Grey's *First Book of Astronomy.* A picture of a solar eclipse with the shadow sharply defined is often used erroneously to illustrate a lunar eclipse. The latter can be demonstrated best in color, to show the reddening.

As in all books, the illustrations and text should be consistent. On page 50 of Branley's *Nine Planets* the text, which does not distinguish between oppositions and favorable oppositions, limits the close approaches of Mars to many fewer than the very clear diagram by Helmut Wimmer shows.

One look at a good picture of the earth in space will bring the question, "What holds it up?" Some books have been satisfied with throwing in the magic word "gravity" in italics or capital letters and perhaps buttressed with an exclamation point, but this, without further explanation, only thickens the plot. So inevitable is the question and so fundamental the answer that the treatment of the subject might serve as a kind of touchstone by which to judge the books.

A great number of books, although setting out to be introductory, simply ignore the problem and launch into a detailed description of planetary orbits. Freeman's *Fun with Astronomy* sidesteps the question. "Nowadays we know the earth is not held up by anything... and moves through space in a special way."

You Among the Stars by Herman and Nina Schneider was one of the first books to undertake to explain the fundamental forces. It takes care to describe gravity and then says, "It is the sun's gravity that keeps the earth in its path around the sun. It pulls just strongly enough to keep the earth exactly in place." There is no mention of why it is pulling.

The Golden Book of Astronomy by Wyler and Ames devotes more time to the question and answers it clearly and succinctly, but uses the concept that "centrifugal force" balances the pull of gravity.

All about the Planets by Patricia Lauber uses a more mature but precise vocabulary and her answer is pleasingly clear. "A planet's movement results from the balance of two forces. One is inertia—the tendency to keep moving forever in a straight line. The other is gravity—the pull of the sun. Without the sun's gravity the planet would fly off into space. Without inertia, it would be drawn into the fiery mass of the sun. The balance of the two forces keeps the planet moving around the sun in its orbit." It is worth while to compare the foregoing with *The Nine Planets* by F. M. Branley in which, on page 16, there is a confusing attempt to use nonscientific terms in order to be understood.

It seems imperative that some precise scientific terms be introduced, explained, and used consistently. For a further discussion of this, we refer you to the article "Space Books—Which Ones and Why," by Lloyd Motz and Minnie R. Motz, *Top of the News* May 1961; to the survey of children's science books in *Natural History* December 1961; to the Foreword of the *AAAS Science Book List for Children* page viii; to *The Unreluctant Years* by Lillian Smith, page 182.

The authors of good astronomy books, as are the authors of any good books, are fired with enthusiasm, knowledge, and respect both for their subject and their readers. Too often the books seem to have been "done" rather than written with any pleasure and sense of communication. If the author has a clear picture of the specific level of interest he wants to inform, the material he chooses for inclusion will have a balance and evenness of treatment. Libration in latitude should not be undertaken, for instance, in a book where the word "crater" must be defined.

Once the child has had some of his first questions answered satisfactorily for the time, and has caught a glimpse of the inexorable and fundamental laws of the universe, his interest turns to dimensions. How big? How far? Some authors take advantage of this with a kind of sensationalism, saying "billions and billions of miles" when "millions" is more nearly correct, or dealing in volumes rather than areas and diameters. The vastness of the universe does not need to be magnified.

MISTAKES IN BOOKS

There are certain discrepancies among books which set forth, for instance, the distances from planets to sun or the diameters of the planets. These are superficial and unimportant, but they are often "corrected" in the library books by the children themselves. The diameter of Jupiter is given as 88,000 miles in *Fun with Astronomy,* as 88,700 in *Boys Book of Astronomy* by P. Moore, as 88,690 in *First Book of Astronomy.* All of these are equatorial measurements and are acceptable approximate figures. However, the more appropriate 86,900 is the mean of the polar and equatorial figures and is the one given by Branley in *The Nine Planets.* He explains mean distances, and so does A. T. White in *All About the Stars,* and it is helpful when authors do.

Librarians will always have to do some verbal editing, however, as they use the books. It may be that, as a group, librarians tend to blanch at the word "science"; but there is a need to catch up with our young readers. When such topics as relativity and antimatter are introduced into our older children's books without apology, there is some indication that we can understand more than we have always thought we could.

"This Universe of Space" by Peter M. Millman, eight radio lectures heard on CBC University of the Air, has been published (1961) by the Canadian Broadcasting Corporation, Toronto, and is a clear presentation of pertinent information. *Splendor in the Sky* by G. S. Hawkins is good. The perennial authority *Introduction to Astronomy* by Robert H. Baker is now in its sixth edition.

The problem of book selection for science would be lessened

by a wider knowledge on the part of librarians of some of the fundamentals of the subject, but they will have to rely on expert advice. The *AAAS Science Book List for Children* recommended in *Top of the News*, March 1961, by Jane Davies, is disappointing. Indeed some of the books starred for first purchase in that list were those which were so wisely but adversely criticized by Miss Davies.There are many inclusions in the AAAS list of astronomy books which we cannot recommend.

The new edition of *Stars for Sam* by Maxwell Reed, edited by Paul F. Brandwein, is an example. The older edition, now out of date, was well written and well organized. The new one is disorganized. There has been some unfortunate rewriting of some sections. Compare the end of the paragraph on cepheid variables, old edition page 102, new edition page 124. On page 119, new edition, a light year is defined, and in the next paragraph the term is used incorrectly. On page 24 there is a full page lunar eclipse sequence which is described as "phases of the moon."

Recommended Books

The following is a list of books we found worthy of recommendation, sometimes with reservations. There are very few for the youngest readers insofar as text is concerned. However, there is a great deal to be said for the young children's enjoyment of good illustrations accompanying a more mature text. A librarian recently questioned the wisdom of a young borrower's choice of a science book. "Do you think you can really read that?" she asked. He looked at her and with withering scorn replied, "I can't *read* it. But I can understand it."

This list contains books printed some years ago as well as the newer ones. The basic knowledge and concepts of astronomy change slowly, and a book published five years ago can contain the whole body of well-established information. Old theories are relatively secure, but should never be presented as definitive. New theories are exciting, but they need to be presented tentatively, because they lack the necessary degree of confirmation. Indeed, the newer a theory the more likely it is to be modified, if not discarded; for example, the two Van Allen belts are now thought to be but one. Finally, a newly published book does not necessarily mean one with the latest theories. In fact, there are some which propagate long dead ideas, such as the one that the moon's place of origin was the Pacific Ocean.

Asimov, Isaac. *The Kingdom of the Sun*. Abelard, 1960. Historical approach to astronomy for readers who have a more mature interest; good selection of subject matter within the limits of 150 pages. Very few of the usual oversimplifications. Interesting style. Diagrams but no photographs. Poor paper.

Baker, Robert H. *When the Stars Come Out,* rev. ed., Viking, 1954. History of the science of astronomy. Constellations. Good illustrations.

Baker, Robert H. *Introducing the Constellations*. Viking, 1957.

Binder, Otto. *The Moon, Our Neighboring World*. Golden Press, 1961. Poor binding. Illustration on page 14 underlines the Pacific Ocean theory of the origin of the moon. However, it has a great deal of reliable information and some outstandingly good diagrams and photographs.

Binder, Otto. *Planet, Other Worlds of Our Solar System*. Golden Press, 1961. Poor binding for a library. With some few exceptions (e.g., comets are erroneously linked with asteroids) there is good presentation of information. With each planet, there is a list of vital statistics, often wanted by children. The illustrations are used to convey auxiliary information as well as to illustrate the text. Some information on the sun is included. Not as thorough a discussion of planetary formation theories as in Gallant's *Exploring the Planets*.

Branley, F. M. *A Book of Planets for You,* illus. by Leonard Kessler. Crowell, 1961. A factual book in which the information is accurate. Not an exciting presentation. Illustrations brilliantly colored and sloppy. The text states, "The rings of Saturn are very beautiful." The illustration scarcely bears this out. For young readers.

Branley, F. M. *The Moon, Earth's Natural Satellite,* illus. by Helmut Wimmer. Crowell, 1960. Beautiful and, for the most part, accurate illustrations. Text disorganized and repetitious. Mixture of elementary and advanced information.

Fenton, C. L. *Worlds in the Sky*. Day, 1950. The facts of astronomy rather than the theories. Attractive format and style.

Freeman, Mae and Ira. *Fun with Astronomy*. Random, 1953. The only book at this level with simple experiments to illustrate principles.

Gallant, Roy A. *Exploring Mars*. Doubleday, 1956. Planetary formations in general and the known facts about Mars. Exciting illustrations. (The format of all of Gallant's books is attractive to all ages of children, even into Junior High School.

The treatment of the subjects is mature enough to interest the older children. Some of his illustrators are more successful than others.)

Gallant, Roy A. *Exploring the Moon.* Doubleday, 1956. Emphasis on a now discarded view of the origin of the moon. The excellent photographs of the moon now available make these illustrations ordinary.

Gallant, Roy A. *Exploring the Planets.* Doubleday, 1958. Theories on the formation of planets in more detail than in *Exploring Mars.* A great deal of information well presented and illustrated. A more mature book than the others in the series.

Gallant, Roy A. *Exploring the Sun.* Doubleday, 1957. More mature information than in Zim's book on the subject.

Gallant, Roy A. *Exploring the Universe.* Doubleday, 1956. History of the theories of the origin of the universe presented with an unfortunate attitude toward the ancient astronomers. Otherwise good.

Gamow, George. *The Moon.* Abelard, 1959. Professional physical scientist and a skillful writer with an interesting style. For older children.

Grey, V. *The First Book of Astronomy.* Watts, 1959. A book similar in its aims to *Worlds in the Sky,* better illustrated but not as well written. Refraction is said to be the reason for the sky's blue color; actually, the air molecules scatter the sun's rays, the blue more than the red, so that in the daytime the atmosphere is suffused with bluish-tinted light. Explanation of earth's orbit similar to that of *Golden Book of Astronomy.*

Kees, Boeke. *Cosmic View.* Day, 1960. Subtitle, The Universe in Forty Jumps. The first jumps are outward into space. A new and effective approach to the size of the universe.

LaPaz, Lincoln and Jean. *Space Nomads.* Holiday House, 1961. An astronomer and his daughter writing with excitement and pleasure about their work, mainly the study of meteorites. For older children. In this branch of astronomy, nomenclature is somewhat unsettled. Usually (but not in this book) a meteorite is a meteroid which falls to the ground, while a meteor is one which is consumed in the earth's atmosphere and appears as a "shooting star." It is widely believed that the former are physically related to the asteroids, while the latter are the debris of comets.

Lauber, Patricia. *All about the Planets.* Random House, 1960. The best book on the subject for this age group. Interesting style, no slurring over subtleties, competent discussions of all the theories of the formation of the solar system. An up-to-date discussion of the surface of the moon.

Lauber, Patricia. *The Quest of Galileo.* Garden City, 1959. A book associated with the subject of astronomy, clear discussion of Galileo's experiments on falling bodies.

May, Julian. *Show Me the World of Astronomy.* Pennington Press, 1959. Very good pictures of the night sky in the part on constellations. The remainder of the book is full of errors.

Neely, Henry M. *The Stars by Clock and Fist.* Viking, 1956. How to find and observe the stars.

Neurath, Marie. *Wonders of the Universe.* Max Parrish, 1961. In the same format as the other Max Parrish color books. Easy-looking format, complex subjects, but well explained and illustrated. Types of stars and their life cycles. Sunspots and their magnetic fields. The red shift. Incomplete account of the formation of the earth and other planets.

Page, Lou Williams. *A Dipper Full of Stars,* rev. ed. Follett, 1959. Subtitle, A Beginner's Guide to the Heavens. A book for an older amateur observer, with a good deal of authoritative information about what he will be looking at. Good treatment of the formation of the solar system. Good style.

Rey, H. A. *Find the Constellations.* Houghton, 1954. Enjoyable, if slangy, style. Attractive format. Reproduction of actual night sky not as clear as in May's *Show Me the World of Astronomy.* Planet finder now out of date.

Rudaux, Lucien, and de Vaucouleurs, G. *Larousse Encyclopedia of Astronomy,* with an introduction by F. L. Whipple, Prometheus Press, 1959. A one-volume encyclopedia with detailed authoritative information and fine illustrations, some in color.

Schneider, Herman and Nina. *You Among the Stars.* Scott, 1951. Poor illustrations of astronomical objects, but persuasive pictures of children looking at a night sky.

Schneider, Leo. *Space in Your Future.* Harcourt, 1961. The solar system and the tools of an astronomer in great detail. Very good for older children. Experiments.

Shepherd, Walter. *The Universe.* Longacre, 1960. Double columns, clear print, good illustrations. Theory of relativity introduced with some success.

Tellander, Marian. *Space.* Follett, 1960. Twenty-four pages of restricted vocabulary which undertakes a simple introduction to the solar system, Milky Way, and some constellations. The sun in all illustrations is too small.

White, A. T. *All about the Stars.* Random House, 1954. "All about" the solar system and the stars. Very well written. "Traffic laws of the sky" a good explanation.

Wyler, Rose and Ames, Gerald. *The Golden Book of Astronomy,* rev. ed. Golden Press, 1959. Excellent one-book introduction to all phases of astronomy from time and tides to space travel. Clear style. Good diagrams.

Zim, Herbert S. *Comets.* Morrow, 1957.

Zim, Herbert S. *Shooting Stars.* Morrow, 1958. Not one of his best.

Zim, Herbert S. *The Sun.* Morrow, 1953. The sun's effect upon the earth.

Zim, Herbert S. *The Universe.* Morrow, 1961. Sixty-four pages to deal with the history, methods of investigation, theories of the universe, types of stars. He manages to introduce all of these in a way that will arouse interest.

Zim, Herbert S. and Baker, Robert H. *Stars.* Simon and Schuster, 1961. Subtitle, A Guide to the Constellations, Sun, Moon, Planets, and Other Features of the Heavens. Profusion of colored charts and illustrations.

WHICH ANTHROPOLOGY BOOKS TO CHOOSE FOR CHILDREN? *

Sara Wheeler

Who can be expert in each of the sciences and the humanities, familiar with the latest finds, methodology, and latest trends? It is baffling to choose books in the field of anthropology, which bridges into so many disciplines. Yet knowledge as to *why* others

* Sara Wheeler, "Which Anthropology Books to Choose for Children?" *Top of the News,* 18 (May, 1962), 47–52. Reprinted by permission of the Children's Services Division of the American Library Association and the author.

look, behave, and think the way they do tends to diminish hostility toward others while increasing interest in them. The persistency of childhood attitudes argues for early exposure to such knowledge. In the process, young minds are awakened to new interests in a wide variety of subjects such as language, art, music, religion, social organization, values, customs, industry, technology, law, genetics, archaeology, and folklore.

Fortunately, anthropological findings make agreement on some basic principles possible. Application of these principles to the selection of books for children can aid in the discovery of materials which will contribute to growth and understanding of others, and the avoidance of those materials which would instill half-truths and perpetuate outmoded dogma.

Basic Principles to Consider

The following principles are offered for application to the selection of factual material in anthropology as well as fiction, especially that which attempts to interpret cultures other than our own. Since anthropology has to do with *people,* their basic anatomical and cultural likenesses and differences, and fiction, too, deals largely with people, much anthropological truth and half-truth is fostered by fictional materials. It is desirable that authors writing stories about other peoples live among them for some time, or at least that their writings show an awareness that a people's attitudes and behavior are a reflection of the culture of that particular group. While avoiding books which *preach* brotherhood, select those instead which further understanding and awaken interest in others (sub-cultures in America as well as cultures abroad). Such story material should adhere to the generally recommended standards of style, character, and plot, while demonstrating the effects of an interplay of the various aspects of culture. Well-selected material in fiction, biography, and folklore can do much to awaken and reinforce anthropological interests and understandings.

Here are the basic principles:

1. There can be no *one* perfection because different environments evoke varying responses, making perfect adaptation in one environment, and for one people, imperfect in and for another. *Books that show American culture (or any other) as the ideal which should be adopted by others everywhere violate this principle.* The tendency to blind ourselves to the achievements of others is responsible for many unfortunate statements, such as

this one from J. Carroll Mansfield's *Dawn of Creation:* "On the sandy, southern shores of the lakes roamed dark-skinned men, who probably had intermingled with the more primitive Negroid submen of the hinterlands of Africa." Ruth Benedict and Gene Weltfish, in their *In Henry's Backyard: the Races of Mankind,* made an admirable attempt to correct such distortions. Here the authors say: "... when the caveman lived in Europe about 5,000 years ago, he was still making crude stone axes ... while the Africans were forging them out of iron."

2. Evolution, whether physical or cultural, is *change,* which moves not in a steady line toward greater adaptation to the environment as is often supposed, but in a twisty, windy, often unpredictable manner, lacking the purpose often attributed to it. Not all groups pass through the stone, iron, and bronze ages. Also, the famous Neanderthal Man fossils are much less modern than several scattered fossils of earlier date. *Books which show evolution as always moving in one direction and through similar stages distort the facts.*

3. Imperfections exist in our culture and in all cultures. Therefore, one should *choose books in which people are not idealized.* The acknowledged desirability of getting along with the rest of the world has seen expression in a flood of books which idealize other peoples. However, a particular people which may have evolved and adopted a way that *for them* solves the problem of sibling rivalry at the same time often exhibits less satisfactory solutions to other problems.

4. Nature is basically unfriendly. Always man has had to struggle against the hazards and dangers of his environment, first to evolve as *man* and then to develop his culture. Each culture he has evolved despite these conditions is a remarkable achievement. Still, many realistic and factual writings portray nature as a kindly mother. *Avoid purchase of books which portray nature as benevolent.* Such ideas must later be unlearned.

5. There is a swing in anthropological thinking from emphasis on differences among peoples to emphasis on an all-pervading base of similarities. There is, however, little agreement as to the extent of this common base. With the emphasis on similarities has come neglect of many important differences which are interesting and important. *Authors who overlook basic similarities or differences fail to give a view of man in depth.*

6. Man not only makes culture, he is molded by it. Each of the aspects of cultural traditions he lives with affects his way of

looking at and thinking about himself and the world. *Avoid books which portray man as in full control of himself or as being able to control others;* he has not demonstrated freedom from being controlled by his culture.

7. Cultures result from an interplay of a particular human group (having great variability, plasticity, and potentiality) with its environment, history, and experience. *Avoid oversimplifications.* The most important aspects of a culture are often the least picturesque or comprehensible. *Writing which emphasizes the superficial in discussing one people or comparing several is dangerously deceptive.*

Another form of oversimplification in anthropological writings for children is the watering-down of the content. *How Man Became a Giant* by M. Ilin and E. Segal is oversimplified, verbose, and meandering in its discussion of the emergence of man.

8. Since all aspects of a culture interrelate, an understanding of this relationship contributes to understanding of the whole. *Overemphasis on one cultural facet without regard to its function in the whole culture is to be avoided.* One cannot understand a person of another culture simply by mastering the language; neither can one hope to modify a culture simply by understanding the technological advancement or economy of a people. Traditional attitudes and mores are persistent and pervade every aspect of a culture.

9. All cultures are organized so as to perpetuate and make cohesive the group and to meet the needs of individuals within it for order and satisfaction of basic needs. Therefore, *books which show characters happy in their own environments are generally more valuable than those which advocate the advantages of another way of life.*

10. Some of the recent scientific methods of dating archaeological finds are: fluorine analysis, microchemical tests, x-ray spectrography, crystallographic analysis and estimates of radioactivity. Application of such methods has revealed the Piltdown jaw to be a hoax, has established the great antiquity of the South Africa fossils, and has revealed man and the anthropoid ape to have such sharply contrasting evolutionary differences that they must have diverged from their common ancestral heritage as much as twenty million years ago. *The remoteness of this divergence is seldom understood and taken into account in references to biological evolution (particularly in fiction writing).* Also, comparisons of man and anthropoid apes as they are today

cannot reveal true measures of differences which may have existed at the time of this divergence.

11. Anthropologists themselves disagree as to the number of races represented by peoples on the earth. The fewer the number of races they accept, the larger the number of groups of people that fit nowhere in their racial scheme. *Authors discussing race should make clear that they mean, when speaking of races, particular groups with similar, visible, and generally inheritable characteristics.* Such definitions would, of course, be adhered to throughout their presentations. *Also, books which perpetuate the dangerous but popular fallacies which equate race with religion and/or temperament should be excluded from library collections.*

12. According to the Revised Version of UNESCO Statement on Race, "Available scientific knowledge provides no basis for believing that the groups of mankind differ in their innate capacity for intellectual and emotional development." The importance of *the role of experience in the development of human mental capacities should be more generally and clearly understood. Carefully written and selected books in fact and fiction can contribute greatly to this understanding.*

Reviews and Lists Valuable

As when selecting in other sciences, book selectors can utilize reviews by specialists appearing in such journals as *Natural History* and *Scientific American* (every December a list of children's books is reviewed) and other scientific organs to advantage. Lists put out by the American Association for the Advancement of Science and the National Science Foundation are also of great help for the book selector in anthropology. Also, as in the case of other factual material, the reputation and position of the writer will weigh heavily in the book's favor when laymen are selecting. Fortunately, quite a number of well-known and highly regarded anthropologists have written about their specialization in books suitable for use with children. Their contributions are starred in the list which follows.

Baity, Elizabeth Chesley. *Americans before Columbus.* Illustrated by C. B. Falls. Viking, 1951.

This volume still deserves high recommendation for its well-rounded picture of the varied peoples who inhabited this con-

tinent before the coming of the white man. Clear distinctions
are drawn between different groups rather than lumping them
all together as Indians, and claiming for them more similarities
than facts warrant. Statuses of various groups today are well-
handled, too. Sixth grade and up.

* Braidwood, Robert J. *Archaeologists and What They Do*. Watts,
1960.

A distinguished professor of archaeology at the University
of Chicago, and authority on the archaeology of the Near East,
writes with enthusiasm and authority about his specialization.
He takes the reader on an actual "dig," which includes preparation, excavating, and interpreting finds. Braidwood warns
against the popular tendency to interpret finds, whether bones,
tools, or pottery, as the earliest representatives of their types.
This is an excellent introduction to archaeology as a profession, including, as it does, rewards and frustrations of the
work and preparation necessary for successful work in the field.
Sixth grade and up.

* Cornwall, I. W. and M. Maitland Howard. *The Making of
Man*. Phoenix House, Ltd., London. Dutton, N.Y., 1960.

A lecturer on environmental archaeology at the University
of London presents this story of evolution through chapters
which interpret and explain the importance of particular fossil remains. M. Maitland Howard is responsible for the clarify-
ing black-and-white drawings which appear on nearly every
page, showing such things as tools, shelters, weapons, and
clothing of the particular people being described. The impli-
cation in one caption, "The Completion of Man," that man
is finished is unfortunate. Fourth grade through junior high.

Eberle, Irmingarde. *Big Family of Peoples*. Crowell, 1952.

The author's central concern is the emergence of types or
races of men with differing visible and apparently inheritable
characteristics. That they are all part of the human family
and have no temperamental or intellectual characteristics as
groups is particularly well presented. Sixth grade and up.

* Edel, May (Mandelbaum). *Story of Our Ancestors*. Little, 1955;
and *Story of People; Anthropology for Young People*. Little,
1953.

Physical and cultural evolution and diversity are presented
in these companion volumes, still highly valuable for their
presentation of basic principles and thoroughness. Junior and
senior high.

Kubie, Nora Benjamin. *First Book of Archaeology.* Watts, 1957.

This is slight, but valuable, as a provocative introduction which, through an historical approach, reveals the vast changes in methods and interpretation which have taken place in archaeology. Some of the latest scientific methods of dating finds are skillfully explained. Fifth grade through junior high.

Lisitsky, Gene. *Four Ways of Being Human.* Illus. by C. B. Falls. Viking, 1956.

The diverse ways of the Semang, the Eskimo, the Maori, and the Hopi are described in relation to the various environments, physical characteristics, and histories of these people. The cultures are shown to be logical, ingenious adaptations which have a cohesiveness and meet the needs of the members of each group. This volume is unusually skillfully designed and illustrated and reads like a novel. Junior and senior high.

* Marriott, Alice. *The First Comers; Indians of America's Dawn.* Longmans, 1960.

The writer of *Sequoyah* and *The Black Stone Knife,* editor of *Winter-Telling Stories,* and contributor to books for adults about the Indians reconstructs in this volume ancient Indian civilizations through the description and interpretation of archaeological finds. *The First Comers* is written clearly and enthusiastically, it conveys the many facets of archaeological interpretation, and it warns against careless amateur collecting and recording. Sixth grade and up.

* Mead, Margaret. *Peoples and Places.* World, 1960.

There can be no doubt of the authenticity of this introduction to anthropology, for the writer has been an eminent researcher and writer in this field for many years. Large print and profuse and colorful illustrations invite young readers to become acquainted with several groups of people who live differently because their environments and experiences are different. The reader takes away provocative glimpses of the many aspects of anthropology. Good bibliography. Third grade to junior high.

Scheele, William E. *Prehistoric Man and the Primates.* World, 1957.

Here is the family tree of man presented in black-and-white pictures and slight text. Famous "fossil men" are explained and interpreted. This book fills the need for a browsing book on prehistoric men similar to the ones on prehistoric animals which have been so popular. Fifth grade and up.

* Underhill, Ruth. *First Came the Family.* Morrow, 1958.

The family varies in its form, organization, and authority from one culture to another, but everywhere there *is* the family. A well-known anthropologist introduces readers to much of the similarity and diversity found in various kinship systems. Here is a succinct introduction to an important key to the understanding of people. Sixth grade and up. This author, well known for her *Red Man's America* and other contributions on the American Indian, has recently provided intermediates with stories of Indian and white children in conflict: *Beaverbird* and *Antelope Singer.* Third to fifth grade.

White, Anne Terry. *First Men in the World.* Random, 1953.

This exciting account of man from Stone Age on is set against a background of archaeological interpretation. A minimum of technical verbiage is employed.

POETRY FOR CHILDREN *

Mildred A. Dawson

Children naturally love the lilt and swing, the musical cadences of poetry. With what pleasure the four-year-old recites his favorite Mother Goose rhymes! He still likes to repeat them when he enters school; and he enjoys the less familiar ones that he learns to repeat with his group in simple choral activities, or dramatizes as his classmates speak the lines. Week in and week out, the child finds genuine enjoyment in listening as his teacher reads or recites verse related to on-going activities.

Notwithstanding, many children leave elementary school having lost their relish for poetry. What has happened? Why has literature in verse form become distasteful to them?

Why Children Dislike Poetry

There are several answers to these questions. In the first place, they may have been victims of poorly selected verse, of poems *about* children but not *for* children. For example, "The Barefoot

* From "Poetry for Children," by Mildred A. Dawson, in *Language Arts Leaflet, number 12,* copyright, 1952, by Harcourt, Brace & World, Inc., and reprinted with their permission.

Boy," once commonly offered in children's readers, reflects the mood of the grandfather, not the grandson. Children love short poems rather than long ones, poems portraying action rather than abstract ideas, poems with marked rhyme and rhythm and a musical lilt to the words. Such poems will stir their emotions —feelings of amusement as Simple Simon fishes in a pail, of pleasure in the alliteration of "Sing a Song of Sixpence," of joyful excitement as jolly St. Nick appears and disappears with his racing reindeer, of admiration and patriotism as Barbara Frietchie displays her flag against rebel orders.

In some instances, the children have been asked to read the poems silently. What excuse can there be for their reading verse silently? Poetry is primarily for the ear. In addition, there are problems of reading difficulty. Sentences are often in inverted order, and are broken up into a series of lines so that the ideas are elusive, causing difficulty for immature readers who do not sense the proper stress of key words and phrases. Boys and girls should *listen* to poetry. It should be read aloud by a teacher, smoothly and expressively, in such manner as to convey the thought, reflect the mood, and bring out the music of words, meter, and rhyme. Such a reading requires previous preparation, as well as sympathetic understanding of the child listeners. Let the children listen so that they may more surely continue to enjoy verse throughout their school years.

In the third place, there may have been too much analysis of the poems. If the vocabularly is so unfamiliar and so difficult that children cannot readily catch the ideas and feelings intrinsic in the verse, the poem should not be presented until later, if at all. Where meanings are subtle, abstract, or overly mature, the poetry is not suitable for children. Listening to a poem should resemble seeing pictures flashed from the movie screen— impressions that are immediate, vivid, clear-cut, and freighted with meaning and feeling. True, there will be an occasional unfamiliar word in a poem suited to children. If the context will make the meaning clear, or if the word is unimportant as a factor in general understanding, the teacher need not call attention to this word. Only the key words upon which much of the significance of the poem rests need be cleared up. A brief reference to the word may be part of a preliminary discussion designed to arouse interest in the poem about to be read, but much discussion and analysis of a poem kill interest.

A fourth factor tending to create distaste is compulsory memorization of certain poems. Most children enjoy memorizing all or part of a poem they especially like. However, children differ in their tastes, and each child should choose the poems he wishes to commit to memory. Actually, there is much unconscious memorization among young children. Children are likely to ask the teacher to read again and again the poems they like best. When they hear a poem several times a month, they tend to join the teacher in saying the parts they recall from repeated hearings. Thus, the best kind of memorization is achieved without conscious effort.

SELECTION OF POETRY FOR CHILDREN

What are the principles that underlie a wise selection of poetry for children? Foremost, the poem must have the qualities that appeal to children. It must be musical, with bold rhythm, natural rhymes, words whose sound and rhythm suggest the idea such as, for instance, "gallop and gallop about" in Stevenson's "Windy Nights" or "the midget mew and giant purr" of Farjeon's "A Kitten." The word pictures must be vivid, impressionistic; there must be action, movement, and a familiar theme that is interesting to children. For the most part, the more modern verse has more appeal than that written many decades ago. The Mother Goose rhymes are an exception.

A second principle is that the poems must suit the maturity of the children. Brevity, bold word pictures, action, strong rhythm, repetitive phrases, children and animals that do things—these factors appeal to young children. Ballads and longer narrative poems, with plenty of action but with more plot, appeal to boys and girls at the intermediate level. In between come the eight-year-olds with their liking for the fanciful, as represented in Rose Fyleman's poems, among others. The teacher is referred to *Children and Books,* by May Hill Arbuthnot, for a presentation of the types of poems suitable to children of different ages and varying background experience.

A third principle is that the poems selected should be currently appropriate. Vachel Lindsay's "The Little Turtle" is in point when a child brings in his pet turtle. Elinor Wylie's "Velvet Shoes" is pertinent when fresh, new-fallen snow lies deep on the ground. The primary teacher should have available for use at a moment's notice, a poem that fits the moment. A convenient file of carefully selected poems is an indispensable aid to the teacher. In connection with science and the social studies, the intermediate-grade teacher should heighten interest in a topic by reading, or making available to the children, closely correlated poetry, a fine poem related to some aspect of the topic.

A fourth principle is that the poems selected must be of high literary quality. Graphic, precisely chosen words and a cameolike expression of ideas are essential to good poetry. Verse of cheap quality does not stimulate the fine emotional reactions that are aroused by true poetry; it does not bear the repetition that leads to memorization; it is not desirable for choral speaking. Good poems, like high-grade cloth, wear well and bring the customer back for more.

USING POETRY IN CHORAL SPEAKING

A method of using poetry that merits detailed consideration is choral speaking, in which children interpret verse as several voices speak in unison. Sometimes there may be solo parts, but usually small groups repeat lines or stanzas in turn. Preferably speaking groups should not number more than twelve, if enunciation is to be clear-cut and if theme and mood are to be sympathetically conveyed. The values of choral speaking are many. The children derive great joy from responding orally to the rhythm and melody of the poetry. As they strive with their companions for a group effect, they gain a sense of social solidarity and, at the same time, tend to lose a tendency to be either shy or overly aggressive in expressing themselves. A permanent love for good literature is encouraged. While it is preferable that a teacher have special training in the techniques for choral speech, she can do a reasonably good job with it if she herself loves poetry and understands children.

The teacher untrained in choral speaking must avoid certain dangers, however. It is very easy for a group to fall into a monotonous, singsong rendition. If the children are keenly conscious of the sense and mood that the poem is to convey, they will change the tempo of lines and the pitch and volume of their voices; at the same time they will inflect and modulate their voices so as to interpret the meaning of the words in the poem. If a poem is meaningfully presented when it is introduced, and if the teacher reads it in an interpretative way, the children are unlikely to lapse into a singsong performance.

The danger of selecting mediocre verse has already been mentioned. In working to achieve the best interpretation, a poem will have to be repeated again and again in various choral effects. Only a genuinely fine poem can have appeal after so many repetitions.

Just as children in a group tend to sing too loudly, so in choral speaking this same tendency is likely to appear. With children, loud voices tend to be harsh or rasping. If any one voice is clearly dominant, the total effect is spoiled. Enunciation must be clear and precise, the voice flexible and well controlled. Whenever voices grow loud, it is best to stop at once, recall the meanings and feelings to be expressed, and encourage light but rich tones on the part of the speakers. One child with poor enunciation can destroy the clarity of the unison voice. Each child can easily sense the need for speaking with clarity and speaking with precision; therefore choral speaking can bring about great improvements in the speech of individual children.

Perhaps the simplest way to initiate choral speaking is to let the group join in as the teacher reads a favorite bit of familiar verse. Even in the first grade where formalized choral speaking is not advocated, children enjoy joining with the teacher in saying nursery rhymes. At the same time, they benefit from the speech practice. A second way of initiating choral speech is through dramatic reading in which the children read assigned parts in a story or in narrative poems incorporating conversation. In such reading, they learn to read interpretatively.

In the elementary school, four types of choral speech are most suitable: *unison, refrain, antiphonal,* and *line-a-child.* In unison reading, the whole group speaks as one. While a finished performance can be expected only of upper-grade children, young children so enjoy saying rhymes and brief poems together that unison speaking is commonly used with them. In the refrain type of reading the teacher, or perhaps a more accomplished or confident child, reads the major part of the poem. The group chime in on the refrain, such as saying "Dinkums, dunkums, little gray Billy Goat." Antiphonal effects are secured as the class is divided into two groups, perhaps boys as one group and girls as the other. In line-a-child performances, each child says a line or two, making a conscious attempt to pick up quickly where the preceding speaker has just left off. "One, Two, Buckle My Shoe" is a good rhyme for introducing this type of speaking.

The teacher must prepare carefully before she reads a choral-speaking selection to her class. She must respond to the meaning and mood of every phrase and line, and must reveal the rhyme and rhythm patterns. After the key ideas have been cleared up through discussion, the children should assist in working out the arrangements, whether antiphonal, line-a-child, or unison interspersed with solo. In the first trial performances, all should be alert to poor articulation and to phrasing that clouds meaning instead of revealing it. Many authorities suggest that the teacher conduct the speaking much as she would conduct a song, using her right hand to indicate tempo and the left to control volume.

With experience, the teacher and her children will gain more and more facility in bringing out key thoughts and feelings. Changes in pace, shifts in voice inflections, pauses to lend emphasis will be used to secure desired effects.

SUMMARY

Poetry suited to the maturity and experiences of the pupils, poetry to which they listen rather than read in silence or stumble through orally, poems that are memorized voluntarily on the basis of personal choice, and poems that are doubly enjoyed in simple choral arrangements—such poetry will be loved by children at all levels of the elementary school.

Professional References

Arbuthnot, May Hill, *Children and Books*. Scott, Foresman & Co., Chicago, Ill. 1947. Chapters 3–10.

Dawson, Mildred A., *Teaching Language in the Grades*. World Book Company, Yonkers, New York. 1951. Ch. 5, pp. 90–92; 234–39.

Rasmussen, Carrie, *Speech Methods in the Elementary School*. The Ronald Press, New York. 1949.

Werner, Lorna S., *Speech in the Elementary School*. Row, Peterson & Company, Evanston, Ill. 1947. Pp. 75–122.

Collections

Association for Childhood Education, *Sung under the Silver Umbrella*. The Macmillan Company, New York. 1935.

Brewton, John, *Under the Tent of the Sky*. The Macmillan Company, New York. 1937.

Brown, Helen A., and Heltman H.J., *Let's-Read-Together Poems*. Row, Peterson & Company, Evanston, Ill. 1949.

Geisner, Barbara and Suter, Antoinette, *Very Young Verses*. Houghton Mifflin Company, Boston. 1945.

McFarland, Wilma, *For a Child: Great Poems Old and New*. Westminster Press, Philadelphia. 1947.

HELPING CHILDREN
ENJOY POETRY *

May Hill Arbuthnot

> Teacher, scholar, lecturer and author, friend of books
> and of children, Mrs. Arbuthnot needs no introduction
> to librarians. We asked her what librarians can do to
> foster in children the enjoyment of poetry. Here is her
> answer, written on planes and in airports as she "ca-
> reened around California" on a lecture tour.

In promoting the enjoyment of poetry with children and youth,
librarians have one great advantage. They have the books. Teachers may have the children—all of them, daily and intimately,
but they rarely have in their classrooms an adequate number of
books to serve as baits to poetry-tasting.

So first of all, make attractive displays of your poetry for
children and youth. This is a privilege today when poetry comes
gaily dressed and decorated as it should always have been. A
riotous and colorful array of *Mother Goose* editions will set the
children hunting for their favorite jingles. Stevenson, Milne, and
Eleanor Farjeon are gaily illustrated. The newer poets—Harry
Behn, David McCord, Gwendolyn Brookes, William Jay Smith,
and John Ciardi are published in editions as appealing to look at
as to read. Two especially beautiful books pictorially are Aileen
Fisher's *Going Barefoot* and Robert Frost's *Come With Me*. The
jackets of all these and the books themselves are eye-catchers for
your bulletin boards and tables.

Then, read poetry to your children and young people every
time you have a chance. Begin or end a story hour with some
poems, and read new ones more than once. Nonsense verse has
sure appeal and leads naturally into light verse, which in turn

* May Hill Arbuthnot, "Helping Children Enjoy Poetry," *Wilson Library
Bulletin* 36 (January, 1962), 377. Reprinted from January 1962 Wilson Library
Bulletin by courtesy of The H. W. Wilson Company, New York with per-
mission of the author.

leads to lyrics, and there you are, right at the heart of authentic poetry with Robert Frost and Walter De La Mare to lead the way.

Introduce children and youth to modern anthologies until they know what they are and how fascinating they can be. Try having a lot of these on hand for your story hour, and ask a child to choose a poem about whatever he thinks of—a dog, a fairy, a rainy day, an airplane, and then find a poem about his subject in one of your wonderful anthologies. This may sound risky, but actually it is about 95 per cent safe and sure. It is a game that amuses the children and by the way of it, they discover the fun and adventure of exploring a new collection of poems.

If you discover a group of children or young people who groan, "Oh, not poetry!", it means one of several things. They have been fed poems too old, too difficult or too "precious" for them. Or they have been set to analyzing poetry—finding all the figures of speech, marking the meter, putting the poem into their own words, picking out the most beautiful line or some such nonsense. The cure for these victims is, take it easy. Begin with nonsense verse or the simplest and most objective verses about everyday experiences and activities. After all, you don't start children's musical experiences with symphonies and sonatas. Even John Ciardi, a serious adult poet and poetry critic, starts his own children with nonsense or humorous verse. But please note his verses are never banal doggerel, but skillfully written by a master craftsman.

Another starting point for reluctant poetry-tasters is the narrative or story poem, long or short. The rapid, on-going meter of verse heightens the sense of action and makes the ballad irresistible to children. From "The Night Before Christmas" for the youngest, to the gory old Scotch-English ballads for the oldest, the story poem will hold them enthralled.

In conclusion, never forget that, like music, poetry is an aural art. It should be spoken and heard to be fully understood and enjoyed, so read poetry aloud whenever you have a chance. Even at your loan desks, when there isn't a mob, have a book of poems on hand, show it to your youthful customer and say casually, "Listen to this and see if you like it," and read a short one. Even our young teen-age sophisticates, when they hear poems vigorously and unaffectedly read, say wonderingly, "Read it again." While the children bounce enthusiastically and cry, "Sing it again!" That is your reward.

BIOGRAPHIES FOR TEEN-AGERS *

Learned T. Bulman

Despite the fact that the biographies discussed in this article are aimed at the younger reader, I have more than once found myself so engrossed in the book at hand that midnight had long passed without my knowledge. Every one of them had something to teach me, and many of them are loaded with factual data that had managed to escape me in a reasonably voracious reading life. If they can do this for me, why not for the teen-ager?

It should be emphasized at this time that many of these works are the narrative or story form often called fictionalized biography. No doubt this has annoyed some English teachers, but one must ask himself what one expects the student to get from reading a biography. If you are seeking great works of literature—even juvenile literature—this is the area in which you are least likely to find them. Few, if any, would fall into the classic status. Only occasionally is there a bright star who would be considered a juvenile Harold Lamb, Emil Ludwig, or Hesketh Pearson. What then is the value of these pattern pieces?

It has been my impression that biographies are frequently assigned with the idea of encouraging the student to make something of himself (?) through the vicarious experience of reading about one who has succeeded. They are also assigned to let the youngster view the whole person (whoever he may be), not just the popular or historical memory of him. To succeed in either of these aims, as far as the middling reader is concerned, there are certain requisites. The author must have presented his facts entertainingly or at least succeeded in sustaining interest. He must not philosophize too much into the why of the subject. And usually he must have accomplished all this in 300 pages or less.

* Learned T. Bulman, "Biographies for Teen-Agers," *English Journal*, 47 (November, 1958), 487–94. Reprinted with the permission of the National Council of Teachers of English and Learned T. Bulman.

The subject is not as important, if the librarian or teacher is a good salesman. Mary Ann Bickerdyke or Joseph Pulitzer—though not well known to this age—will be eagerly read if properly introduced.

It should be understood that this paper is written from the viewpoint of a public librarian. For that very reason, it is mandatory that the rather different attitude such a person assumes when asked for a biography by a student be clarified. The public librarian is seldom acquainted with the individual's I.Q., reading score, or other pedagogical measurements. He is equally unaware of how well the student does, or better, approaches his school work. This does not for a moment imply that he does not know personally the many students who come to him, and recognize their seeming potential. Again, the problem is not the student who will come in and ask for Sandburg or someone similar suggested by the teacher. The problem students are those who can read better and are not doing so, and those who can just about read!

For those who can just read, but have somehow reached junior or senior high school, books by Ronald Syme, Clara Judson, or even some of the Landmark and World Landmark titles might help. As good as we think the latter are for informing the fourth, fifth, and sixth graders about United States and world historical events and leaders, we do not as a rule recommend them to the older students. However, some of these Random House titles that may be the answer for the slow readers are Sterling North's *Abe Lincoln* and *George Washington,* Vincent Sheean's *Thomas Jefferson,* John Gunther's *Alexander the Great,* and Emily Hahn's *Leonardo da Vinci.* The majority of the books that will be discussed in this paper will be aimed at the neither good nor bad, but just middling reader.

After this possibly long-winded, but necessary, introduction to the author's status and attitudes, it is best to push immediately into the subject at hand—namely biographies written for teenagers. Our main concern will be the publishers' dream designation of "12 to 16," on occasion, "14-up," which so often of recent years has appeared on the inside flap of the dust cover of these books.

The firm of Julian Messner, Inc., is head and shoulders above all other publishing houses in this field. Their Shelf of Biographies has in its (forgive the expression) stable of authors, some really good writers. One out of three of the better biographies would seem to be published by Messner, although there are no figures to substantiate such a statement. Other houses have one or two people who consistently turn out good material, but, with these exceptions, the biographies that have excited our interest have been non-series items. Books no longer in print have been avoided. That your library may have them is fine, but why frustrate those teaching in new schools, whose libraries, equally new, cannot obtain such material?

FOUR PROLIFIC WRITERS

We will first consider the more prolific writers. In this category are: Jeannette Covert Nolan, Jeanette Eaton, Shannon Garst, and Marguerite Vance. Although no two necessarily follow the same pattern, all four of them use the narrative approach to a greater or lesser degree and all are formula writers. Of the four, . . . Eaton and Nolan are the best literary artists.

Much of what is said about Nolan is equally true of Eaton. There is such similarity of approach that some of their works could have been done by either. They have both written top-notch items as well as one or two that aren't quite as interesting. They, as will be true of most of our authors, deal in blacks and whites. Their subjects are either good or bad; there is little or no attempt at gradation.

Jeannette Covert Nolan is a Messner author. She usually averages 180 to 190 pages per book, always has a bibliography, and usually has an index. She has written about Abraham Lincoln, Andrew Jackson, Benedict Arnold, Clara Barton, Florence Nightingale, Eugene Field, George Rogers Clark, O. Henry, John Brown, and La Salle. A few of her books are geared to the average 10- to 14-year-old reader; the rest are for the 12 to 16 age. They seem to be well researched, are well written, very readable, and add flesh and blood to what occasionally could be a skeletal subject.

Jeanette Eaton has used a number of publishers. She does not always have bibliographies and indexes. She averages 250 pages, although her *Trumpeter's Tale* (Louis Armstrong) is 191 and *Leader by Destiny* (George Washington) is 402. She is also a good researcher and reporter and has several items that are for a little older audience than those of Nolan. Other of her books still in print are *David Livingston; Gandhi; Lone Journey* (Roger Williams); *Narcissa Whitman; Eleanor Roosevelt;* and *Young Lafayette.*

Shannon Garst is a western devotee. All of her work is devoted to mountain men, Indians, scouts, and legendary figures of the West and Southwest. Her research is good. The vocabulary and style (which is choppier than in most books we will discuss) recommend her for those restless readers who will find that many of her subjects would make good television heroes—or already have. Wild Bill Hickock, James Bowie, Kit Carson, and Crazy Horse are samples of such figures. On the other hand, not all of her subjects are as well known outside of their home grounds as are most of the people covered by other authors for this age. Other of her books feature Big-foot Wallace (of the Texas Rangers), Chief Joseph of the Nez Perces, Jim Bridger, Joe Meek, Custer, Buffalo Bill, Sitting Bull, and William Bent.

Marguerite Vance is a romanticist. All of her biographies concern women who either have been great themselves, or have helped their men to become so. There is a storybook quality, an almost preciousness, that will appeal to the teen-age girls who enjoy historical fiction, but this does not detract from evident care for factual writing. She is our "thinnest" author, more often reading 160 pages than 180. There is never a bibliography or an index. All of these facts make her particularly inviting to the nonreading girl who has to read a biography, but is afraid of getting a book which looks like one. To date Vance has written for Dutton: *Empress Josephine; On Wings of Fire* (Nathaniel Hawthorne's daughter, Rose, who became Mother Alphonsa); *Elizabeth Tudor; Jacksons of Tennessee; Lady Jane Grey; Marie Antoinette; Lees of Arlington; Martha, Daughter of Virginia* (Washington); and *Flight of the Wildling* (Elizabeth of Austria).

Selected Biographies

Turning to less prolific authors, we come first to Rachel Baker who has written five excellent biographies which, on a rating scale, would place her almost at the top. Even more important, she has often chosen almost impossible people to write about and yet succeeded admirably. Her first and longest (248 pages) book, *First Woman Doctor* (the story of Elizabeth Blackwell, M.D.), has had many foreign editions. She next chose an even lesser known subject, William Thomas Green Morton, a pioneer in the use of ether. In 1950 her *Chaim Weizmann* vividly told not only the story of Weizmann, but made one aware of Israel's battle to again become a nation. Her other titles are *Sigmund Freud* and *Angel of Mercy* (Dorothea Lynde Dix). Miss Baker writes sympathetically and has the ability to become part of her subject. One sees, with Miss Dix, the inhuman conditions of the insane, and one experiences, with Dr. Blackwell, the vicissitudes of a woman pioneering in a man's field. Messner publishes Baker's books which average 180 to 224 pages with index and, where possible, bibliography.

One is often of two minds when one learns of a new biography for teen-agers. Why did the author choose that particular person to write about, and why, in some cases, wasn't it done sooner? Alvin F. Harlow, an established author, with work in many fields, brings such thoughts to mind. Why he chose Joel Chandler Harris (Uncle Remus), Henry Bergh (founder of the ASPCA), and Bret Harte is less important than that he has done a good job with them. Careful research and a good index, in all but the Harris book, make them fine items for book reports. His earlier books, the Harris, Harte, and Theodore Roosevelt, ran from 278 to 307 pages. His more recent works, which also include an Andrew Carnegie and a family work on the Ringlings of circus fame, run about 180 pages each. All six are part of the Messner Shelf.

Our next three authors have written only three or four biographies each and have very little in common. Of all the authors mentioned in this article, Alice Desmond comes the closest to adult writing and usually is marked "14 and up." There is a tremendous amount of research evident in her work. She has two things in common with Vance: She writes about women and her books lack indexes. But there, any similarity ends. Her writing is more scholarly than Vance's and her books are about twice as long (278 to 307 pages). She offers a bibliography, a number of photographs and pictures, and, to date, has been published by Dodd, Mead. Four of her biographies—*Alexander Hamilton's Wife; Glamorous Dolly Madison; Martha Washington;* and *Bewitching Betsy Bonaparte* (American wife of Napoleon's brother, Jerome)—have successfully painted a picture of the dress, living conditions, politics, and general thinking of their respective times. Like most of our authors, she takes the liberty of inventing dialogue and thought for her subjects. At no time, however, does it seem forced or unlikely. This is another whose works should be equally useful to social studies as well as to English classes.

Manuel Komroff has done biographies of Julius Caesar, Mozart, Marco Polo, and Napoleon. He averages 180 to 190 pages, always indexes, usually has a bibliography, and has been published by Messner and Knopf. He uses simple language in a third-person storybook style. He does not offer much shading in his characterizations; they are either good or bad, but seldom some of both. He has a short staccato sentence style that may bother some readers, and likes to repeat points he fears may be missed. For all of this, his material seems well researched and is clearly reported.

A comparatively new name to this field is Iris Noble. Her biography of *Nellie Bly* appeared almost simultaneously with those by Nina Brown Baker and by Mignon Rittenhouse, but was judged superior to the others. Her next book was *Joseph Pulitzer,* and her most recent is *Clarence Darrow.* She enjoys writing about people with a mission. The first of her subjects wished to bring recognition and respect for women in the field of journalism. The next, who incidentally provided *Nellie Bly* her step to fame, wanted to bring *all* the news to his readers. Methods were unimportant as long as the true story was printed. His greatest mission was probably forcing the recognition of journalism as a respected profession demanding specialized training. The last of Miss Noble's knights has been best remembered for his penchant to champion the underdog in legal battle—particularly the one who represented a cause. His successes and failures filled many a column in his day. Miss Noble's journalistic background is evident in her work. She sometimes speaks in headlines, but never at the expense of lesser necessary information. There is a feeling of immediacy in all of these titles which average 191 pages, have index and bibliography, and are also published by Messner.

A specialist in yet a different way is Shirley Graham. Her forte is Negroes—well or lesser known for their part in the formation of our nation. Subjects for her books are Phyllis Wheatley, a little-known slave poetess of the American Revolutionary War period; Benjamin Banneker, born a freeman, who was known in the late 1700's for his knowledge of astronomy, his published almanac, and his help in laying out the city of Washington, D.C.; Frederick Douglass, escaped slave during the Civil War, who used his journalistic and oratorical skills to help free his people; Booker T. Washington; and Dr. George Washington Carver, whose biography Miss Graham coauthored with George Lipscomb. Shirley Graham writes with a true feeling for her subjects—

giving them dimension in a style that is lively and yet, when necessary, detailed. One can rejoice at each success of a character and feel, not pity, but the determination to try again after each failure. All of these books have been printed by Messner, run from 180 to 240 pages, and usually have an index and bibliography.

A book that won the 1955 Newbery award and one that was a runner-up for it in 1957 are worthy of discussion here. The first is Jean Lee Latham's 251-page *Carry on, Mr. Bowditch,* published by Houghton, Mifflin. This is actually recommended for the 10 to 14 age level but is a really accomplished piece of writing. Miss Latham has succeeded in making a comparatively unknown person come alive on every page of her book. Unlike a number of the Newbery winners, which seem to be chosen by librarians more because they have a beauty of writing (usually lost on the child) than because they tell a good story and do it well, *Carry on, Mr. Bowditch* has been well received by the youngsters and may be just the book to give to the not-so-good reader who needs a book with bounce. Miss Latham's *Trail Blazer of the Seas,* about Matthew Maury, is not as interesting a book or subject, and her *On Stage, Mr. Jefferson* stops much too soon in Joseph Jefferson's life to be a really acceptable biography.

The runner-up referred to is Leo Gurko's *Tom Paine, Freedom's Apostle.* It is published by Thomas Crowell, has 213 pages and an index. In general format it reminds one of the Messner titles. It is written in the third person, and the writing is superior to that in most of the titles mentioned up to now. It calls a spade a spade and in no way tries to whitewash either Paine or the great men he dealt with in his lifetime. Gouverneur Morris, John Adams, even George Washington are seen as they were and not as legend has made them.

Our next concern will be with those writers who have succeeded in benefiting us with one or two items of significance. Such a person is Phyllis Wynn Jackon whose *Golden Footlights* pleased us so much that on a visit to San Francisco we went out of our way to learn more about that merry madcap named Lotta Crabtree. Although little known to recent generations, in her day she was second to none in the world of musical comedy. Her rise from dancing and singing as a child for miners in the riproaring camps of the old West to stardom on Broadway is vivid and enjoyable reading. Holiday House has printed this 310-page chapter in the history of musical comedy.

A title that has worn itself out several times on our shelves is *The Great Houdini* by Beryl Williams and Samuel Epstein, a husband and wife team who together and separately have written on a wide range of subjects. Nothing thrills a youngster more than a peek into the unknown, and what could be more mysterious than the secrets of a great magician and escape artist? The authors have brought the excitement of success, and enough explanation of how some of Houdini's tricks were achieved, to make every youngster who reads this pass on the good word. Bibliography and index are provided in this 182-page offering from Messner.

The constant need for first-class biographies of women is aided by Nina Brown Baker, a prolific writer who has directed much of her material to a younger audience. Of those intended for older readers, her books on Garibaldi, Bolivar, and Juarez are notable additions to this genre of writing. To our mind, however, her very best is *Cyclone in Calico*. It is the story of Mary Ann Bickerdyke—a rough, salty housewife who worked tirelessly as nurse, cook, and friend in battle hospitals of the Civil War. Not content with remaining in the larger cities, she followed the troops, knowing that often more lives were lost in those hours immediately after battle than on the battle field. An extensive bibliography and most complete index are found in this 278-page Little, Brown publication.

Long before the cry for a stronger science training was made, a number of notable scientists' lives were being tailored for the teen-age market. The author who has done the most accomplished job in this field is Elma Ehrlich Levinger. Of her three offerings, *Albert Einstein* is probably the most accurate and detailed. This is understandable when one remembers that Galileo and Leonardo da Vinci did not have about them reporters who could immortalize their extemporizing. *Galileo* is the most fictionalized, the author having fewer records to work with. Da Vinci, fortunately, left copious notebooks. All three books have index and bibliography, average 175 to 190 pages, and are printed by Messner.

Also from the Messner presses are the lives of Michael Faraday and Isaac Newton by Harry Sootin. If it is possible to give life and feeling to a biography of a scientist, Sootin has done it. This remark is made because perusal of many such books has shown that the single-mindedness of these great men has frequently caused them to lead a semi-sheltered, almost dull life.

One scientist who led anything but a dull life, despite a crippling disability that for many might have been a handicap, was Charles Proteus Steinmetz. Sigmund Lavine, whose *Wandering Minstrels We* is an excellent dual life of Gilbert and Sullivan, of light opera fame, has done an equally fascinating job for the genius of electricity, often called the Wizard of Schenectady. Steinmetz's active interest in civic affairs, his tremendous influence at Union College, his hobbies of cacti, orchids, and wild and domesticated animals are combined into a highly readable and entertaining volume of 241 pages, printed by Dodd, Mead.

The middling to poor male student often is unable to settle down with a biography of Gandhi, Julius Caesar, or even George Rogers Clark. Eaton's story of Louis Armstrong and even Shannon Garst's tales of Bowie and Hickock may not work. The next, and too often only, answer is a sports personality. Unfortunately one cannot get excited over the caliber of the sports biographies extant. Gene Schoor, Milton Shapiro, Joe Trimble and others have manufactured lives of our sports heroes of the day, but they seldom have much to say, due no doubt to the fact that there just isn't much to write about these people. It is only the occasional *Lou Gehrig* by Frank Graham that succeeds in attaining some stature in this field.

Biography Series

There is one series of biographies that rates special commendation. These books do not specifically fall into the framework that has been set up for this paper but the high quality of authorship and the compactness of presentation make them of particular value to the better high school reader. The Alfred A. Knopf publishing company has, for several years, been printing the Great Lives in Brief series. Authors such as Andre Maurois, Rumer Godden, Albert Guerard, and Stewart Holbrook have succeeded in capturing in 205 or 206 pages the very being of such people as Hans Christian Andersen, Napoleon III, and Alexandre Dumas. The smallness of the books should in no way discourage English and social studies teachers from not only accepting but encouraging reports on volumes from the series. Albert Guerard's *Napoleon* (the First) and Ruth Moore's *Charles Darwin* are good examples of these masterpieces of distillation which should and often do encourage the student reader to hunt out larger and more detailed biographies of the same people.

A series of biographies that most teachers may not consider inclusive enough for book reports, but which we think particularly well done, are the art biographies by Elizabeth Ripley. She has managed to digest in 70 pages, illustrated with black and white reproductions of the better works of these masters, an almost crystal-like view of such fine painters as Van Gogh, Rembrandt, Michelangelo, Goya, da Vinci, and Rubens. At a time when television has blessed us with Omnibus, the Leonard Bernstein lectures on music for children, and discussion of art by teachers like Meyer Schapiro, we could do worse than to recommend these thin, but informative works published by Oxford University Press.

This is by no means an exhaustive list of biographies for this age. The reader has no doubt thought of several fine individual biographies that could or should have been part of this paper. No attempt has been made to include all the fields that biography covers. Several authors who have a number of biographies were purposely omitted because they are dull.

Our purpose in writing this paper was to act as a proxy reader and reporter. It has been our observation that the average English teacher seldom has the time to read many of the books that are written purposely for the teen-ager. This, we hope, may have eased that work.

which should and often do encourage the student reader to hunt
out larger and more detailed biographies of the same people.

A series of biographies that most teachers may not normally
consider enough for book reports, but which we think particularly well done, are the art biographies by Elizabeth Ripley, the
best-rounded to digest in 70 pages, illustrated with black and
while reproductions of the better works of these artists, as almost invariable view of each one we see, of Van Gogh, Rembrandt, Michelangelo, Goya, da Vinci, and Rubens. Was a time
when education has blessed in with Continho, the Eskimal here-
with lectures on music for children, and discussion of art by
teachers in... begins, we could do worse than to recommend these titles, but Informative books published by Oxford
University Press.

This is by no means an exhaustive list of biographies for this
age. The reader has no doubt thought of several that individual
biographies that could or should have been part of this paper.
No attempt has been made to include all the fields that biography covers. Several authors who have a number of biographies
were purposely omitted because they are dull.

Our purpose in writing this paper was to act as a proxy reader
and reporter. It has been our observation that the average English reader seldom has the time to read many of the books that
we submit purposely for the teen-ager. This we hope may have
spied that work.

INDEX

INDEX

A

ALA Booklist, 93, 101
ALA Notable Children's Books, 93
Abbott, J., 133–34
Adam, B. P., 45, 263, 265, 272, 274
Adams, J. D., 8
Alcott, L. M., 37, 76, 134, 163
Alice's Adventures in Wonderland, 196, 304
Alm, R. S., 351
American Antiquarian Society (Worcester, Massachusetts), 157
American Association of School Librarians, 115
American Library Association, 97, 146, 300, 303
An Ample Field, 96
Andersen, H. C., 9, 59, 133, 162, 273, 286
Anderson, M., 100
Andrews, S., 279
Annixter, P., 361
Anthropology books, 397
   list of, 401–404
   principles of selecting, 398
Anzilotti, R., 299–301, 302
Arbuthnot, M. H., 18, 45, 85, 264, 269–70, 272, 406, 409, 410
Ardizzone, E., 186
Asbjörnsen, P., 277, 280, 284
Association for Childhood Education International, 146
Astronomy books, 388
   illustrations in, 390
   list of, 393–97
Atwater, M., 50
Atwater, Richard and Florence, 57, 74, 165, 167, 170
Austin, M., 238
Averill, L. A., 64, 66
Awards, children's book,
   Caldecott, 147, 175–76, 178, 181
   Carnegie Medal, 183
   Kate Greenaway Medal, 198
   Newbery, 147, 174–76, 178
   Regina Medal, 175

B

Bailey, M., 31
Baker, A., 74, 335
Baker, N. B., 419
Baker, R., 415–16
Barbauld, A. L., 131–32, 141
Barry, F., 148–49
Baruch, D., 3, 267, 268
Basic Book Collections, 103
Batchelder, M., 148
Battledore, 131, 138
Becker, M. L., 6
Becktel, L. Seaman, 146
Benary-Isbert, M., 39, 42, 45
Bennett, R., 53
Bequest of Wings, 45, 345
Berelson, B., 29
Betzner, J., 44, 45, 273–74
Beust, N. E., 148, 255
Bibliotherapy, 20, 41. *See also* **Therapeutic Reading,** 31
   list of books about, 34–39
Biography, 3, 317, 412
   series books about, 420–21
Bishop, C. H., 44, 59, 162, 167
Blake, W., 132, 205
Book evaluation, 71, 74, 78, 81, 351
Book selection, 12, 89, 96, 100, 108, 115
   criteria for, 97–98, 114
   exercise in, 114
Book Week, 174, 179, 188
   artists of posters for, 190
   slogans for, 190
Books, Children and Men, 71
Books For the Teen Age, 364
Books, Young People and Reading Guidance, 30
Boston, L. M., 76
Boyd, J., 108
Bradshaw, F., 29
Branley, F., 17
Bright, V., 299
Brink, C. R., 166, 167, 169
Bro, M., 38, 359–60
Brooke, L. L., 74, 161

Brooks, A., 29
Brooks, W., 56
Brown, M., 59, 77
Buck, P., 314
Bugbee, E., 354
Bulletin of the Center for Children's Books, 93, 101
Bulman, L. T., 412
Burrows, A. T., 30
Burton, D. L., 46, 357
Burton, V. L., 162, 167, 237, 239
Butterworth, R. F., 64, 67

C

Cahoe, E., 30
Caldecott Medal, 147, 175–76, 178, 181
Caldecott, R., 77, 147, 175–76, 178, 181, 197–98, 203–204
Carlyle, T., 21
Carnegie, A., 183–84
Carnegie Medal, 183
  winners of, 187
Carpenter, F., 278
Carr, C., 47, 51
Carroll, L., 81, 84, 139, 140, 163, 304
  tercentenary of, 309
Cavanna, B., 36, 356
Chambellan, R. P., 175, 180–81
Chapbooks, 131, 136
Chase, M. E., 217
Chase, R., 277
Chicago Daily Tribune, 143
Children and Books, 406
Children's Book Council, 147, 174, 188
Children's Books Too Good to Miss, 85
Children's Catalog, 103, 363
Children's libraries, 144, 146, 255
"Choose Something Like a Star," 177
Choral speaking, 407–409
Clark, A. N., 39, 44
Classics, 81, 92, 99, 158, 166
  abridged, 92, 160–61
  definition of, 159
  list of, 161–66
  rewritten, 76, 77, 160
Clippinger, E. E., 248
Coleridge, S. T., 271
Collins, B., 131
Collodi, C., *see* Lorenzini, C.

Colum, P., 281
Comenius, J. A., 130
Comics, 46, 51
  appeal of, 47–49
  substitutes for, 49–50, 53–63
Commager, H. S., 156
Compton's Pictured Encyclopedia, "How to Tell a Story" (Sawyer), 248
Coolidge, O., 113
Corey, S. M., 29
Courlander, H., 277
Craig, J. C., 64, 66
Crane, W., 138
A Critical History of Children's Literature, 45, 152
Crosby, M., 25, 26, 30
Crouch, M., 183
Cruikshank, G., 138, 196, 204
Cummings, E., 270
Curry, C. M., 248

D

Daly, M., 38, 357–58
Darling, R. L., 23, 30
Dasent, G., 280, 282
Davis, M. G., 290, 292
Dawson, M. A., 404, 409
Day, T., 131, 139, 140–41
De Angeli, M., 24, 39, 44
De Jong, M., 44
De La Mare, W., 9, 77, 135, 175, 186, 254, 272
Depew, O., 271
Desmond, A., 416
Developmental needs, 20, 26
  case study of, 27–28
  list of, 22
Developmental reading, 20
Developmental task, definition of, 22
Dewey, J., 145, 147–48
Djurklou, G., 281
Dodgson, C. L., *see* Carroll, L.
Door in the Wall, 24
Douglas, M. P., 148
du Bois, W. P., 56
Duff, A., 41, 43, 45, 345

E

Eakin, M. K., 115
Eaton, A. T., 155

Eaton, J., 414
Edes, M. E., 166, 304
Edgeworth, M., 132, 139, 143, 148–49
Edwards, M. A., 357
Egoff, S. A., 135
Elkins, D., 23, 29
Emery, A., 356
Enright, E., 37, 44, 167
Epics, 282, 283
Ersted, R., 148
Estes, E., 24, 32, 37, 39, 44, 49, 61, 165, 167
Ets, M. H., 57, 235, 239
Evaluating Library Resources for Elementary School Libraries, 119
Evans, E., 197
Ewing, J. H., 139, 198

F

Fadiman, C., 10, 12, 75
Fairy tales. *See* Folktales
Fargo, L. F., 108
Farjeon, E., 186
Farley, W., 28, 37
Federici, Y., 108
Felsen, H. G., 35, 357
Fenner, P., 28, 55, 158
Ferris, H., ed., 45
Field, C. W., 118
Field, W. T., 270
Fillmore, P., 281
Flack, M., 38, 39, 161, 162, 237, 239
Fletcher, D., 91
Folk tales, 72–73, 75–76, 244, 263, 269, 277, 279, 286, 315
American, 292
Danish, 281
Finnish, 281
Norwegian, 279, 284
Swedish, 281
Forbes, E., 167, 361
Foreign books, 339
purchasing list of, 343–44
France, A., 77
François, A., 204
Frank, J., 18, 159, 313
Frederic G. Melcher Scholarship, 177
Freeman, M., and I., 17
From Rollo to Tom Sawyer, 153
Frost, A. B., 197
Frost, R., 177

G

Gág, W., 54–55, 90, 161
Gagliardo, R., 172
Gardiner, J., 108
Garnett, E., 185
Garst, S., 415
Gates, D., 17, 33, 35, 37, 44, 49, 50, 81, 270–71, 327
Gateways to Readable Books, 98
Gaver, M. V., 119
Geisel, T. S., 53, 118, 167, 236, 239
Godden, R., 9, 41, 359
Goodrich, S., 133, 141
Goudge, E., 184
Graham, S., 417
Grahame, K., 8, 61, 76, 77, 135, 162, 349
Gray, E. J., 37, 38, 44
Greco, E., 303
Green, I. S., 178
Greenaway, K., 77, 132, 138, 198
Grimm, J. L., and W. C., 133, 162, 195–96, 204, 245, 251–52, 277, 280
Guiding children through reading, 3, 8, 14, 20, 31, 40, 46, 51
Guilfoile, E., 225
Gunderson, A. G., 232

H

Hackett, F., 273
Hale, L., 164
Hanna, G. R., 26, 30
Hargreaves, A. *See* Liddell, A. P.
Harnett, C., 185
Harris, J. C., 134, 296
Havighurst, R. J., 22, 29
Haviland, V., 89, 279
Hayes, F., 44
Hays, M. B., 286
Hazard, P., 71, 153, 238
Hazeltine, A. I., 37, 175, 179, 180
Heinlein, R. A., 368
Heller, F., 25–26, 30
Henne, F., 29, 148
Henry, M., 17, 28, 36, 58, 167, 169
Herrick, V. E., 29
Hewins, C., 144, 173
History of children's literature, 109, 125, 135, 142, 152, 158, 166, 172, 178, 183, 188

History of children's literature (*cont.*)
   notable collections in, 135, 157
   notable magazines in, 144
Hollowell, L., 264, 274
Horn Book Magazine, 78, 93, 101, 117, 147, 153, 154
Hornbook, 128
Horrell, R. C., 263, 269
Humorous books for children, 56–58, 84, 235, 345
Hunt, C. W., 175, 179, 180, 189
Hunt, M. L., 44

I

Illustrations, 195, 201, 205, 237, 377–78, 390
   children's preferences in, 205
Illustrators, 77, 195, 201
Indiana State Education Report, 145
Informational books, 375, 383. *See also* Science
   criteria for, 378–79
   definition of, 375–76
Interests, children's, 15, 17, 27–28
Irving, W., 133, 164, 198, 297

J

Jacobs, J., 277, 278, 286
Jacobs, L. B., 3
James, W., 28
Jones, J. O., 45
Jordan, A. M., 78, 153
Journal of Educational Sociology, 47
Journal of Experimental Education, 47
Junior Booklist, 363
Junior Bookshelf, 101, 187
Junior Reviewers, 101

K

Kalevala, 283
Kate Greenaway Medal, 186
Kidder, E., 300
"The King's Breakfast," 182
Kipling, R., 84, 135, 163, 164, 237, 290–91, 293
Kircher, C. J., 43, 45, 339
Kjelgaard, J., 50
Kolson, C. J., 63

Komroff, M., 416–17
Krauss, R., 205, 314

L

Lagerlöf, S., 83, 283
Lamb, C., and M., 9, 132
Lambert, J., 352–53, 354
Lang, A., 277, 279
Larrick, N., 14, 30
Lathrop, D., 175
Lauber, P., 391
Lawson, R., 54, 165, 234–35, 238
Leaf, M., 54, 347
Lear, E., 196
LeGrand, 17
Lenski, L., 24, 37, 44, 328
Levarie, N., 19
Levinger, E. E., 419
Lewis, C., 45
Libraries. *See* Children's libraries, School libraries
Library Journal, 117
Liddell, A. P., 304
Lofting, H., 57, 164, 233–34, 238
Long, H. G., 108
Longer Flight, 43, 45
Lorenzini, C., 60, 162, 299, 302
Loveman, A., 327

M

McAllister, M. K., 26, 30
McCloskey, R., 61–62, 77, 90, 165, 167
McGinley, P., 35, 58, 79, 80
MacGregor, E., 17
McGuffey Readers, 143
MacManus, S., 277
MacRae, D., and E., 388
Magazines for children, 118
   criteria for selecting, 119
Malter, M. S., 64, 67
Massey, M., 146
Mathiews, F. K., 174, 189
Maxwell, W., 360
Meader, S. W., 49, 50
Means, F. C., 44
Meigs, C., 45, 152
Melcher, F. C., 147, 154, 155, 172, 189, 190
   scholarship in honor of, 177
Merlino, C. P., 299–301

Meschler, M. J. (Rev.), 246, 248
Millay, E. St. V., 8
Miller, B. M., 147, 154, 174
Millett, E., 362
Milne, A. A., 40–41, 76, 164, 182, 346–47
Minarik, E. H., 118
Minority groups,
  biography of, 417–18
  realistic fiction about, 324–25, 328, 335
Mitchell, L. S., 148
Mitchell, M., tr. (Hazard), 71
Moe, J., 277, 280, 284
Monro, H., 232
Montgomery, L. M., 31, 38, 62
Monvel, B. de, 198–99, 203
Moore, A. C., 77, 133, 146–47, 153, 154, 195, 256
Moore, A. E., 44, 45
Morgan, J. E., 46
Morley, C., 178
Mother Goose, 131, 239
  origins of, 240–42
Mumford, E. W., 188
Munson, A., 96
My Roads to Childhood, 77, 195
Myths, 84, 245, 281–82, 285
  Greek, 245
  Norse, 281–82, 285

N

Nash, O., 18
National Society for the Study of Education, 149
Natural History Magazine, 117, 401
Negroes, 324–25, 335
  American folk tales of, 296
  biographies of, 417–18
  criteria for stories of, 336
  lists of books about, 338
Nesbitt, E., 8, 74, 82, 155–56
New England Primer, 128–29, 143
New York Herald Tribune, 101, 142, 146, 364
The New York Times, 101, 142–43, 189
Newbery, J., 130–31, 175, 180
Newbery Medal, 147, 174–76, 178
  study of books awarded, 63, 66
Newell, E., 40

Nicholson, W., 200–201
Noble, I., 417
Nolan, J. C., 414
Norton, M., 18, 184–85

O

O'Faolian, S., 273
Orbis Pictus, 130
Osborne Collection, 135
Osborne, E., 137–38

P

Parables, 246
Parent's Guide to Children's Reading, 14
Patee, D., 154–55, 156–57
Pease, H., 50, 327
Perrault, C., 72, 73, 131
Peter Parley. *See* Goodrich, Samuel
Petersham, M., and M., 150
Pinocchio, Statue of, 299, 302
Poetry, 7, 212–44, 404, 410
  beginning, 411
  collections of, 409
  difficulty of, 404
  selection of, 406–407
Potter, B., 11, 77, 161, 199
Powell, L. C., 365
Power, E., 108
Proof of the Pudding, 158
Public libraries
  methods of selecting books for, 100
  service to children in, 144, 146
Publishers
  children's preferences in, 63
Pyle, H., 77, 134, 144, 164, 165, 199–200

R

Rankin, M., 63, 66
Ransome, A., 11, 185
Rasmussen, C., 409
Ravielli, A., 74
Rawlings, M., 37, 167, 361
Reading Ladders for Human Relations, 26, 30
Realistic fiction, 32, 33, 34, 44, 315–17, 318, 337

Realistic fiction *(cont.)*
  criteria for evaluating, 361
  list of, 44
Reece, B. H., 243–44, 248
Regina Medal, 175
Regional stories, 328
  definition of, 332
  see also Minority groups
Religious books, 246–47, 317
  exercise on selecting, 114
Rey, H. A., 57, 167
Ripley, E., 421
Robinson, E. R., 300
Robinson, R. E., 63
Rollins, C., 335
Rosenbach Collection, 157
Ross, E. S., 277
Rousseau, J. J., 131, 139
Rudisill, M., 205
Ruskin, J., 195–96
Russell, D. H., 21, 23, 29, 45

                           S

St. Nicholas Magazine, 118, 199–200
Sapieha, Princess P., 320
Saturday Review, 101, 108
Sauer, J. L., 318
Sawyer, R., 37, 44, 62, 112, 248, 277
School libraries,
  methods of selecting books for, 100
  service to children in, 147, 148
School Library Journal, 93
Schroeder, I., 302
Science books, 384, 388, 397
  book reviews of, 116–17
  criteria for selecting, 385–87
Science fiction, 365, 368
  criteria for evaluating, 370
  definition of, 366, 369
  history of, 367
Scott, M., 119
Selsam, M. E., 118, 383
Sendak, M., 201
Senior Booklist, 363
Seredy, K., 37, 39, 44, 166
Series books, 50
  biography in, 91, 420–21
  social studies in, 50, 91, 117
Suess, Dr., *pseud. See* Geisel, T. S.
Shedlock, M. L., 253, 256
Sherwood, M. M., 140

Shippen, K., 114
Shrodes, C., 21, 29, 45
Sister Mary Jerome, 30
Sister Mary Joan Patricia, 239
Smith, D. V., 142, 232
Smith, L. H., 42, 45, 92, 266, 271, 272,
  391
Smith, N. A., 277
Smith, N. B., 22, 29
Social studies books, selection of, 117
Spain, F. L., 100
Sprague, R., 112
*Standard Catalog for High School Li-
  braries,* 103–104, 363, 364, 365
*Standards for School Library Pro-
  grams,* 115
Stevenson, R. L., 76, 135, 163, 223, 243
Stolz, M., 38, 44, 358–59
Stong, P., 54, 235, 239
Story hour, 255
Storytelling, 248, 255
  books about, 253
  sources of stories for, 252, 253–54
Strang, R., 98
Streatfeild, N., 62
Strickland, R. G., 236
Sunday School Libraries, 143

                           T

Tall tales, 293–94
Taylor, A., and J., 132–33, 141
Taylor, E., ed., 195–96
Taylor, P. B., 268–69
*A Teacher's Guide to Children's
  Books,* 14
Television for children, 15–16, 221
Tenniel, J., 196–97, 307
Tews, R. M., 26–27, 30
Thomas, I., 157–58
Thomas, K. E., 240, 248
Thompson, G. C., 64, 67
Thompson, M. W., 355
Thorne-Thomsen, G., 277, 280, 284,
  286
Thorndike, R. L., 47, 52
"Three Owls," 146–47
Thurber, J., 54
Time for Poetry, 18
Toksvig, S., ed., 273, 276
Travers, P., 57, 165, 167, 233, 235, 239,
  349

Trimmer, S. K., 132
Tunis, J. R., 36, 39, 44

U

Ungerer, T., 204
The Unreluctant Years, 45, 92
Untermeyer, L., 18

V

Van Loon, H., 83, 175
Vance, M., 415
Venturi, V., 303
Viguers, R. H., 78, 156
Vipont, E., 185
"Vocabularized" books, 75–76, 79, 80, 91

W

Walker, M., 359
Waples, D., 29
Ward, L., 35, 90, 150
Washington Post, 143
Webb, H. A., 365
Weekes, B. E., 263, 266, 274
Weingarten, S., 23, 29
Weisgard, L., 239

Wells, H. G., 324
Werner, L. S., 410
Wertham, F., 46
West, J., 37, 189
Wheeler, S., 397
White, D. N., 264
White, E. B., 18, 61, 76, 167, 238, 239
White, G., 196, 197
Wickenden, D., 360–61
Wiggin, K. D., 277
Wilder, L. I., 165, 167
Willett, M. A., 108
Williams, G., 18
Williams, M., 82
Witty, P., 20, 29, 30, 52
Wofford, A., 120, 121
World Book Encyclopedia, "Literature for Children," 125

Y

Yashima, T., 45, 314
Yates, E., 24, 337
Your Child's Reading Today, 159

Z

Zim, H. S., 375
Zimmerman, W. G., 63